changing the way the world learns[SM]

To get extra value from this book for no additional cost, go to:

http://www.thomson.com/wadsworth.html

thomson.com is the World Wide Web site for Wadsworth/ITP
and is your direct source to dozens of on-line resources.
thomson.com helps you find out about supplements,
experiment with demonstration software, search for a job,
and send e-mail to many of our authors. You can even
preview new publications and exciting new technologies.

thomson.com: *It's where you'll find us in the future.*

Critical Thinking and Popular Culture

Reading and Writing the American Experience

Peter Elias Sotiriou
Los Angeles City College

Wadsworth Publishing Company
An International Thomson Publishing Company

Belmont, CA • Albany, NY • Bonn • Boston • Cincinnati • Detroit
Johannesburg • London • Madrid • Melbourne • Mexico City • New York
Paris • Singapore • Tokyo • Toronto • Washington

English Editor: Karen Allanson
Editorial Assistant: Ryan Vesely
Project Editor: Angela Mann
Marketing Manager: Chaun Hightower
Text Designer: Vargas/Williams/Design
Print Buyer: Karen Hunt
Copy Editor: Donald Pharr
Permissions Editor: Robert Kauser
Art Editor: Roberta Broyer
Compositor: TBH/Typecast, Inc.
Printer: Banta/Harrisonburg

This book is printed on acid-free recycled paper

Printed in the United States of America
1 2 3 4 5 6 7 8 9 10

For more information, contact Wadsworth Publishing Company, 10 Davis Drive,
Belmont, CA 94002, or electronically at *http://www.thomson.com/wadsworth.html*

International Thomson Publishing Europe
Berkshire House 168-173
High Holborn
London, WC1V 7AA, England

International Thomson Editores
Campos Eliseos 385, Piso 7
Col. Polanco
11560 México D.F. México

Thomas Nelson Australia
102 Dodds Street
South Melbourne 3205
Victoria, Australia

International Thomson Publishing Asia
221 Henderson Road
#05-10 Henderson Building
Singapore 0315

Nelson Canada
1120 Birchmount Road
Scarborough, Ontario
Canada M1K 5G4

International Thomson Publishing Japan
Hirakawacho Kyowa Building, 3F
2-2-1 Hirakawacho
Chiyoda-ku, Tokyo 102, Japan

International Thomson Publishing GmbH
Königswinterer Strasse 418
53227 Bonn, Germany

International Thomson Publishing Southern Africa
Building 18, Constantia Park
240 Old Pretoria Road
Halfway House, 1685 South Africa

Library of Congress Cataloging-in-Publication Data

Sotiriou, Peter Elias.
    Critical thinking and popular culture : reading and writing the
American experience / Peter Elias Sotiriou.
        p.   cm.
    Includes index.
    ISBN 0-534-23592-1
    1. Readers—popular culture.   2. Popular culture—United States—
Problems, exercises, etc.   3. English language—Rhetoric—Problems,
exercises, etc.   4. Critical thinking—Problems, exercises, etc.
5. Report writing—Problems, exercises, etc.   6. College readers.
I. Title.
PE1127.P6S68   1997
808'.0427—dc21
                                                                97-11642

Contents

Chapter 5

Popular Culture in Speeches   219

Chapter 6

The Research Paper on Popular Culture   261

List of Logical Practices and Fallacies

Introduction

to think critically (p. 2)   to use reasoned practices to carefully and accurately formulate a response to a question you have posed

Chapter 1

to define (p. 21):   to state a word's meaning

   logical definition (p. 22):   lists the class and characteristics of a term

   extended definition (p. 22):   places a term in larger disciplinary context

   circular definition (p. 22):   uses the same term or synonym in the definition

to analyze (p. 23):   to study the structure and significance of an idea or object

to infer (p. 24):   to further explain an idea or object using evidence in the text and your conclusions about the evidence

Chapter 2

metaphor making (p. 72):   comparing two seemingly unlike objects or ideas

simile (p. 73):   using *like* or *as* in a metaphorical comparison

symbol making (p. 73):   using objects or characters that are part of a work's narrative but also have metaphorical significance

ambiguity (p. 74):   having several possible meanings

   semantical ambiguity (p. 74):   word or phrase that can be analyzed in two or more ways

paradox (p. 74):   a seemingly contradictory phrase or statement that on closer analysis is illuminating

oxymoron (p. 74):   a contradiction in terms

hyperbole (p. 75): a thought-provoking exaggeration

identifying mood and tone
   tone (p. 75): literary author's attitude toward her subject
   mood (p. 75): feeling a reader gets from a literary work

identifying satire and sarcasm
   satire (p. 75): criticism of society
   sarcasm (p. 75): strong criticism of society

Chapter 3

to sequence (p. 113): to understand and predict the stages in a narrative
to predict (p. 114): to correctly anticipate what will come next in a narrative
to evaluate (p. 115): to judge, determining the worth of an object or idea

Chapter 4

to generalize (p. 176): to summarize from many specific details
   sound generalization (p. 177): conclusion drawn from accurate, sufficient, and representative evidence

   unqualified
   generalization (p. 177): conclusion that is true of every specific instance it explains
   qualified generalization (p. 177): conclusion supported by evidence a percentage of the time
   hasty generalization (p. 178): conclusion made from either insufficient or incorrect evidence

induction (p. 178): process of making a general statement from a body of specific evidence

false dilemma (p. 178): statement making one choose between two extreme positions

to deduce (p. 179): to use a general statement and details to come to a new conclusion

syllogism (p. 179): three parts of a deduction
   major premise (p. 179): the generalization
   minor premise (p. 179): the detail statement
   conclusion (p. 179): the synthesis of the generalization and the detail statement
bandwagon appeal (p. 179): asks one to be like or join a specific group
appeal to authority (p. 179): encourages one to use a product or accept a belief because it is endorsed by a famous person

connotation (p. 180):   what a word suggests
  positive (p. 180):   the word's pleasing associations
  negative (p. 180):   the word's harsh associations
  neutral (p. 180):   the word's associations that are neither positive nor negative
denotation (p. 181):   a word's dictionary meaning

Chapter 5

causation (p. 222):   how events produce a result
  necessary (p. 223):   requires that the cause be present for the event to occur
  sufficient (p. 223):   a cause that may lead to an effect
  necessary and sufficient (p. 223):   requires that the cause be present and be the only one present
  contributory (p. 223):   one cause among many that affects a particular condition
causal oversimplification (p. 224):   making a contributory cause a sufficient cause
post hoc (p. 224):   assuming that the most recent cause is the sufficient cause
slippery slope (p. 224):   claiming that one event becomes the cause of a chain reaction of events
comparison (p. 224):   objects, people, or ideas grouped in the same class
  false (p.224):   objects, people, or ideas from different classes grouped in the same class
analogy (p. 225):   the linkage of two seemingly different items to show their commonality
  false (p. 225):   more dissimilarities than similarities in the comparison
argument ad hominem (p. 225):   to criticize an individual through name calling
circumstantial argument
ad hominem (p. 226):   calling the circumstances of an individual's life into question in order to criticize her position

Chapter 6

to synthesize (p. 262):   to combine several ideas to construct a new argument
to create (p. 263):   to come upon an entirely new insight as a result of one's research

Preface

Critical Thinking and Popular Culture is a textbook for students in second-semester composition courses who want to apply critical thinking practices to their college writing. Critical thinking has become an important practice in freshman writing courses because both students and teachers realize that college writing not only needs to be organized and clear, but also analytical. In applying critical thinking practices to their reading and writing, students can both effectively analyze and make appropriate inferences from the texts they examine, investigating the texts' organization, logic, and unstated assumptions.

To be a critical thinker involves using reasoned practices to respond carefully and accurately to a particular question. Yet critical thinking is a practice that is not easily defined because its activities are informed by the discipline that it examines. For example, being a critical thinker in biology does not involve all of the same practices that one uses in analyzing literature. *Critical Thinking and Popular Culture* examines the critical practices that one often applies to humanities and social science material. It does so in an original way because the readings, the writing assignments, and the critical thinking practices are all integrated into one textbook. Most courses in critical thinking and composition require a reader and a separate critical thinking text.

As its title suggests, *Critical Thinking and Popular Culture* investigates those practices that students need to apply to texts in popular culture, particularly American popular culture. This textbook is based upon the pedagogical assumption that critical practices are most effectively learned in the context of reading and writing in one engaging subject. Therefore, you will note that all the readings deal with selected aspects of popular culture: photography, fiction, television, advertisements, and speeches. There are other aspects of popular culture that this text does not treat intensively: popular film, professional and collegiate sports, popular music, rock concerts, and so on. Yet the critical practices that students learn in these six chapters can be applied to those aspects of popular culture that are not treated in this textbook.

The text is divided into an introduction and six chapters, each chapter dealing with a particular aspect of popular culture. In the introduction, students will be presented with successful ways to read and write critically: how to construct arguments, how to comment on what has been read, and how to effectively use reading journals. In each of the following six chapters, the topic in popular culture is introduced and the various critical practices related to the topic are presented to allow students to effectively analyze the popular culture issue in question. Chapter 6 is a culminating chapter because students rely on most or all of the critical practices that they have learned up to that point to compose a research paper on some aspect of popular culture. Since all of the readings in the text deal with various aspects of popular culture, by the end of the text, students will be able to make an informed choice regarding their research paper topic, so their research will in fact be a "term" project. The topic they choose may come from one of the topics they have already explored in the previous chapters, or it may be an entirely new topic in popular culture that a student wants to examine. All the formal essays that students complete in this textbook, including the term paper, encourage students to compose their writing in drafts that are evaluated both by their peers and their instructor, so the writing process is an integral part of this critical thinking textbook.

How the Textbook Is Organized

There are eight major sections in each of the six chapters that students will complete:

1. Introduction: In this first part of each chapter, students are introduced to significant issues surrounding the particular area of popular culture that they will study.

2. Critical Practices: Here students are introduced to the various critical thinking activities that apply to the topic on popular culture examined in the chapter.

3. Recapping: Students are given a summary of the popular culture topic as well as the critical practices that apply to the topic.

4. Reading Selections: In chapters 1–5, four challenging and usually long excerpts are presented, which analyze the particular topic in question. These selections come from scholarly publications, popular sources, contemporary American fiction, and transcripts of political and popular culture speeches.

5. Critical Explorations: Reading: After each selection, there are five questions that students can use as they reread the material. These reading selections are not easily understood in one reading, and these questions thus encourage students' critical rereading of each text.

6. Critical Explorations: Writing: With the exception of Chapter 6, each chapter has four or five formal writing topics on the material examined in the particular chapter. Chapter 6 includes ten writing options. These topics encourage students to apply the critical practices that they have learned to the texts they have read or to popular culture texts of their own choosing in forming a critical essay response.

7. Student Writing: Each chapter presents a student essay response to one of the writing topics for that chapter. Students are encouraged to read this essay draft critically as they respond to the five questions concerning its content, structure, and style. This essay will show students how an individual at their level of composition ability responded to a topic on popular culture, and it may also provide them with ideas for composing their own essay responses.

8. Peer Responses: This final section to each chapter includes five questions that students can use once they have completed a draft of their writing topic. Students may use these questions to revise their draft, to allow peers and their instructor to respond to their draft, or to help them critically examine their peers' drafts. These questions examine each draft's organization and the critical practices that the writers employed to analyze their topic.

Critical Thinking and Popular Culture is a challenging text that will prepare composition students for many of the reading and writing activities that they will be asked to complete in upper-division college courses. Once students have worked through these six chapters, they will be able to analytically examine shorter and longer texts in the humanities and social sciences: identifying these texts' unstated assumptions, recognizing and applying logical practices to their own writing and to the texts of others, and synthesizing material from several sources, thus cogently expressing their responses to a variety of cultural works.

Acknowledgments

I have several people to thank for the completion of *Critical Thinking and Popular Culture.* First, Angie Gantner, former managing editor at Wadsworth, patiently encouraged me to begin this project. And Angela Mann, project editor, meticulously and professionally moved this textbook through its several stages.

I would also like to thank reviewers Robert L. Arend, Miramar College; Judith Bank, Los Medanos College; Jon Bates, Southwestern College; Vicky Daley, Stephen F. Austin State University; Joseph F. Dunne, Saint Louis Community College; Louie Edmundson, Chattanooga State Technical Community College; Michael Hogan, Southeast Missouri State University; Margaret Hyde, Evergreen Valley College; Katherine Ploeger, California State University at Stanislaus; Priscilla Rockwel, Rio Hondo College; Mary Jane Ross, Glendale Community College; Anne Wiegard, SUNY @ Cortland; and particularly Vic Mortimer of Ohio State University, who carefully read two revisions of *Critical Thinking and Popular Culture* and provided several thoughtful suggestions that I incorporated into the final manuscript.

I would like to thank my students, who are always the source for my textbook projects. During the spring semester of 1995, I piloted the bulk of this manuscript with my students in a second-semester composition course entitled, Critical Thinking, Reading, and Writing, and six of these students agreed to have drafts of their essays published. I would also like to thank Darwin Aronoff, emeritus librarian, who combed through our library to find relevant reading selections; Penelope Choy, colleague, who provided me with the "Miss Clairol" selection; and Gregg Segal, colleague, whose provocative photographs form part of Chapter 1.

Finally, as always, I want to thank my wife, Vasi, and my sons, Elia and Dimitri, who have lived with this project for the past four years, during my sabbatical in Greece and here. They are my patient and faithful partners in all the important work that I do.

Introduction: Writing and Reading Critically

Constructing Arguments

Before you begin the reading and writing explorations in the following six chapters of this textbook, it is helpful for you to consider how essays are written, particularly how arguments in essays are constructed. From the other writing courses that you have taken, you most likely know how college essays are organized: how the introduction introduces the points you intend to cover, the body in several paragraphs explains each point, and the conclusion summarizes or synthesizes the points that you have made in your essay. You have likely also learned how to introduce textual material or personal experience as evidence for the main points your essay is making. In this

1

composition and critical thinking textbook, you will move beyond being able to effectively organize and support your essay. In various writing activities throughout this textbook, you will examine your main point to see how convincing it is, and you will learn how to analyze the evidence you select in order to support this point. In the first five chapters, you will not only be introduced to a topic in popular culture, but you will also examine practices that will make you a more critical reader and writer of material in popular culture. In this way, you will develop critical practices that will help make your college essays more convincing, or *cogent*. In several important ways, after you have completed these six chapters, your writing will take on greater clarity and authority.

Throughout this textbook you will be developing your critical thinking abilities through focused reading and writing activities. You can define *critical thinking* as using reasoned practices to carefully and accurately formulate a response to a question you have posed.

What Is an Argument?

As you begin writing about popular culture, the first questions you need to consider are these: What constitutes an effective argument? How can I ensure that the argument I introduce in my essay is cogent? In order to answer these questions, you need to understand what an argument is.

An argument is related to the following terms: topic, issue, and claim. A *topic* is simply a particular subject matter that you are considering. Let's say you begin studying Chapter 3 in this textbook. You would be studying the topic of television. An *issue* is a more specific part of a topic. An issue that Neil Postman explores concerning the topic of television (Selection 9) is the relationship between language and learning. Note that an issue does not express a particular point of view. Rather, it merely divides up the topic. Finally, a *claim* is a statement about a topic or issue that expresses an individual's belief about the issue. In regard to television and language, a claim about this issue could be the one Postman makes in Selection 9: television is a visual medium that does not encourage language development.

Where does argument fit into these related terms? An *argument* is simply a more reasoned and more researched claim. Arguments rather than claims are what you want to express in your college essays. Yet note how all these terms are related. That is, you will probably be relying on all of them before you formulate your argument.

Consider this situation leading to the construction of an argument: you have always been attracted to the topic of television and especially interested in the issue of television learning and language learning. You begin with a claim that television learning is unlike language learning. After some research, your argument becomes this: television viewing actually retards language learning.

Note also what this argument about television viewing is *not*. It is not a description of television. That is, this argument does not provide you with the characteristics of television. Nor is this argument an explanation of television. It does not clarify a particular television procedure or operation. Finally, this argument is not a summary, or a retelling of the main points in the Postman selection. An argument consistently states the writer's reasoned belief on a topic: an original statement expressing a point of view. In this case, the writer's point of view is a negative one concerning television viewing and language development.

Arguments come in various forms. They may be stated as a cause or causes of a particular effect. Some sociologists and psychologists have constructed the argument that children who watch several hours of television a day tend to be more violent than those who do not. In their argument, television viewing becomes a cause of increased violent behavior among children. (You will study arguments relying on causes in Chapter 5.) Arguments can also be written as analogies, or comparisons between two objects. More will be said about analogies in Chapter 5, on speeches and popular culture. In regard to advertisements, some critics have concluded that television ads are like visual works of art. These critics see that television commercials have artistic as well as persuasive value. In this analogy, they compare a commercial to a visual artwork, such as a painting or sculpture.

In a sense, an argument is shaped by the audience to which it is directed. The *audience* is simply the reader or the listener of the argument. A writer forming an argument about television for sociologists may be inclined to use more statistical evidence than if she were presenting this argument to an audience of parents, for which specific stories about television viewing and children would perhaps be more effective.

Arguments are always shaped by circumstances. That is, arguments are rhetorical statements. *Rhetoric*, as you will learn in greater detail in Chapter 5, is the art of persuasion. Arguments persuade, but each audience brings a different set of beliefs to the argument. In forming her argument and selecting her evidence, a writer or speaker therefore needs to consider the beliefs and practices of the particular audience and construct her arguments accordingly.

All arguments are built upon two basic ways of thinking: induction and deduction. These two thinking practices will be analyzed in detail in Chapter 4, on advertising and commercials. For now, consider how these two kinds of thinking work to form an argument. An *induction* is a conclusion that one draws based upon experience or experiment. In the above cause–effect argument that children who watch television tend to be more violent, the researchers have conducted experiments examining violent behavior in children who watch television. The results of their experiments led to their conclusion about television viewing and violence. The inductive argument always moves from the *specific* experience (the eyewitness account or the experimental data) to the *general* statement, or conclusion.

A *deductive argument* uses the premises of an induction to draw a conclusion about a specific case. In the above induction about television and violence, a psychologist may be studying the violent behavior of Marco, a seven-year-old. The psychologist may conclude that Marco's watching eight hours of children's television a day is one of the causes of his violent behavior. The deduction would follow this pattern of thought: (1) Excessive television viewing may be a cause of violence in children. (2) Marco is expressing violent behavior. (3) Marco may be watching too much television. The psychologist's deductive argument could be worded this way: one of the causes of Marco's violent behavior may be his excessive television viewing. Deductions are valid only if the original induction, called the major premise, is valid. You will learn more about how to determine the validity of deductions in Chapter 4.

Arguments can be divided into three basic types: the pro–con, the logical, and the analytical. The *pro–con argument* presents both sides of an issue. This argument usually organizes political debates. In pro–con argumentation, an audience listens to both sides of an issue. In the above example on television and violence, an audience would listen to both sides of the debate, which addressed the following question: Does television cause violent behavior? Often, opposing teams present each side of the argument.

The *logical argument* is one that examines the forms of thinking of an argument. The logical argument asks the following kinds of questions: What are the premises in a deduction? Are these premises valid? What is the induction? What type of evidence is used to arrive at this general statement? For example, in logically analyzing the argument on television and violence, one would evaluate the general statement and the evidence used to make the connection between television viewing and violence. The evaluator would rely upon logical criteria to make this assessment.

The *analytical argument* is one that carefully examines textual material in order to determine whether a particular claim can be made. For example, a writer who claims that television viewing does not contribute to violent behavior among children would examine evidence from personal research or from that of others to support or deny this claim. Analytical arguments may use both pro–con and logical arguments as evidence. The analytical argument is the major type that you will develop in your written responses in this textbook. You will be reading texts on popular culture, and you will be analyzing the evidence from these texts and from texts of your own choosing in order to develop your own argument. Consider the following two analytical arguments, which you will consider in Chapters 3 and 4:

1. The Rodeo car advertisement speaks to a young, affluent, athletic American male.

2. The television program *Grace Under Fire* presents socially relevant topics and develops complex characters.

The evidence one uses to support these claims would come from the Rodeo ad's visual and written text or from moments in one or several episodes of *Grace Under Fire*. Essays like these are successful if the writer knows *what* evidence to analyze and *how* to analyze the evidence she chooses. You will learn ways to successfully analyze texts in popular culture in Chapter 1, on American beliefs and needs.

With each of the arguments you write on popular culture, it is wise to write down the answers to the following questions as you form and revise your argument:

1. What is my topic?
2. What issue concerning this topic interests me?
3. What claim do I want to make about this issue?
4. What is my argument concerning this issue?

What Types of Evidence Are Arguments Built On?

The strength of each of your arguments relies on the accuracy of the *evidence* that you present in your essay. Other words that you will hear related to evidence are *reasons* and *support*. Evidence and arguments have a necessary relationship to each other because your argument is altered as you analyze your evidence. In fact, a lack of evidence may require that you give up on your argument entirely. For example, if you do not have several studies that support the relationship between violence and television viewing, then you may not be able to present a cogent analytical argument showing this cause–effect relationship. Evidence is what you present in the body, or middle, of your essay.

Evidence may originate from experimental research. This sort of evidence is often called *data*. As a college student, the evidence that you find frequently comes from sources that you read. This type of support is called *textual evidence*. Many of the arguments that you will construct from the topics on popular culture in this text will be supported by textual evidence, or the selections you have read and excerpts you quote.

Evidence can also come from personal experience, or what you see yourself doing as well as your observations of others. In an essay asking how a consumer is affected by commercials, you could use some of your own buying experiences to construct and support your argument. In some cases, using evidence from your own experiences is compelling support for your argument.

Much will be said about evaluating the nature of evidence in order to support your argument in Chapters 4 and 5. For now, realize that all your evidence must be *accurate* and *clear*. Also, you should see how your accumulation of accurate and clear evidence continually questions and revises your argument. Never assume that because you have set up an argument, you must find evidence to fit the argument. If you find much evidence to support your argument, then you can state your argument more strongly. If you find less evidence or contradictory evidence, you may need to qualify your argument. In the above example on television and violence, you may need to say that in "some cases" television is a cause of violent behavior if you come upon conflicting experimental studies. Remember that every issue worthy of argument has two sides.

Continue to see your argument and your evidence as forever interconnected, with the nature of the evidence transforming the argument. Let your evidence allow you to keep an open mind about your argument. Remember that the purpose of writing an argumentative essay is to attempt to find the truth in a particular claim. As you have seen in the above examples on television and violence, truth is always shaped by its context, or its rhetorical situation. Very rarely is the truth of a statement unchanging. In many areas of popular culture, the truth is difficult to pinpoint, yet this fact does not allow you to say whatever seems right. Assume that textual evidence, scientific data, and personal experience, if clearly stated and honestly interpreted, will allow you to construct a cogent analytical argument.

What Are the Necessary Stages in Constructing an Argument?

Constructing clear analytical arguments is a process, as I have suggested in the discussion of evidence and arguments. Neither arguments nor evidence emerge full blown. As you think, gather evidence, and put your ideas in writing, you are constantly rethinking your argument.

You have likely already studied the *writing process*, or the three interrelated stages of composing, commonly called *prewriting, drafting,* and *revising.*

Prewriting includes the research you do in preparation for your writing: the books and articles you read, the notes you take on this material, and the questions you ask about this material. Prewriting is an essential stage in the writing process because it questions the strength of your claim and determines the quality and quantity of the evidence you can use. The ancient Greek rhetoricians referred to this stage in composing a speech as *invention,* or generating ideas on a particular topic. *Invention* is a powerful word because it suggests that you create your argument. It is important to see yourself at this prewriting stage as developing an argument that may never have been previously put forth. Consider it your original statement on the topic in question.

When you prewrite, it is wise to jot down your ideas, many of which you may not end up using in your final draft. Jotting down ideas in this prewriting stage is often referred to as *brainstorming.* Brainstorming need not be in any logical order—that is, it may mix up general information with more detailed material. Brainstormed material is best written down in informal lists that you refer to when you begin drafting your essay.

Once you have devoted time to thinking through your topic, to collecting your information, and to brainstorming, you are ready to begin drafting. At this stage in the writing process, you should have some idea of what you want to say. You should at least be able to state a claim and list the evidence you have to support this claim. The *drafting stage* is a more formal writing stage. Yet do not expect that what you write at this time is your final word on your topic. When you draft, you change your ideas, rewrite your claim into an argument, and rearrange your evidence to best support your argument. Rewriting and rearranging are most easily done on a word processor.

Before you begin your first draft, you may want to jot down your ideas in a more formal outline or visual map, in which you separate your argument from your evidence and from your conclusion. At this time you should refer to your brainstorming lists and organize general and specific levels of information. More will be said about brainstorming, outlining, and visual mapping in Chapter 6, which discusses the research paper on popular culture.

During this drafting stage, it is wise to share your writing with others— with your peers and with your instructor. Listen to their comments. See how you can reconsider what you have written. During these conferences, clearly explain your argument and present your evidence to your peers and your instructor. Often your oral explanations to others help clarify what you have written. Yet also listen to yourself. Do not feel that you must rewrite unless you agree with the suggestions of your peers and your instructor. In each of the writing assignments in the six chapters of this textbook, you will be provided with questions to apply both to your drafts and to those of your peers in the activity titled "Peer Responses." You will also be able to evaluate drafts of student essay responses in the Student Writing activities.

It is wise to let your draft sit for a while—a day or two. Then reread it; see how it sounds and make additional changes. Seeing your draft fresh will provide you with additional ways to improve what you have said. Your instructor and your peers may ask to read your first draft and often your second draft. With each set of comments, make further changes to your argument, and add or delete evidence.

The last step is the revising stage. *Revising* is simply rethinking your draft. As you have seen in the drafting stage, revising is a necessary part of drafting. Revising is especially important after you receive feedback on your drafts. Revising is not simply adding and deleting material. In the argumentative essay, revising is most importantly rethinking your argument, reconsidering your premises, and evaluating your evidence. Of the three stages in writing, revising is the most challenging.

At the very end of your revising stage, you are ready to edit your draft. *Editing* is simply reading your draft for formal concerns—grammar, usage, and correct format. Editing is a mechanical process, and it is best completed if you are not thinking about the content of your essay.

Once you have edited your essay, you are ready to submit your final draft. Yet you should never consider your final draft as the last word on your argument. If you had more time, your final draft could be revised even further. With every writing activity that you do in or out of college, you will be under a time constraint. Your final draft is simply the best writing that you can produce given the time that you have been allotted.

Much more will be said about the writing process in Chapter 6, which discusses the research paper on popular culture.

Recapping

Constructing cogent arguments is the goal of most successful college writing. Arguments are reasoned claims that are supported by carefully researched or considered evidence. Arguments and evidence are consistently interwoven—the evidence informs the argument, and the argument informs the evidence.

The three most common types of arguments are the pro–con, the logical, and the analytical. Essays on popular culture are most often analytical arguments that examine and evaluate textual material.

All effective argumentative writing follows the three stages of the writing process: prewriting, drafting, and revising. Each stage influences and is influenced by the other, so you should not consider the three stages of the writing process as separate activities.

Reading Critically

Much of the work that you do in college in the humanities and social sciences involves careful reading. Critical thinking is an essential part of what you do when you read these materials; critical thinking is not just a practice you apply to your writing. You will find that in this textbook the readings are often quite long. Because of the length of most of the selections, you will be able to see how an author constructs, and sometimes revises, her argument and how a wealth of evidence can be used to develop this argument.

You can apply the concepts of topic, claim, and argument that you learned in the previous section to these selections and to your college reading in general. As well as applying these questions to your writing, you can also ask the following questions of the writings of others:

1. What topic has the author selected?
2. What claim is being made?
3. Is a convincing argument put forth?

As with your own writing, when you read, you constantly need to sift through the evidence to see how the evidence either supports the argument or calls it into question.

In moving beyond the issues of topic, claim, and argument, you will also examine the following questions:

1. How can critical reading be seen as a carefully considered dialogue?
2. Why is it important to mark the texts that you read?

3. How can your writing of reading journals help you read critically?
4. How are critical reading and critical writing related?

How Is Reading a Dialogue?

You no doubt know what a face-to-face dialogue is. You speak to an individual, and that person replies. Often what you say in this conversation alters what you know about a particular topic. You ask or answer various questions, and so does your partner. This movement from question to answer revises what you and your partner know about the topic in question.

Reading can also be seen as a dialogue. As you read, you are creating a voice that speaks to you, answering the questions that you may have or providing you with knowledge that will further your understanding of a topic. This voice is the author's, or your construction of the author's voice. In critical reading, you are listening very carefully to the voice that you hear in the selection. You listen to the voice of the author, and you assess the value of what this constructed voice says. The challenge in any kind of reading is that, unlike in a face-to-face dialogue, the reader must construct the author's voice. A critical reader poses the following questions to this voice:

1. Is what you say accurate?
2. How can what you say about a particular topic help me further understand this topic?
3. What point of view do you have about this topic? How do I agree or disagree with what you say?

You will likely say that when you read, you do not hear a voice as you do when you are talking to someone in conversation. It is true that the voice of the author in the reading is silent. This is the challenge of any kind of reading. Nonetheless, the author's voice directs your reading. When you are enjoying what you are reading, you can anticipate what the author will say next. In a sense, your voice complements the voice in the reading. When the reading is complicated, you have difficulty predicting where the author is heading. It seems as if the author is speaking to an audience that has excluded you. As a critical reader, you need to determine the audience to which the author is speaking and what you need to know to become an active member of this audience.

Why Is Marking a Selection Helpful?

This critical reading dialogue is best encouraged if you mark up the selection as you read and reread. Your comments become your responses to what the reading is saying to you. You have probably already learned how to locate the main idea and major details in a reading selection. Some teachers encourage you to identify a main idea in a paragraph by underlining it once and to note major details by underlining them twice.

As a critical reader, you need to go beyond a summary of a selection—that is, merely identifying main ideas and major details. As with your own writing, you want to identify the argument of a selection and comment on how sound it is. Some critical readers note in the margin "arg." or "argument" next to where they believe the author's main point is to be found. At other times, when the argument is not directly stated or is unclearly stated, the critical reader writes out the argument of the selection in the margins. He may also comment on whether he believes this argument is convincing or whether he questions it.

You may write your marginal comments at any time during your reading, but these comments are often most helpful during your second reading. Throughout this textbook, you will be asked to reconsider what you have read in the section titled "Critical Explorations: Reading." It is often wise to initially read through the selection quickly to get a sense of the selection's organization and the major points that the author makes. During the second and ensuing readings, you can more easily locate the significant parts of the selection and make comments that you find necessary in the margins. All these comments are your proof that you are responding to the text in dialogue. They help construct the author's voice. These comments also save you time when you are writing about the selection because they direct you to what you have found important.

When you critically read, particularly when you critically read the longer selections in this textbook, you may pose questions that may remain unanswered even after you have finished reading and rereading the selection. You should consider these questions as necessary starting points to further understand the reading. As in face-to-face dialogue, you often gather important knowledge by asking questions. A question mark in the margin next to a particularly difficult sentence or sentences is an appropriate response, and a specific question regarding a part of or the entire selection does not necessarily show that you have failed in your reading. Posing the right kinds of questions can open a reading up for you. It is your way of asking the author a question.

In Figure 1.1, you will see how a selection excerpt is successfully marked, with comments and questions in the margins to help construct the author's voice. These comments are intended to show you how critical reading is an ongoing, active dialogue.

How Is the Reading Journal Important?

Another way to make the readings speak is by writing informal journals after you have read. These journals can serve many purposes. They can summarize what you have read, or they can present your immediate responses to

Note: Malls are not immediately understood.

How is the mall like a world of magic?

Note: Author compares malls to historical events and to myths.

Note: the qualifier here.

management: the control of temperature, lighting, merchandise, and events. 11) The mall's special space is achieved by enclosure, protection, and control. Those are its secrets, the keys to the kingdom, the whole mall game. Within the environment established by those elements, a mall can contain five department stores or none, one level or six; it can be a brand-new building or deposit itself in the shell of an old one; it can thrive in Alaska or Hawaii, in the desert or on the beach; it can put in skating rinks and roller coasters and historical markers; it can be as small as a garage or as big as a country, and it will still be a mall.

12) These are also the elements that make the mall an extremely efficient and effective selling machine—but that is a subject for the daytime. At night the mall reveals other implications that contribute to its selling success; but they are also intriguing to consider on their own. For when you have a space that you have separated from the outside world, and the ability to create your own world inside, governed by your own rules, what you have is the ability to make magic. You've got yourself a house of fantasy.

13) For after all, isn't this sense of separated, protected privileged space common to the special worlds of history and myth, from the castles and walled cities of medieval Europe and the Forbidden City of China to the enchanted wood, the city in the sky or under the sea, the Shangri-La[3] in the mystic mountains of fantasy? These are the necessary conditions for magic places apart from the ordinary world: through the looking glass, up the beanstalk, down the rabbit hole, off to the Emerald City. Such magic places may also be separated by time (whether places that time forgot or places in the far future or the distant past accessible only by time travel) and by a combination of time and space (as in the *Star Wars* saga—"long, long ago in a galaxy far, far away . . ."). So it is no wonder the mall is full of themes and suggestions of the past and an intergalactic[4] future.

14) But of course the mall is not completely inaccessible from the real world—in fact, it's convenient, with plenty of free parking. It is instead a special space within the usual world where the imagination is given strong suggestions for fantasy. And there is a model for that kind of environment.

15) I saw that, too, on this night in the empty mall, as I stood at the second-level railing and looked down into the center court. I saw the white pools of

Figure 1.1   A Successfully Marked Page

the reading. If the reading is difficult, you can say why. If you disagree with a premise in the reading, you can explain your disagreement. Finally, if the reading is going to be used in a writing assignment, you can explain how you plan to use it.

The composition theorist Ann Berthoff* has discussed the dialectical note-book, what I call the dialogic journal, in which you draw a line down the middle of the paper, copy an important excerpt from the reading on one side, and comment on this excerpt on the other. The dialogic journal is particularly helpful when you find important sections of the reading that you simply can-not comment on fully in the margins. The dialogic journal allows you to be-gin explaining the insights that you have come upon in your reading.

Reading journals again become the evidence that you are having a con-versation with the reading. The journal is like the transcript of what you are saying to the author. As a journal, your conversation with the reading is in-formal, so do not focus on your form and style, and do not fret if your re-sponses at this time are not entirely logical.

Figures 1.2 and 1.3 show you how the reading journal and dialogic jour-nal look. Note that in both examples, you identify the reading selection, list the page number, and date the entry. These entries are best placed in a bound notebook that lists your entries in chronological order.

How Can Reading Critically Help My Writing?

Too often in composition courses, students separate their reading assign-ments from their writing assignments. They assume that their reading has lit-tle to do with their writing. You need to start considering the ways that your critical reading allows you to become a better critical writer.

You have already seen how similar the questions are that you ask of a reading and that you ask of your writing. In both activities, you ask the same three questions: What is the topic? What is the claim? What is the argument?

Further, when you are reading critically, you are applying the very same critical practices that you use in your writing. For example, in Chapter 4 you will be learning about generalizations and you will be analyzing the kinds of generalizations that ads use. If you have been analyzing the generalizations used in the readings of Chapter 4—if you have been considering how a writer qualifies her generalizations and how she makes her generalizations convincing—then you will have had practice in analyzing the generalizations in the ad you write about. It will then be easier for you to locate and com-ment cogently on the generalizations that the ad makes.

If reading is a dialogue with the author, then you are always responding in some way to the reading: in informal phrases, questions, and comments. Put differently, you are always writing about your reading. This informal

---

*Ann E. Berthoff, *The Making of Meaning* (Upper Montclair, NJ: Boynton/Cook, 1981), 122.

Secrets of the Shopping Mall, page 61, 2/12/98

I think I've got an idea for a term paper topic here. I like what Kowinski is saying about how malls are a part of a world of fantasy. When I go to the malls, I get the feeling that I'm at Disneyland. What is it about Disneyland and malls that are similar? And why does this fantasy world make people want to buy? Kowinski talks about how malls are separated from space and time: "... the mall is full of the themes of the past and an intergalactic future." In many ways, so are the attractions at Disneyland. Maybe I could write about the fantasy world of the mall with a lot of first-hand observation as a part of my evidence.

Figure 1.2   A Sample Reading Journal Entry

Secrets of the Shopping Mall, p. 61, 2/13/98

Quotation	Response
"what you have is the ability to make magic. You've got yourself a house of fantasy." (61)	I've never thought of a mall as a magical place. But I guess Kowinski is right. There must be magic attached to those countless shoppers who go to the mall and buy nothing.
"For after all, isn't this sense of separated, protected, privileged space common to the special worlds of history and myth ... ?" (61)	I like how Kowinski makes the mall part of an event in history and an American myth. I think that historians in the future will talk about the importance of malls to our culture. Also, we're short on myths these days. Could malls be one of the myths of our time?

Figure 1.3   A Sample Dialogic Journal Entry

writing—comments in the margins and reading journals—can serve as the starting point for your more formal writing.

Recapping

Critical thinking involves both careful reading and careful writing. Critical reading can be seen as thoughtful, sustained dialogue with the author. In this dialogue, the critical reader determines what the voice of the author is saying and poses questions to the author. These questions and comments are best placed as glosses in the margins during a rereading of the selection. Critical reading is also aided by reading journals—informal notations about the selection. In many important ways, reading critically helps one become a more critical writer.

Chapter 1

Analyzing Beliefs and Needs We Live By

Introduction

From the moment of your birth, you are immersed into a set of beliefs and needs that helps determine how you think and act throughout your lifetime. Many needs are shared by everyone in the world, for they ensure human survival. For example, all people need food and shelter to survive. As an infant, you made it very clear to your parent or guardian when you were hungry, cold, hot, or wet. Your crying was a sign to the adult world that you needed food and a more comfortable shelter.

Along with these needs are beliefs that are passed on to you from your family and society. Some are beliefs that your family members have learned from their country, others from their culture. Like the need for food and shelter, many of these beliefs are so basic that you and your family take them for granted. In this sense, many of your beliefs are an unconscious part of your thinking and behavior.

In America, these beliefs are complicated and contradictory because the United States is a history of immigrant populations. At times the immigrants' cultural beliefs go against what established Americans seem to believe. For example, your immigrant culture may tell you to live with your parents until you marry, whereas your teachers, school counselors, and friends may advise you to move out of your family home right after you graduate from high school.

In what ways do your country and culture affect your thoughts and actions? There are innumerable beliefs that inform American thinking. Yet there are seven issues that speak most directly to the selections and questions that you will be examining in this textbook:

1. an understanding of family: the ways American family members relate to and care for one another
2. an understanding of gender: what Americans believe a woman and a man are capable of accomplishing
3. the use of science and technology: the role that Americans see science and technology playing in solving human problems
4. equal opportunity: whether Americans believe that anyone, from whatever gender, class, race, or ethnic group, has an equal chance at success in America
5. wealth and beauty: whether Americans believe that monetary wealth and beauty ensure happiness
6. an understanding of success in life: whether Americans believe that life is basically a happy or unhappy experience
7. patriotism: how much respect Americans have for their history and for their country's policies

In the first part of this chapter, I will be discussing each of these beliefs from an American perspective. These beliefs will serve you throughout this textbook as you examine the various aspects of American life: short fiction (Chapter 2), television programming (Chapter 3), advertising (Chapter 4), speeches on popular culture (Chapter 5), and your own researched topic on an aspect of American popular culture (Chapter 6).

The Family

In the United States, the family has undergone a revolution in the past twenty-five years. Single parents make up a large percentage of the families today, whereas in the fifties and before, single parents and divorced parents were in the minority.

What has remained through these generations of change is some sort of family structure, and each of us brings to our experiences a particular attitude toward family. Some Americans believe that the nuclear family (mother, father, and children) is the best way to raise children. For example, television shows in the fifties such as *Leave It to Beaver* and *Father Knows Best* portrayed the happy nuclear family: caring mothers and fathers who could, together, solve any problems their children faced.

Today, with more single-parent families, there is the counter-belief that a single parent (usually a mother) can do just as well to ensure the well-being of her family. And many television shows in the sixties, seventies, and eighties portrayed the success of single parenting. In the late sixties and early seventies the television program *Julia* was popular, portraying an African American nurse who was quite capable of caring for her son, Corey, on her own.

What America does not believe, or any other country for that matter, is that children can raise themselves. Everyone sees the need for some sort of family structure in the rearing of children.

What has emerged in the American media today are several conflicting pictures of the family: the image of the harmonious nuclear family—with a loving mother and father—the image of a single parent providing all that her children need, and the image of divorced parents remarrying and being able to effectively care for both their own children and their stepchildren. In American advertising and television comedies and dramas, you will see these images being used. But these images are usually idealized, so the difficulties that any one of these family structures faces are rarely examined in any detail.

Gender

Just as the American family has undergone revolutionary change in the past generation, so has the concept of gender—particularly America's understanding of a woman's role in society. In the fifties, as so many television shows and commercials attest, the woman's place was almost always in the home, tending to her family, whereas the man's central task was to work, providing for his wife and children. Today, most American women work while at the same time being a wife and mother. And in the past twenty years, the media has focused more on the professional woman and less on her traditional roles as wife and mother.

Like the beliefs surrounding the family, American beliefs about gender are conflicting. Many older Americans support the traditional role of woman as homemaker and that of the man as provider and protector of his family. Yet a growing number of Americans see the male and female as equals, both on the job and at home. Fathers are now sometimes praised if they cook, clean, and tend to the children. These traditional female activities often do not take away from the new American male's masculine identity.

Therefore, in the next three chapters, when you analyze American fiction, television shows, and commercials, you need to be sensitive to the belief system about gender that the work suggests. Often, you will not be told how men and women in the particular story, program, or commercial are understood. It will be up to you to determine their status. What is clear is that gender is a major issue in American literature and media today. How we respond to these works is often based on whether we agree with a work's attitude toward men and women.

Science and Technology

Many Americans believe that science and technology can solve any problem that humanity faces. For some, technology has almost become a religion. Further, these believers in technology state that sophisticated machines and materials will greatly improve the quality of their lives. Technology will extend their life span and make physical tasks easier. For this reason, the scientist and the doctor are usually seen as respected professionals in America. In the technical knowledge of these specialists, many Americans see an answer to their hopes and fears.

The American media generally show the world of science and technology in this positive light. American commercials for medical care or drugs often use doctors and scientists for expert testimony, and many American television programs and movies explore the future possibilities of science and technology. Moreover, many media works focus on such topics as cloning, robotics, and space travel.

Yet, like the issues of the family and gender, there is an American counterargument to the benefits of technology. A growing number of Americans have come to distrust technology, believing that it is quickly destroying planet Earth. Food and cosmetic commercials sometimes refer to the natural ingredients in their products to speak to those who see technology as an enemy of their world. Selection 1 in this chapter will discuss the meaning of the "natural look" in makeup.

Equal Opportunity

Like the beliefs concerning gender and family, the concept of equal opportunity has also changed dramatically in recent years. A generation ago, it was usually the white male in America who had the greatest opportunities for important jobs and wealth.

Due to the efforts of civil rights activists and civil rights legislation from the sixties to today, minorities and women have been given greater opportunities in education, work, and housing. Most Americans now believe that any American—of whatever race, ethnicity, and gender—should be given the same rights and privileges. Still other Americans hold chauvinistic beliefs. These people believe that their race or sex is superior and that they should be granted America's best opportunities and greatest wealth.

In the past twenty years, the American media have responded to civil rights activists and federal law. Advertisements and television programs are beginning to show an America of many colors: a Bill Cosby, a Connie Chung, and a Geraldo Rivera, to name only a few minority media stars. Yet many civil rights activists and scholars argue that the colors and faces may have changed on television, but racism in the media still exists. These are questions that you will explore in Chapter 3.

America may not be a country of equal opportunity, yet the media portray this belief in many ways. As a critical observer of the media, you need to see how this belief in equal opportunity is shown. Are minorities and women portrayed in a positive light? Is the media's perception of a particular minority accurate? When is a minority portrayed in a racist way?

Wealth and Beauty

America is a country that often sends the message to its people that self-reliance and hard work will lead to monetary success. For many Americans, personal success in a capitalist society is synonymous with the accumulation of material wealth; so the more money you make, the more successful you are. The media often encourage this materialistic belief, highlighting the multimillion-dollar contracts of athletic superstars, movie actors, and entertainment executives and creating popular television series such as *Beverly Hills 90210* about the very wealthy.

As a critical observer of this American belief, you need to examine how subtly wealth has become a part of what you see and hear: the expensive clothing television actors wear, the fast, top-of-the-line cars they drive. Ask yourself if the poor are portrayed honestly on television. For example, are the poor ever seen as attractive and productive members of society, or are they most often shown as depressed and unfulfilled?

Related to this belief in the power of wealth is an emphasis on physical beauty. Media personalities (news reporters, movie and television actors, models in magazines, and actors in commercials) are usually attractive. They have nicely proportioned, thin bodies and ageless faces. As an observer of these media personalities, one begins to feel that the attractive person is normal and the average-looking person abnormal.

Again, you need to begin asking the following critical questions: How do these images of physical beauty affect me? Do these personalities minimize my appearance or my self-respect? What attributes, other than physical beauty, define my appreciation of a person? Why are wealth and beauty so important in selling products?

The Belief in a Happy Ending

Related to this American belief in wealth and beauty are questions about the nature of life. Is life always joyful? Can money and beauty ensure life's happiness? Or does life have pain, for the rich and the poor, the beautiful and the unattractive? Most all of us want a life free of serious pain. Yet all of us know that pain exists, and some of us realize that it visits all of us at one time or another. Certain cultures and philosophies focus on how one deals with life's conflicts. For example, the ancient Greek Stoics saw life as painful, and they provided a world view that attempted to deal with this pain.

Yet the American media frequently focus on the "happy ending" version of life. Most television shows present easy solutions to difficult life problems. American commercials most often present smiling, beautiful faces, so life's pain is often overlooked.

Again, as a critical observer of the American media, you need to examine whether the situation comedy, drama, or commercial is one that best explains the human story being portrayed and one that helps describe your own experiences.

Patriotism

It is natural for every American, or citizen of any other country, to want to love and respect his or her country. The question about patriotism is not whether one should be patriotic but the degree of patriotism one should have in order to be a responsible citizen. For example, when is it patriotic to criticize a particular action of your government? Is it ever not right to praise the practices of another country or political system?

You will often see patriotism emerge in the media in political campaigning, political commercials, and speech making. In Chapter 5, you will be critically examining two American political speeches, and you will be see how patriotic beliefs are used by political figures.

As with the other beliefs that we have examined so far, you will see that patriotism has different meanings for a wide range of American citizens. In studying political texts, especially, you need to see how the belief in love of country is used. Is the individual politician or political party using patriotism in a thoughtless way? Are you being encouraged to support any American practice simply because it is American? Or are you given historical and social evidence for why you should respect and be proud of your country?

Sometimes the American flag is shown in a political commercial or the colors red, white, and blue used to arouse the passions of American patriots. For these patriots, the American flag represents unqualified support for America, an acceptance of the slogan "America: love it or leave it!" In these cases, the flag and its colors lead to a kind of "knee-jerk" patriotic response for certain spectators. At other times, you may see a rock musician or a political activist wearing an American flag as a shirt, dress, or pants. Rather than indicating her patriotism, she may be suggesting a less-respectful attitude toward her country. As a critical observer of how patriotic or anti-American beliefs are used in America, you need to ask whether you are being forced into a patriotic or unpatriotic position, or whether you are being reasoned into one.

These seven American beliefs are important ones to consider as you work through the various chapters of this text. All of these chapters will deal with *American popular culture*, which I define as American practices and experiences that are available to, and practiced by, the vast majority of Americans: commercial television, popular music, sports, politics, and so on. You will notice that this definition of American popular culture does not include many of the arts, such as theater, classical music, and literature, that are more often appreciated by the wealthy and educated of our country.

As you examine the selections in the various chapters of this text, you will find that American fiction, television shows, and commercials deal on many levels with the issues of family, gender, wealth, and beauty that I have presented in this introduction. These works often express their attitudes toward these issues in subtle ways. For example, a commercial may be advertising an automobile and use as background an example of the American family and American wealth. It is this background that you will be critically examining. Moreover, in the political speeches that you will analyze, these seven American topics also help convey each speech's meanings.

I will be referring loosely to all the works you examine in this textbook as *texts*, so both written works, such as speeches, and visual material, such as television commercials and photographs, will be called texts. You will learn more about the definition of *text* in Selection 1.

Critical Practices

There are some important ways to read and interpret American beliefs, whether you find them in a political speech or in a commercial. There are three key critical practices you will need: (1) defining the concept you are using, (2) analyzing the text you are studying, and (3) making appropriate inferences about the text. To define, analyze, and infer are critical practices that you will use not only in understanding American beliefs but also in studying all aspects of American popular culture.

To Define

Before you begin to study American popular culture, you need to know how certain concepts in popular culture are being used. Concepts such as beliefs, myths, culture, and gender are essential when you investigate the unstated meanings of commercials and television shows. Yet you will find that these concepts vary in meaning, depending on how they are used and who uses them. What *myth* means to a student of American popular culture is different from what it means to a scholar of classical Greek mythology. What you need to do is to define a term as carefully as you can based upon the needs of your study. *To define* is to state the meaning of a word. For example, how is the term *myth* used by those studying American popular culture? Before you begin using this term, you need to define it so that your audience knows how you are using it.

There are two basic types of definitions: a *logical definition* and an *extended definition*. There is another type of definition that you should avoid using—a *circular definition*.

A definition is *logical* if it lists the essentials of a particular term. A logical definition is written precisely and clearly. Logical definitions usually begin generally and end specifically. The general part of a definition is called its *class*, the specific part its *characteristics*.

A logical definition of *myth* used in popular culture would say something like this: "A myth is a belief, set of beliefs, story, or set of stories that a group of people uses to explain their customs and their institutions." Note that "religious rites" is not included in this definition of *myth* as it would be if the term were defined by a classics scholar or anthropologist. Note also that the classification under which the definition would fit is belief and story, whereas the more detailed characteristics of a myth include customs and institutions. You could create a chart defining a myth in popular culture in this way:

Term	Classification	Characteristics
myth	belief/story	customs and institutions

Do you see how the characteristics (customs and institutions) further explain the classification, listing what these beliefs and stories are concerned with?

An *extended* definition places a term into a larger context, showing how other studies use the term and comparing how it is understood in these various studies. You usually find extended definitions in an essay where the writer of the extended definition often examines the history of the word (its etymology). She studies what characteristics the term shares with other disciplines, where these characteristics differ, as well as the more common and less common uses of the term.

Note that the way *myth* is used in cultural studies differs from its more traditional definition used by classicists and anthropologists. For example, a definition used by classicists would say that it is "a story of unknown authorship explaining a natural or human phenomenon, using gods and heroes." The classicist's definition could be charted this way:

Term	Classification	Characteristics
myth	story	unknown origin, explaining natural and human phenomena, using gods and heroes

You could write an entire essay on the common and uncommon definitions of *myth*. You could examine what elements these definitions share, where they differ, and the reasons why the definition changes with each discipline.

Circular definitions are those that use the term or its synonym somewhere in the definition itself. In this sense, the definition "goes in circles." It ends where it begins—with the same or similar word. A circular definition of *myth* could be the following: "A myth is a story of a natural or human phenomenon using mythological figures likes gods and heroes." Note here how "mythological" is used to describe the characteristics of a myth. If you do not know what a myth is, how can you determine what mythological figures are?

When writing your own definitions, remember that you cannot use the same term both in its general sense (myth) and in its specific sense (mythological figure). To say that a myth uses mythological figures is not to logically move from a general sense of the word to its more specific characteristics.

To Analyze

To analyze is to perform the most important activity in any critical task. In the activities you will complete in this text, analysis is the central practice you will be performing. In defining, you determine *what* you are examining. Moreover, in analyzing, you determine the *structure* and *significance* of what you are studying.

Analysis can be broadly defined as the study of what makes up something: the tracing of things to their essentials. For our purposes, the analysis of cultural texts involves uncovering the unstated beliefs that explain a particular text or texts: a television program, a commercial, a photograph, a political speech, and so on.

Analysis forms the central activity of critical thinking. As an overarching activity, it cannot be easily compartmentalized into a method with specific steps to follow. Analysis provides a system for any critical thinking, but this system or method is influenced by what you are studying.

However, there are certain basic questions that you can bring to any selection in this book. By answering these questions, you are analyzing the text before you. You are determining its essentials, or unstated premises, that inform the text. The key questions that you bring to these texts include these:

1. How is the text organized? Where is its main argument or focus? And how does it present this argument or focus? Through examples? Emotional appeal? Both a photograph and a political speech have an organization. A photograph has a focus, a political speech an argument.

2. What is the nature of the evidence? Are the details convincing or unconvincing? For example, in your mayor's speech, how does he try to convince you that your city needs a tax hike? Or in a photograph depicting a "typical" American family, what details do you find that create an overall focus or mood?

   In analysis, you continually move from the argument to the evidence. You touched on this movement in the introduction to this text. The evidence encourages you to re-form the argument, while the argument makes you re-study the details. In writing an essay of your own, you perform this same type of analytical movement from argument, or thesis, to the evidence you select to support your argument.

3. Is the argument convincing? Or is the overall effect of the work successful? By considering what a text says and how it says it, you come to judge it. That is, you identify what is effective and ineffective about the text. For example, if you are impressed with the beauty of a photograph, your analysis will allow you to say why. You will be able to discuss what the photograph's overall effect is and how the photographer achieves this effect. Moreover, if you are examining a political speech, you practice a similar sort of analysis. You determine what the speaker is saying, the evidence she uses, and the speech's overall success. More will be said about constructing political arguments in Chapter 5.

Analysis involves a constant sifting through of evidence, a careful restructuring of what the text is saying, and an assessment of the text's overall effect. Your analytical abilities improve as you continue to ask these questions in various texts. Although you cannot apply a set formula to every text that you study in order to analyze it effectively, you will learn as you analyze several texts what to emphasize: the argument, the detail, or your assessment. Developing your analytical abilities is an ongoing challenge.

Consider the following photograph, and apply these analytical questions to it:

1. What is it saying? How is it organized?
2. What details do you see in the composition?
3. Is the overall effect successful or unsuccessful? Why?

To Infer

Once you have analyzed a text, you may want to study it more carefully. Often when you move beyond your analysis, you make inferences about the text. *To infer* is to further explain your responses to a text, using both the evidence in the text and your conclusions about this evidence. Inferences are often conclusions that are not literally in the text but become clear from your careful study of the evidence that is there.

Inference making involves reasoned guessing. The conclusion you draw that goes beyond the evidence in the text is one that can be supported with reasons. Wild guessing is not inference making. If, in the photograph you have been analyzing, you were to say that the young man with the gun seems to be wealthy, you would need to provide reasons for your inference.

Inference making is at the heart of identifying beliefs in the texts of American popular culture. Just as the aim of successful commercials or political speeches is to mask many of the premises that make up these texts, it is your task to make the appropriate inferences to articulate these unstated beliefs. Inference making is also central to the reading of short fiction, which you will examine in Chapter 2.

Gregg Segal, "Steven and Veronica, Monrovia, California, 1993"

Like analysis, inference making improves with practice. No single method can serve every text in order for you to draw cogent inferences. Yet all inference making in popular culture centers around the following questions:

1. What type of evidence or detail is used in a text?
2. Does this evidence fit into a particular pattern? Does this pattern suggest an issue that is not directly mentioned in the text?

   Let's say that you are studying a photograph of seven people, gazing at the flag of the United States with their hands over their hearts. You would likely infer that this photograph is representing American patriotism. You could further infer that this photograph is presenting a positive attitude toward American patriotism. Yet you would be making an unsubstantiated inference if you concluded that this photograph was condemning Canada and Mexico, America's neighbors. Nowhere does the evidence in this photograph refer to the geographical neighbors of the United States.

3. Is any of the evidence or are any of the details peculiar? What do you make of this peculiarity? Does this peculiarity remind you of an idea or person not directly mentioned in the text?

Let's return to the imaginary photograph of the reverent American patriots and change it somewhat. Assume that of the seven people saluting the American flag, one man is not. He has his back to the flag and has been positioned in the very center of the composition. You would likely make a different inference here—one that would assume that a respect for the American flag is in question. Moreover, you would be incorrect to infer that the photograph was expressing a pro-Canadian or pro-Mexican position. Again, there is no evidence in the photograph to make this inference.

Now see what inferences you can make from the photograph you previously analyzed (p. 25).

Recapping

The American culture, like any culture in the world, is founded upon certain beliefs. Of course, not everyone in America follows each one of these beliefs. Yet the media tend to present a picture of an America with a consistent set of ideas and ways to behave. The beliefs that most directly explain American popular culture center on the following issues: family, gender, science and technology, equal opportunity, wealth and beauty, life as joy or pain, and patriotism.

You can begin to critically examine these beliefs that inform American popular culture by (1) defining the concepts that you use to describe these practices, (2) analyzing the texts of popular American culture, and (3) making appropriate inferences about these texts. To effectively define, analyze, and infer are practices that require much thought and practice. These are the basic activities of critical thinking, and you will rely on them whenever you study any aspect of American popular culture.

Reading Selections **1–4**

The following four reading selections will give you a better understanding of how to analyze texts in American popular culture. The first selection is from two chapters of a textbook titled *Signs in Contemporary Culture*. The author, Arthur Asa Berger, introduces you to the study of *semi-*

otics, a practice that analyzes signs, or the ways that words, pictures, and actions indicate meaning. Semiotics will provide you with another way to understand American popular culture by revealing what is suggested in the practices of daily life. The second selection is from a chapter of a book titled *The Signs of Our Time,* by Jack Solomon. In this chapter, Solomon analyzes American popular culture by explaining five myths. In some ways, the Solomon selection is similar to this chapter's introduction on the seven American beliefs. You will note that Solomon uses some of the semiotic terms that Berger has introduced.

Selections 3 and 4 will show you how semiotics can be used to examine cultural beliefs. In Selection 3, William Severini Kowinski analyzes those American beliefs that are represented by the American mall in chapters from his full-length study titled *The Malling of America.* In Selection 4, the great French theorist Roland Barthes explains many French cultural beliefs by analyzing the spectacle of wrestling in his essay "The World of Wrestling." These two selections will provide you with expert examples of how to analyze daily cultural practices.

Selection 1

"Signs and Images" and "No Sign as Sign"
Arthur Asa Berger

These two chapters, from *Signs in Contemporary Culture,* are written in a straightforward manner.

Arthur Asa Berger is a professor of communications and has written on culture and its relationship to the media. In the first part of "Signs and Images" Berger defines five semiotic terms, then uses them to analyze common human experiences. In "No Sign as Sign," Berger shows you how inaction is also a sign by analyzing several daily actions in which not acting is suggestive. He then analyzes the cultural significance of not wearing makeup, examining what two American thinkers—Ralph Waldo Emerson and Mircea Eliade—have to say about nature and nudity.

These chapters are easy to read, though some of the terms may be difficult to understand at first. Your job is to carefully study the semiotic terms, learning their meanings and comparing one term to another. Then see how Berger applies his knowledge of these terms to the daily experiences that he analyzes. Your knowing these terms will both help you understand the following three selections in this chapter and provide you with terms to use in your writing about cultural texts.

Reading–Writing Preparation

Before you read this selection, you may want to answer the following questions in writing or discussion:

1. What do you think the word *sign* means? Consider its use in the following two statements: (a) Stop at the stop sign. (b) Last year's earthquake is a sign of more disaster to come.

2. When someone takes a photograph, what do you think the viewer of this photograph sees?

Chapter Fifteen
Signs and Images

1 Signs are generally composed of a number of different elements, each of which itself may function as a sign. Some signs, of course, are extremely simple—such as an arrow indicating where one should go to arrive at a desired destination. But most signs are much more complicated than that, and we usually find ourselves with a number of things to consider in the analysis of a sign.

2 Let me suggest some terms we might use in dealing with signs so that when I use a word we will know precisely what I have in mind. We will proceed from the simple to the complicated.

3 *Signemes or Sign Elements.* These are the most fundamental elements in a sign, elements that cannot be broken down further. They are the most simple signs. A bubble in a glass of champagne would be a sign element or signeme. So would the light yellow color champagne has.

4 *Signs.* Signs are more complex than signemes and might be called complex signs, except that it is a bit unwieldly to use that term all the time. We define a sign as something which stands (or can be made to stand) for something else or which can be used to stand for something else. Signs are collections of signemes. Thus, a champagne bottle is a sign that contains many different sign elements: wire, gold foil, a label, and so on.

5 *Icon.* An icon is a collection of visual signs, as in a photograph, a frame from a film, a "still" from a television program, an advertisement, etc. An icon, such as a photograph, might show people wearing certain clothes or costumes in certain settings doing certain activities: and all of these phenomena are signs which can be read for meaning.

6 *Sign Assemblage.* This is a collection of signs of an auditory as well as visual nature that occurs in a relatively short passage of time. I wish to have a way of considering sound effects and music as signs in specific situations and I am using sign assemblage for this purpose. A sign assemblage is part of a narrative or text.

7 *Text.* This is a term which is used, conventionally, to mean a systematically related collection of signs in a narrative, such as a film, television program, play, and so on. We use it, loosely, to mean "the subject of our analysis" (which means that newspaper and magazine advertisements also are texts, though relatively simple texts). Thus, the CBS National News, *Raiders of the Lost Ark*, poems, a Burger King commercial, *A Passage to India*, an advertisement in *Playboy*, songs, as well as descriptive, expository, and argumentative materials, are all texts, though some are more complex and challenging than others.

8 This system of categories or definitions has deficiencies, but it does allow us to discuss signs more systematically and with more specificity.

9 Let me offer an example of how these terms might be used in the analysis of a wedding as a text.

Signeme/ Sign Elements	Bubbles in champagne
Sign	Champagne bottle
Icon	Photograph of bride and groom drinking champagne
Sign Assemblage	Sounds and smells, when photograph was being snapped

From Arthur Asa Berger, *Signs in Contemporary Culture*, pp. 114–126. ©1984 by Arthur A. Berger, 1989. Reissued by Sheffield Publishing Company, Salem, Wisconsin. Reprinted by permission of the publisher.

Text	The wedding itself, from beginning to end

A champagne bottle is a rather complex sign, made up of signemes such as foil, wire, a label, a certain brand name (which is an indicator of the quality, cost, or value of the champagne itself), a yellow wine, bottles, etc.—all of which might be analyzed.

10   Why, we might ask, do we have champagne at weddings and other celebrations? One reason might be that good champagne is relatively expensive, so serving champagne is an indicator of one's wealth (and power) and that one wants to give one's guests the "very best." Champagne is also full of life and vitality: it has bubbles that signify these things. Champagne is sparkling and effervescent. When we drink champagne we "take in" this life and make it part of ourselves. Good champagne is also quite delicious and has the virtue of going with almost all dishes. So it is champagne we drink at weddings, at Bar Mitzvahs, at festive parties . . . champagne to signify taste, to signify class, to signify life.

11   There is also something sexual about the way champagne spurts out of its bottle which is another reason champagne is used at weddings. Champagne functions as a kind of metaphor for sexual relations: it is not for nothing that the bride throws a bouquet of flowers away, symbolizing the fact that she is to be "deflowered." Opening a bottle of champagne is, then, a symbolic rehearsal of male orgasm.

12   Technically, only wine made in the Champagne region of France can be called champagne. But now champagne has become an appellation[1] used for an entire genre of sparkling white wines. So, in one sense, champagne is a case-study in the appropriation[2] of a sign, and champagne-style wines are now neither rare nor expensive—though fine champagne is both.

---

1. appellation: a name
2. appropriation: the use of

Photography

13   The photograph has come a long way since 1826 when photography was born. Nicéphore Niépce's picture of a view from his window is often cited as the first photograph. It is a crude and grainy shot of a garden. Since that time our technology and our attitudes toward photography have changed considerably. We now have cameras that don't use film, cameras that produce photographs just seconds after we have snapped the shutter, and disc cameras which promise (in the advertisements) "decision-free" photography.

14   As the camera has changed from a crude machine to a gadget to a highly sophisticated device, our conceptions of photography have also evolved. It is fair to say that photography is now seen by many critics as an art form of major importance. Prints of great photographs by masters such as Ansel Adams and Diane Arbus now sell for thousands of dollars, and there are presently numerous art galleries devoted only to photography.

15   There is developing a body of criticism, also, including works such as Susan Sontag's *On Photography* and Roland Barthes's *Camera Lucida.* One important notion of many critics interested in photography is that the photograph is not just a simple reflection of reality. Thus Howard S. Becker writes in an essay, "Aesthetics and Truth:"

> When people make or use photographs for scientific or scholarly purposes, they do not strive for unique visions or personal styles. Instead, they want material that helps them answer a question taken seriously in an established community concerned with such questions. Such photographs are frequently made in a standardized fashion, so accepted in the user community that its members think it the only way such pictures can be made. But every choice embodied in those images—of framing, lens, lighting, printing—is a choice that could have been made differently, with a

different photographic result. (*Society*, July/August 1980:27–28)

What Becker points out is that there are all kinds of aesthetic decisions to be made in even the most straightforward shot. The camera does not run by itself or, as Becker puts it, "photographs do not record reality neutrally."

16 The photographer, in a sense, creates the reality of the photograph. This "reality" is affected by the lighting to a great degree. Strong lighting, which negates shadows and imparts a two-dimensionality to the persons or objects being photographed, yields a very different effect than soft lighting. The chiaroscuro effect, in which there are strong lights and darks, conveys a different attitude to the viewer from flat lighting or other kinds of lighting. And lighting is only one of the components of the photograph.

17 (The idea that the camera merely reflects reality is responsible for the notion many people have that television always tells the truth. People believe this because, as they tell you, "seeing is believing." What people do not think about—and this applies equally to still photographs—is that what they see on television is what someone wants them to see. Sometimes what the television camera doesn't show is more important than what it does. The camera always records a particular person's perspective or point of view which may be part of the truth but not all the truth.)

18 In short, there is much room for judgment in the taking of photographs and in the making of the photographs. Every photograph reflects a number of things about the photographer who took it: his or her technical ability, aesthetic sensibility, social and political orientation, and values, to name some of the more important considerations.

19 Just as the photograph reflects what the photographer knows, what we see in a photograph reflects what we know. What we know, believe, and are affects what we get out of a given photograph. As John Berger writes in *Ways of Seeing*, "the way we see things is affected by what we know or what we believe." (1972:8) (Sociologists often discuss the same thing when they talk about selective perception and selective inattention—the way people see only what they want to see and don't see what they don't wish to see.)

20 Photographs are one important form of image, for Berger, which he defines as a "sight which has been recreated or reproduced." He adds, "It is an appearance, or a set of appearances, which has been detached from the place and time in which it first made its appearance and preserved—for a few moments or a few centuries." (1972:9, 10) These images provide "direct testimony about the world which surrounded other people at other times," and thus are of value to the social historian—even though the "way of seeing" of the photographer must be taken into account. We must also take into account the ways of seeing of the people at large—their assumptions about reality, the good life, beauty, taste, and so on.

21 For the average person, a photograph is a way of capturing a moment in time and preserving it. People take photographs at events of special meaning to them: weddings, bar mitzvahs, parties, and convocations,[3] for example. It is as if some kind of a visual image were required to certify that something happened. These photos have an existential[4] significance. They say, "look, we exist!" And when we take photographs of ourselves in front of monuments, cathedrals in France, with natives in exotic lands, we are preserving a record of our exploits. "Look," say these photographs, "I've had adventures, I've seen things, I've done things." (I'm making a distinction here between snapshots of ourselves on our travels and portraits that we take which usually do not show us doing anything, but just being ourselves.)

22 In his essay, "The Image-Freezing Machine," Stanley Milgram points out that photographs not

---

3. convocations: meetings

4. existential: focusing on daily life

only create their own reality but also often affect reality. He writes:

> There is a universe of events that we smell and a universe that we hear; there is also a universe of events whose existence is embodied in photographs. Thus each year we eagerly await the official Chinese Communist May Day photograph to see who is photographed alongside the chairman and who has been displaced. The official photograph is not only a reflection of the political reality, but itself solidifies that reality and becomes an element in it. The question, therefore, is to what degree events that exist in photographs exert an effect outside the photograph. Does a photograph act back on and shape the real world? (*Society,* November/December 1976:12)

Milgram's answer to this questions is "yes!" The photograph has a double valence:[5] it both reflects and affects reality.

23   The photographic image permeates our culture. There are photographs in our books, magazines, newspapers, on the walls of our houses, on billboards, in advertising of all sorts. We are bombarded by so many photographs that we seldom take a moment to examine them and consider the reality they present to us and the effects they may be having upon us. It might be worthwhile examining them carefully, taking them seriously.

---

5. valence: force

Chapter Sixteen
No Sign as Sign

---

24   No sign is also a sign. Since we are sign-giving and sign-interpreting animals and since for much of our lives we are involved with this kind of activity, no signs or absent signs (where signs are expected) also communicate something to us. Let me suggest some areas where a lack of signs is a sign, and say a bit about what these absent signs reveal.

Area	Meaning
Phone rings but caller says nothing	Prankster, pervert, or wrong number and embarrassment
Dog not barking at murderer	Master revealed as killer
No response to stimuli	Catatonic[6]
Not doing what is expected of you	Aggressive passivity
No brain waves	Dead
No reply to letter	Rejection, lack of decision, letter misplaced

25   One of the few laws that social scientists seem to have discovered about people is that the "law of reciprocity" usually operates. We feel we should *get* and amount equal to what we *give* (though there are, I admit, aberrations such as the potlatch[7]), that we should be treated fairly and justly. Closely allied to this principle is the matter of feedback. We feel that when we give a sign to someone, such as saying "hello," we

---

6. catatonic: describing a mental illness in which the body becomes rigid

7. potlatch: ceremonial feast among Native Americans in which gifts are exchanged

should get an appropriate response—some form of greeting or reply. When we don't get the response we expect, we take it as a sign of something. Saying nothing can speak volumes.

26   It isn't always possible to determine what "absent" signs mean—when we get a phone call and nobody answers, it could be a pervert or a criminal calling to see whether anyone is home. But it also could be someone who got a wrong number, recognized that the voice answering the phone was wrong, and simply hung up. When a person doesn't say anything and doesn't hang up, then we know something fishy is going on and should, so people from the phone company tell us, hang up immediately.

27   The dog *not* barking during a murder is a different sort of thing. Here it is important to recognize that the dog *should* have been barking—since, presumably, dogs bark at strangers—so when the dog doesn't bark, that becomes a sign of something. Or, to be more precise, someone—namely the dog's owner or someone the dog knows.

28   Not doing anything when something is expected of you is a form of hostile behavior labeled "passive aggression" by some and "aggressive passivity" by others. Passive–aggressive people are angry and express this by not doing their fair share which, usually, leads to a response by others who adopt the same tactics. This kind of behavior tears relationships apart, because the partners in the passive–aggressive scenario keep mounting the stakes, keep refusing to do more and more of what is expected of them so that eventually, without striking a blow, they come to hate one another. What makes this so insidious is that nothing *seems* to be happening; a wife keeps putting off mending something for her husband, a husband "forgets" to pick up something his wife asked him to get at the supermarket, and so on. Before long, conscious and unconscious resentments poison the relationship and we are left with people who have literally done *nothing* to one another—with vengeance.

The Natural Look: (No Makeup)

29   The natural look is best described in terms of what it is not—it is a "look" in which no makeup is used, no lipstick, no eye shadow, no cosmetics of any kind. It is based on the rejection of cosmetics, of that which is "artificial" and contrived. It is only meaningful, then, in the context of a beauty system in which, at one pole, there is glamour and cosmetics, and at the other pole, diametrically[8] opposed, there is beauty and naturalness.

30   Nature is an important word in the American mind. Whether it is true or not, we see ourselves (and have done so for centuries) as living in nature in contrast to the Europeans (in particular) who we see as living in history and having culture, institutions, and other resources that go with this circumstance. We stress our natural state and its concomitants:[9] purity, honesty, simplicity, and so on.

31   Thus the natural look, which is a contradiction in terms if you think about it, is more than just a style; it is a sign of a certain orientation toward life and society. It is a kind of statement about oneself and one's philosophy. It reflects an essentially pastoral longing—for the simple life of shepherdesses and herdsmen in some simple and ideal society. In such a state one has escaped from history, from institutions, from complexity, and troubles, and one has attained a paradisiacal state.

32   This longing for an escape to nature has deep roots in the American experience. The Puritans came to America to establish a Holy Commonwealth in nature in the early 1600s and our writers and poets have celebrated our natural state for hundreds of years. Consider, for example, the concluding lines of Emerson's poem, "America, My Country," which was written in 1833:

> *Land without history, land lying all*
> *In the plain daylight of the temperate zone,*
> *Thy plain acts*

---

8. diametrically: directly

9. concomitants: those elements that accompany

Without exaggeration done in day;
Thy interests contested by their manifold good
*   sense,*
In their own clothes without the ornament
Of bannered army harnessed in uniform.
Land where—and 'tis in Europe counted a
*   reproach—*
Where man asks questions for which man was
*   made.*
A land without nobility, or wigs, or debt.
No castles, no cathedrals, and no kings;
Land of the forest.

These lines describe the philosophical stance implied by the natural look. What is stressed here? Such things as daylight, plain acts, no ornaments or fancy uniforms (i.e., fancy clothes) and, of course, no wigs.

33 Whether Americans really are living in nature is beside the point; we have traditionally idealized it and used our alleged naturalness as a means of establishing an identity and as a way of reflecting our egalitarian[10] and spiritual values. We see ourselves as living in nature and that is what is important, since people act on the basis of their perceptions of reality, not reality itself.

34 There is, I believe, a still deeper and more profound meaning to the natural look, American attitudes about naturalness, and our repudiation of Europe, history, and culture. This meaning has to do with the extension of the natural look to what might be called the natural state—the one that existed before the Fall. In the garden of Eden, Adam and Eve lived in a natural paradise and in a state of nudity. They had no knowledge of good and evil. It was only after they disobeyed God and ate from the tree of knowledge and *recognized that they were naked* that Adam and Eve were expelled from Paradise.

35 What Mircea Eliade writes, in *The Sacred and The Profane*, about baptismal nudity is relevant here:

---

10. egalitarian: describing the belief that people should have equal rights

Baptismal nudity too bears a meaning that is at once ritual and metaphysical. It is abandoning "the old garment of corruption and sin, which the baptized person takes off in imitation of Christ, the garment with which Adam was clothed after his sin"; but it is also return to primitive innocence, to Adam's state before the fall. "Oh admirable!" Cyril writes. "Ye were naked before the eyes of all and felt no shame. Because verily ye bear within you the image of the first Adam, who was naked in Paradise and felt no shame." (1961:134)

From this perspective, the natural look has a symbolic significance full of implications. On one level it is a kind of "antistyle" statement, a repudiation of "the made-up look" and all that goes with it. On another level, it is connected with American attitudes toward nature and attitudes connected with nature: egalitarianism, simplicity, honesty, individualism, and freedom. (This is contrasted with European decadence and sensuality, for example.)

36 On a still deeper level, the natural look is connected with a desire to regain paradise and escape from guilt and shame. (I doubt that the person adopting the natural look is aware of the symbolic significance of the act. People seldom are aware of the full meaning or significance of what they do, wear, say, and so on.) This desire for paradise is, in itself, pregnant with meaning, for in paradise there is, Cyril tells us, "no shame." Eliade argues that movements like nudism reflect a "nostalgia" for Eden and are camouflaged or degenerated forms of religious behavior. Nudism and movements for complete sexual freedom represent, he says:

the desire to re-establish the paradisiacal state before the Fall, when sin did not exist and there was no conflict between the pleasures of the flesh and conscience. (1961:207)

It would seem, then, that the natural look is a sign that suggests some kind of anxiety about guilt

and sexuality, on the personal level—an anxiety that can be escaped by a return to natural paradise or, at the very least, a step in that direction.
37   *Note:* I realize there is also a natural look that involves makeup of a special kind—to give the effect of naturalness. I would imagine that the same dynamics and meaning apply to this natural look as well as to the no-makeup natural look.

Critical Explorations: Reading

Answer the following questions as you reread the two Berger chapters. Rather than asking you to rephrase this material, these questions encourage you to critically explore the definitions Berger introduces and the inferences he makes about American popular culture. You may use these questions and your answers for your reading or dialogic journal.

1. The first section of "Signs and Images" carefully defines key semiotic terms: signeme, sign, icon, sign assemblage, and text. Use the following chart to divide up the essential parts of each definition:

Term	Classification	Characters or Examples

2. In paragraphs 9–12, Berger makes many inferences about the use of champagne. List the inferences he makes, and cite the evidence he uses for making these inferences. Do you think these inferences are accurate ones?
3. Reread the Stanley Milgram extract in paragraph 22. What do you think he means by the question "Does a photograph act back on and shape the real world?" How would you answer this question?
4. In paragraph 25, Berger introduces the law of reciprocity. He explains how this concept works through the use of examples. Study these examples; then formulate your own definition of the law of reciprocity.
5. The subsection "The Natural Look: (No Makeup)" can be seen as a carefully argued short essay. Analyze this short essay (para-

graphs 29–37). What is Berger's argument? What evidence does he use to support his argument? Is his argument convincing?

Selection 2

"Of Myths and Men: Culture's Hidden Frames"
Jack Solomon

This selection is a chapter from Professor Jack Solomon's *The Signs of Our Time: The Secret Meanings of Everyday Life.* This chapter is an analysis of the cultural forces that explain aspects of American culture: its media, toys, food, buildings, and so on. This is one of his early chapters, in which Solomon identifies five myths that explain American cultural practices. Compare what Solomon says to what you have read in the introduction to this chapter, and see whether Solomon's focus is similar.

Jack Solomon is an English professor, and he uses what he has learned in analyzing literature to understand nonliterary texts such as commercials and popular movies.

This is a very readable selection. Solomon writes in a witty, sometimes conversational style. He is well-read, and he uses material from many disciplines—not only literature but science and philosophy as well. In almost every case, Solomon gives some background on the figures he refers to—Roland Barthes in paragraph 9, William Blake in paragraphs 15 and 16, and Thomas Kuhn in paragraph 34. As you read, see how these figures and their ideas help you better understand the five myths that Solomon explores. Also note that Solomon uses some of the semiotic terms that you were introduced to in Selection 1.

Reading–Writing Preparation

Before you read this selection, you may want to answer the following questions in writing or discussion:

1. When you consider your childhood, what recollections do you have? Are they positive or negative? Do you think that most Americans believe that childhood is a time of pleasure?

2. How do you think money is regarded in the United States? What attitudes do you think most Americans have about those who are wealthy and about what wealth can do for the average American?

Of Myths and Men: Culture's Hidden Frames

A mythology reflects its region.

Wallace Stevens

1   As I stared at the cover of the January 26, 1987, issue of *Time* magazine, three battered G.I.'s stared back at me beneath a bold headline. "*PLATOON*," it read, "Viet Nam as It Really Was."

2   And so *Time*, in a feature story on Oliver Stone's Oscar-winning film, charted yet another cinematic contribution to the ever-unfolding mythology of Vietnam—a mythology that has included *Apocalypse Now, The Deer Hunter, The Hanoi Hilton, Full Metal Jacket*, the "Rambo" films, and even *The Green Berets*. More such films will appear in the years to come as Americans continue to tell and retell the story of Vietnam, weaving a mythic web that future generations may well compare with Homer's epic tales of the Trojan War.

3   You may be surprised that I call the stories of the Vietnam War a "mythology," comparing them with the legends of the ancient Greeks. Surely fifty thousand American dead and over a million Vietnamese casualties are hardly the stuff of fiction and fantasy. No, such a war was no myth. It was an all too real national and international catastrophe from which we are still recovering. And yet, when we look at the Vietnam War from a semiotic perspective, seeking to understand the many interpretations that it has endured, we find the clear outline of history blurring into the gray depths of mythology. Here, the objective clarity of events yields to ideology;[1] combat slips into code; and the "truth" of experience—"Viet Nam as it really was"—becomes hostage to the teller of the tale.

4   But whose myth should we believe? John Wayne's or Francis Ford Coppola's? Oliver Stone's or Sylvester Stallone's? Believe Wayne, and Vietnam appears as Lyndon Johnson wanted it to appear: a war against totalitarianism,[2] a noble-minded defense of freedom. Believe Coppola, and the war was a moral fiasco that corrupted America just as the Belgian Congo corrupted Kurtz, the fallen missionary in Joseph Conrad's *Heart of Darkness*. For Stallone, Vietnam has all the moral complexity of a "He-Man" cartoon, while in Oliver Stone's *Platoon*, the war is reframed as a myth of male initiation, the story of a young soldier coming to manhood in a contest

Reprinted by permission of The Putnam Publishing Group/Jeremy P. Tarcher, Inc. From Solomon, Jack. *The Signs of Our Time.* © 1988 by Jack Fisher Solomon, Ph.D.

1. ideology: belief system of a dominant group

2. totalitarianism: governmental system that controls all and does not allow dissent

between surrogate[3] fathers. Is this, finally, what Vietnam was all about?

5   Certainly not to a Vietnamese peasant. Nor to the women who waited at home while their sons and lovers fought it out in a distant jungle. Nor even to many of the men who were there. The same events take on a very different appearance depending on who is looking at them. In this sense, the war can be viewed as a sign, as an experience surrounded by a mythology whose meaning refers more to the values of its interpreters than to the actual conflict. To put this another way, *Time*'s headline is misleading: no single version of the war can represent "Viet Nam as it really was." There are only versions, stories erected within a mythic frame.

6   The myths of Vietnam have been particularly visible in the photographic imagery that the war produced. In the late 1960s, when American revulsion to the war began to reach its peak, the iconic image of a naked child running away from her napalmed village, or of a Vietcong guerrilla grimacing as a bullet shatters his brains, told a story of American brutality and callousness that literally and figuratively left Hanoi's brutality and callousness out of the picture. But in the 1980s, as Americans forgot the moral ambiguities of the war amid a general patriotic revival spearheaded by the Reagan presidency, the picture was reversed. Images of middle-aged men running their trembling hands over the black marble walls of the Vietnam War Memorial tell the tale of American suffering in Vietnam, but leave Vietnamese suffering outside the frame. Meanwhile, the "Rambo" films propagate a mythology of betrayal, blaming the American failure in Vietnam on the antiwar movement, and offering the figure of a machine gun–wielding Sylvester Stallone as a symbol of vicarious revenge for battles lost.

7   For the French semiotician Roland Barthes, photographs do an especially good job of propagating cultural myths. That's because we assume they mirror reality; a photographic image presents itself to us as an absolutely neutral[4] representation of its subject. A camera, supposedly, never lies. In fact, however, any photograph—whether taken by a photojournalist in the Vietnam jungles or by Dad with his Kodak in the backyard—can be stage-managed. Just look at your family photo album. How many pictures show the family gathered round, smiling brightly, despite the quarrel that broke out only moments before? By telling, or sometimes forcing, Mom, Dad, and Junior to say "cheese," we manufacture images of the happy families we want to believe in, even if that's not what our family is like at all.

8   Similarly, when you look at the photographic image of a fashion model, you're not really seeing the natural representation of a human being. Through the careful orchestration of light, camera angle, background, airbrush, and so on, a fashion photographer doesn't so much capture as *manufacture* an image—an image that represents not the model but a cultural ideal of human beauty. Just think of the way that Cheryl Tiegs and Christie Brinkley have become figures symbolic of a particular "look" that our culture admires. The finished photograph covers all this up by pretending to represent its subject as she "really" looks, but this is a myth. The *Cosmo* Girl, for instance, and the model who portrays her, are not really one and the same. The model is the fashion photographer's raw material for the myth, but while the model is real, the image manufactured for the cover of *Cosmopolitan* is not.

9   Photographs don't create myths by accident, however. In a book appropriately titled *Mythologies*, Barthes explores the way that photographs produce a "reality effect" that conceals the ideological motives of the culture behind them. Probing beneath the surface of a *Paris-Match* cover photo featuring a black African soldier devotedly saluting the French flag, for example, Barthes sees more than an innocent image of a man dressed in

---

3. surrogate: substitute

4. neutral: without a point of view

a French uniform. Instead, he decodes the way in which a colonial power naturalizes its own ideology. The editors of *Paris-Match* picked this photograph because they wanted their readers to believe "here is the image of a devoted French soldier." But the picture was not so innocent as that because, in presenting the apparent equality of devotion among all those who serve under the French flag, it distracted its viewer from noticing the fact that the African soldier was really serving in the army of his conquerors. His apparent contentment belied the simmering resentment that would eventually lead to violent uprisings against French rule. For Barthes, the photograph was simply part of a cultural mythology, actually a sort of propaganda, in which colonial power was framed so as to appear to be both natural and necessary, part of the proper order of things.

10 Barthes intended his essays in *Mythologies* to be subversive, and (in the semiotic sense) they were, for each was intended to jolt the French out of their cultural complacency and force them to confront their own ideological presuppositions. What Barthes meant to do was compel his readers to look under the surface of ordinary images and objects of their daily lives in order to see the cultural forces that were producing them. To understand those forces, French readers would have to know the historical circumstances that brought them into being. They couldn't "read" the photograph in the *Paris-Match* cover, for example, without knowing the history of the French colonial experience in Africa. Semiotic understanding, in other words, requires historical understanding, and one of the major tasks of semiotics is to reveal the histories behind our perceptions.

11 Indeed, you might look at *The Signs of Our Time* as a sort of American "Mythologies," a probing into the histories and meanings of some of the most common objects, images, and beliefs of American culture. For American society, too, is permeated through and through with cultural myths that present themselves as realities, as "life as it really is." But life, as the semiotician sees it, never presents itself to us in such a straightforward manner. Between our perceptions and the realities we perceive there always lies a cultural myth. Let's take five classic cultural "myths," which appear as inseparable parts of the natural world to most people, and look at them the way a semiotician would see them.

The Myth of Childhood

12 Consider, for example, our perception of childhood. For most of us, childhood is a stage of life separate from adulthood, a time of innocence set off against the experience of grown-up life. It seems only natural to view childhood this way. How else *could* we look at it? "Quite otherwise," history answers, for as Roger Sale explains in his book *Fairy Tales and After: From Snow White to E. B. White:*

> In our sense, children and childhood did not exist until recent centuries. . . . If there were any stages in the growth of children, they were simply before and after infancy. This is easily seen in medieval and early Renaissance depictions of the Seven Ages of Man and in portraits of royal and noble children in that period. There are no children there, at least not as we think of them, but babes in arms . . . and then people of varying sizes all of whom have adult faces. People we think of as children look like midgets.

13 Our perception of the child has changed owing to a major shift in the way families make their livings. Before the Industrial Revolution of the eighteenth and nineteenth centuries, most European families lived on the land. Farm life necessitated the full participation of everyone in the economic life of the family, and so youngsters whom we would now regard as being barely out of infancy were expected to do their share of the work. With little distinction between an "adult's" and a "child's" responsibilities, few distinctions were made between children and adults. Children were thus seen *as* adults, albeit smaller and weaker ones.

14   The distinctions that we now make between childhood and adulthood began to emerge once the Industrial Revolution shifted the center of economic activity from the farm to the factory and office. During the eighteenth and nineteenth centuries, the majority of Europe's population moved from the country to the city and, consequently, the children of the new economic order generally had less work to do. You don't have to feed the pigs or plough any fields when you live in an urban setting. Father earned the family's wages and mother took care of the house, but the kids were left with few responsibilities of their own. In response, a new myth of childhood emerged, declaring that children shouldn't have to work or bear adult responsibilities at all, but should be free to play and to learn.

15   By the end of the eighteenth century, child labor thus began to be viewed for the first time as a kind of violation of nature, an evil intrusion into the lives of innocent children. We can catch an early glimpse of the emerging sensibility by reading William Blake's *Songs of Innocence,* poems in which he often depicts the plight of exploited children sent to work before they even had a chance to *be* children. In the poem "The Chimney Sweeper," for example, a young London chimney sweep tells us his story:

> *When my mother died I was very young,*
> *And my father sold me while yet my tongue*
> *Could scarcely cry " 'weep! 'weep! 'weep! 'weep!"*
> *So your chimneys I sweep, and in soot I sleep.*

16   Blake's chimney sweeps dream of an angel who will set them free and take them to heaven, but they wake to cold days and hard work. By the early nineteenth century, however, children began to appear *as* angels, or at least as superior beings, in the poetry of William Wordsworth, who perhaps did more to construct the myth of childhood than anyone else. In his great "Ode on Intimations of Immortality from Recollections of Early Childhood," Wordsworth addresses the child as a kind of infant philosopher, a "Mighty Prophet" and "Seer[5] blest," whose "exterior semblance[6] doth belie/Thy soul's immensity." No one could have written that in the middle ages, when children were regarded as being born in the wrath of original sin, saved only by the rituals of the Church.

17   By the mid-nineteenth century, the myth of childhood as we know it today was pretty much in place. That was the period in which child-labor laws first began to reform the exploitation of young children in the workplace, and public education made schooling a reality for more European youngsters than ever before. Protected from the corrupting pressures of the working world, the child began to assume an aura[7] of innocence that continues into the present day.

18   The myth of childhood innocence has all the sentimental attractiveness of a tale written by A. A. Milne or Kenneth Grahame, but it is still only a myth. At present, it appears that a new myth may be emerging, one not of childhood innocence but of childhood experience. The fact that teachers are now being asked to educate students about the danger of AIDS, for example, is a sign that adults now suspect—or fear—that their children are sexually active and must be warned and protected. Birth-control clinics and substance-abuse treatment on grade-school campuses are a far cry from the world of *Winnie the Pooh* or *The Wind in the Willows.*

19   In short, the myth of childhood innocence is weakening all around us, but it's not going down without a fight. The resurgence of interest in stuffed toys, particularly Edwardian-style[8] teddy bears, signals a nostalgic desire for the innocent icons of a bygone era. The appearance of elabo-

---

5. seer: prophet

6. semblance: appearance

7. aura: atmosphere

8. Edwardian: referring to the reign of the British king Edward VII (1901–1910)

rate rocking horses in the more expensive toy stores is another sign of this nostalgia for the icons of the Victorian-Edwardian nursery. However, the self-conscious revival of such emblems of mythical childhood suggests that this is a last-ditch effort, and that the children of the future will be seen differently from the way they are seen now.

Myths of Gender

20 Perhaps the most naturalized of all the cultural myths that frame our perceptions of reality are the myths of gender and sexual identity. We normally assume that sexual traits are something determined by nature rather than by culture, by sheer biology, not ideology, but that's not entirely the case. The ideological motivations behind our perceptions of the sexes can be revealed by semiotic analysis.

21 You'll recognize the myths of gender as sets of opposite psychological and social traits: "men are rational," "women are intuitive"; "men are active," "women are passive"; "men are ambitious," "women are nurturing"; "a man's place is in the office," "a woman's place is in the home." The belief that a man can find fulfillment in his career but that a woman's happiness lies at home and with her family was a particularly potent cultural myth in the 1950s and 1960s, but though we now live in an era of feminist myth and consciousness, the old myth is still going strong. We don't have to look at Phyllis Schlafly's attacks on the Equal Rights Amendment to find signs of the continuing authority of the myth. A glance at a simple advertisement can tell us all we need to know, particularly when it pretends to be challenging what we might call the "myth of the happy housewife."

22 In a recent Whirlpool magazine ad, a woman chats happily on her kitchen telephone, waiting for the dishwasher to finish. The scene's relative darkness indicates it's evening, suggesting that the woman has probably come home from work,

eaten dinner, and changed into jeans, a sweater, and flats before seeing to the dishes. In other words, the setting implies that this is no housecoat-and-apron drudge of the 1950s; this is a modern liberated woman. But even though she has shed her apron and has apparently gotten a job of her own, she's still associated with the kitchen and the telephone. We don't see a man in the kitchen, and we don't see the woman doing any office "homework"—as we commonly see men doing in advertisements featuring products (such as computers) aimed at male audiences. Furthermore, a televised version of the same ad reveals that the woman on the phone is talking to her mother about dishwasher noise. According to the myth of the happy housewife, this is the sort of thing that women discuss with one another.

23 Although the ad pretends to adapt itself to the liberated 1980s, it has actually only updated the myth of the happy housewife. The modern woman in the ad doesn't look like a fifties-era housewife but, like her earlier counterpart, she is associated with the kitchen, the telephone, and her mother. Even in an age of feminist consciousness, we can still find the American Housewife in an advertisement that appears to say one thing—"Whirlpool announces the end of the noisy dishwasher"—but is really a sign of the enduring patriarchal[9] vision of American womanhood, the traditional belief that "a woman's place is in the home."

24 A more subtle gender myth lurks behind our belief that women are the more beautiful sex. "Men see," the myth says, "but women are to be seen." "Men are voyeurs,"[10] as Freud put it, "women are exhibitionists." There is a long history behind this myth that the English art critic John Berger explores in his book *Ways of Seeing*. Berger analyzes the history of the nude in

---

9. patriarchal: referring to the father; male control

10. voyeur: one who looks on

Western art, pointing out how nude portraiture has always assumed a male viewer gazing upon a female subject. Such paintings, he insists, are created *by* men, *of* women, *for* men. The modern version of this genre is, of course, the *Playboy* centerfold. Even though the famous *Cosmopolitan* centerfold of Burt Reynolds proved that women like to look at men too, the predominant cultural myth still holds that ogling is a male prerogative. Women have been taught to turn their gazes inward, to watch themselves being watched, conscious of being forever on display. Men are accordingly associated with binoculars and telescopes, women with mirrors.

25   In attempting to subvert the myths of gender that have so long dominated American consciousness, feminists have developed their own myths. During the 1970s women disregarded the passive, nurturing housewife and invented the superwoman—iconically represented by the comic-book character of Wonder Woman—who can have it all: career, family, and sex appeal. But this myth put so much pressure on women that some began to crack under the strain in the 1980s, abandoning their careers to return to the haven of the home. A mythic compromise is slowly emerging that puts less pressure on women and allows more latitude to their desires, requiring them to be neither housewives nor superwomen. In the new myth, sex roles will be less strictly defined, leaving more room for "house husbands" and female breadwinners, but allowing women to be just wives and mothers if they so desire.

The Money Myth

26   So, there are myths of childhood and myths of gender, fundamental frames within which we define our sense of self-identity. But what about the ordinary *objects* in our lives? They too are defined mythologically. Take the money in your wallet, or the change in your purse. Have you ever asked yourself what money really is? Paper and metal and marks on your banker's balance sheet? Of course not. These are just the *signs* by which we represent wealth, tokens for the purposes of economic exchange. But what do these tokens represent? What myths surround them?

27   In semiotic terms, the ultimate significance of money is purely mythological. I'm not referring to the fact that our paper currency is no longer backed by an equivalent quantity of gold at Fort Knox, or that our so-called "silver" coins are really silver, copper, and nickel sandwiches. Even if the dollar were still backed up by gold, or if pure silver coins were still in general circulation, this would still not explain why gold and silver are so precious to us. These metals are of no strategic value. They are too soft to be fashioned into weapons or tools or into anything useful. Yet their value is legendary, and the origin of that value lies in myth, not in the metals themselves.

28   Often an object becomes valuable because it is rare, and gold and silver indeed owe part of their value to their scarcity. But that is not the ultimate cause of their preciousness. Rather, gold and silver became precious in the ancient world because of their *resemblance* to other precious things: gold, to the brightness of the sun that rises every morning and returns with renewed strength every spring to begin a new season of growth; and silver, to the brightness of the moon that waxes and wanes through the months, associated in the ancient world with feminine fertility. More importantly, gold, which neither rusts nor tarnishes, resembles unchanging, incorruptible immortality itself. Year after year, century after century, gold remains unchanged, like that most precious mythical possession of all, eternal life. When the medieval alchemists[11] searched for the key to transforming base metals into gold, they were not looking for a way to make a fast buck; they were seeking immortality. They believed if they could find the secret of gold, they could unlock the secrets of eternity.

---

11. alchemists: medieval scientists who claimed that they could turn base metal to gold

29　Although we are no longer conscious of the original mythical significance of gold, it still retains the aura it has always held. We still purchase it in times of economic uncertainty as a kind of talismanic[12] protection against inflation and international catastrophe. Prophets of impending doom commonly counsel their flocks to store food, stock weapons, and buy gold—even though in a real crisis I doubt that anyone would stop to barter for ingots. Food and weapons are the essentials, not symbolic bits of precious metal. Interestingly enough, though, it is gold that costs over $400 an ounce.

30　Even something as solid and enduring as the value of gold is grounded in mythological belief. Gold, finally, is also a sign, an icon of all that we desire as mortals in a dangerous world. Gold can grant us neither immortality nor permanent economic security. But it is divine insofar as it resembles immortal things, and its divinity has lost none of its mythic luster even in an age that has substituted science for superstition, an age that believes it has finally transcended the myths of the past to see the world in the clear light of scientific knowledge.

Science or Myth?

31　Is science the answer to mythology, the one way to see things as they really are? Can we escape from cultural myth by adopting a purely scientific attitude? Not exactly, according to the semiotician, for science is also a kind of mythology.

32　To say that science is mythological, however, is not at all the same as saying that it is untrue or that it is in any sort of real competition with religious mythologies. Religious myths frame the invisible world of the spirit, the realm of belief and desire; scientific myths frame the world of the senses, the material reality that we see and expe-

rience. Scientific theory demands empirical[13] testing and support; religion requires only faith. The fact that scientists cannot explain everything in the universe is not a valid reason for rejecting science in favor of religion. The two mythologies are simply incommensurate[14] and should not be compared with each other as competing views of the world. Many scientists are religious, but this does not mean that their science is in any way undermined by belief. Einstein believed in God —whom he called the Old One—but this didn't make him believe in the geocentric universe presupposed by the myth of Creation.

33　There are two ways in which science is mythological. First, like any myth, it causes us to look at the world through a frame. Nonscientists commonly believe that the scientist merely observes things and objectively describes their behavior for the sake of knowledge alone, but that is not the way science works. First, a scientist doesn't investigate something unless he or she has a reason for looking at it. Sometimes this interest is sheer ambition, sometimes it is political; for example, German physicists in the 1930s sought to discredit Einstein's work because Einstein was a Jew—they called his theories "Jewish physics." Most of the time, however, a scientist does something because that is what his or her peers are doing. To put this another way, there is an *historical* component to scientific investigation that scientists and nonscientists alike often ignore.

34　In his groundbreaking study of the history of science, *The Structure of Scientific Revolutions*, Thomas Kuhn argues that most scientists engage in what he calls "normal science"; that is, they conduct the research projects that are accepted by the scientific establishments in which they work. Astronomical investigation, for example, is a part

---

12.　talismanic: referring to magical powers

13.　empirical: referring to testing requiring experiments

14.　incommensurate: unable to be compared

of the normal science of the twentieth century, while astrology, which was an acceptable part of medieval science, is not. Psychologists and psychiatrists are accredited by modern scientific institutions, but students of the paranormal[15] and of ESP are still relegated to the margins of scientific inquiry. Phrenology, or the tracing of specific character traits back to the shape of one's skull, was a popular tool for nineteenth-century criminology, but is entirely discredited in twentieth-century science.

35　The paradigms[16] of normal science can differ from place to place as well as from time to time. In modern China, for example, the theory and practice of acupuncture is not just a part of the normal training of a Chinese physician, it may be the only treatment he or she is taught to use. If on a business trip to Peking you have a toothache, an eye problem, or even appendicitis, expect acupuncture to be a part of your treatment. But don't expect it in New York or Boston, for while American physicians are allowed to dabble in acupuncture, it is still not an accepted part of the American medical community. What is normal in China is met in America with amusement and sometimes incredulity. In Kuhn's terms, American and Chinese physicians each operate within different "paradigms," or within different frameworks, of medical practice—what a semiotician would call different "myths."

36　There is a second sense in which modern science is mythological. Consider how often you are exhorted to buy something because it contains "beta carotene," or because "nine out of ten doctors agree" about it, or because it will end your pain with "ibuprofen." Advertisers seek to dazzle us with technical or scientific terms because science and technology have become the dominant mythology of our times. The language of science has become an almost sacred tongue today, a discourse known only to the initiated which the rest of us must accept from the scientist on faith. Compare the sacred Latinity of the Catholic priesthood with the language on a medical prescription. Physicians, too, have their own Latinate jargon that divides them from the nonmedical laity.

37　Indeed, scientists have become the "priests" of a new kind of materialistic religion, the religion of scientific expertise. Where we once consulted oracles and priests about the nature of the universe and of the future, we now go to scientific experts, even when their expertise is more limited than their pronouncements would suggest. When Linus Pauling published his opinion that vitamin C could cure the common cold, for example, thousands of Americans began to gobble down vitamin supplements, even though Pauling's two Nobel Prizes do not include one in medicine. Scientific celebrities like Carl Sagan and Stephen Jay Gould are consulted on everything from "nuclear winter" to race relations in South Africa. And Isaac Asimov is sure to be found on any panel delegated to predict what our lives will be like in the twenty-first century.

38　Like any religion, however, science can fall victim to its own promises if those promises are not borne out. Having replaced the soothsayers[17] and witch doctors of the past, scientists today are expected to foresee the future, and when they fail in their predictions they must often endure public criticism. Consider the beating the U.S. Geological Survey took when it failed to predict the magnitude of the Mount St. Helens explosion. Or the mounting impatience of many Californians who want to know precisely *when* "the Big One" (the great quake everyone is predicting will occur within the next quarter century) will occur. Government agencies consult the scientific community to learn what effect industrial air pollution will have on future weather patterns and are given two conflicting answers:

---

15. paranormal: relating to events unexplained by established scientific means

16. paradigms: patterns or models

17. soothsayers: those who predict the future

either there will be a "greenhouse effect," which will heat up the earth, or there will be a cooling trend due to the blockage of solar heat by dust particles in the air. Scientists are not dismayed by such uncertainty, but the nonscientists who consult them certainly are.

39 Perhaps more seriously, we have come to believe in a scientific myth that science is capable of curing every human ill, and blame the scientist when the cure is not forthcoming. You know the old complaint: "We can put a man on the moon, why can't we cure the common cold?" Gay activists accuse the medical establishment of deliberate betrayal as years pass without a cure for AIDS. Cancer patients thumb their noses at the medical experts and head south for laetrile clinics in Tijuana. And faith healers move in with their prescientific treatments when science fails to provide relief.

40 Whenever the myth of science fails, myths of religion reemerge with renewed strength. It is probably no accident that in the 1980s America experienced a resurgence of orthodox religious fervor at a time when science and technology no longer seemed to be providing satisfactory answers to our deepest questions about our place in the universe. Nonscientists tend to confuse the scientist's search for physical origins—the Big Bang,[18] the beginnings of life on earth—with religion's search for the Absolute. Reputable scientists, however, don't pretend to deliver absolute knowledge, and are perfectly aware that their theories are often incomplete. Evolutionary theory, for example, which isn't really a theory anymore but an established fact of the normal science of twentieth-century biology, is still itself in a process of evolution. Scientists disagree among themselves about the precise mechanisms of evolution, but few doubt the overall truth of the theory. Confident of their own absolute and unchanging knowledge, however, religious Crea-

tionists[19] leap in with a triumphant "I told you so" every time biologists differ among themselves, but this simply misses the point. The myth of science presupposes theoretical uncertainty and approximation. It expects its framing paradigms to change as scientific knowledge changes. Science grows through a dynamic process of theoretical conjecture and experimental verification; religion cites preestablished textual authorities. You simply can't compare the two.

The Myth of Progress

41 Everyone knows the old adage "you can't stop progress," which usually means that you shouldn't oppose some technological invention or industrial development scheme. But the belief in progress is older than modern technology. It first made its appearance during the eighteenth-century Enlightenment, when philosophers like Voltaire saw the rise of rational thought and the decline of the Catholic Church as a sign of social progress. By the early nineteenth century, the German philosopher G. W. F. Hegel had declared that all human history is necessarily progressive, that society becomes freer and more rational with every passing epoch of civilization. And so there emerged a general "myth of progress," which held that social progress was an inevitable product of history, and optimistically looked to the future for better and better things.

42 The astounding technological advances of the twentieth century—the way we have gone from the Wright brothers to the moon in but half a century—have often been taken as proof of the inevitability of human progress. Equating technological progress with social and moral progress, the defenders and exponents of the virtues of technology often accuse their opponents of being against progress itself. But the myth of progress, both social and technological, is beginning to

---

18. Big Bang: astronomical theory that says the universe was created by a huge explosion

19. creationists: those who believe that the Earth was created literally as the Bible describes it

weaken in the face of Auschwitz, Hiroshima, and Chernobyl.[20] The population explosion and the worldwide pollution of the earth point to a dismal, not promising, future. Plenty of optimists are still around who denounce the prophets of "gloom and doom," but the certainty of future improvement and perfection promised by the myth of progress is being sorely tested.

43   The myths that frame our perceptions and beliefs are generally invisible to us *as myths* so long as they seem to correspond to reality. Once the frame begins to appear, the myth's authority weakens and a new myth takes its place. The authority, for example, of the Creation myth found in the Bible was shattered by mid-nineteenth-century discoveries in geology and biology, and with it the authority of traditional religion itself. Similarly, the myth of progress is now being exposed and undermined at a moment when human events seem more irrational and violent than ever before. The myth of progress is accordingly being replaced today by a "myth of uncertainty" in an uncertain age.

44   We can discover the traces of an emerging myth of uncertainty by looking at some of the changes in attitude that have occurred within the scientific community in recent years. For example, when Darwin formulated his theory of evolution, he assumed—believing in the myth of progress as he did—that species evolved into higher and more progressive forms as the years went by, eventually culminating in man. But modern evolutionary scientists, like Stephen Jay Gould, who have rejected the myth of progress now argue that evolution is a more or less random process, a history of accidents leading neither to "higher" nor to "improved" species. Evolutionary change, the new myth suggests, is just a dice throw.

45   Similarly, whereas Sir Isaac Newton invented the calculus to predict with certainty the motion of any object in space, contemporary physicists now believe in a general "uncertainty principle." First formulated in the 1920s by the German physicist Werner Heisenberg, it holds that a physicist can never be certain of the position of an atomic particle in space. All that he or she can calculate is the *probable* behavior of the atom. The old deterministic[21] certainty is gone.

46   Of course, scientists like Gould or Heisenberg don't regard their observations as the product of a myth; they view them as discoveries and truths, and at the moment, they *are* truths, because they have not been challenged by any contrary evidence. The myth of uncertainty itself is still quite young and has not yet been falsified by experience. Nor has it been contradicted by history. Living in the shadow of nuclear weapons, the population explosion, and the unchecked destruction of our environment, we face an uncertain future indeed. No wonder everything appears chancy to us. And I expect that the myth of uncertainty will only grow in authority as long as the world hovers on the brink of destruction.

47   This doesn't mean, however, that the myth of uncertainty is the final word on the nature of the universe. It's just another way of viewing things. Will there someday be a final myth that we can settle on as the "truth" of things at last? How fine it would be to be able to answer this question in the affirmative, but, as a semiotician, I'm afraid I must demur.[22] If the last frame ever crumbles and reality shines on us in its pure unmediated[23] being, semiotics itself will vanish and will perhaps be the last myth to fall.

---

20. Auschwitz, Hiroshima, and Chernobyl: World War II German death camp, Japanese city hit by atomic bomb to help end World War II, site of Russian nuclear reactor disaster of the eighties

---

21. deterministic: describing the idea that all events are determined by a sequence of causes

22. demur: pause

23. unmediated: without any explanation or discussion

Critical Explorations: Reading

Reread the Solomon selection; as you do, answer the following five questions, which will encourage you to critically examine the text. You will be considering some of the terms Solomon uses and analyzing several of the more thought-provoking statements he makes. You may answer these questions in your reading or dialogic journal.

1. Solomon frequently uses the concept of myth to explain how Americans interpret their culture. However, nowhere in this chapter does he succinctly define *myth*. Reread paragraphs 1–7, and construct your own definition of *myth* that would effectively describe how it is related to the five issues Solomon presents in this selection. Be sure that your definition has both a general and specific component.

2. In paragraph 10, Solomon states, "Semiotic understanding, in other words, requires historical understanding, and one of the major tasks of semiotics is to reveal the histories behind our perceptions." Carefully analyze this statement. How is history related to semiotics? What can you infer from Solomon's use of the plural term "histories" instead of the singular term "history" to describe semiotic understanding?

3. Reread paragraph 24. What is the effect on women in seeing themselves as objects of male desire? That is, what power relationship is established between men and women when "men see" and "women are exhibitionists"?

4. In paragraph 36, Solomon makes a peculiar comparison between the language used by doctors writing prescriptions and the Latin used in the Catholic mass. Analyze further the semiotic suggestions behind a medical language that is Latinate and obscure. What does this language suggest about the American medical profession?

5. In paragraph 46, Solomon refers to scientific observations in the following way: "at the moment, they *are* truths, because they have not been challenged by any contrary evidence." This is an untraditional understanding of truth. What is the more common definition of *truth,* and how does Solomon's understanding differ? Finally, why does Solomon refer to several "truths" instead of a single "truth"?

Selection 3

from *The Malling of America: An Inside Look at the Great American Paradise*
William Severini Kowinski

This excerpt is three chapters from William Severini Kowinski's examination of American malls. In these chapters, Kowinski makes a thorough study of the Greengate Mall, located in Greengate, Pennsylvania. Kowinski incorporates an understanding of American beliefs and the American media to analyze the unstated assumptions that help explain this mall. Kowinski examines such issues as the size of the stores in this mall, the positioning of these stores, how this mall resembles the downtowns of many small American cities, and the mall's overall design. These chapters are part of a larger study of several malls in the United States that Kowinski undertook over a two-year period.

This excerpt incorporates many of the American beliefs that you have studied in the introduction to this chapter. Kowinski's careful examination of Greengate can serve as a model for you to semiotically study the shopping centers and malls with which you are familiar.

Kowinski's style is clear, captivating, and playful. His argument is based on three extended comparisons: the mall is theater, the mall is television, and the mall is Disneyland. As you read, focus on these comparisons to see how they help you understand the attraction that malls have for American shoppers. Also ask yourself if you agree with these comparisons as they relate to your experiences in malls.

Reading–Writing Preparation

Before you read this selection, you may want to answer the following questions in writing or discussion:

1. Why do you think shopping malls are so popular with American consumers?

2. Why do you think the young go to malls? The elderly? Housewives?

Chapter 5
Secrets of the Shopping Mall

1   At this point an event of such glamour and such radiance occurred that you forgot the name all over again. It could be compared to arriving in an unknown city at night, intoxicated by the strange lighting and the ambiguities of the streets. . . . At once the weight of the other years and above all the weight of distinguishing among them slipped away. You found yourself not wanting to care. Everything was guaranteed, it always had been, there would be no future, no end, no development, except this steady wavering like a breeze that gently lifted the tired curtains day had let fall.

—John Ashbery
Three Poems

2   A little overwhelmed by the swirl of sights and sounds, by the information I'd been collecting from Harry Overly and others about how the mall operates, I sought sanctuary one night in McSorley's, the only bar at Greengate. McSorley's keeps later hours than the rest of the mall, so after the shop managers have banged down their electro-shutters and made their night deposits, and after the last extraterrestrial teenager has abandoned the video game panels and phoned home, and all the shoppers have melted into the night, mall people and other regulars meet and mingle for a while at the bar, grousing[1] about rents, talking merchandising strategy, gossiping, flirting, and raising a little hell. Some may honor the Greengate tradition of sliding down the railing of the dormant escalator on their way out. One spring night, as legend has it, a somewhat sodden[2] group slid right into an Easter display of live ducks, causing the whole mall to quack.

3   I sat among the menagerie of mall rats, barflies, and potential duck terrorists, treating my mental wounds with cognac, and then wandered out into the empty mall alone. The mall courts were dimmer than usual (all the stores were dark) but there was enough light for the maintenance crew to clean the floors and empty the refuse containers. They even kept the piped-in music on; they Muzaked while they worked.

4   I sat on a bench on the second level and looked across the court. Since the lighting was different, the court looked different. Greengate's basic layout is the model of the American shopping mall: It is fully enclosed, with two levels, three big department stores, and about a hundred shops, services, and eating places. The large central section has a two-level department store at each end and two parallel rows of shops on

---

Reprinted from William Severini Kowinski, *The Malling of America: An Inside Look at the Great Consumer Paradise,* by permission of William Morrow and Company, Inc. © 1985 by William Severini Kowinski.

---

1. grousing: grumbling
2. sodden: drunken

each level, separated on the first floor by a wide, plazalike central court, with the space above it open to the high ceiling; and on the second level by the railings that surround the central court, making the aisles in front of the second-level shops into a kind of continuous balcony.

5   Jutting off the central court is a long side court, again with two parallel rows of shops, the food court (the area of tables between fast-food outlets), and another department store at the end. (Because department stores are typically at the ends of the courts, they are often called "anchors.") Greengate has benches and planters in several places, and a central-court fountain that shoots water nearly to the ceiling. It has some interesting architectural touches, due perhaps to the relatively unusual conjunction, for a small town, of a major mall developer—the Rouse Company, known for its innovativeness—and a major designer—Victor Gruen Associates, the premier mall-design firm in the country.

6   Now when the mall was devoid of people and movement, I could take note of that architecture; I could look at the mall simply as space, and try to see what had been done with that space. I looked at its size and scale. It felt comfortable, intelligible, not overwhelmingly large but big enough to be a bit mysterious, to warrant walking around and exploring. I saw the wide shiny courts, the gleaming silver escalator ending in the kind of tile you associate with the outside, in a plaza or a sunny path around a garden. There was a staircase, too; it looked like a staircase that should be inside a building, even a house, yet its wide landings overlooked a broad square and two rows of storefronts along an indoor street. All the elements that didn't seem to belong together were here, nevertheless, in a kind of harmony, with a strange feeling—perhaps inevitable in the emptiness of night—of magic.

7   Then suddenly I knew why, or anyway I started to find my way to why. My next perceptual jolt was the sudden realization that this space was special, that it could break so many rules and preconceptions because it was com-pletely separated from the rest of the world. It was its own world, pulled out of time and space, but not only by windowless walls and a roof, or by the neutral zone of the parking lot between it and the highway, the asphalt moat around the magic castle. It was *enclosed* in an even more profound sense—and certainly more than other mere buildings—because all these elements, and others, psychologically separated it from the outside and created the special domain within its embrace. It *meant* to be its own special world with its own rules and reality. That was the first and most essential secret of the shopping mall.

8   Its space is also special because it is *protected*. The mall banishes outside threats of disruption and distraction: No cars are allowed in the mall, no traffic, noise, or fumes. The natural world can't even intrude; there's no rain or snow, heat or cold, no seasonal changes—not even gathering clouds to cause concern. This space is protected so that people will not be distracted or feel threatened; they'll relax and open themselves to the environment, and trust it. That must be part of the reason why very little is allowed in the mall that is larger, faster, or more powerful than a person.

9   The mall is also *controlled* space. This essential element is clearly implied in the official definition of a shopping center that I read in a publication of the Urban Land Institute, an organization that works closely with the mall industry. The operative part of that definition is: "a group of architecturally unified commercial establishments built on a site which is planned, developed, owned and managed as an operating unit . . ." Unity, preplanning, single and centralized management (and Harry's rules) are the instruments by which the mall creates its special conditions, by which it controls the environment created by enclosure and protection.

10   The process begins with the mall's careful design: The developer selects what goes into it, from concrete to conceptual statement, from tenants to trees. Then the process continues in the day-by-day management: the control of temperature, lighting, merchandise, and events.

11   The mall's special space is achieved by enclosure, protection, and control. Those are its secrets, the keys to the kingdom, the whole mall game. Within the environment established by those elements, a mall can contain five department stores or none, one level or six; it can be a brand-new building or deposit itself in the shell of an old one; it can thrive in Alaska or Hawaii, in the desert or on the beach; it can put in skating rinks and roller coasters and historical markers; it can be as small as a garage or as big as a country, and it will still be a mall.

12   These are also the elements that make the mall an extremely efficient and effective selling machine—but that is a subject for the daytime. At night the mall reveals other implications that contribute to its selling success; but they are also intriguing to consider on their own. For when you have a space that you have separated from the outside world, and the ability to create your own world inside, governed by your own rules, what you have is the ability to make magic. You've got yourself a house of fantasy.

13   For after all, isn't this sense of separated, protected privileged space common to the special worlds of history and myth, from the castles and walled cities of medieval Europe and the Forbidden City of China to the enchanted wood, the city in the sky or under the sea, the Shangri-La[3] in the mystic mountains of fantasy? These are the necessary conditions for magic places apart from the ordinary world: through the looking glass, up the beanstalk, down the rabbit hole, off to the Emerald City. Such magic places may also be separated by time (whether places that time forgot or places in the far future or the distant past accessible only by time travel) and by a combination of time and space (as in the *Star Wars* saga—"long, long ago in a galaxy far, far away . . ."). So it is no wonder the mall is full of themes and suggestions of the past and an intergalactic[4] future.

14   But of course the mall is not completely inaccessible from the real world—in fact, it's convenient, with plenty of free parking. It is instead a special space within the usual world where the imagination is given strong suggestions for fantasy. And there is a model for that kind of environment.

15   I saw that, too, on this night in the empty mall, as I stood at the second-level railing and looked down into center court. I saw the white pools of light, the areas of relative darkness, the symmetrical aisles and gleaming escalator, the bracketed store facades, the sudden strangeness of live trees and plants indoors. It was as if I were standing on a balcony, looking down on a stage, waiting for the show to begin.

16   That was it. This is theatrical space. The mall is a theater.

17   At Greengate the theatrical element is fairly explicit. Over the center court are a series of arches—a subtle proscenium—lined with double rows of white lights in marquee array. These lights also surround the cupola[5] over the landing of the center stairs, and are incorporated into the design of many mall stores. In comparison to downtown, the stores are brighter and glitzier; even the banks, staid and sturdy on Main Street, are sprightly and open at the mall. On Halloween, the vice-presidents and loan officers dress up as ghouls and goblins, and on the mall's Country and Western Days the tellers wear cowboy hats. The mall environment is itself a magic theater—trees grow out of the tiled floor! Plants flourish without sun or rain!

18   But even before the theatrical effects, the conditions for theater are set by design and management. For a space to be a theater, the outside rules of time and space must be banished. The mall keeps out such reference points—not only its windowless enclosure but its very uniformity (one mall resembling another) means it could be anywhere. It is placeless. Many malls banish all

---

3. Shangri-La: a hidden paradise

4. intergalactic: between galaxies in space

5. cupola: small dome

sense of time by eliminating clocks, and although Greengate has a large but unobtrusively decorative clock above center court, it neutralizes time by controlling light and sound—morning, noon, and night, they are the same. The mall doesn't allow the appearance of aging—the stores are forever new in an environment that is forever now. It is timeless.

19 The mall is kept squeaky clean, the stores bright, the fountains gushing, the greenery fresh —or at least those are management's goals. The effect is one of almost unreal perfection. Moreover, this continuous, flowing environment with no reference to the outside—this sense of a special world—permits a kind of unity of experience within an effortless enclosure that is something like the classical theater's unities of time, place, and action. It's all here, now. The mall concentrates the drama, suspends disbelief.

20 For theater, after all, is largely a matter of light and darkness. The mall at night suggests this most strongly. The idea is to darken all distractions and to focus audience attention with light. For the mall, the process begins with excluding the outside in order to concentrate on what is happening inside. To do that, the basic environment must be created and maintained. The audience must not be distracted; it must be lulled into receptivity[6] by a comfortable, sweet neutrality.

21 Then comes the shaping of what is in the spotlight, what's on the stage. For once the mall's space is enclosed, protected, and controlled, it can be further designed to create almost any fantasy within it. Like a theater in which *King Lear*[7] might be followed the next night by *Camelot*[8] and the next by the Jacksons in concert, the mall is a Never-Never-Land that says let's pretend. What is pretended can be virtual anything. The mall is, in a word, malleable, and that becomes another key to its success.

22 There are essential differences between theater and the mall, too; between the kind and intent of the fantasies created in each. But the similarities were fascinating as I gazed out over the mall: silent and still, with its dramatic lighting, its props and staging, and the costumed mannequins in store windows. It looked like a stage anticipating the play, a movie set on down-time, waiting to be brought alive.

---

6. receptivity: a state of acceptance

7. *King Lear*: great Shakespearean tragedy

8. *Camelot*: sixties musical about King Arthur and his court

Chapter 6
Mousekatecture on Main Street

23 So much for the theater—what is the show? Greengate Mall looks like a set for many potential plays, movies, and television shows—a little *Our Town*,[9] a bit of *High Noon*,[10] a touch of *Star Wars*, a piazza from Fellini[11] thrown into an atmosphere out of *Ozzie and Harriet*, as well as a little of *The Twilight Zone* (or maybe a lot). But what is the central image that pulls all these other images together?

---

9. *Our Town*: famous early-twentieth-century American play by Thornton Wilder about small-town America

10. *High Noon*: famous Western film (1952)

---

11. Fellini: famous twentieth-century Italian film director

24   Pondering this problem at home, I happened on help. I saw a tiny wire-service story in the local paper, not much more than a filler in a page of advertisements. It was about how shopping malls were becoming community centers. By now that wasn't news to me, except perhaps that it was happening elsewhere and to an impressive extent. The article quoted a few mall industry people, a public relations director or two, and one writer. His name was Ralph Keyes, and the quote selected was from his book *We, the Lonely People*. "Malls aren't part of the community," he wrote. "They are the community."

25   That was a pretty strong statement. Keyes evidently also saw something special in malls, something that made them more than shopping centers. I got in touch with Ralph Keyes, and it turned out that although his interest in malls began when he was a reporter for *Newsday* on Long Island, he now lived across the state of Pennsylvania from me, near Allentown. He was kind enough to send me a copy of his book and an earlier article he'd done on teenagers at Walt Whitman Mall on Long Island.

26   He also put me in touch with Richard Francaviglia, a young professor of geography at Antioch College. Geography is one of the old disciplines (like landscape architecture) that studies such new phenomena as the organization of cities and the nature of theme parks, phenomena that have escaped or transcended traditional academic categories. Even so, as Francaviglia told me in a letter, he had a tough time getting his academic colleagues to take malls seriously. When he read one of his papers on malls at a Popular Culture Association convention in Chicago, "It nearly started a riot," his letter said. "Quite literally, scholars were yelling back and forth at each other—and me. It was all very stimulating, but while we were arguing, 20 million people were shopping in malls and generally enjoying themselves."

27   What Francaviglia apparently wanted to know was *why*? Why were all those people at malls? What were the malls doing to attract them? In two articles for scholarly journals that he sent me, he came up with some ingenious answers.

28   Two of the now conventional observations about the mall are that, because it has become such a community center, it is "the new Main Street," and, because of the bright array of consumer products, it is a "Disneyland for adults." Francaviglia not only demonstrated deeper meaning in each of these ideas, he showed how they were connected. In the process he answered my question: What is the central image that brings all the mall theatrics together?

29   Francaviglia began by analyzing "Main Street U.S.A.," the centerpiece of Disneyland and Disney World, the world-famous amusement parks. These parks are, it should be noted, commercial environments that are preplanned, enclosed, protected, and controlled (and therefore might just as well be called "shopping malls for kids").

30   Francaviglia was interested in how Walt Disney took the popular mythology about small towns and created a brilliant but artificial design for Main Street U.S.A. Francaviglia began by pointing out that there are two basic kinds of Main Street in the real America. The most common kind is the Main Street that is not only the principal business district but also the "main drag"—the road that leads through town. Essentially this Main Street is both for pedestrians conducting business and social affairs, and for cars and trucks passing through. This, in fact, is the kind of Main Street that Greensburg's is—it's part of Route 66, the principal north-south artery, and has a substantial amount of truck traffic rumbling along it for that reason.

31   The other and much less frequently encountered type is the Main Street that has only one way in and out; the other end of it leads to a town square or village green. So the destination of cars on this Main Street has to be Main Street itself. As Francaviglia pointed out, this is the kind of Main Street most often portrayed in movies and on television, especially when the

purpose is to evoke small-town nostalgia. The reasons for that are obvious: This kind of Main Street is quieter and more peaceful; it doesn't have the roar of traffic crashing through town on its way from somewhere to somewhere else. The town square itself makes it even more peaceful, pedestrian-oriented, and probably prettier.

32   But Disney took this second and rarer kind of Main Street and did it one better: He put town plazas at both ends, enclosing it completely. Furthermore, cars and trucks were banned altogether from Disney's Main Street, and as Francaviglia noted, such clearly enclosed space creates a strong, if mostly unconscious, psychological confidence that no car *could* ever be on this street. It is a toy street, a fantasy, a Main Street of dreams.

33   So Disney, who had already outdone inventors who merely try to build a better mousetrap by inventing a better mouse—the sweet, lovable, suburban-head-of-household Mickey Mouse— now evoked small-town nostalgia by building a better Main Street. He based Main Street U.S.A. on the Main Street of Marceline, Missouri, as it was when he was a boy growing up there. But besides enclosing it, he encased it in the mistiness of memory. Part of Disney's genius was his ability to make fantasies concrete, and he did this with Main Street U.S.A. by improving on reality.

34   Marceline's Main Street had been (in Francaviglia's words) ". . . rutted and rilled and horse manure helped turn it into a soupy quagmire in wet weather. . . . Gaunt telephone poles with many cross arms, rather than trees, bordered the sidewalks." But Disney's Main Street U.S.A. was lined with shapely trees, and not only the occasional horse droppings but everything else was cleaned up immediately, to keep this street as pristine[12] as any gold-paved avenue of paradise.

35   There were also no sleazy bars, dingy luncheonettes, seedy pool halls, or dirty jail cells arrayed along Disney's Main Street. There were only pleasant, clean, colorful, and nostalgic small-town stores which seemed to shimmer with remembered magic.

36   Disney employed another device to achieve his effects which I found particularly intriguing. The buildings along Main Street U.S.A. are not only better than life, they are smaller; according to Francaviglia, they are five-eighths the size of actual stores on real streets. This scaling-down appeals psychologically to both children and adults; children find the smaller spaces more comfortable and comprehensible—more their size—while the adults, as Francaviglia writes, "are reminded of trips back to childhood haunts; everything is much smaller than one remembers."

37   Francaviglia goes on to make the connection with the enclosed shopping mall. The rows of stores are set up as on a street, but the street of the mall is also clearly enclosed. Except for auto shows, a car in the mall is unthinkable, and the mall's street is bounded by plazas or courts. Francaviglia claims that so-called pedestrian malls in real downtowns that are created by blocking off real streets never really succeed in subliminally convincing customers that they are safe from traffic. But the mall does, because its street is obviously—theatrically—enclosed and artificial.

38   Like Disney's street, the shopping mall plans and carries out a consistent design so that the mall's street looks unified, quaint yet familiar. The mall also excludes the rougher elements of real downtowns—no dives or pool halls here— and like the Disney versions, the stores are smaller than stores on town streets.

39   So the resemblance goes beyond enclosure, protection, and control. It struck me that the basic image the mall delivers—what this stage was set up to be—is a simplified, cleaned-up, Disneyfied fantasy version of Main Street U.S.A. Francaviglia doesn't claim that mall designers copied directly from Disney, but mall people that I met all praised the Disney parks. Still, it's worth noting that Disneyland and the first enclosed malls were being built at about the same time.

---

12. pristine: unspoiled

40   Suddenly it seems so obvious, and all too ironic: The "new Main Street" for Greensburg was not just a metaphor for the mall as the major retail and community center of town. It was literally true: The mall was the new "Main Street."

41   The mall not only acted like a Main Street, it was designed to be one. But not the real one—an archetypal[13] Main Street, designed to fulfill

---

13. archetypal: original; relating to the model upon which all things are made

wishes and longings and to allay fears; it was meant to embody a dream and keep out the nightmares. So Greengate Mall's Main Street was an idealization of Greensburg's Main Street, with just the right touch of obvious artificiality to make it permanently extraordinary. It was also cleaner, dryer, more comfortable, more convenient, better scaled and designed for walking, apparently safer, brighter—and in the final irony, more nostalgically reminiscent of small-town Main Street life. The mall was Old-fashioned Bargain Days, every day of every year.

Chapter 7
Cosmallogy

42   The Main Street of Greengate mall confirmed what Francaviglia was saying. The store facades and signs impart a kind of friendly quaintness, a nostalgic peaceful brightness. But not only do stores like Hickory Farms, the Plantation Country Store, or Tobacco Village suggest a sleepy country town in an era before the roar of cars and the hugeness of steel and glass high-rises; so do the scale and design of the street itself. That's why this atmospheric creation can turn Video Concepts, the Program Store, and Radio Shack into the equivalent of the butcher, the baker, and the candlestick maker.

43   The mall design conveys an image, an ideal, of a small, controllable environment that is quiet, prosperous, and neighborly, where good citizens keep the streets clean and safe and the storekeepers take scrupulous care of their shops and their customers. This may be a technologically controlled kingdom, but Big Brother is invisible behind the friendly haze of nostalgic, suggested, half-enacted dreams.

44   The mall shops have appropriated not only the nostalgic look of Disney's Main Street but their smaller size as well. This happens to make

physical sense here, for with the mall itself providing exterior walls and roof, the shop's structure doesn't have to do as much. These stores are essentially partitioned spaces within a building.

45   The smaller size also makes economic sense for tenants who need to get as much productivity out of high-rent space as possible. Fortunately, they've generally found they can generate more business in a smaller space than they could on a real street. They can leave it to the mall itself to provide a sense of openness and peacefulness, while the shops create a sense of excitement by squeezing the merchandise together into a continuous crush of color, texture, and product. This contrast is also carried out in lighting—the stores are usually much brighter and brasher than the more demure[14] mall courts.

46   The coincidence of physical requirements and fantasy-producing design is seen in other aspects of the mall—for example, why mall shops don't have doors. Because of enclosure, they actually need doors only when they are locked up

---

14. demure: sedate or serious

for the night. There is no snow or wind to keep out. All that's really necessary is the locked shutters that most mall shops use. But psychologically the absence of doors makes looking in and entering the store practically effortless. For even more friendly than an open door is no door at all. The entrance positively beckons; it is a surprise and an invitation.

47   The mall also incorporates other fantasy elements found on Disney's Main Street U.S.A. The mall courts function as public squares, the greenery as gardens and parks—all scaled down to a quaint and comprehensible size. Just as Disney's street eventually leads to Sleeping Beauty's castle, the mall's Main Street leads to the department stores, the consumer equivalent of a citadel[15] of wonders.

48   The courts are often the most blatantly theatrical sections of the mall, and they serve many fantasy functions. When displays are here they are the public markets or the fairgrounds; when a performance is under way, they are the bandstand in the park. Greengate's major center-court attraction is the fountain shooting water high in the air, as in an outdoor park. The court is large enough to have a plaza atmosphere, with its tiles and terraces, benches and greenery, suggesting a European village square.

49   There is an innate theatricality about such places; Giorgio de Chirico in particular caught this quality in his supposedly surrealistic paintings in the early twentieth century. Of Chirico, art critic Robert Hughes wrote, "What fascinated him in the squares and arcades of Perrara and Turin—the cities from which most of his motifs came—was not their solid architectural reality but their staginess."

50   But for all this effective stage setting, there is something at work here that goes beyond clever design. The question arises: Can these parallel strips of stores on a toy Main Street of polished brick really work magic? How can this be such a powerful and attractive fantasy that it compensates for what's missing—like the sky, or a little bit of fleshly disorder? How can people accept roofed over trees, patently artificial effects, and outdoor cafés that aren't really outdoors?

51   There is perhaps one more element that explains this acceptance, that accounts for the believability of the mall's fantasy world. The idea began with Ralph Keyes. It was his explanation for why people buy the mall fantasy. "Television," Keyes said. "The mall *is* television."

52   He didn't mean just that the mall is TV's delivery system: that what TV proposes, the mall disposes. He was talking about the management of people's perceptions of space and reality, the elements that persuade people to suspend their disbelief. *The magic of television!*

53   The mall is a visual experience. It's TV that you walk around in. "People-watching" is what people do in the mall when they aren't "looking for something" to buy. The images they see in the mall are from television; and how they see and accept these images has been conditioned by watching television.

54   "People have gotten used to two-dimensional effects, to cardboard reality," Keyes maintained. "That's what they see on television, and they accept it."

55   In particular, television shows from *Ozzie and Harriet* to *Happy Days* produced visual dramatic images of small towns. They were simplified and cosmeticized: a few endlessly repeated sets, characters, and relationships, all encased in squeaky-clean nostalgia, but since they all appeared complete, in everybody's living room every week, they assumed an undeniable reality. It was all there, scaled down to the small screen.

56   From family sitcoms and homey westerns to the sixty-second and thirty-second dramas of commercials, television makes the mall's relentlessly upbeat and minimalist[16] Main Street easier to accept. For millions of urban and suburban viewers, the television image may be the

---

15. citadel: fortified place; stronghold

16. minimalist: simplified, sparse

only visual idea they have of small-town Main Street. For residents of real small towns, this Main Street may be equally convincing on another level: It may be what they wish their reality was, and they wish it hard enough to make it so.
57 Advertising uses this kind of suggestion (as opposed to suggestiveness) even more extensively, and more pointedly. TV commercials try to communicate quickly with a repertoire[17] of visual images that suggest places and the feelings associated with them. They didn't invent all these images and associations, but through repetition they've made a virtual iconography of them. In advertising talk, the image "says" something. If you want to "say" glamour and romance, you "say" Paris, and if you want to "say" Paris with an image, you show the Eiffel Tower. The Eiffel Tower "says" Paris, which "says" all kinds of glamorous and exciting things about the product, and what will happen to you if you buy it.
58 The mall shrewdly makes use of these perceptual habits created by TV. It "says" Main Street with some Disneyesque design elements and a few props. The same technique is used in theme restaurants and shops. It's relatively cheap to do, and it works great.
59 What is true of the perception of Main Street is also true of the perception of many other kinds of places, from western towns and sailing ships to grand hotels and space ships: All these places have been seen in movies and on television—and perhaps *only* there. Media images dominate ideas about these places. The mall can make use of these simplified images to create its own fantasies, even beyond the principal one of Main Street.
60 It occurred to me that perceptual habits learned through hours and hours of television watching may also account for something else the mall seems to manage easily: its incongruities.[18] The mall jumbles so many kinds of

stores and services, from brokerage offices to cotton-candy stands, singles bars to interfaith chapels, that otherwise don't go together. But to a population used to seeing a bloody murder followed by a candy-bar commercial, followed by soap opera sex, a religious revival, and a public TV fund drive, nothing much would seem incongruous. Compared to what is shown in sequence on one TV channel, or what is available at any moment on many channels as the viewer switches through them, the eclecticism[19] of the mall has to be considered mild.
61 The similarities of television and the mall go on and on. Both of them lull and stimulate simultaneously. Watching TV, we can be everywhere without being anywhere in particular. And basically, television and the mall are in the same business: entertainment in order to sell products. Advertisers pay for TV programs so people will watch the commercials, and the commercials themselves try to sell products by being entertaining. In the mall, product sales are also based on how attractive and entertaining the mall environment and its stores are. The mall is like three-dimensional television.
62 Television advertises attractive ways of life and the products associated with them in its programming, and its commercials tell little stories; the line between programs and ads is therefore often blurred. At the mall, the line between "programs" and "advertising" is almost nonexistent. The fantasy of Main Street is there to sell products. Because that's what all of this—the theater, the sets, the costumes and props—is for. The mall industry even has a name for what it's all about: They call it The Retail Drama.

Critical Explorations: Reading

Use these five questions as guides to rereading the Kowinski excerpt. By answering these ques-

---

17. repertoire: collection

18. incongruities: lack of agreement

19. eclecticism: a borrowing from many systems

tions, you will better understand how Kowinski uses semiotics to analyze the Greengate Mall. You may want to answer some or all of these questions in your reading or dialogic journal.

1. Reread paragraphs 7, 8, and 9. Then summarize a mall's three characteristics. How do these three characteristics differ from those that come to your mind when you study a shopping center or store that is not part of a mall?

2. In paragraph 13, Kowinski compares the Greengate Mall to the Emerald City, the imaginary city in *The Wizard of Oz*. Consider several characteristics of the Emerald City as you may remember it from the book *The Wizard of Oz* or from the movie. Then compare these characteristics to those Kowinski provides of the Greengate Mall. Do you think his comparison is an accurate one?

3. In paragraphs 17 and 18, Kowinski compares the Greengate Mall to a theater. List the characteristics of a theater that Kowinski says also apply to the Greengate Mall. Is this comparison a convincing one for you?

4. In paragraphs 51–62, Kowinski compares the world of the mall to that created by television. Reread these paragraphs and list those characteristics of the television world that also describe a mall. Do you agree with some or all of this comparison?

5. Review the seven American beliefs discussed in the introduction to this chapter. Which of these beliefs does Kowinski use in his analysis of the Greengate Mall?

Selection 4

"The World of Wrestling"
Roland Barthes

This essay is from a famous anthology written by Roland Barthes titled *Mythologies*, which ana-

lyzes the hidden premises that explain several everyday French practices. Roland Barthes was an influential critical theorist who wrote both on popular French culture and literary theory. Much of his literary work is a careful semiotic analysis of specific literary texts. Written in the sixties, "The World of Wrestling" is one of Barthes's earlier essays.

Before you begin reading this selection, realize that Barthes is referring not to the Olympic sport but to the "spectacle" of professional wrestling—the "show" in which winners and losers are decided before the match ever begins. Barthes bases his essay on a series of comparisons between the spectacle of wrestling and practices that do not at first seem to have any relationship to wrestling. An expert semiotician, Barthes articulates the unstated, comparing wrestling to drama, algebra, and Christianity.

Barthes writes in a very careful, suggestive style that is captured well in this translation. This selection is more difficult than the previous three, particularly because of Barthes's educated vocabulary and his detailed and qualified writing style. As you read, check the footnotes, which will help explain the most difficult terms. Like the previous selection on shopping malls, Barthes uses comparisons to explain what wrestling is, comparing wrestling to the theater and to algebra. As you read, ask yourself how these comparisons further Barthes's argument.

Reading–Writing Preparation

Before you read this selection, you may want to answer the following questions in writing or discussion:

1. What are some of the outrageous actions that you have seen used in professional wrestling?

2. Why do you think people pay to see the staged actions of professional wrestling?

The World of Wrestling

The grandiloquent truth of gestures on life's great occasions.
Baudelaire

1   The virtue of all-in wrestling is that it is the spectacle of excess. Here we find a grandiloquence[1] which must have been that of ancient theatres. And in fact wrestling is an open-air spectacle, for what makes the circus or the arena what they are is not the sky (a romantic value suited rather to fashionable occasions), it is the drenching and vertical quality of the flood of light. Even hidden in the most squalid Parisian halls, wrestling partakes of the nature of the great solar spectacles, Greek drama and bullfights: in both, a light without shadow generates an emotion without reserve.

2   There are people who think that wrestling is an ignoble sport. Wrestling is not a sport, it is a spectacle, and it is no more ignoble to attend a wrestled performance of Suffering than a performance of the sorrows of Arnolphe or Andromaque.[2] Of course, there exists a false wrestling, in which the participants unnecessarily go to great lengths to make a show of a fair fight; this is of no interest. True wrestling, wrongly called amateur wrestling, is performed in second-rate halls, where the public spontaneously attunes itself to the spectacular nature of the contest, like the audience at a suburban cinema. Then these same people wax[3] indignant because wrestling is a stage-managed sport (which ought, by the way, to mitigate its ignominy[4]). The public is completely uninterested in knowing whether the contest is rigged or not, and rightly so; it abandons itself to the primary virtue of the spectacle, which is to abolish all motives and all consequences: what matters is not what it thinks but what it sees.

3   This public knows very well the distinction between wrestling and boxing; it knows that boxing is a Jansenist[5] sport, based on a demonstration of excellence. One can bet on the outcome of a boxing-match: with wrestling, it would make no sense. A boxing-match is a story which is constructed before the eyes of the spectator; in wrestling, on the contrary, it is each moment which is intelligible, not the passage of time. The spectator is not interested in the rise and fall of fortunes; he expects the transient image of certain passions. Wrestling therefore demands an immediate reading of the juxtaposed meanings, so that there is no need to connect them. The logical conclusion of the contest does not interest the wrestling-fan, while on the contrary a boxing-match always implies a science of the future. In other words, wrestling is a sum of spectacles, of which no single one is a function: each moment imposes the total knowledge of a passion which rises erect and alone, without ever extending to the crowning moment of a result.

---

1. grandiloquence: the use of high-flown words

2. In Molière's *L'École des Femmes* and Racine's *Andromaque*. (Molière, Racine: famous-seventeenth century French playwrights)

From *Mythologies* by Roland Barthes, translated by Annette Lavers. Translation copyright © 1972 by Jonathan Cape Ltd. Reprinted by permission of Hill and Wang, a division of Farrar, Straus & Giroux, Inc.

---

3. wax: become

4. mitigate its ignominy: lessen its shame

5. Jansenist: believer in the ideas of a seventeenth-century French Catholic bishop

4   Thus the function of the wrestler is not to win; it is to go exactly through the motions which are expected of him. It is said that judo contains a hidden symbolic aspect; even in the midst of efficiency, its gestures are measured, precise but restricted, drawn accurately but by a stroke without volume. Wrestling, on the contrary, offers excessive gestures, exploited to the limit of their meaning. In judo, a man who is down is hardly down at all, he rolls over, he draws back, he eludes defeat, or, if the latter is obvious, he immediately disappears; in wrestling, a man who is down is exaggeratedly so, and completely fills the eyes of the spectators with the intolerable spectacle of his powerlessness.

5   This function of grandiloquence is indeed the same as that of ancient theatre, whose principle, language and props (masks and buskins[6]) concurred in the exaggeratedly visible explanation of a Necessity. The gesture of the vanquished wrestler signifying to the world a defeat which, far from disguising, he emphasizes and holds like a pause in music, corresponds to the mask of antiquity meant to signify the tragic mode of the spectacle. In wrestling, as on the stage in antiquity, one is not ashamed of one's suffering, one knows how to cry, one has a liking for tears.

6   Each sign in wrestling is therefore endowed with an absolute clarity, since one must always understand everything on the spot. As soon as the adversaries are in the ring, the public is overwhelmed with the obviousness of the roles. As in the theatre, each physical type expresses to excess the part which has been assigned to the contestant. Thauvin, a fifty-year-old with an obese and sagging body, whose type of asexual hideousness always inspires feminine nicknames, displays in his flesh the characters of baseness, for his part is to represent what, in the classical concept of the *salaud*, the 'bastard' (the key-concept of any wrestling-match), appears as organi-

cally[7] repugnant. The nausea voluntarily provoked by Thauvin shows therefore a very extended use of signs: not only is ugliness used here in order to signify baseness, but in addition ugliness is wholly gathered into a particularly repulsive quality of matter: the pallid collapse of dead flesh (the public calls Thauvin *la barbaque*, 'stinking meat'), so that the passionate condemnation of the crowd no longer stems from its judgment, but instead from the very depth of its humours.[8] It will thereafter let itself be frenetically embroiled[9] in an idea of Thauvin which will conform entirely with this physical origin: his actions will perfectly correspond to the essential viscosity[10] of his personage.

7   It is therefore in the body of the wrestler that we find the first key to the contest. I know from the start that all of Thauvin's actions, his treacheries, cruelties and acts of cowardice, will not fail to measure up to the first image of ignobility he gave me; I can trust him to carry out intelligently and to the last detail all the gestures of a kind of amorphous[11] baseness, and thus fill to the brim the image of the most repugnant bastard there is: the bastard-octopus. Wrestlers therefore have a physique as peremptory[12] as those of the characters of the *Commedia dell'Arte*, who display in advance, in their costumes and attitudes, the future contents of their parts: just as Pantaloon can never be anything but a ridiculous cuckold, Harlequin an astute servant and the Doctor a stupid pedant, in the same way Thauvin will never be anything but an ignoble traitor, Reinières (a tall blond fellow with a limp body and unkempt hair) the moving image of passivity, Mazaud

---

6. buskins: covers worn by ancient actors in tragedy

7. organically: in a fashion that shows a complex interrelationship

8. humours: moods or states of mind

9. frenetically embroiled: frantically entangled

10. viscosity: thickness or stickiness

11. amorphous: without shape

12. peremptory: absolute

(short and arrogant like a cock) that of grotesque conceit, and Orsano (an effeminate teddy-boy first seen in a blue-and-pink dressing-gown) that, doubly humorous, of a vindictive *salope*, or bitch (for I do not think that the public of the Elysée-Montmartre, like Littré, believes the word *salope* to be a masculine).

8   The physique of the wrestlers therefore constitutes a basic sign, which like a seed contains the whole fight. But this seed proliferates, for it is at every turn during the fight, in each new situation, that the body of the wrestler casts to the public the magical entertainment of a temperament which finds its natural expression in a gesture. The different strata of meaning throw light on each other, and form the most intelligible of spectacles. Wrestling is like a diacritic[13] writing: above the fundamental meaning of his body, the wrestler arranges comments which are episodic but always opportune, and constantly help the reading of the fight by means of gestures, attitudes and mimicry which make the intention utterly obvious. Sometimes the wrestler triumphs with a repulsive sneer while kneeling on the good sportsman; sometimes he gives the crowd a conceited smile which forebodes an early revenge; sometimes, pinned to the ground, he hits the floor ostentatiously to make evident to all the intolerable nature of his situation; and sometimes he erects a complicated set of signs meant to make the public understand that he legitimately personifies the ever-entertaining image of the grumbler, endlessly confabulating[14] about his displeasure.

9   We are therefore dealing with a real Human Comedy, where the most socially-inspired nuances of passion (conceit, rightfulness, refined cruelty, a sense of 'paying one's debts') always felicitously[15] find the clearest sign which can re-ceive them, express them and triumphantly carry them to the confines of the hall. It is obvious that at such a pitch, it no longer matters whether the passion is genuine or not. What the public wants is the image of passion, not passion itself. There is no more a problem of truth in wrestling than in the theatre. In both, what is expected is the intelligible representation of moral situations which are usually private. This emptying out of inferiority to the benefit of its exterior signs, this exhaustion of the content by the form, is the very principle of triumphant classical art. Wrestling is an immediate pantomime, infinitely more efficient than the dramatic pantomime, for the wrestler's gesture needs no anecdote, no decor, in short no transference in order to appear true.

10   Each moment in wrestling is therefore like an algebra which instantaneously unveils the relationship between a cause and its represented effect. Wrestling fans certainly experience a kind of intellectual pleasure in *seeing* the moral mechanism function so perfectly. Some wrestlers, who are great comedians, entertain as much as a Molière character, because they succeed in imposing an immediate reading of their inner nature: Armand Mazaud, a wrestler of an arrogant and ridiculous character (as one says that Harpagon* is a character), always delights the audience by the mathematical rigour of his transcriptions, carrying the form of his gestures to the furthest reaches of their meaning, and giving to his manner of fighting the kind of vehemence and precision found in a great scholastic disputation,[16] in which what is at stake is at once the triumph of pride and the formal concern with truth.

11   What is thus displayed for the public is the great spectacle of Suffering, Defeat, and Justice.

---

13. diacritic: mark used to distinguish one sound from another

14. confabulating: chatting

15. felicitously: happily

16. scholastic disputation: argumentation originally used by medieval Christian scholars

*In Molière's *L'Avare*. [Barthes's note.]

Wrestling presents man's suffering with all the amplification of tragic masks. The wrestler who suffers in a hold which is reputedly cruel (an arm-lock, a twisted leg) offers an excessive portrayal of Suffering; like a primitive Pieta,[17] he exhibits for all to see his face, exaggeratedly contorted by an intolerable affliction. It is obvious, of course, that in wrestling reserve would be out of place, since it is opposed to the voluntary ostentation of the spectacle, to this Exhibition of Suffering which is the very aim of the fight. This is why all the actions which produce suffering are particularly spectacular, like the gesture of a conjuror who holds out his cards clearly to the public. Suffering which appeared without intelligible cause would not be understood; a concealed action that was actually cruel would transgress the unwritten rules of wrestling and would have no more sociological efficacy than a mad or parasitic gesture. On the contrary suffering appears as inflicted with emphasis and conviction, for everyone must not only see that the man suffers, but also and above all understand why he suffers. What wrestlers call a hold, that is, any figure which allows one to immobilize the adversary indefinitely and to have him at one's mercy, has precisely the function of preparing in a conventional, therefore intelligible, fashion the spectacle of suffering, of methodically establishing the conditions of suffering. The inertia of the vanquished allows the (temporary) victor to settle in his cruelty and to convey to the public this terrifying slowness of the torturer who is certain about the outcome of his actions; to grind the face of one's powerless adversary or to scrape his spine with one's fist with a deep and regular movement, or at least to produce the superficial appearance of such gestures: wrestling is the only sport which gives such an externalized image of torture. But here again, only the image is involved in the game, and the spectator does not

wish for the actual suffering of the contestant; he only enjoys the perfection of an iconography.[18] It is not true that wrestling is a sadistic spectacle: it is only an intelligible spectacle.

12   There is another figure, more spectacular still than a hold; it is the forearm smash, this loud slap of the forearm, this embryonic punch with which one clouts the chest of one's adversary, and which is accompanied by a dull noise and the exaggerated sagging of a vanquished body. In the forearm smash, catastrophe is brought to the point of maximum obviousness, so much so that ultimately the gesture appears as no more than a symbol; this is going too far, this is transgressing the moral rules of wrestling, where all signs must be excessively clear, but must not let the intention of clarity be seen. The public then shouts 'He's laying it on!', not because it regrets the absence of real suffering, but because it condemns artifice: as in the theatre, one fails to put the part across as much by an excess of sincerity as by an excess of formalism.

13   We have already seen to what extent wrestlers exploit the resources of a given physical style, developed and put to use in order to unfold before the eyes of the public a total image of Defeat. The flaccidity of tall white bodies which collapse with one blow or crash into the ropes with arms flailing, the inertia of massive wrestlers rebounding pitiably off all the elastic surfaces of the ring, nothing can signify more clearly and more passionately the exemplary abasement of the vanquished. Deprived of all resilience, the wrestler's flesh is no longer anything but an unspeakable heap spread out on the floor, where it solicits relentless reviling and jubilation. There is here a paroxysm[19] of meaning in the style of antiquity, which can only recall the heavily underlined intentions in Roman triumphs. At other times, there is another ancient posture which appears in the coupling of the wrestlers, that of the

---

17. *Pietà*: representation of the Virgin Mary grieving over her crucified Son

18. iconography: the art of pictorial representation

19. paroxysm: an intensification

suppliant who, at the mercy of his opponent, on bended knees, his arms raised above his head, is slowly brought down by the vertical pressure of the victor. In wrestling, unlike judo, Defeat is not a conventional sign, abandoned as soon as it is understood; it is not an outcome, but quite the contrary, it is a duration, a display, it takes up the ancient myths of public Suffering and Humiliation: the cross and the pillory. It is as if the wrestler is crucified in broad daylight and in the sight of all. I have heard it said of a wrestler stretched on the ground: 'He is dead, little Jesus, there, on the cross,' and these ironic words revealed the hidden roots of a spectacle which enacts the exact gestures of the most ancient purifications.

14   But what wrestling is above all meant to portray is a purely moral concept: that of justice. The idea of 'paying' is essential to wrestling, and the crowd's 'Give it to him' means above all else 'Make him pay'. This is therefore, needless to say, an immanent justice. The baser the action of the 'bastard', the more delighted the public is by the blow which he justly receives in return. If the villain—who is of course a coward—takes refuge behind the ropes, claiming unfairly to have a right to do so by a brazen mimicry, he is inexorably pursued there and caught, and the crowd is jubilant at seeing the rules broken for the sake of a deserved punishment. Wrestlers know very well how to play up to the capacity for indignation of the public by presenting the very limit of the concept of Justice, this outermost zone of confrontation where it is enough to infringe the rules a little more to open the gates of a world without restraints. For a wrestling-fan, nothing is finer than the revengeful fury of a betrayed fighter who throws himself vehemently not on a successful opponent but on the smarting image of foul play. Naturally, it is the pattern of Justice which matters here, much more than its content: wrestling is above all a quantitative sequence of compensations (an eye for an eye, a tooth for a tooth). This explains why sudden changes of circumstances have in the eyes of wrestling

habitués[20] a sort of moral beauty: they enjoy them as they would enjoy an inspired episode in a novel, and the greater the contrast between the success of a move and the reversal of fortune, the nearer the good luck of a contestant to his downfall, the more satisfying the dramatic mime is felt to be. Justice is therefore the embodiment of a possible transgression;[21] it is from the fact that there is a Law that the spectacle of the passions which infringe it derives its value.

15   It is therefore easy to understand why out of five wrestling-matches, only about one is fair. One must realize, let it be repeated, that 'fairness' here is a role or a genre, as in the theatre: the rules do not at all constitute a real constraint; they are the conventional appearance of fairness. So that in actual fact a fair fight is nothing but an exaggeratedly polite one: the contestants confront each other with zeal, not rage; they can remain in control of their passions, they do not punish their beaten opponent relentlessly, they stop fighting as soon as they are ordered to do so, and congratulate each other at the end of a particularly arduous episode, during which, however, they have not ceased to be fair. One must of course understand here that all these polite actions are brought to the notice of the public by the most conventional gestures of fairness: shaking hands, raising the arms, ostensibly avoiding a fruitless hold which would detract from the perfection of the contest.

16   Conversely, foul play exists only in its excessive signs: administering a big kick to one's beaten opponent, taking refuge behind the ropes while ostensibly invoking a purely formal right, refusing to shake hands with one's opponent before or after the fight, taking advantage of the end of the round to rush treacherously at the adversary from behind, fouling him while the referee is not looking (a move which obviously only

---

20. habitués: common frequenters of amusement places; regulars

21. transgression: crime

has any value or function because in fact half the audience can see it and get indignant about it). Since Evil is the natural climate of wrestling, a fair fight has chiefly the value of being an exception. It surprises the aficionado,[22] who greets it when he sees it as an anachronism and a rather sentimental throwback to the sporting tradition ('Aren't they playing fair, those two'); he feels suddenly moved at the sight of the general kindness of the world, but would probably die of boredom and indifference if wrestlers did not quickly return to the orgy of evil which alone makes good wrestling.

17　Extrapolated, fair wrestling could lead only to boxing or judo, whereas true wrestling derives its originality from all the excesses which make it a spectacle and not a sport. The ending of a boxing-match or a judo-contest is abrupt, like the full-stop which closes a demonstration. The rhythm of wrestling is quite different, for its natural meaning is that of rhetorical amplification: the emotional magniloquence,[23] the repeated paroxysms, the exasperation of the retorts can only find their natural outcome in the most baroque[24] confusion. Some fights, among the most successful kind, are crowned by a final charivari, a sort of unrestrained fantasia where the rules, the laws of the genre, the referee's censuring and the limits of the ring are abolished, swept away by a triumphant disorder which overflows into the hall and carries off pell-mell wrestlers, seconds, referee and spectators.

18　It has already been noted that in America wrestling represents a sort of mythological fight between Good and Evil (of a quasi-political nature, the 'bad' wrestler always being supposed to be a Red). The process of creating heroes in French wrestling is very different, being based on ethics and not on politics. What the public is look-ing for here is the gradual construction of a highly moral image: that of the perfect 'bastard'. One comes to wrestling in order to attend the continuing adventures of a single major leading character, permanent and multiform like Punch or Scapino, inventive in unexpected figures and yet always faithful to his role. The 'bastard' is here revealed as a Molière character or a 'portrait' by La Bruyère,[25] that is to say as a classical entity, an essence, whose acts are only significant epiphenomena[26] arranged in time. This stylized character does not belong to any particular nation or party, and whether the wrestler is called Kuzchenko (nicknamed Moustache after Stalin[27]), Yerpazian, Gaspardi, Jo Vignola or Nollières, the aficionado does not attribute to him any country except 'fairness'—observing the rules.

19　What then is a 'bastard' for this audience composed in part, we are told, of people who are themselves outside the rules of society? Essentially someone unstable, who accepts the rules only when they are useful to him and transgresses the formal continuity of attitudes. He is unpredictable, therefore asocial. He takes refuge behind the law when he considers that it is in his favour, and breaks it when he finds it useful to do so. Sometimes he rejects the formal boundaries of the ring and goes on hitting an adversary legally protected by the ropes, sometimes he re-establishes these boundaries and claims the protection of what he did not respect a few minutes earlier. This inconsistency, far more than treachery or cruelty, sends the audience beside itself with rage: offended not in its morality but in its logic, it considers the contradiction of arguments as the basest of crimes. The forbidden move becomes dirty only when it destroys a quantitative

---

22. aficionado: devotee or fan

23. magniloquence: pompous way of speaking

24. baroque: ornamental style

---

25. La Bruyère: seventeenth-century French writer and moralist

26. epiphenomena: phenomena that occur with and seem to result from others

27. Stalin: leader of the Soviet Union from 1924 to 1953

equilibrium and disturbs the rigorous reckoning of compensations; what is condemned by the audience is not at all the transgression of insipid official rules, it is the lack of revenge, the absence of a punishment. So that there is nothing more exciting for a crowd than the grandiloquent kick given to a vanquished 'bastard'; the joy of punishing is at its climax when it is supported by a mathematical justification; contempt is then unrestrained. One is no longer dealing with a *salaud*[28] but with a *salope*[29]—the verbal gesture of the ultimate degradation.

20   Such a precise finality demands that wrestling should be exactly what the public expects of it. Wrestlers, who are very experienced, know perfectly how to direct the spontaneous episodes of the fight so as to make them conform to the image which the public has of the great legendary themes of its mythology. A wrestler can irritate or disgust, he never disappoints, for he always accomplishes completely, by a progressive solidification of signs, what the public expects of him. In wrestling, nothing exists except in the absolute, there is no symbol, no allusion, everything is presented exhaustively. Leaving nothing in the shade, each action discards all parasitic meanings and ceremonially offers to the public a pure and full signification, rounded like Nature. This grandiloquence is nothing but the popular and age-old image of the perfect intelligibility of reality. What is portrayed by wrestling is therefore an ideal understanding of things; it is the euphoria[30] of men raised for a while above the constitutive ambiguity of everyday situations and placed before the panoramic view of a univocal[31] Nature, in which signs at last correspond to causes, without obstacle, without evasion, without contradiction.

21   When the hero or the villain of the drama, the man who was seen a few minutes earlier possessed by moral rage, magnified into a sort of metaphysical[32] sign, leaves the wrestling hall, impassive, anonymous, carrying a small suitcase and arm-in-arm with his wife, no one can doubt that wrestling holds that power of transmutation[33] which is common to the Spectacle and to Religious Worship. In the ring, and even in the depths of their voluntary ignominy, wrestlers remain gods because they are, for a few moments, the key which opens Nature, the pure gesture which separates Good from Evil, and unveils the form of a Justice which is at last intelligible.

Critical Explorations: Reading

Reread the Barthes selection. As you do, answer the five questions below. In this reading, focus on the ways Barthes examines the event of wrestling as a unique spectator experience. The answers to these questions may be used in your reading or dialogic journal.

1. In paragraph 2, Barthes says that "wrestling is not a sport, it is a spectacle." This seems to be the crux of his argument in this essay. What distinction is he making between spectacle and sport? How does this distinction relate to his understanding of wrestling as a sport?

2. In paragraph 3, Barthes contrasts boxing to wrestling through a treatment of the characteristics of each. Reread this paragraph, and list the characteristics he presents for wrestling and for boxing.

3. In paragraph 7, Barthes compares wrestling to *Commedia dell'Arte*. Through inferences you can make in this paragraph, explain what you think *Commedia dell'Arte* is. How does this reference to *Commedia dell'Arte* help

---

28. *salaud:* dirty fellow

29. *salope:* sexually promiscuous woman

30. euphoria: feeling of well-being

31. univocal: having a single meaning

32. metaphysical: dealing with concepts beyond the physical.

33. transmutation: a change from one state to another

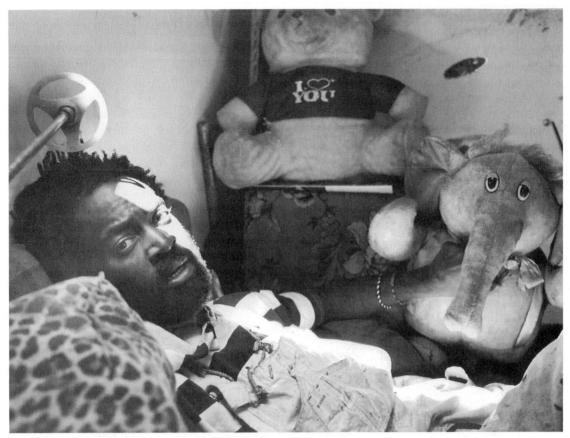

Gregg Segal, "Anonymous Man, Los Angeles, CA 1994"

you understand Thauvin, the wrestler whom Barthes examines in this paragraph?

4. In paragraph 9, Barthes notes that "what the public [wrestling fans] wants is the image of passion, not passion itself." What distinction is he making here? How is the image of passion different from passion itself?

5. In paragraph 20, Barthes refers to the perfection of wrestling—"the image of the perfect intelligibility of reality." Reread paragraphs 20–21 to determine how Barthes is defining *perfection*. How does this understanding of perfection help summarize Barthes's conception of wrestling?

Critical Explorations: Writing

The following are four topics for reasoned essays on popular culture. Once you select a topic and begin composing, have your draft read by your peers and professor. You may use any material you have read in the chapter introduction as well as in the selections as background for your essay.

1. Analyze the photograph above. First, explain what you see in as much detail as you can. Analyze these visual details. How are they organized? Then make responsible inferences from these details. What American beliefs does this photo seem to be projecting? You

may use the semiotic terms introduced by Arthur Asa Berger in Selection 1 in your analysis.

2. Choose any photograph or portrait—a family photo, a portrait in an art book or art history text, or a picture in a magazine. Describe the details you see. Analyze these details. Then infer what cultural beliefs the work seems to be suggesting. Attach a copy of the photo or portrait to your final draft. You may use the semiotic terms defined by Arthur Asa Berger in your analysis.

3. William Kowinski does a careful semiotic analysis of shopping malls in Selection 3. Choose another community event involving sales that you are familiar with: a state fair, a computer display show, an automobile show, a flea market, a garage sale, and so on. Describe the event in as much detail as you can. Then identify and analyze the unstated cultural meanings that you believe explain this communal event.

4. Roland Barthes semiotically analyzes the world of French wrestling (Selection 4). Pick an American sport or spectacle you know well: football, basketball, car racing, the spectacle of American wrestling, and so on. Discuss the essentials of how the sport or spectacle is played. Then focus on those aspects of the game or spectacle that seem to have semiotic significance. What cultural beliefs about gender, heroism, cooperation, victory, and defeat does the sport or spectacle reveal to you?

Student Writing

Below you will find a student's response to an analysis of the photograph you studied in the introduction to this chapter (page 25); it is his second draft. Read the draft carefully; then answer the questions that follow. Greg responded to the following essay topic:

Introduce and comment on the beliefs that seem to inform so much of American popular culture. Then relate this discussion of beliefs to an analysis of the photo "Steven and Veronica."

Urban Gothic

1   American popular culture is anchored by a set of myths, a belief system that addresses various aspects of the society, including the society's views on equal opportunity, technology, patriotism, wealth and beauty, the happy ending, gender roles and family structure. Concerning gender roles and family, the popular culture's views have changed significantly, allowing for greater individual freedom. Of course, these are broadenings, not shifts, of society's beliefs; traditional manifestations of gender roles and families still constitute a large part of American society. "Steven and Veronica," a portrait of a young couple by photographer Gregg Segal, shows how traditional beliefs can still thrive in modern-day, urban America.

2   America's myths reveal the values and expectations of its society. Equal opportunity, for example, is still struggling in terms of being fully

applied to the society, but, as a whole, American society has been won over to the concept that everyone has a basic set of rights, a concept that was penned over 200 years ago by the Founding Fathers: the right to "life, liberty and the pursuit of happiness." America developed its own unique form of patriotism, based not as much on the idea of an independent nation or of common heritage as it is on the aforementioned declaration, on liberty and equality and the opportunity for a better life. In our society, this "better life" can be defined in terms of wealth and beauty; American myth has made these two qualities the keys to happiness, although it sometimes reminds itself—halfheartedly—that happiness is not guaranteed through these means. Another way of achieving happiness, American society believes, is technology, the application of scientific knowledge we have gained. In general, American society has looked on its technology as solutions to its problems, although there is a growing movement of people who believe that technology is causing more problems than it solves. Nevertheless, the resolution of problems, the pursuit of happiness, is paramount in the American way of life; pain and sadness are to be avoided as much as possible, even as resolutions in the stories of popular entertainment. There has to be a sense, if not of ecstatic, spectacular triumph, of an inner victory, a growth and improvement of character, and appreciation of and contentment with the resolution of one's problems.

3   Although many American myths, like those stated above, have remained constant and part of the American tradition, American views on gender roles and on family have undergone a revolution since the 1950's. Tradition follows that the male is dominant, the breadwinner, protector, and supreme authority of his family; the female takes care of the home, raises the children, and is subservient to her mate. Not counting the aberration caused by World War II, but recognizing that it probably opened the door to what followed, a substantial number of women have entered the male-dominated work force since the 1950's. It was a protracted (and yet ongoing) struggle, but in the past forty years there has been a complete change in American popular culture's views of the working woman.

4   This revolution also played a part in the transformation of the American view of the family. Prior to the Sixties, the most accepted form of the family was the nuclear family: a few children, a father and a mother, with the parents filling the gender roles aforementioned. Nowadays, due in no small part to the growing self-reliance and self-sufficiency of the working woman, divorce has lost its traditional stigma and has become more prevalent in the past two decades; single-parent families are practically the norm. This is also evidenced by television family situation comedies: the nuclear families of "Father Knows Best" and "Leave It to Beaver" have been replaced with the single parents of "Murphy Brown" and "Blossom" (although the character of the family in the latter sitcom recently remarried); the nuclear families that have remained are the dysfunctional Conners ("Roseanne"), Bundys ("Married...with Children") and "The Simpsons," and the campy descendants of the 50's shows. Moreover, unorthodox family structures (homosexual parents, for example) are gaining attention if not acceptance, thanks in large part to another constituent of the television medium, the daytime talk show.

5   Despite these transformations, traditional gender roles and family structures are thriving in America. American popular culture has not shifted its views in that it has embraced the new and discarded the old, but it has become more open and accepting of the possibilities—of women's abilities in the workplace, and of the different permutations of the family. The preservation of tradition is not merely attributed to the rural, often conservative families of America's "Heartland," but is also due to immigrant families, whose native cultures have a more traditional belief system.

6   Gregg Segal's photograph embodies the survival of these traditional, one might even say primitive, cultural myths. In it we see a young couple in front of a parked bus. The man is standing, holding a gun in his right hand and looking into the eyes of his seated mate, cradling her with his left hand. She is carrying a dog, and is looking up at her lover. Iconographically, the photograph makes certain statements. Traditionally considered a phallic symbol, the gun represents male power, virility, and capacity for violence. The presence of the dog may allude back to iconography used in art since before the Renaissance, when dogs in paintings—usually found near women—represented fidelity, faithfulness of the women to their spouse. The man's position, with a firm hold on both the gun and his woman, standing a full head higher than her, is overtly an icon of male domination and power. His facial expression is vague, and can be interpreted as anything from a firm, caring gaze to dictatorial hostility; one might see this as a sign of male emotional inaccessibility. He appears to be Latino, and therefore from a culture where males are traditionally dominant, the culture that lent American culture the term "machismo"—virility, dominance of women, aggression, violence. The young woman, however, is looking up at her man, in admiration, perhaps, in subservient love, with maybe just a bit of apprehension, vulnerable at his blatant masculinity. The Virgin Mary, symbol of the perfect woman and perfect mother in Christian religion, is almost invariably portrayed as seated in religious art from early Christian times through the Renaissance, and although this may be reaching quite a bit, it may have some connection with the young lady being seated as opposed to standing up. She is holding Fido, the sign of fidelity (one should not read too much into the position and the expression of the dog, for dogs probably do not care much about their poses in pictures). The most telling part of her icon, however, is the word printed on the bus right above her head: "COMMAND." Perhaps she is bidding him to command her. An alternate interpretation, that he is commanding her, seems to be not as strong as the word would probably have been placed closer to him, rather than above and a little behind her head, to achieve that effect.

7   The text itself appears to be a portrait of a young, modern, urban couple still somehow clinging to the traditional, perhaps crude and primal, values once exclusively embraced by America. Symbols of tradition—much like the old Middle American couple in Grant Wood's painting *American Gothic*—alive and well in present-day Los Angeles.

1. Reread paragraphs 2 and 3. How does Greg introduce and organize his discussion of American beliefs and myths? Do you think this is an intelligent way to organize these beliefs? Can you provide another way to organize this material?

2. At the end of paragraph 4, Greg presents an interesting cause–effect relationship between the kinds of families portrayed on evening television situation comedies and the discussion of families one sees on daytime talk shows. What relationship is he establishing here? What additional discussion about daytime talk shows could you include here to make this relationship clearer, or more specific, for the reader?

3. Reread paragraph 6. What is Greg's argument here regarding what the photo "Steven and Veronica" is communicating? How does Greg's argument relate to his previous analysis of American values and beliefs?

4. Are there any additional details in the photo that you think Greg could include in paragraph 6, or in another paragraph, to further support his argument?

5. Consider Greg's conclusion in paragraph 7 that "Steven and Veronica" is a photo that relies on traditional values. Do you agree? Or do you see other, less traditional values suggested in this photograph?

Peer Responses

Use some or all of these questions to respond to your peer's draft. Comment as specifically as you can so that your peer can use your comments to effectively revise her draft.

1. Read your peer's introduction. Is the photograph or popular culture event adequately identified? Are the cultural assumptions mentioned that will be analyzed in the essay? Is there anything else that you would want to add here?

2. Choose one paragraph that analyzes the cultural beliefs that inform the photo or event. How well developed is this paragraph? Are there any elements in its organization that could be improved? Are there any sentences that could be phrased more clearly?

3. Locate the first paragraph that introduces the photo or cultural event. Are there any details that you think should be included here to make this paragraph clearer? Are there any details that you would want to omit?

4. Locate one paragraph that you think is well organized. Explain why you believe this paragraph is successful.

5. Locate a sentence or sentences that carefully analyze the photo or cultural event. Say why this part of the draft is effective. Then locate a sentence or sentences that do not analyze the photo or event as effectively. Explain how the analysis here can be improved.

Chapter 2

Literature About Popular Culture

Introduction

Popular culture is so much a part of American thinking that writers have begun to examine it in their short stories and novels. In this chapter, you will be critically examining selections from American fiction that focus on American popular culture. This literature relates to the beliefs we analyzed in Chapter 1. In each of the four selections in this chapter, you will see how the various characters express these beliefs in their statements and actions. You will also be able to infer how each writer feels about these American beliefs. Therefore, you will have a richer understanding of these beliefs as you study television, advertising, and speech making in the chapters that follow.

These literary texts are not as widely read in America as best-sellers are or as popular as television programs and commercials. In this chapter, you will learn about the critical practices used in reading formal literature. These practices are, at times, different from the ones you use in analyzing the media.

How does one read and write about literature? What is literature, after all, that asks you to read it differently from a best-selling romance? Or is there any real difference between a novel or short story and a formulaic romance? Much has been written on these questions, and you will find that there is little agreement. Some scholars believe that a novel or short story is no different from a best-selling romance, whereas others see literature as unique, requiring critical reading practices not used in popular fiction. This is a question you will be considering as you complete this introduction and read the four literary selections.

Characterization and *narration* are terms that are used in analyzing any kind of fiction. (You will be considering these same two terms in the next chapter on television.) Critics of literature, like television reviewers, talk about characters that are stereotyped or multidimensional. *Stereotypical* characters are those that are not lifelike and are easily predictable, whereas *multidimensional* characters are analyzed for their complexity and impression of realism. Literary characters tend to be multidimensional. For example, in the excerpt from *White Noise* that you will be reading, Babette is not the typical happy housewife seen in American commercials, but one with specific problems caused by an American technology that overwhelms her. As critical readers, we can learn about our own involvement with American technology by analyzing her thoughts and actions. In contrast, characters in popular romances tend to be stereotyped. The jealous lover or the strong, handsome man acts in ways that readers are familiar with. The jealous lover pines for his woman, suspecting her every action, or the handsome hero protects his woman, never frightened or in doubt.

The questions one needs to ask of literary characters of popular culture are these:

1. In what ways are they believable?

2. In what ways are they unique?

3. In what ways are they memorable?

4. How are their actions consistent with the kind of character the author has created?

5. How do they help us understand the American beliefs we live by?

Similarly, literary narratives or plots are similar to those in television situation comedies and dramas. A story is told, either on television or in a novel, and you attempt to determine the outcome. But unlike half-hour or hour television narratives, novels on popular culture take several hours to read, so their narratives tend to be more complex. However, the questions you ask of fiction narratives are the same ones you bring to television narratives:

1. Is the story line easy to follow or complex?
2. Are the actions in the story believable?

Just like the oversimplified story line in a television drama, you can fault a novel for an easily anticipated outcome. Something in the narrative needs to keep you guessing, just as the events in your own life often do not have a conclusion that you can easily determine.

Moreover, like advertisements on television and radio and in magazines, you must be alert to the language that the writer of fiction selects. You need to see how the language in the work helps create a particular feeling in you. In this excerpt from the first chapter of *White Noise,* the narrator describes the returning college students in this way: "Their summer has been bloated with criminal pleasures, as always." As a critical reader of word associations, you need to consider what the words *bloated* and *criminal* suggest about these students. *Bloated* can relate to overindulgence and loss of control, and *criminal* is associated with breaking the law. Are these students overfed on technological pleasures? Are they really breaking the law, or is their life-style lawless or undisciplined? These are questions whose answers you will find as you continue to read about these students.

Unlike commercials and television shows, in fiction you also need to be aware of point of view. That is, who is telling the story? In television drama and commercials, several characters speak, presenting their respective points of view. In fiction, characters may speak, but they speak through the eyes of a particular narrator. In novels, you will find three kinds of narrative viewpoints: first person, omniscient, and limited omniscient. In the first-person narrative, the point of view is "I" or "we"—actual characters in the work telling the story. The first-person perspective is limited because the reader sees everything through one perspective (the narrator's). In first-person narration, readers may also experience a sense of *irony,* because they may know more than the narrator about the actions and characters in the novel.

In omniscient narration, the story is told from the point of view of an outsider who, as a god-like figure, is aware of all that happens in a story. With an omniscient narration, told in the third person "he, she, they," readers can get into the minds of all the characters. In limited-omniscient narration, the point of view is still third person, but the narrator reports the story from the perspective of one of the characters. Therefore, we do not learn as much about the narration as we would from an omniscient point of view. Yet we get to understand this particular character in greater depth than we would if the story were told from an omniscient point of view.

Writers of fiction use these three points of view to fit their particular purposes. For the sake of the story line, they may not want the reader to know more than their characters, so they may use a first-person or limited-omniscient point of view. In other cases, they may want the reader to be all-knowing, so an omniscient point of view is appropriate.

In this century, novelists, in an attempt to portray their characters more intimately, have developed a *stream of consciousness* narrative technique that sacrifices the details of the story's action to get into the often distorted and confusing thoughts of their characters. For many readers, reading this type of fiction is demanding because the story line is often interrupted by the thoughts of the characters.

Critical Practices

As with the previous texts that you have examined on popular culture, you need to bring specific critical practices to the reading of fiction.

Metaphor Making

The most significant difference between nonliterary and literary texts is that literary texts tend to use more metaphorical language. These metaphors are often those you have not considered before. Lyrical poetry is almost completely metaphorical, whereas metaphors form some of the description in fiction. A *metaphor* is simply a comparison between two seemingly unlike objects or ideas, whose differences help you better understand the object or idea described.

You were introduced to comparisons in Selections 3 and 4 in the previous chapter. If you recall, Kowinski compared malls to various other entities and Barthes compared wrestling to the theater. You were asked to see how helpful these comparisons were to understanding the topics that these authors examined. In critically analyzing a metaphor, you need to see how an apparently inappropriate comparison sheds light on your understanding of a character or action in the novel. In the excerpt from *The Crying of Lot 49* (Selection 8), Thomas Pynchon describes Oedipa's understanding of Southern Californians this way: "Though she knew even less about radios than about Southern Californians, there were to both outward patterns a hieroglyphic sense of concealed meaning, of an intent to communicate." In this excerpt, the narrator first presents a metaphor of the Southern Californian as a radio, then compares them both to hieroglyphics.

Critically analyzing metaphors requires considering the relationship between the object described—called the *tenor*—to its comparison, or *vehicle.* In the Pynchon excerpt, the tenor is the Southern Californian and the vehicle to describe it is a radio—for most readers, a machine that they know how to operate but do not understand how it works. It is often best to place tenor and vehicle side by side, then to list the associations that this comparison provides. As you examine a metaphor, you may choose to refer to a dictionary and thesaurus.

Look at how you can consider the metaphor of the radio as a hieroglyphic:

Tenor	Vehicle	Associations
radio	hieroglyphic	ancient picture writing, symbols and signs, hard to master, writing that is difficult to understand

You can find many of these suggestions for the word *hieroglyphics* in a dictionary or a thesaurus. Your first reaction is likely this: "How are radios like hieroglyphics? I understand what is said on the radio; I don't understand hieroglyphics." Like all effective metaphor makers, Pynchon wants you at first to reject the comparison, then to reconsider it, and finally to begin to see new ways of comparing the two items. Southern Californians and radios are fairly new historical events, whereas hieroglyphics are old. Yet maybe the message that one gets from the radio and from living in Southern California is as mysterious as hieroglyphics are. Perhaps there are unstated, semiotic meanings in all three items that are being compared.

Metaphors can also be phrased so that the comparison is more direct. In the Pynchon novel, the narrator could have said, "Southern Californians are like hieroglyphics." When *like* or *as* is used in a metaphorical comparison, the metaphor becomes a *simile*. Though stated differently, a simile is no different from a metaphor. The critical practices you use to analyze both are the same. One can say either that a simile is a special kind of metaphor or that a metaphor is a special kind of simile.

By stretching your logical capacities so that you are asked to make far-reaching comparisons, metaphors allow you to experience an object or event from a fresh perspective. This is the purpose of literature. It recreates the world for you.

Symbol Making

Related to metaphors in literary works are symbols. *Symbols* are objects or characters that are part of a novel's or short story's narrative yet whose meaning is also metaphorical. Symbols often serve to summarize the central idea or mood of a literary work. In DeLillo's *White Noise*, for example, white noise is itself a part of the narrative. It becomes the anonymous sounds that technology makes—computer hums, electrical noises, and so on. These sounds infiltrate and deaden human thinking. Thus, white noise becomes the symbol for the anonymous face of technology. It is a particularly effective summary for the mood of the entire novel.

Analyzing Ambiguity, Paradox, Oxymoron, and Hyperbole

In the texts that you studied in Chapter 1, you were encouraged to analyze their arguments. In analytical texts, or texts that explain, ambiguity and equivocation are practices that are discouraged. In philosophy, *semantical ambiguity* is defined as the use of a word or phrase that can be analyzed in two or several ways. For example, a word such as *brutality* has different significance when it is used in separate disciplines. To a law professor, brutality has specific legal significance. Particular physical actions are considered brutal; others are characterized as violent or mischievous. To a novelist, brutality may be seen in a less confining way. Brutality describes emotional states as well as physical actions. A character's stare may be seen as brutal. Such a description would not be accepted in a court of law. In analytical writing, such as legal essays, terms need to be defined in specific, limiting ways, but in descriptive writing, such as novels, a term gathers meaning through the particular way that the writer uses it.

Furthermore, in analytical works, once you define a term, you need to consistently apply this definition in the rest of your essay. *Equivocation* is a logical error in which you use the same term in two or more different ways in the same argument.

In literature, writers have a different understanding of ambiguity and equivocation. Being unclear is sometimes their intent. In recreating the world, literature does not necessarily clarify life's experiences, as would effective analytical writing. In literature, *ambiguity* is the intentional use of a term in more than one way. Occasionally, a novelist uses a pronoun ambiguously. That is, she wants to show that she is referring to more than one character. For example, she could end one of her chapters in the following way: "She cast her hostile stare at them." The "them" may refer to several characters, none of whom are identified by name. This confusion or ambiguity may be exactly what the novelist intends. She may want to refer to the several people her character is thinking of and keep their identities in doubt until the next chapter, or to suggest that the character herself does not know who exactly is the target of her hostility.

Similar to ambiguity in literature is *paradox*—a phrase or statement that seems contradictory but, on closer study, is illuminating. John Donne, the great seventeenth-century British poet, ends a religious sonnet with the following confusing statement: "Death, thou shalt die." How, the reader asks, can death die? Such a statement in an analytical paper would sound absurd, but in this sonnet, the speaker wants to show that the human being overcomes death in eternal life and, by doing so, puts an end to death.

Similar to a paradoxical statement in literature is an *oxymoron*—a contradiction in terms. In a novel, a character considering a confusing compliment could say to himself, "That was surely an unflattering compliment." Outside the novel's context, one could ask a logical question: How can a compliment ever be unflattering? Isn't this a contradiction in terms? But, in the complexity of human relationships, these contradictions do occur. People sometimes do compliment in order to insult politely or subtly. And writers often use oxymorons in order to express these contradictions.

Finally, writers can exaggerate to get their point across. A writer may speak of the "eternity of grief" that his character is experiencing. In measured psychological terms, this would be an inexact way of describing grief, for how can a human being experience an immeasurable amount of grief? Yet in literature, such exaggeration—known as *hyperbole*—is an effective way of recreating the mental or emotional state of a character. For in describing grief as eternal, the writer has captured the feeling that we have all had at times: that our grief will never end.

Identifying Mood and Tone

All these literary practices create the *tone* of a particular work—that is, the attitude the writer has for his story—and its *mood*, or the feeling the reader gets from the work. You infer a work's mood and tone from the actions and statements of the characters and from the language that the writer uses to create character and action. The tone of the work is often described as sympathetic, critical, or very critical. When a writer criticizes, sometimes humorously, the society she creates, she is writing *satire*. When her tone is very critical of her society, you can describe her tone as *sarcastic*. You will likely identify a satirical tone in several of the works that you will read in this chapter. Each work finds fault with specific aspects of American popular culture, and these faults are at times expressed in a sort of dark humor.

Although the reading of literature does not require you to use a set of exact practices, you are still using critical practices. In understanding how a writer recreates experiences, you consider life's complexities and mysteries. These are emotions that are difficult to describe, like taboo thoughts or impossible story lines. Yet by analyzing the literary text, you do come upon convincing interpretations, just as you do with nonliterary texts. You will find that reading literature requires its own kind of logic.

Recapping

The reading of literature requires critical practices, yet these practices are not necessarily those that you have learned to use in analyzing arguments in essays. The central practice in literary reading is understanding metaphorical language. You also find that in critically reading literature, you come upon illogical statements and phrases. Yet in analyzing paradoxes, oxymorons, and hyperboles, you learn to understand the complexities in human events that logical statements about these events would not capture.

The practices you have been introduced to in this chapter are just a few of those that students of literature use to analyze fiction. Yet these activities are the ones that will best help you critically examine the four selections in this chapter, and they are also those that most clearly show you how literary analysis is different from the critical practices you have used so far in analyzing arguments in essays.

Reading Selections   **5–8**

The four reading selections in this chapter come from American novels and a short story about popular culture. All have a satirical tone to them because they find that the human character is compromised in our technological world. In interesting ways, these selections examine the beliefs that you studied in Chapter 1. The first selection is from Jerzy Kosinski's *Being There.* His topic is American television and how it influences one's character and behavior. Chance, the protagonist, is a peculiar character because his most significant human contact is the television, which he has been raised on. In the second selection, from *White Noise,* Don DeLillo describes an American family of the eighties: divorced parents with children and stepchildren. His focus is on how technology affects each of them: how their decisions and actions are shaped by television, commercials, and computers.

The third selection, Helena María Viramontes's short story "Miss Clairol," describes a young woman who is dependent on American cosmetics and advertising to redefine herself and her relationship to her daughter. The world of advertising and the mystery surrounding beauty products become the background in which mother and daughter relate to each other. The fourth and final selection is from the second chapter of Thomas Pynchon's *The Crying of Lot 49.* This is an unusual story about intrigue in Southern California with characters who act bizarrely. Part of the reason for the mystery in this work is American technology, whose influence the characters do not fully understand.

Selection 5

from *Being There*
Jerzy Kosinski

In *Being There,* Jerzy Kosinski has written a satire on American culture that focuses on the ways various characters respond to his main character, Chauncey Gardiner, known as Chance. Chance is an orphan who has been cared for since birth by a character named Old Man. Chance's only job is to tend to Old Man's garden, situated in his large estate, in exchange for his room and board. Yet Old Man has no real contact with Chance. In fact, the most important contact Chance has with other humans is the television. Almost everything Chance knows he has learned on television. Therefore, his character is peculiar in many ways.

The section of *Being There* that you will read comes from the first half of the novel, in which Chance has been taken in by a wealthy couple—

Mr. Rand and EE—after he has been removed from his home following the death of Old Man. What is interesting in this excerpt is how Chance's character has been shaped by television and the surprising responses influential people have to Chance.

This excerpt is easy to read. The sentence structure is straightforward, the vocabulary is fairly easy, and the story line is uncomplicated. What will require careful thought is your determining why Chance seems to act so strangely and why influential people are attracted to him. Kosinski will not give you his answers to these questions, so you will have to make inferences from the evidence you have in the selection.

Reading–Writing Preparation

Before you read this selection, you may want to answer the following questions in writing or discussion:

1. What kind of knowledge do you get from television?

2. What do you think makes media stars popular?

Being There

1 Chance watched TV in his room. The President's speech at the luncheon of the Financial Institute was telecast on several channels; the few remaining programs showed only family games and children's adventures. Chance ate lunch in his room, continued to watch TV, and was just about to fall asleep when Rand's secretary called.

2 "The executives of the THIS EVENING television program have just phoned," she said excitedly, "and they want you to appear on the show tonight. They apologized for giving you such short notice, but they've only just now heard that the Vice President will be unable to appear on the show to discuss the President's speech. Because Mr. Rand is so ill, he will, of course, also be unable to appear, but he has suggested that you—a financier who has made so favorable an impression on the President—might be willing to come instead."

3 Chance could not imagine what being on TV involved. He wanted to see himself reduced to the size of the screen; he wanted to become an image, to dwell inside the set.

4 The secretary waited on the phone.

5 "It's all right with me," said Chance. "What do I have to do?"

6 "You don't have to do anything, sir," she said cheerfully. "The producer himself will pick you up in time for the show. It's a live program, so you have to be there half an hour before it goes on. You'll be THIS EVENING's main attraction tonight. I'll call them right back; they'll be delighted with your acceptance."

7 Chance turned on the TV. He wondered whether a person changed before or after appearing on the screen. Would he be changed forever or only during the time of his appearance? What part of himself would he leave behind when he finished the program? Would there be two Chances after the show: one Chance who watched TV and another who appeared on it?

8 Early that evening, Chance was visited by the producer of THIS EVENING—a short man in a dark suit. The producer explained that the President's speech had heightened interest in the nation's economic situation. ". . . and since the Vice President won't be able to appear on our show

Excerpt from *Being There*. © 1970 by Jerzy Kosinski, reprinted by permission of Harcourt Brace & Company.

tonight," he continued "we would be very grateful to have you tell our viewers exactly what is going on in the country's economy. Occupying, as you do, a position of such intimacy with the President, you are a man ideally suited to provide the country with an explanation. On the show you can be as direct as you'd like to be. The host won't interrupt you at all while you're talking, but if he wants to break in he'll let you know by raising his left forefinger to his left eyebrow. This will mean that he wants either to ask you a new question or to emphasize what you've already said."

9   "I understand," said Chance.

10   "Well, if you're ready, sir, we can go; our make-up man will have to do only a minor touch-up." He smiled. "Our host, by the way, would be honored to meet you before the show goes on."

11   In the large limousine sent by the network, there were two small TV sets. As they drove along Park Avenue, Chance asked if a set could be turned on. He and the producer watched the program in silence.

12   The interior of the studio looked like all the TV studios Chance had ever seen on TV. He was escorted quickly to a large adjoining office and offered a drink, which be refused; instead, he had a cup of coffee. The host of the show appeared. Chance recognized him instantly; he had seen him many times on THIS EVENING, although he did not like talk shows very much.

13   While the host talked on and on to him, Chance wondered what was going to happen next and when he would actually be televised. The host grew quiet at last, and the producer returned promptly with a make-up man. Chance sat in front of a mirror as the man covered his face with a thin layer of brownish powder. "Have you appeared on television a lot?" asked the make-up man.

14   "No," said Chance, "but I watch it all the time."

15   The make-up man and the producer chuckled politely. "Ready," said the make-up man, nodding and closing his case. "Good luck, sir." He turned and left.

16   Chance waited in an adjacent room. In one corner stood a large, bulky TV set. He saw the host appear and introduce the show. The audience applauded; the host laughed. The big, sharp-nosed cameras rolled smoothly around the stage. There was music, and the band leader flashed on the screen, grinning.

17   Chance was astonished that television could portray itself; cameras watched themselves and, as they watched, they televised a program. This self-portrait was telecast on TV screens facing the stage and watched by the studio audience. Of all the manifold things there were in all the world—trees, grass, flowers, telephones, radios, elevators—only TV constantly held up a mirror to its own neither solid nor fluid face.

18   Suddenly the producer appeared and signaled Chance to follow him. They walked through the door and on past a heavy curtain. Chance heard the host pronounce his name. Then, as the producer stepped away, he found himself in the glare of the lights. He saw the audience in front of him; unlike the audiences he had seen on his own TV set, he could not distinguish individual faces in the crowd. Three large cameras stood on the small square stage; on the right, the host sat at a leather-padded table. He beamed at Chance, rose with dignity, and introduced him; the audience applauded loudly. Imitating what he had so often seen on TV, Chance moved toward the vacant chair at the table. He sat down and so did the host. The cameramen wheeled the cameras silently around them. The host leaned across the table toward Chance.

19   Facing the cameras and the audience, now barely visible in the background of the studio, Chance abandoned himself to what would happen. He was drained of thought, engaged, yet removed. The cameras were licking up the image of his body, were recording his every movement and noiselessly hurling them into millions of TV screens scattered throughout the world—into rooms, cars, boats, planes, living rooms, and bed-

rooms. He would be seen by more people than he could ever meet in his entire life—people who would never meet him. The people who watched him on their sets did not know who actually faced them; how could they, if they had never met him? Television reflected only people's surfaces; it also kept peeling their images from their bodies until they were sucked into the caverns of their viewers' eyes, forever beyond retrieval, to disappear. Facing the cameras with their unsensing triple lenses pointed at him like snouts, Chance became only an image for millions of real people. They would never know how real he was, since his thinking could not be televised. And to him, the viewers existed only as projections of his own thought, as images. He would never know how real they were, since he had never met them and did not know what they thought.

20   Chance heard the host say: "We here in the studio are very honored to have you with us tonight, Mr. Chauncey Gardiner, and so, I'm sure, are the more than forty million Americans who watch THIS EVENING nightly. We are especially grateful to you for filling in on such short notice for the Vice President, who was unfortunately prevented by pressing business from being with us tonight." The host paused for a second; there was complete silence in the studio. "I will be frank, Mr. Gardiner. Do you agree with the President's view of our economy?"

21   "Which view?" asked Chance.

22   The host smiled knowingly. "The view which the President set forth this afternoon in his major address to the Financial Institute of America. Before his speech, the President consulted with you, among his other financial advisers. . . ."

23   "Yes . . . ?" said Chance.

24   "What I mean is . . ." The host hesitated and glanced at his notes. "Well . . . let me give you an example: the President compared the economy of this country to a garden, and indicated that after a period of decline a time of growth would naturally follow. . . ."

25   "I know the garden very well," said Chance firmly. "I have worked in it all of my life. It's a good garden and a healthy one; its trees are healthy and so are its shrubs and flowers, as long as they are trimmed and watered in the right seasons. The garden needs a lot of care. I do agree with the President: everything in it will grow strong in due course. And there is still plenty of room in it for new trees and new flowers of all kinds."

26   Part of the audience interrupted to applaud and part booed. Looking at the TV set that stood to his right, Chance saw first his own face fill the screen. Then some faces in the audience were shown—they evidently approved his words; others appeared angry. The host's face returned to the screen and Chance turned away from the set and faced him.

27   "Well, Mr. Gardiner," the host said, "that was very well put indeed, and I think it was a booster for all of us who do not like to wallow in complaints or take delight in gloomy predictions! Let us be clear, Mr. Gardiner. It is your view, then, that the slowing of the economy, the downtrend in the stock market, the increase in unemployment . . . you believe that all of this is just another phase, another season, so to speak, in the growth of a garden. . . ."

28   "In a garden, things grow . . . but first, they must wither; trees have to lose their leaves in order to put forth new leaves, and to grow thicker and stronger and taller. Some trees die, but fresh saplings replace them. Gardens need a lot of care. But if you love your garden, you don't mind working in it, and waiting. Then in the proper season you will surely see it flourish."

29   Chance's last words were partly lost in the excited murmuring of the audience. Behind him, members of the band tapped their instruments; a few cried out loud bravos. Chance turned to the set beside him and saw his own face with the eyes turned to one side. The host lifted his hand to silence the audience, but the applause continued, punctuated by isolated boos. He rose slowly and motioned Chance to join him at center stage, where he embraced him ceremoniously. The applause mounted to uproar. Chance stood

uncertainly. As the noise subsided, the host took Chance's hand and said: "Thank you, thank you, Mr. Gardiner. Yours is the spirit which this country so greatly needs. Let's hope it will help usher spring into our economy. Thank you again, Mr. Chauncey Gardiner—financier, presidential adviser, and true statesman!"

30 He escorted Chance back to the curtain, where the producer gently took him in hand. "You were great, sir, just great!" the producer exclaimed. "I've been producing this show for almost three years and I can't remember anything like it! I can tell you that the boss really loved it. It was great, really great!" He led Chance to the rear of the studio. Several employees waved to him warmly, while others turned away.

31 After dining with his wife and children, Thomas Franklin went into the den to work. There was simply not enough time for him to finish his work in the office, especially as Miss Hayes, his assistant, was on vacation.

32 He worked until he could no longer concentrate, then went to the bedroom. His wife was already in bed, watching a TV program of commentary on the President's speech. Franklin glanced at the set as he undressed. In the last two years, Franklin's stock market holdings had fallen to one third of their value, his savings were gone, and his share in the profits of his firm had recently diminished. He was not encouraged by the President's speech and hoped that the Vice President or, in his absence, this fellow Gardiner, might brighten his gloomy predicament. He threw off his trousers clumsily, neglecting to hang them in the automatic trouser-press which his wife had given him on his birthday, and sat down on the bed to watch THIS EVENING, which was just starting.

33 The host introduced Chauncey Gardiner. The guest moved forward. The image was sharp and the color faithful. But even before that full face materialized clearly on the screen, Franklin felt he had seen this man before somewhere. Had it been on TV, during one of the in-depth inter-

views through which the restless cameras showed every angle of a man's head and body? Perhaps he had even met Gardiner in person? There was something familiar about him, especially the way he was dressed.

34 He was so absorbed in trying to remember if and when he had actually met the man that he did not hear at all what Gardiner said and what it was exactly that had prompted the loudly applauding audience.

35 "What was that he said, dear?" he asked his wife.

36 "Wow!" she said, "how did you miss it? He just said that the economy is doing fine! The economy is supposed to be something like a garden: you know, things grow and things wilt. Gardiner thinks things will be okay!" She sat in bed looking at Franklin ruefully.[1] "I told you that there was no need to give up our option on that place in Vermont or to put off the cruise. It's just like you—you're always the first one to panic! Ha! I told you so! It's only a mild frost—in the garden!"

37 Franklin once again stared distractedly at the screen. When and where the devil had he seen this fellow before?

38 "This Gardiner has quite a personality," his wife mused. "Manly; well-groomed; beautiful voice; sort of a cross between Ted Kennedy and Cary Grant. He's not one of those phony idealists, or IBM-ized technocrats."

39 Franklin reached for a sleeping pill. It was late and he was tired. Perhaps becoming a lawyer had been a mistake. Business . . . finance . . . Wall Street; they were probably better. But at forty he was too old to start taking chances. He envied Gardiner his looks, his success, his self-assurance. "Like a garden." He sighed audibly. Sure. If one could only believe that.

40 On his way home from the studio, alone in the limousine, watching TV, Chance saw the host

---

1. ruefully: sorrowfully

with his next guest, a voluptuous actress clad in an almost transparent gown. He heard his name mentioned by both the host and his guest; the actress smiled often and said that she found Chance good-looking and very masculine.

41 At Rand's house, one of the servants rushed out to open the door for him.

42 "That was a very fine speech you made, Mr. Gardiner." He trailed Chance to the elevator.

43 Another servant opened the elevator door. "Thank you, Mr. Gardiner," he said. "Just 'thank you' from a simple man who has seen a lot."

44 In the elevator Chance gazed at the small portable TV set built into a side panel. THIS EVENING was still going strong. The host was now talking to another guest, a heavily bearded singer, and Chance once again heard his name mentioned.

45 Upstairs, Chance was met by Rand's secretary: "That was a truly remarkable performance, sir," the woman said. "I have never seen anyone more at ease, or truer to himself. Thank goodness, we still have people like you in this country. Oh, and by the way, Mr. Rand saw you on television and though he's not feeling too well he insisted that when you got back you pay him a visit."

46 Chance entered Rand's bedroom. "Chauncey," said Rand, struggling to prop himself up in his enormous bed. "Let me congratulate you most warmly! Your speech was so good, so good. I hope the whole country watched you." He smoothed his blanket. "You have the great gift . . . of being natural, and that, my dear man, is a rare talent, and the true mark of a leader. You were strong and brave, yet you did not moralize. Everything you said was directly to the point."

47 The two men regarded each other silently.

48 "Chauncey, my dear friend," Rand went on, in a serious and almost reverential manner. "You will be interested in the fact that EE is chairman of the Hospitality Committee of the United Nations. It is only right that she should be present at the U.N. reception tomorrow. Since I won't be able to escort her, I would like you to do so for me. Your speech will be uppermost in many people's minds, and many, I know, would like very much to meet you. You will escort her, won't you?"

49 "Yes. Of course I'll be glad to accompany EE."

50 For a moment, Rand's face seemed blurred, as if it were frozen inwardly. He moistened his lips; his eyes aimlessly scanned the room. Then he focused them on Chance. "Thank you, Chauncey. And . . . by the way," he said quietly, "if anything should happen to me, please do take care of her. She needs someone like you . . . very much."

51 They shook hands and said good-bye. Chance went to his room.

52 On the plane back to New York from Denver, EE thought more and more about Gardiner. She tried to discover a unifying thread in the events of the last two days. She remembered that when she first saw him after the accident, he did not seem surprised; his face was without expression, his manner calm and detached. He behaved as if he had expected the accident, the pain, and even her appearance.

53 Two days had passed, but she did not know who he was and where he had come from. He steadily avoided any talk about himself. The day before, while the servants were eating in the kitchen and Chance was asleep, she had carefully gone through all of his belongings, but there were no documents among them, no checks, no money, no credit cards; she was not able to find even the stray stub of a theater ticket. It puzzled her that he traveled this way. Presumably, his personal affairs were attended to by a business or a bank which remained at his instant disposal. For he was obviously well-to-do. His suits were hand-tailored from an exquisite cloth, his shirts handmade from the most delicate silks and his shoes handmade from the softest leather. His suitcase was almost new, though its shape and lock were of an old-fashioned design.

54 On several occasions she had attempted to question him about his past. He had resorted to one or another of his favorite comparisons drawn on television or taken from nature; she guessed that he was troubled by a business loss, or even a

bankruptcy—so common nowadays—or perhaps by the loss of a woman's love. Perhaps he had decided to leave the woman on the spur of the moment and was still wondering if he should return. Somewhere in this country there was the community where he had lived, a place which contained his home, his business, and his past.

55   He had not dropped names; nor had he referred to places or events. Indeed, she could not remember encountering anyone who relied more on his own self. Gardiner's manner alone indicated social confidence and financial security.

56   She could not define the feelings that he kindled in her. She was aware that her pulse raced when she was near him, aware of his image in her thoughts and of the difficulty she had in speaking to him in cool, even tones. She wanted to know him, and she wanted to yield to that knowledge. There were innumerable selves that he evoked in her. Yet she was not able to discover a single motive in any of his actions, and for a brief instant she feared him. From the beginning, she noticed the meticulous care he took to insure that nothing he said to her or to anyone else was definite enough to reveal what he thought of her or of anyone or, indeed, of anything.

57   But unlike the other men with whom she was intimate, Gardiner neither restrained nor repulsed her. The thought of seducing him, of making him lose his composure, excited her. The more withdrawn he was, the more she wanted him to look at her and to acknowledge her desire, to recognize her as a willing mistress. She saw herself making love to him—abandoned, wanton,[2] without reticence or reserve.

58   She arrived home late that evening and called Chance, asking him whether she could come to his room. He agreed.

59   She looked tired. "I am so sorry I had to be away. I missed your television appearance—and I missed you," she murmured in a timid voice.

---

2. wanton: sexually unrestrained

60   She sat down on the edge of the bed; Chance moved back to give her more room.

61   She brushed her hair from her forehead, and, looking at him quietly, put her hand on his arm. "Please don't . . . run away from me! Don't!" She sat motionless, her head resting against Chance's shoulder.

62   Chance was bewildered: there was clearly no place to which he could run away. He searched his memory and recalled situations on TV in which a woman advanced toward a man on a couch or a bed or inside a car. Usually, after a while, they would come very close to each other, and, often they would be partly undressed. They would then kiss and embrace. But on TV what happened next was always obscured: a brand-new image would appear on the screen: the embrace of man and woman was utterly forgotten. And yet, Chance knew, there could be other gestures and other kinds of closeness following such intimacies. Chance had just a fleeting memory of a maintenance man who, years ago, used to come to the Old Man's house to take care of the incinerator. On several occasions, after he was through with the work, he would come out into the garden and drink beer. Once he showed Chance a number of small photographs of a man and woman who were completely naked. In one of these photographs, a woman held the man's unnaturally long and thickened organ in her hand. In other, the organ was lost between her legs.

63   As the maintenance man talked about the photographs and what they portrayed, Chance scrutinized them closely. The images on paper were vaguely disturbing; on television he had never seen the unnaturally enlarged hidden parts of men and women, or these freakish embraces. When the maintenance man left, Chance stooped down to look over his own body. His organ was small and limp; it did not protrude in the slightest. The maintenance man insisted that in this organ hidden seeds grew, and that they came forth in a spurt whenever a man took his pleasure. Though Chance prodded and massaged his organ, he felt nothing; even in the early

morning, when he woke up and often found it somewhat enlarged, his organ refused to stiffen out: it give him no pleasure at all.

⁶⁴ Later, Chance tried hard to figure out what connection there was—if any—between a woman's private parts and the birth of a child. In some of the TV series about doctors and hospitals and operations, Chance had often seen the mystery of birth depicted: the pain and agony of the mother, the joy of the father, the pink, wet body of the newborn infant. But he had never watched any show which explained why some women had babies and others did not. Once or twice Chance was tempted to ask Louise about it, but he decided against it. Instead, he watched TV, for a while, with closer attention. Eventually, he forgot about it.

⁶⁵ EE had begun to smooth his shirt. Her hand was warm; now it touched his chin. Chance did not move. "I am sure . . ." EE whispered, "you must . . . you do know that I want us, want you and me to become very close. . . ." Suddenly, she began to cry quietly, like a child. Sobbing and blowing her nose, she took out her handkerchief and patted her eyes; but still she kept on crying.

⁶⁶ Chance assumed that he was in some way responsible for her sorrow, but he did not know how. He put his arms around EE. She, as if expecting his touch, leaned heavily against him, and they tumbled over together on the bed. EE bent over his chest, her hair brushing his face. She kissed his neck and forehead; she kissed his eyes and his ears. Her tears wet his skin, and Chance smelled her perfume, all the while thinking of what he should do next. Now EE's hand touched his waist, and Chance felt the hand exploring his thighs. After a while, the hand withdrew. EE was not crying any longer; she lay quietly next to him, still and peaceful.

⁶⁷ "I am grateful to you, Chauncey," she said. "You are a man of restraint. You know that with one touch of your hand, just one touch, I would open to you. But you do not wish to exploit another," she reflected. "In some ways you are not

really American. You are more of a European man, do you know that?" She smiled. "What I mean is that, unlike men I have known, you do not practice all of those American lovers'-lane tricks, all of that fingering, kissing, tickling, stroking, hugging: that coy meandering³ toward the target, which is both feared and desired." She paused, "Do you know that you're very brainy, very cerebral,⁴ really, Chauncey, that you want to conquer the woman from within her very own self, that you want to infuse in her the need and the desire and the longing for your love?"

⁶⁸ Chance was confused when she said that he wasn't really American. Why should she say that? On TV, he had often seen the dirty, hairy, noisy men and women who openly declared themselves anti-American, or were declared so by police, well-dressed officials of the government and businessmen, neat people who called themselves American. On TV, these confrontations often ended in violence, bloodshed, and death.

⁶⁹ EE stood up and rearranged her clothes. She looked at him; there was no enmity⁵ in her look. "I might just as well tell you this, Chauncey," she said. "I am in love with you. I love you, and I want you. And I know that you know it, and I am grateful that you have decided to wait until . . . until . . ." She searched, but could not find the words. She left the room. Chance got up and patted down his hair. He sat by his desk and turned on the TV. The image appeared instantly.

Critical Explorations: Reading

Reread the excerpt from *Being There*. As you do, consider these five questions, which should help you understand the particular role that television plays in this novel—in the shaping of Chance's character and in the development of the American culture in general. You may want to answer

---

3. coy meandering: playful wandering

4. cerebral: intellectual

5. enmity: bitter hatred

some or all of these questions in your reading or dialogic journal.

1. In paragraphs 3, 7, and 17, the narrator presents Chance's reflections on television. Study Chance's thoughts. What is he saying about the specific ways that television influences his perceptions of the world?

2. In paragraph 19, Chance considers how television communicates. Reread this paragraph and analyze the ways that television communication is different from face-to-face communication.

3. In paragraphs 31–39, Kosinski introduces the character of Thomas Franklin. Reread this section and describe Thomas. How does he differ from Chance, and why do you think Kosinski puts this character into the narrative?

4. In paragraphs 54 and 55, EE considers Chance's character as one without history. How has Chance's connection with television made him ahistorical?

5. This excerpt ends in the following way: "Chance got up and patted down his hair. He sat by his desk and turned on the TV. The image appeared instantly." Why is this an appropriate ending? In what ways can television be described as appealing to one's instant gratifications? And in what ways is Chance's character shaped by the immediate gratification he gets from television?

Selection 6

from *White Noise*
Don DeLillo

These are the beginning four chapters of Don DeLillo's novel *White Noise*. Here you will be in- troduced to the major characters in this work: Jack Gladney, his wife Babette, their children from several marriages, as well as Jack's colleagues at the college where he is professor of Hitler Studies, of all things.

The central question DeLillo asks in this novel is this: How has technology shaped American popular culture? In fact, one can say that every character in *White Noise* represents a different response to this question. By analyzing these characters as they attempt to understand their technological world, you will be able to examine this key question that DeLillo poses.

Like Kosinski, DeLillo writes an uncomplicated story with a generally straightforward vocabulary. Your reading challenge is to infer as much as you can about the characters, particularly Jack Gladney; his wife, Babette; and his friend Murray Siskind. Each has peculiar interests and fears. And each makes an interesting statement about popular culture. Finally, from the characters' actions and from the details in popular culture that DeLillo describes, you can express the mood of this selection. That is, what are your feelings about the cultural world that DeLillo creates?

Reading–Writing Preparation

Before you read this selection, you may want to answer the following questions in writing or discussion:

1. Can you think of any common technological objects that seem to have encouraged people to communicate with one another?

2. Can you think of any common technological objects that seem to have discouraged people from communicating with one another?

Chapter 1
White Noise

1   The station wagons arrived at noon, a long shining line that coursed through the west campus. In single file they eased around the orange I-beam sculpture and moved toward the dormitories. The roofs of the station wagons were loaded down with carefully secured suitcases full of light and heavy clothing; with boxes of blankets, boots and shoes, stationery and books, sheets, pillows, quilts; with rolled-up rugs and sleeping bags; with bicycles, skis, rucksacks, English and Western saddles, inflated rafts. As cars slowed to a crawl and stopped, students sprang out and raced to the rear doors to begin removing the objects inside; the stereo sets, radios, personal computers; small refrigerators and table ranges; the cartons of phonograph records and cassettes; the hairdryers and styling irons; the tennis rackets, soccer balls, hockey and lacrosse sticks, bows and arrows; the controlled substances, the birth control pills and devices; the junk food still in shopping bags—onion-and-garlic chips, nacho thins, peanut creme patties, Waffelos and Kabooms, fruit chews and toffee popcorn; the Dum-Dum pops, the Mystic mints.

2   I've witnessed this spectacle every September for twenty-one years. It is a brilliant event, invariably. The students greet each other with comic cries and gestures of sodden[1] collapse. Their summer has been bloated with criminal pleasures, as always. The parents stand sun-dazed near their automobiles, seeing images of themselves in every direction. The conscientious suntans. The well-made faces and wry looks. They feel a sense of renewal, of communal recognition. The women crisp and alert, in diet trim, knowing people's names. Their husbands content to measure out the time, distant but ungrudging, accomplished in parenthood, something about them suggesting massive insurance coverage. This assembly of station wagons, as much as anything they might do in the course of the year, more than formal liturgies or laws, tells the parents they are a collection of the like-minded and the spiritually akin, a people, a nation.

3   I left my office and walked down the hill and into town. There are houses in town with turrets[2] and two-story porches where people sit in the shade of ancient maples. There are Greek revival[3] and Gothic[4] churches. There is an insane asylum with an elongated portico, ornamented dormers and a steeply pitched roof topped by a pineapple finial.[5] Babette and I and our children by previous marriages live at the end of a quiet street in what was once a wooded area with deep ravines. There is an expressway beyond the backyard now, well below us, and at night as we settle into our brass bed the sparse traffic washes past, a remote and steady murmur around our sleep, as of dead souls babbling at the edge of a dream.

4   I am chairman of the department of Hitler studies at the College-on-the-Hill. I invented Hitler studies in North America in March of

---

1. sodden: dull from drunkenness or humidity

---

2. turrets: small towers

3. Greek revival: architecture that imitates the Classical Greek style

4. Gothic: medieval style known for its pointed arches and tall columns

5. finial: small ornament at the top of a gable

1968. It was a cold bright day with intermittent winds out of the east. When I suggested to the chancellor that we might build a whole department around Hitler's life and work, he was quick to see the possibilities. It was an immediate and electrifying success. The chancellor went on to serve as adviser to Nixon, Ford and Carter before his death on a ski lift in Austria.

5   At Fourth and Elm, cars turn left for the supermarket. A policewoman crouched inside a boxlike vehicle patrols the area looking for cars parked illegally, for meter violations, lapsed inspection stickers. On telephone poles all over town there are homemade signs concerning lost dogs and cats, sometimes in the handwriting of a child.

Chapter 2
White Noise

6   Babette is tall and fairly ample; there is a girth and heft to her. Her hair is a fanatical blond mop, a particular tawny[6] hue that used to be called dirty blond. If she were a petite woman, the hair would be too cute, too mischievous and contrived. Size gives her tousled aspect a certain seriousness. Ample women do not plan such things. They lack the guile[7] for conspiracies of the body.

7   "You should have been there," I said to her.

8   "Where?"

9   "It's the day of the station wagons."

10   "Did I miss it again? You're supposed to remind me."

11   "They stretched all the way down past the music library and onto the interstate. Blue, green, burgundy, brown. They gleamed in the sun like a desert caravan."

12   "You know I need reminding, Jack."

13   Babette, disheveled, has the careless dignity of someone too preoccupied with serious matters to know or care what she looks like. Not that she is a gift-bearer of great things as the world generally reckons them. She gathers and tends the children, teaches a course in an adult education program, belongs to a group of volunteers who read to the blind. Once a week she reads to an elderly man named Treadwell who lives on the edge of town. He is known as Old Man Treadwell, as if he were a landmark, a rock formation or brooding swamp. She reads to him from the *National Enquirer*, the *National Examiner*, the *National Express*, the *Globe*, the *World*, the *Star*. The old fellow demands his weekly dose of cult mysteries. Why deny him? The point is that Babette, whatever she is doing, makes me feel sweetly rewarded, bound up with a full-souled woman, a lover of daylight and dense life, the miscellaneous swarming air of families. I watch her all the time doing things in measured sequence, skillfully, with seeming ease, unlike my former wives, who had a tendency to feel estranged from the objective world—a self-absorbed and high-strung bunch, with ties to the intelligence community.

14   "It's not the station wagons I wanted to see. What are the people like? Do the women wear plaid skirts, cable-knit sweaters? Are the men in hacking jackets? What's a hacking jacket?"

15   "They've grown comfortable with their money," I said. "They genuinely believe they're entitled to it. This conviction gives them a kind of rude health. They glow a little."

---

6. tawny: dark yellow

7. guile: cunning

16 "I have trouble imagining death at that income level," she said.

17 "Maybe there is no death as we know it. Just documents changing hands."

18 "Not that we don't have a station wagon ourselves."

19 "It's small, it's metallic gray, it has one whole rusted door."

20 "Where is Wilder?" she said, routinely panic-stricken, calling out to the child, one of hers, sitting motionless on his tricycle in the backyard.

21 Babette and I do our talking in the kitchen. The kitchen and the bedroom are the major chambers around here, the power haunts, the sources. She and I are alike in this, that we regard the rest of the house as storage space for furniture, toys, all the unused objects of earlier marriages and different sets of children, the gifts of lost in-laws, the hand-me-downs and rummages. Things, boxes. Why do these possessions carry such sorrowful weight? There is a darkness attached to them, a foreboding. They make me wary not of personal failure and defeat but of something more general, something large in scope and content.

22 She came in with Wilder and seated him on the kitchen counter. Denise and Steffie came downstairs and we talked about the school supplies they would need. Soon it was time for lunch. We entered a period of chaos and noise. We milled about, bickered a little, dropped utensils. Finally we were all satisfied with what we'd been able to snatch from the cupboards and refrigerator or swipe from each other and we began quietly plastering mustard or mayonnaise on our brightly colored food. The mood was one of deadly serious anticipation, a reward hard-won. The table was crowded and Babette and Denise elbowed each other twice, although neither spoke. Wilder was still seated on the counter surrounded by open cartons, crumpled tinfoil, shiny bags of potato chips, bowls of pasty substances covered with plastic wrap, flip-top rings and twist ties, individually wrapped slices of orange cheese. Heinrich came in, studied the scene carefully, my only son, then walked out the back door and disappeared.

23 "This isn't the lunch I'd planned for myself," Babette said. "I was seriously thinking yogurt and wheat germ."

24 "Where have we heard that before?" Denise said.

25 "Probably right here," Steffie said.

26 "She keeps buying that stuff."

27 "But she never eats it," Steffie said.

28 "Because she thinks if she keeps buying it, she'll have to eat it just to get rid of it. It's like she's trying to trick herself."

29 "It takes up half the kitchen."

30 "But she throws it away before she eats it because it goes bad," Denise said. "So then she starts the whole thing all over again."

31 "Wherever you look," Steffie said, "there it is."

32 "She feels guilty if she doesn't buy it, she feels guilty if she buys it and doesn't eat it, she feels guilty when she sees it in the fridge, and she feels guilty when she throws it away."

33 "It's like she smokes but she doesn't," Steffie said.

34 Denise was eleven, a hard-nosed kid. She led a more or less daily protest against those of her mother's habits that struck her as wasteful or dangerous. I defended Babette. I told her I was the one who needed to show discipline in matters of diet. I reminded her how much I liked the way she looked. I suggested there was an honesty inherent in bulkiness if it is just the right amount. People trust a certain amount of bulk in others.

35 But she was not happy with her hips and thighs, walked at a rapid clip, ran up the stadium steps at the neoclassical high school. She said I made virtues of her flaws because it was my nature to shelter loved ones from the truth. Something lurked inside the truth, she said.

36 The smoke alarm went off in the hallway upstairs, either to let us know the battery had just died or because the house was on fire. We finished our lunch in silence.

Chapter 3
White Noise

---

37   Department heads wear academic robes at the College-on-the-Hill. Not grand sweeping full-length affairs but sleeveless tunics puckered at the shoulders. I like the idea. I like clearing my arm from the folds of the garment to look at my watch. The simple act of checking the time is transformed by this flourish. Decorative gestures add romance to a life. Idling students may see time itself as a complex embellishment, a romance of human consciousness, as they witness the chairman walking across campus, crook'd arm emerging from his medieval robe, the digital watch blinking in late summer dusk. The robe is black, of course, and goes with almost anything.

38   There is no Hitler building as such. We are quartered in Centenary Hall, a dark brick structure we share with the popular culture department, known officially as American environments. A curious group. The teaching staff is composed almost solely of New York émigrés,[8] smart, thuggish, movie-mad, trivia-crazed. They are here to decipher the natural language of the culture, to make a formal method of the shiny pleasures they'd known in their Europe-shadowed childhoods—an Aristotelianism[9] of bubble gum wrappers and detergent jingles. The department head is Alfonse (Fast Food) Stompanato, a broad-chested glowering[10] man whose collection of prewar soda pop bottles is on permanent display in an alcove. All his teachers are male, wear rumpled clothes, need haircuts, cough into their armpits. Together they look like teamster officials assembled to identify the body of a mutilated colleague. The impression is one of pervasive bitterness, suspicion and intrigue.

39   An exception to some of the above is Murray Jay Siskind, an ex-sportswriter who asked me to have lunch with him in the dining room, where the institutional odor of vaguely defined food aroused in me an obscure and gloomy memory. Murray was new to the Hill, a stoop-shouldered man with little round glasses and an Amish beard. He was a visiting lecturer on living icons and seemed embarrassed by what he'd gleaned so far from his colleagues in popular culture.

40   "I understand the music, I understand the movies, I even see how comic books can tell us things. But there are full professors in this place who read nothing but cereal boxes."

41   "It's the only avant-garde we've got."

42   "Not that I'm complaining. I like it here. I'm totally enamored of this place. A small-town setting. I want to be free of cities and sexual entanglements. Heat. This is what cities mean to me. You get off the train and walk out of the station and you are hit with the full blast. The heat of air, traffic and people. The heat of food and sex. The heat of tall buildings. The heat that floats out of the subways and the tunnels. It's always fifteen degrees hotter in the cities. Heat rises from the sidewalks and falls from the poisoned sky. The buses breathe heat. Heat emanates from crowds of shoppers and office workers. The entire infrastructure[11] is based on heat, desperately uses up heat, breeds more heat. The eventual heat death of the universe that scientists love to talk about is already well underway and you can feel it happening all around you in any large or medium-sized city. Heat and wetness."

---

8. émigré: a person forced to emigrate for political reasons; in this case, one who has emigrated

9. Aristotelianism: belief in the philosophy of the Classical Greek philosopher Aristotle

10. glowering: staring angrily

11. infrastructure: internal workings

43 "Where are you living, Murray?"

44 "In a rooming house. I'm totally captivated and intrigued. It's a gorgeous old crumbling house near the insane asylum. Seven or eight boarders, more or less permanent except for me. A woman who harbors a terrible secret. A man with a haunted look. A man who never comes out of his room. A woman who stands by the letter box for hours, waiting for something that never seems to arrive. A man with no past. A woman with a past. There is a smell about the place of unhappy lives in the movies that I really respond to."

45 "Which one are you?" I said.

46 "I'm the Jew. What else would I be?"

47 There was something touching about the fact that Murray was dressed almost totally in corduroy. I had the feeling that since the age of eleven in his crowded plot of concrete he'd associated this sturdy fabric with higher learning in some impossibly distant and tree-shaded place.

48 "I can't help being happy in a town called Blacksmith," he said. "I'm here to avoid situations. Cities are full of situations, sexually cunning people. There are parts of my body I no longer encourage women to handle freely. I was in a situation with a woman in Detroit. She needed my semen in a divorce suit. The irony is that I love women. I fall apart at the sight of long legs, striding, briskly, as a breeze carries up from the river, on a weekday, in the play of morning light. The second irony is that it's not the bodies of women that I ultimately crave but their minds. The mind of a woman. The delicate chambering and massive unidirectional flow, like a physics experiment. What fun it is to talk to an intelligent woman wearing stockings as she crosses her legs. That little staticky sound of rustling nylon can make me happy on several levels. The third and related irony is that it's the most complex and neurotic and difficult women that I am invariably drawn to. I like simple men and complicated women."

49 Murray's hair was tight and heavy-looking. He had dense brows, wisps of hair curling up the sides of his neck. The small stiff beard, confined to his chin and unaccompanied by a mustache, seemed an optional component, to be stuck on or removed as circumstances warranted.

50 "What kind of lectures do you plan giving?"

51 "That's exactly what I want to talk to you about," he said. "You've established a wonderful thing here with Hitler. You created it, you nurtured it, you made it your own. Nobody on the faculty of any college or university in this part of the country can so much as utter the word Hitler without a nod in your direction, literally or metaphorically. This is the center, the unquestioned source. He is now your Hitler, Gladney's Hitler. It must be deeply satisfying for you. The college is internationally known as a result of Hitler studies. It has an identity, a sense of achievement. You've evolved an entire system around this figure, a structure with countless substructures and interrelated fields of study, a history within history. I marvel at the effort. It was masterful, shrewd and stunningly preemptive. It's what I want to do with Elvis."

52 Several days later Murray asked me about a tourist attraction known as the most photographed barn in America. We drove twenty-two miles into the country around Farmington. There were meadows and apple orchards. White fences trailed through the rolling fields. Soon the signs started appearing. THE MOST PHOTOGRAPHED BARN IN AMERICA. We counted five signs before we reached the site. There were forty cars and a tour bus in the makeshift lot. We walked along a cowpath to the slightly elevated spot set aside for viewing and photographing. All the people had cameras; some had tripods, telephoto lenses, filter kits. A man in a booth sold postcards and slides—pictures of the barn taken from the elevated spot. We stood near a grove of trees and watched the photographers. Murray maintained a prolonged silence, occasionally scrawling some notes in a little book.

53 "No one sees the barn," he said finally.

54 A long silence followed.

55 "Once you've seen the signs about the barn, it becomes impossible to see the barn."

56 He fell silent once more. People with cameras left the elevated site, replaced at once by others.

57 "We're not here to capture an image, we're here to maintain one. Every photograph reinforces the aura. Can you feel it, Jack? An accumulation of nameless energies."

58 There was an extended silence. The man in the booth sold postcards and slides.

59 "Being here is a kind of spiritual surrender. We see only what the others see. The thousands who were here in the past, those who will come in the future. We've agreed to be part of a collective perception. This literally colors our vision. A religious experience in a way, like all tourism."

60 Another silence ensued.

61 "They are taking pictures of taking pictures," he said.

62 He did not speak for a while. We listened to the incessant clicking of shutter release buttons, the rustling crank of levers that advanced the film.

63 "What was the barn like before it was photographed?" he said. "What did it look like, how was it different from other barns, how was it similar to other barns? We can't answer these questions because we've read the signs, seen the people snapping the pictures. We can't get outside the aura. We're part of the aura. We're here, we're now."

64 He seemed immensely pleased by this.

Chapter 4
White Noise

65 When times are bad, people feel compelled to overeat. Blacksmith is full of obese adults and children, baggy pantsed, short-legged, waddling. They struggle to emerge from compact cars; they don sweatsuits and run in families across the landscape; they walk down the street with food in their faces; they eat in stores, cars, parking lots, on bus lines and movie lines, under the stately trees.

66 Only the elderly seem exempt from the fever of eating. If they are sometimes absent from their own words and gestures, they are also slim and healthy-looking, the women carefully groomed, the men purposeful and well dressed, selecting shopping carts from the line outside the supermarket.

67 I crossed the high school lawn and walked to the rear of the building and toward the small open stadium. Babette was running up the stadium steps. I sat across the field in the first row of stone seats. The sky was full of streaking clouds. When she reached the top of the stadium she stopped and paused, putting her hands to the high parapet[12] and leaning into it to rest diagonally. Then she turned and walked back down, breasts chugging. The wind rippled her oversized suit. She walked with her hands on her hips, fingers spread. Her face was tilted up, catching the cool air, and she didn't see me. When she reached the bottom step she turned to face the seats and did some kind of neck stretching exercise. Then she started running up the steps.

68 Three times she ascended the steps, walked slowly down. There was no one around. She worked hard, hair floating, legs and shoulders working. Every time she reached the top she leaned into the wall, head down, upper body throbbing. After the last descent I met her at the edge of the playing field and embraced her, putting my hands inside the sweatband of her gray cotton pants. A small plane appeared over

---

12. parapet: defensive wall

the trees. Babette was moist and warm, emitting a creaturely hum.

69 She runs, she shovels snow, she caulks the tub and sink. She plays word games with Wilder and reads erotic classics aloud in bed at night. What do I do? I twirl the garbage bags and twist-tie them, swim laps in the college pool. When I go walking, joggers come up soundlessly behind me, appearing at my side, making me jump in idiotic fright. Babette talks to dogs and cats. I see colored spots out of the corner of my right eye. She plans ski trips that we never take, her face bright with excitement. I walk up the hill to school, noting the whitewashed stones that line the driveways of newer homes.

70 Who will die first?

71 This question comes up from time to time, like where are the car keys. It ends a sentence, prolongs a glance between us. I wonder if the thought itself is part of the nature of physical love, a reverse Darwinism[13] that awards sadness and fear to the survivor. Or is it some inert element in the air we breathe, a rare thing like neon, with a melting point, an atomic weight? I held her in my arms on the cinder track. Kids came running our way, thirty girls in bright shorts, an improbable bobbing mass. The eager breathing, the overlapping rhythms of their footfalls. Sometimes I think our love is inexperienced. The question of dying becomes a wise reminder. It cures us of our innocence of the future. Simple things are doomed, or is that a superstition? We watched the girls come round again. They were strung out now, with faces and particular gaits, almost weightless in their craving, able to land lightly.

72 The Airport Marriott, the Downtown Travelodge, the Sheraton Inn and Conference Center.

73 On our way home I said, "Bee wants to visit at Christmas. We can put her in with Steffie."

74 "Do they know each other?"

---

13. Darwinism: belief in the evolutionary theories of Charles Darwin, the nineteenth-century English biologist

75 "They met at Disney World. It'll be all right."

76 "When were you in Los Angeles?"

77 "You mean Anaheim."

78 "When were you in Anaheim?"

79 "You mean Orlando. It's almost three years now."

80 "Where was I?" she said.

81 My daughter Bee, from my marriage to Tweedy Browner, was just starting seventh grade in a Washington suburb and was having trouble readjusting to life in the States after two years in South Korea. She took taxis to school, made phone calls to friends in Seoul and Tokyo. Abroad she'd wanted to eat ketchup sandwiches with Trix sticks. Now she cooked fierce sizzling meals of scallion bushes and baby shrimp, monopolizing Tweedy's restaurant-quality range.

82 That night, a Friday, we ordered Chinese food and watched television together, the six of us. Babette had made it a rule. She seemed to think that if kids watched television one night a week with parents or stepparents, the effect would be to deglamorize the medium in their eyes, make it wholesome domestic sport. Its narcotic undertow and eerie diseased brain-sucking power would be gradually reduced. I felt vaguely slighted by this reasoning. The evening in fact was a subtle form of punishment for us all. Heinrich sat silent over his egg rolls. Steffie became upset every time something shameful or humiliating seemed about to happen to someone on the screen. She had a vast capacity for being embarrassed on other people's behalf. Often she would leave the room until Denise signaled to her that the scene was over. Denise used these occasions to counsel the younger girl on toughness, the need to be mean in the world, thick-skinned.

83 It was my own formal custom on Fridays, after an evening in front of the TV set, to read deeply in Hitler well into the night.

84 On one such night I got into bed next to Babette and told her how the chancellor had advised me, back in 1968, to do something about my name and appearance if I wanted to be taken seriously as a Hitler innovator. Jack Gladney

would not do, he said, and asked me what other names I might have at my disposal. We finally agreed that I should invent an extra initial and call myself J. A. K. Gladney, a tag I wore like a borrowed suit.

85 The chancellor warned against what he called my tendency to make a feeble presentation of self. He strongly suggested I gain weight. He wanted me to "grow out" into Hitler. He himself was tall, paunchy, ruddy, jowly, big-footed and dull. A formidable combination. I had the advantages of substantial height, big hands, big feet, but badly needed bulk, or so he believed—an air of unhealthy excess, of padding and exaggeration, hulking massiveness. If I could become more ugly, he seemed to be suggesting, it would help my career enormously.

86 So Hitler gave me something to grow into and develop toward, tentative as I have sometimes been in the effort. The glasses with thick black heavy frames and dark lenses were my own idea, an alternative to the bushy beard that my wife of the period didn't want me to grow. Babette said she liked the series J. A. K. and didn't think it was attention-getting in a cheap sense. To her it intimated dignity, significance and prestige.

87 I am the false character that follows the name around.

Critical Explorations: Reading

As you reread the four chapters from *White Noise*, answer these questions. All will test your abilities at inference making, allowing you to examine the hidden forces that help explain the characters' statements and actions. You may respond to these questions in your reading or dialogic journal.

1. Reread paragraph 13. Describe Babette, as seen from Jack's eyes. Is she a stereotyped housewife or a unique characterization? What evidence do you have for your answer?

2. In paragraph 21, Jack asks this question: "Why do these possessions carry such sorrowful weight?" What evidence do you have in these four chapters that possessions bring sorrow and are oppressive?

3. In paragraphs 52–64, Jack describes the barn viewing that has become a popular activity in Blacksmith. How is this activity peculiar? How is it shaped by technology?

4. Reread paragraph 82. What metaphors are used to describe television? Analyze them, showing what these metaphors say about television's effect on its viewers.

5. Reread paragraphs 85–87. What does Jack mean when he says of himself "I am the false character that follows the name around"? That is, what sort of character is Jack, and how has his culture shaped his personality?

Selection 7

"Miss Clairol"
Helena María Viramontes

This short story is from a young Chicana fiction writer. Born and raised in East Los Angeles, Viramontes examines women who survive under difficult social and economic conditions. In "Miss Clairol," Viramontes develops the relationship between a young Chicana mother and her ten-year-old daughter, who live in poverty.

What ties "Miss Clairol" to the previous two works of fiction in this chapter is Viramontes's focus on the materials of popular culture and advertising: hair dyes, false eyelashes, nail polish, and so on. As with the characters in *Being There* and *White Noise*, these materials of American popular culture shape the behavior of the mother and daughter.

"Miss Clairol" is also a story that is easy to follow. There are only two characters to study:

the mother and daughter. Unlike the previous two selections, which describe white Americans in popular culture, "Miss Clairol" provides a Chicana's perspective on American popular culture. Therefore, you will see the occasional Spanish phrase that the mother and daughter use when speaking to each other. There is much to infer from the details in this story. By the end of your reading, can you determine the story's time period, the kind of mother Arlene is, the sort of daughter Champ is, and the beliefs that help explain Arlene's actions? As with *White Noise,* the details in "Miss Clairol" create a particular mood. After you have read this selection, put into words your feelings about the world that Viramontes has created.

Reading–Writing Preparation

Before you read this selection, you may want to answer the following questions in writing or discussion:

1. Why do you think people buy beauty products?

2. How do you think ads for beauty products affect how women understand and appreciate themselves?

Miss Clairol

1   Arlene and Champ walk to K-Mart. The store is full of bins mounted with bargain buys from T-shirts to rubber sandals. They go to aisle 23, Cosmetics. Arlene, wearing bell bottom jeans two sizes too small, can't bend down to the Miss Clairol boxes, asks Champ.

2   –Which one mamá–asks Champ, chewing her thumb nail.

3   –Shit, mija,[1] I dunno.–Arlene smacks her gum, contemplating the decision.–Maybe I need a change, tú sabes.[2] What do you think?–She holds up a few blond strands with black roots. Arlene has burned the softness of her hair with peroxide; her hair is stiff, breaks at the ends and she needs plenty of Aqua Net hairspray to tease and tame her ratted hair, then folds it back into a high lump behind her head. For the last few months she has been a platinum "Light Ash" blond, before that a Miss Clairol "Flame" redhead, before that Champ couldn't even identify the color—somewhere between orange and brown, a "Sun Bronze." The only way Champ knows her mother's true hair color is by her roots which, like death, inevitably rise to the truth.

4   –I hate it, tú sabes, when I can't decide.– Arlene is wearing a pink, strapless tube top. Her stomach spills over the hip bugger jeans. Spits the gum onto the floor.–Fuck it.–And Champ follows her to the rows of nailpolish, next to the Maybelline rack of make-up, across the false eyelashes that look like insects on display in clear, plastic boxes. Arlene pulls out a particular color of nailpolish, looks at the bottom of the bottle for the price, puts it back, gets another. She has a tattoo of purple XXX's on her left finger like a ring. She finally settles for a purple-blackish color, Ripe Plum, that Champ thinks looks like the

---

1. *mija:* my daughter

2. *tú sabes:* you know

---

color of Frankenstein's nails. She looks at her own stubby nails, chewed and gnawed.

5 Walking over to the eyeshadows, Arlene slowly slinks out another stick of gum from her back pocket, unwraps and crumbles the wrapper into a little ball, lets it drop on the floor. Smacks the gum.

6 –Grandpa Ham used to make chains with these gum wrappers–she says, toeing the wrapper on the floor with her rubber sandals, her toes dotted with old nailpolish.–He started one, tú sabes, that went from room to room. That was before he went nuts–she says, looking at the price of magenta eyeshadow.–Sabes que?[3] What do you think?–lifting the eye shadow to Champ.

7 –I dunno know–responds Champ, shrugging her shoulders the way she always does when she is listening to something else, her own heartbeat, what Gregorio said on the phone yesterday, shrugs her shoulders when Miss Smith says OFELIA, answer my question. She is too busy thinking of things people otherwise dismiss like parentheses, but sticks to her like gum, like a hole on a shirt, like a tattoo, and sometimes she wishes she weren't born with such adhesiveness. The chain went from room to room, round and round like a web, she remembers. That was before he went nuts.

8 –Champ. You listening? Or in lala land again?–Arlene has her arms akimbo[4] on a fold of flesh, pissed.

9 –I said, I dunno know.–Champ whines back, still looking at the wrapper on the floor.

10 –Well you better learn, tú sabes, and fast too. Now think, will this color go good with Pancha's blue dress?–Pancha is Arlene's comadre. Since Arlene has a special date tonight, she lent Arlene her royal blue dress that she keeps in a plastic bag at the end of her closet. The dress is made of chiffon, with satin-like material underlining, so that when Arlene first tried it on and strutted about, it crinkled sounds of elegance. The dress fits too tight. Her plump arms squeeze through, her hips breathe in and hold their breath, the seams do all they can to keep the body contained. But Arlene doesn't care as long as it sounds right.

11 –I think it will–Champ says, and Arlene is very pleased.

12 –Think so? So do I mija.–

13 –They walk out the double doors and Champ never remembers her mother paying.

14 It is four in the afternoon, but already Arlene is preparing for the date. She scrubs the tub, Art Labo[5] on the radio, drops crystals of Jean Nate into the running water, lemon scent rises with the steam. The bathroom door ajar, she removes her top and her breasts flop and sag, pushes her jeans down with some difficulty, kicks them off, and steps in the tub.

15 –Mija. MIJA–she yells.–Mija, give me a few bobby pins.–She is worried about her hair frizzing and so wants to pin it up.

16 Her mother's voice is faint because Champ is in the closet. There are piles of clothes on the floor, hangers thrown askew and tangled, shoes all piled up or thrown on the top shelf. Champ is looking for her mother's special dress. Pancha says every girl has one at the end of her closet.

17 –Goddamn it Champ.–

18 Amidst the dirty laundry, the black hole of the closet, she finds nothing.

19 –NOW–

20 –Alright, ALRIGHT. Cheeze amá,[6] stop yelling–says Champ, and goes in the steamy bathroom, checks the drawers, hairbrushes jump out, rollers, strands of hair, rummages through bars of soap, combs, eyeshadows, finds nothing; pulls open another drawer, powder, empty bottles of oil, manicure scissors, kotex, dye instructions crinkled and botched, finally, a few bobby pins.

---

3. *sabes que?*: Do you know what?

4. akimbo: with hands on hips and elbows bent outward

5. Art Labo: sixties rock and roll disc jockey

6. *cheeze amá*: loved one

21 After Arlene pins up her hair, she asks Champ,–Sabes que? Should I wear my hair up? Do I look good with it up?–Champ is sitting on the toilet.

22 –Yea, amá, you look real pretty.–

23 –Thanks mija–says Arlene, Sabes que? When you get older I'll show you how you can look just as pretty–and she puts her head back, relaxes, like the Calgon commercials.

24 Champ lays on her stomach, T.V. on to some variety show with pogo stick dancers dressed in outfits of stretchy material and glitter. She is wearing one of Gregorio's white T-shirts, the ones he washes and bleaches himself so that the whiteness is impeccable. It drapes over her deflated ten year old body like a dress. She is busy cutting out Miss Breck models from the stacks of old magazines Pancha found in the back of her mother's garage. Champ collects the array of honey colored haired women, puts them in a shoe box with all her other special things.

25 Arlene is in the bathroom, wrapped in a towel. She has painted her eyebrows so that the two are arched and even, penciled thin and high. The magenta shades her eyelids. The towel slips, reveals one nipple blind from a cigarette burn, a date to forget. She rewraps the towel, likes her reflection, turns to her profile for additional inspection. She feels good, turns up the radio to . . . your love. For your loveeeee, I will do anything, I will do anything, forrr your love. For your kiss . . .

26 Champ looks on. From the open bathroom door, she can see Arlene, anticipation burning like a cigarette from her lips, sliding her shoulders to the ahhhh ahhhhh, and pouting her lips until the song ends. And Champ likes her mother that way.

27 Arlene carefully stretches black eyeliner, like a fallen question mark, outlines each eye. The work is delicate, her hand trembles cautiously, stops the process to review the face with each line. Arlene the mirror is not Arlene the face who has worn too many relationships, gotten too little sleep. The last touch is the chalky, beige lipstick.

28 By the time she is finished, her ashtray is full of cigarette butts, Champ's variety show is over, and Jackie Gleason's[7] dancing girls come on to make kaleidoscope patterns with their long legs and arms. Gregorio is still not home, and Champ goes over to the window, checks the houses, the streets, corners, roams the sky with her eyes.

29 Arlene sits on the toilet, stretches up her nylons, clips them to her girdle. She feels good thinking about the way he will unsnap her nylons, and she will unroll them slowly, point her toes when she does.

30 Champ opens a can of Campbell soup, finds a perfect pot in the middle of a stack of dishes, pulls it out to the threatening rumble of the tower. She washes it out, pours the contents of the red can, turns the knob. After it boils, she puts the pot on the sink for it to cool down. She searches for a spoon.

31 Arlene is romantic. When Champ begins her period, she will tell her things that only women can know. She will tell her about the first time she made love with a boy, her awkwardness and shyness forcing them to go under the house, where the cool, refined soil made a soft mattress. How she closed her eyes and wondered what to expect, or how the penis was the softest skin she had ever felt against her, how it tickled her, searched for a place to connect. She was eleven and his name was Harry.

32 She will not tell Champ that her first fuck was a guy named Puppet who ejaculated prematurely, at the sight of her apricot vagina, so plump and fuzzy.–Pendejo[8]–she said–you got it all over me.–She rubbed the gooey substance off her legs, her belly in disgust. Ran home to tell Rat and Pancha, her mouth open with laughter.

33 Arlene powder puffs under her arms, between her breasts, tilts a bottle of *Love Cries* perfume and dabs behind her ears, neck and

---

7. Jackie Gleason: film and television personality who had successful comedies in the fifties and sixties

8. *Pendejo:* stupid one

breasts for those tight caressing songs which permit them to grind their bodies together until she can feel a bulge in his pants and she knows she's in for the night.

34   Jackie Gleason is a bartender in a saloon. He wears a black bow tie, a white apron, and is polishing a glass. Champ is watching him, sitting in the radius of the gray light, eating her soup from the pot.

35   Arlene is a romantic. She will dance until Pancha's dress turns a different color, dance until her hair becomes undone, her hips jiggering and quaking beneath a new pair of hosiery, her mascara shadowing under her eyes from the perspiration of the ritual, dance spinning herself into Miss Clairol, and stopping only when it is time to return to the sewing factory, time to wait out the next date, time to change hair color. Time to remember or to forget.

36   Champ sees Arlene from the window. She can almost hear Arlene's nylons rubbing against one another, hear the crinkling sound of satin when she gets in the blue and white shark-finned Dodge. Champ yells goodbye. It all sounds so right to Arlene who is too busy cranking up the window to hear her daughter.

Critical Explorations: Reading

Answer these five questions as you reread this short story. In exploring these questions, you will better understand how advertised products sold in department stores become a major focus in the lives of these two characters. You may want to respond to these questions in your reading or dialogic journal.

1. When does this story take place? Select appropriate details in the story that allow you to infer a particular time.

2. How would you describe the relationship that Arlene has with her daughter, Champ? In what ways is it shaped by the commercial world advertised in the media and sold in K-Mart?

3. In paragraph 4, the author compares the false eyelashes that Arlene sees to insects: "false eyelashes that look like insects on display in clear, plastic boxes." Analyze this simile. What associations come to mind? In what ways does this insect simile serve to describe the other cosmetics that Arlene uses?

4. In paragraphs 31 and 35, Arlene is described as a romantic. In what ways are Arlene's romantic beliefs shaped by her economic circumstances? And in what ways does the commercial world of cosmetics affect Arlene's understanding of being romantic?

5. Why do you now think this story is titled "Miss Clairol"? Who is Miss Clairol in the advertising world, and in what ways do you think Arlene is influenced by Miss Clairol—both the product and the American female figure that Miss Clairol represents?

Selection 8

from *The Crying of Lot 49*
Thomas Pynchon

Thomas Pynchon's *The Crying of Lot 49* can be seen as a satirical portrait of American culture. In this excerpt, Chapter 2, Pynchon creates Southern California as he understands it. The central character, Oedipa Maas, is on a peculiar mission to Southern California to secure a music deal with Metzger Inverarity, who was once a famous child actor. Oedipa's husband, Mucho Maas, is a disk jockey in Northern California.

Most of this chapter is set in a Southern California hotel, where the music deal is made. What the characters discuss and the television programming the characters watch in the hotel room help explain how technology has contributed to the bizarre life-styles that these people have.

Of the four selections in this chapter, this one is the most difficult. The vocabulary is at times obscure, and the sentences are often long. Furthermore, the story is complicated because the reader must follow both what Oedipa and Metzger are doing and saying while at the same time study the old movie the two are watching. The two narratives are related. As in the Kosinski and DeLillo selections, these characters are strange, and the story's actions are at times peculiar. This strangeness helps you determine the kind of satire that Pynchon develops. After you have read this story, you should be able to answer the following questions: What is the mood of the story? What is its tone? What exactly is Pynchon satirizing?

Reading–Writing Preparation

Before you read this selection, you may want to consider the following questions in writing or discussion:

1. In what ways is television present in our everyday activities?

2. How are large urban areas in the United States impersonal?

Chapter 2
The Crying of Lot 49

1   She left Kinneret, then, with no idea she was moving toward anything new. Mucho Maas, enigmatic, whistling "I Want to Kiss Your Feet," a new recording by Sick Dick and the Volkswagens (an English group he was fond of at that time but did not believe in), stood with hands in pockets while she explained about going down to San Narciso for a while to look into Pierce's books and records and confer with Metzger, the co-executor. Mucho was sad to see her go, but not desperate, so after telling him to hang up if Dr Hilarius called and look after the oregano in the garden, which had contracted a strange mold, she went.

2   San Narciso lay further south, near L.A. Like many named places in California it was less an identifiable city than a grouping of concepts—census tracts, special purpose bond-issue districts, shopping nuclei, all overlaid with access roads to its own freeway. But it had been Pierce's domicile,[1] and headquarters: the place he'd begun his land speculating in ten years ago, and so put down the plinth course of capital on which everything afterward had been built, however rickety or grotesque, toward the sky; and that, she supposed, would set the spot apart, give it an aura. But if there was any vital difference between it and the rest of Southern California, it was invisible on first glance. She drove into San Narciso on a Sunday, in a rented Impala. Nothing was happening. She looked down a slope, needing to squint for the sunlight, onto a vast sprawl of houses which had grown up all together, like a well-tended crop, from the dull brown earth; and she thought of the time she'd opened a transistor radio to replace a battery and seen her first printed circuit. The ordered swirl of houses and streets, from this high angle, sprang at her now with the same unexpected, astonishing clarity as the circuit card had. Though she knew even less about radios than about Southern Californians, there were to both outward

1. domicile: legal residence

patterns a hieroglyphic sense of concealed meaning, of an intent to communicate. There'd seemed no limit to what the printed circuit could have told her (if she had tried to find out); so in her first minute of San Narciso, a revelation also trembled just past the threshold of her understanding. Smog hung all around the horizon, the sun on the bright beige countryside was painful; she and the Chevy seemed parked at the centre of an odd, religious instant. As if, on some other frequency, or out of the eye of some whirlwind rotating too slow for her heated skin even to feel the centrifugal[2] coolness of, words were being spoken. She suspected that much. She thought of Mucho, her husband, trying to believe in his job. Was it something like this he felt, looking through the soundproof glass at one of his colleagues with a headset clamped on and cueing the next record with movements stylized as the handling of chrism, censer, chalice might be for a holy man, yet really tuned in to the voice, voices, the music, its message, surrounded by it, digging it, as were all the faithful it went out to; did Mucho stand outside Studio A looking in, knowing that even if he could hear it he couldn't believe in it?

3   She gave it up presently, as if a cloud had approached the sun or the smog thickened, and so broken the "religious instant," whatever it might've been; started up and proceeded at maybe 70 mph along the singing blacktop, onto a highway she thought went toward Los Angeles, into a neighborhood that was little more than the road's skinny right-of-way, lined by auto lots, escrow services, drive-ins, small office buildings and factories whose address numbers were in the 70 and then 80,000's. She had never known numbers to run so high. It seemed unnatural. To her left appeared a prolonged scatter of wide, pink buildings, surrounded by miles of fence topped with barbed wire and interrupted now and then by guard towers: soon an entrance whizzed by, two sixty-foot missiles on either side and the

name YOYODYNE lettered conservatively on each nose cone. This was San Narciso's big source of employment, the Galactronics Division of Yoyodyne, Inc., one of the giants of the aerospace industry. Pierce, she happened to know, had owned a large block of shares, had been somehow involved in negotiating an understanding with the county tax assessor to lure Yoyodyne here in the first place. It was part, he explained, of being a founding father.

4   Barbed wire again gave way to the familiar parade of more beige, prefab, cinderblock office machine distributors, sealant makers, bottled gas works, fastener factories, warehouses, and whatever. Sunday had sent them all into silence and paralysis, all but an occasional real estate office or truck stop. Oedipa resolved to pull in at the next motel she saw, however ugly, stillness and four walls having at some point become preferable to this illusion of speed, freedom, wind in your hair, unreeling landscape—it wasn't. What the road really was, she fancied, was this hypodermic needle, inserted somewhere ahead into the vein of a freeway, a vein nourishing the mainliner L.A., keeping it happy, coherent, protected from pain, or whatever passes, with a city, for pain. But were Oedipa some single melted crystal of urban horse, L.A., really, would be no less turned on for her absence.

5   Still, when she got a look at the next motel, she hesitated a second. A representation in painted sheet metal of a nymph holding a white blossom towered thirty feet into the air; the sign, lit up despite the sun, said "Echo Courts." The face of the nymph[3] was much like Oedipa's, which didn't startle her so much as a concealed blower system that kept the nymph's gauze chiton[4] in constant agitation, revealing enormous vermillion-tipped[5] breasts and long pink thighs at each flap. She was smiling a lipsticked and public smile, not quite a hooker's but nowhere

---

2. centrifugal: describing a force moving outward around a circle

3. nymph: beautiful maiden goddess

4. chiton: undergarment worn by ancient Greeks

5. vermillion: scarlet red

near that of any nymph pining away with love either. Oedipa pulled into the lot, got out and stood for a moment in the hot sun and the dead-still air, watching the artificial windstorm overhead toss gauze in five-foot excursions. Remembering her idea about a slow whirlwind, words she couldn't hear.

6   The room would be good enough for the time she had to stay. Its door opened on a long courtyard with a swimming pool, whose surface that day was flat, brilliant with sunlight. At the far end stood a fountain, with another nymph. Nothing moved. If people lived behind the other doors or watched through the windows gagged each with its roaring air-conditioner, she couldn't see them. The manager, a drop-out named Miles, maybe 16 with a Beatle haircut and a lapelless, cuffless, one-button mohair suit, carried her bags and sang to himself, possibly to her:

Miles's Song

Too fat to Frug,[6]
That's what you tell me all the time,
When you really try'n' to put me down,
But I'm hip,
So close your big fat lip,
Yeah, baby,
I may he too fat to Frug,
But at least I ain't too slim to Swim.

7   "It's lovely," said Oedipa, "but why do you sing with an English accent when you don't talk that way?"

8   "It's this group I'm in," Miles explained, "the Paranoids. We're new yet. Our manager says we should sing like that. We watch English movies a lot, for the accent."

9   "My husband's a disk jockey," Oedipa trying to be helpful, "it's only a thousand-watt station, but if you had anything like a tape I could give it to him to plug."

10   Miles closed the door behind them and started in with the shifty eye. "In return for what?" Moving in on her. "Do you want what I

think you want? This is the Payola[7] Kid here, you know." Oedipa picked up the nearest weapon, which happened to be the rabbit-ear antenna off the TV in the corner "Oh," said Miles, stopping. "You hate me too." Eyes bright through his bangs.

11   "You *are* a paranoid," Oedipa said.

12   "I have a smooth young body," said Miles, "I thought you older chicks went for that." He left after shaking her down for four bits for carrying the bags.

13   That night the lawyer Metzger showed up. He turned out to be so good-looking that Oedipa thought at first They, somebody up there, were putting her on. It had to be an actor. He stood at her door, behind him the oblong pool shimmering silent in a mild diffusion of light from the night-time sky, saying, "Mrs. Maas," like a reproach. His enormous eyes, lambent,[8] extravagantly lashed, smiled out at her wickedly; she looked around him for reflectors, microphones, camera cabling, but there was only himself and a debonair bottle of French Beaujolais, which he claimed to've smuggled last year into California, this rollicking lawbreaker, past the frontier guards.

14   "So hey," he murmured, "after scouring motels all day to find you, I can come in there, can't I?"

15   Oedipa had planned on nothing more involved that evening than watching *Bonanza* on the tube. She'd shifted into stretch denim slacks and a shaggy black sweater, and had her hair all the way down. She knew she looked pretty good. "Come in," she said, "but I only have one glass."

16   "I," the gallant Metzger let her know, "can drink out of the bottle." He came in and sat on the floor, in his suit. Opened the bottle, poured her a drink, began to talk. It presently came out that Oedipa hadn't been so far off, thinking it was an actor. Some twenty-odd years ago, Metzger had been one of those child movie stars,

---

6. Frug: rock and roll dance popular in the sixties

7. payola: fifties scheme in which disk jockeys were paid by record companies to play certain songs

8. lambent: radiant

performing under the name of Baby Igor. "My mother," he announced bitterly, "was really out to kasher[9] me, boy, like a piece of beef on the sink, she wanted me drained and white. Times I wonder," smoothing down the hair at the back of his head, "if she succeeded. It scares me. You know what mothers like that turn their male children into."

17   "You certainly don't look," Oedipa began, then had second thoughts.

18   Metzger flashed her a big wry couple rows of teeth. "Looks don't mean a thing any more," he said. "I live inside my looks, and I'm never sure. The possibility haunts me."

19   "And how often," Oedipa inquired, now aware it was all words, "has that line of approach worked for you, Baby Igor?"

20   "Do you know," Metzger said, "Inverarity only mentioned you to me once."

21   "Were you close?"

22   "No. I drew up his will. Don't you want to know what he said?"

23   "No," said Oedipa, and snapped on the television set. Onto the screen bloomed the image of a child of indeterminate sex, its bare legs pressed awkward together, its shoulder-length curls mingling with the shorter hair of a St Bernard, whose long tongue, as Oedipa watched, began to swipe at the child's rosy cheeks, making the child wrinkle up its nose appealingly and say, "Aw, Murray, come on, now, you're getting me all wet."

24   "That's me, that's me," cried Metzger, staring, "good God."

25   "Which one?" asked Oedipa.

26   "That movie was called," Metzger snapped his fingers, "*Cashiered*."

27   "About you and your mother."

28   "About this kid and his father, who's drummed out of the British Army for cowardice, only he's covering up for a friend, see, and to redeem himself he and the kid follow the old regiment to Gallipoli,[10] where the father somehow builds a midget submarine, and every week they slip through the Dardanelles[11] into the Sea of Marmara[12] and torpedo the Turkish merchantmen, the father, son, and St Bernard. The dog sits on periscope watch, and barks if he sees anything."

29   Oedipa was pouring wine. "You're kidding."

30   "Listen, listen, here's where I sing." And sure enough, the child, and dog, and a merry old Greek fisherman who had appeared from nowhere with a zither,[13] now all stood in front of phony-Dodecanese[14] process footage of a seashore at sunset, and the kid sang.

Baby Igor's Song

'Gainst the Hun and the Turk, never once do we shirk,
My daddy, my doggie and me.
Through the perilous years, like the Three Musketeers,
We will stick just as close as can be.
Soon our sub's periscope'll aim for Constantinople,
As again we set hopeful to sea;
Once more unto the breach, for those boys on the beach,
Just my daddy, my doggie and me.

Then there was a musical bridge, featuring the fisherman and his instrument, then the young Metzger took it from the top while his aging double, over Oedipa's protests, sang harmony.

31   Either he made up the whole thing, Oedipa thought suddenly, or he bribed the engineer over at the local station to run this, it's all part of a plot, an elaborate, seduction, *plot*. O Metzger.

32   "You didn't sing along," he observed.

---

9. kasher: to make kosher, or to follow Judaic law in preparing food

10. Gallipoli: peninsula in eastern Turkey

11. Dardanelles: strait in Turkey linking the Aegean Sea to the Sea of Marmara

12. Sea of Marmara: a sea in Turkey

13. zither: a stringed musical instrument

14. Dodecanese: Greek islands in the Aegean Sea

33   "I didn't *know*," Oedipa smiled. On came a loud commercial for Fangoso Lagoons, a new housing development west of here.

34   "One of Inverarity's interests," Metzger noted. It was to be laced by canals with private landings for power boats, a floating social hall in the middle of an artificial lake, at the bottom of which lay restored galleons, imported from the Bahamas; Atlantean fragments of columns and friezes from the Canaries; real human skeletons from Italy; giant clamshells from Indonesia—all for the entertainment of Scuba enthusiasts. A map of the place flashed onto the screen, Oedipa drew a sharp breath, Metzger on the chance it might be for him looked over. But she'd only been reminded of her look downhill this noon-time. Some immediacy was there again, some promise of hierophany:[15] printed circuit, gently curving streets, private access to the water, Book of the Dead. . . .

35   Before she was ready for it, back came *Cashiered*. The little submarine, named the "Justine" after the dead mother, was at the quai, singling up all lines. A small crowd was seeing it off, among them the old fisherman, and his daughter, a leggy, ringletted nymphet who, should there be a happy ending, would end up with Metzger; an English missionary nurse with a nice build on her, who would end up with Metzger's father; and even a female sheepdog with eyes for Murray the St Bernard.

36   "Oh, yeah," Metzger said, "this is where we have trouble in the Narrows. It's a bitch because of the Kephez minefields, but Jerry has also recently hung this net, this gigantic net, woven out of cable 2½ inches thick."

37   Oedipa refilled her wine glass. They lay now, staring at the screen, flanks just lightly touching. There came from the TV set a terrific explosion. "Mines!" cried Metzger, covering his head and rolling away from her. "Daddy," blubbered the Metzger in the tube, "I'm scared." The inside of the midget sub was chaotic, the dog galloping to and fro scattering saliva that mingled with the spray from a leak in the bulkhead, which the father was now plugging with his shirt. "One thing we can do," announced the father, "go to the bottom, try to get *under* the net."

38   "Ridiculous," said Metzger. "They'd built a gate in it, so German U-boats could get through to attack the British fleet. All our E class subs simply used that gate."

39   "How do you know that?"

40   "Wasn't I there?"

41   "But," began Oedipa, then saw how they were suddenly out of wine.

42   "Aha," said Metzger, from an inside coat pocket producing a bottle of tequila.

43   "No lemons?" she asked, with movie-gaiety. "No salt?"

44   "A tourist thing. Did Inverarity use lemons when you were there?"

45   "How did you know we were there?" She watched him fill her glass, growing more anti-Metzger as the level rose.

46   "He wrote it off that year as a business expense. I did his tax stuff."

47   "A cash nexus,"[16] brooded Oedipa, "you and Perry Mason, two of a kind, it's all you know about, you shysters."

48   "But our beauty lies," explained Metzger, "in this extended capacity for convolution.[17] A lawyer in a courtroom, in front of any jury, becomes an actor, right? Raymond Burr is an actor, impersonating a lawyer, who in front of a jury becomes an actor. Me, I'm a former actor who became a lawyer. They've done the pilot film of a TV series, in fact, based loosely on my career, starring my friend Manny Di Presso, a one-time lawyer who quit his firm to become an actor. Who in this pilot plays me, an actor become a lawyer reverting periodically to being an actor. The film is in an air-conditioned vault at one of the Hollywood

---

15. hierophany: interpretation of sacred mysteries

16. nexus: link between individuals of a group

17. convolution: a coiling together

studios, light can't fatigue it, it can be repeated endlessly."

49 "You're in trouble," Oedipa told him, staring at the tube, conscious of his thigh, warm through his suit and her slacks. Presently:

50 "The Turks are up there with searchlights," he said, pouring more tequila, watching the little submarine fill up, "patrol boats, and machine guns. You want to bet on what'll happen?"

51 "Of course not," said Oedipa, "the movie's made." He only smiled back. "One of your endless repetitions."

52 "But you still don't know," Metzger said. "You haven't seen it." Into the commercial break now roared a deafening ad for Beaconsfield Cigarettes, whose attractiveness lay in their filter's use of bone charcoal, the very best kind.

53 "Bones of what?" wondered Oedipa.

54 "Inverarity knew. He owned 51% of the filter process."

55 "Tell me."

56 "Someday. Right now it's your last chance to place your bet. Are they going to get out of it, or not?"

57 She felt drunk. It occurred to her, for no reason, that the plucky trio might not get out after all. She had no way to tell how long the movie had to run. She looked at her watch, but it had stopped. "This is absurd," she said, "of course they'll get out."

58 "How do you know?"

59 "All those movies had happy endings."

60 "All?"

61 "Most."

62 "That cuts down the probability," he told her, smug.

63 She squinted at him through her glass. "Then give me odds."

64 "Odds would give it away."

65 "So," she yelled, maybe a bit rattled, "I bet a bottle of something. Tequila, all right? That you didn't make it." Feeling the words had been conned out of her.

66 "That I didn't make it." He pondered. "Another bottle tonight would put you to sleep," he decided. "No."

67 "What do you want to bet, then?" She knew. Stubborn, they watched each other's eyes for what seemed five minutes. She heard commercials chasing one another into and out of the speaker of the TV. She grew more and more angry, perhaps juiced, perhaps only impatient for the movie to come back on.

68 "Fine then," she gave in at last, trying for a brittle voice, "it's a bet. Whatever you'd like. That you don't make it. That you all turn to carrion[18] for the fish at the bottom of the Dardanelles, your daddy, your doggie, and you."

69 "Fair enough," drawled Metzger, taking her hand as if to shake on the bet and kissing its palm instead, sending the dry end of his tongue to graze briefly among her fate's furrows, the changeless salt hatchings of her identity. She wondered then if this were really happening in the same way as, say, her first time in bed with Pierce, the dead man. But then the movie came back.

70 The father was huddled in a shellhole on the steep cliffs of the Anzac beachhead, Turkish shrapnel flying all over the place. Neither Baby Igor nor Murray the dog were in evidence. "Now what the hell," said Oedipa.

71 "Golly," Metzger said, "they must have got the reels screwed up."

72 "Is this before or after?" she asked, reaching for the tequila bottle, a move that put her left breast in the region of Metzger's nose. The irrepressibly comic Metzger made crosseyes before replying.

73 "That would be telling."

74 "Come on." She nudged his nose with the padded tip of her bra cup and poured booze. "Or the bet's off."

75 "Nope," Metzger said.

76 "At least tell me if that's his old regiment, there."

77 "Go ahead," said Metzger, "ask questions. But for each answer, you'll have to take something off. We'll call it Strip Botticelli."

---

18. carrion: dead flesh

78 Oedipa had a marvelous idea: "Fine," she told him, "but first I'll slip into the bathroom for a second. Close your eyes, turn around, don't peek." On the screen the "River Clyde," a collier carrying 2000 men, beached at Sedd-el-Bahr in an unearthly silence. "This is it, men," a phony British accent was heard to whisper. Suddenly a host of Turkish rifles on shore opened up all together, and the massacre began.

79 "I know this part," Metzger told her, his eyes squeezed shut, head away from the set. "For fifty yards out the sea was red with blood. They don't show that." Oedipa skipped into the bathroom, which happened also to have a walk-in closet, quickly undressed and began putting on as much as she could of the clothing she'd brought with her: six pairs of panties in assorted colors, girdle, three pairs of nylons, three brassieres, two pairs stretch slacks, four half-slips, one black sheath, two summer dresses, half dozen A-line skirts, three sweaters, two blouses, quilted wrapper, baby blue peignoir[19] and old Orlon muu-muu. Bracelets then, scatterpins, earrings, a pendant. It all seemed to take hours to put on and she could hardly walk when she was finished. She made the mistake of looking at herself in the full-length mirror, saw a beach ball with feet, and laughed so violently she fell over, taking a can of hair spray on the sink with her. The can hit the floor, something broke, and with a great outsurge of pressure the stuff commenced atomizing, propelling the can swiftly about the bathroom. Metzger rushed in to find Oedipa rolling around, trying to get back on her feet, amid a great sticky miasma[20] of fragrant lacquer. "Oh, for Pete's sake," he said in his Baby Igor voice. The can, hissing malignantly, bounced off the toilet and whizzed by Metzger's right ear, missing by maybe a quarter of an inch. Metzger hit the deck and cowered with Oedipa as the can continued its high-speed caroming; from the other room came a slow, deep crescendo of naval bombard-ment, machine-gun, howitzer[21] and small-arms fire, screams and chopped-off prayers of dying infantry. She looked up past his eyelids, into the staring ceiling light, her field of vision cut across by wild, flashing over-flights of the can, whose pressure seemed inexhaustible. She was scared but nowhere near sober. The can knew where it was going, she sensed, or something fast enough, God or a digital machine, might have computed in advance the complex web of its travel; but she wasn't fast enough, and knew only that it might hit them at any moment, at whatever clip it was doing, a hundred miles an hour. "Metzger," she moaned, and sank her teeth into his upper arm, through the sharkskin. Everything smelled like hair spray. The can collided with a mirror and bounced away, leaving a silvery, reticulated[22] bloom of glass to hang a second before it all fell jingling into the sink; zoomed over to the enclosed shower, where it crashed into and totally destroyed a panel of frosted glass; thence around the three tile walls, up to the ceiling, past the light, over the two prostrate bodies, amid its own whoosh and the buzzing, distorted uproar from the TV set. She could imagine no end to it; yet presently the can did give up in midflight and fall to the floor, about a foot from Oedipa's nose. She lay watching it.

80 "Blimey," somebody remarked. "Coo." Oedipa took her teeth out of Metzger, looked around and saw in the doorway Miles, the kid with the bangs and mohair suit, now multiplied by four. It seemed to be the group he'd mentioned, the Paranoids. She couldn't tell them apart, three of them were carrying electric guitars, they all had their mouths open. There also appeared a number of girls' faces, gazing through armpits and around angles of knees. "That's kinky," said one of the girls.

81 "Are you from London?" another wanted to know: "Is that a London thing you're doing?"

---

19. peignoir: woman's dressing gown
20. miasma: poisonous fumes

---

21. howitzer: a cannon that fires shells high into the air
22. reticulated: arranged to resemble a net

Hair spray hung like fog, glass twinkled all over the floor.

82   "Lord love a duck," summarized a boy holding a passkey, and Oedipa decided this was Miles. Deferent, he began to narrate for their entertainment a surfer orgy he had been to the week before, involving a five-gallon can of kidney suet,[23] a small automobile with a sun roof, and a trained seal.

83   "I'm sure this pales by comparison," said Oedipa, who'd succeeded in rolling over, "so why don't you all just, you know, go outside. And sing. None of this works without mood music. Serenade us."

84   "Maybe later," invited one of the other Paranoids shyly, "you could join us in the pool."

85   "Depends how hot it gets in here, gang," winked jolly Oedipa. The kids filed out, after plugging extension cords into all available outlets in the other room and leading them in a bundle out a window.

86   Metzger helped her stagger to her feet. "Anyone for Strip Botticelli?" In the other room the TV was blaring a commercial for a Turkish bath in downtown San Narciso, wherever downtown was, called Hogan's Seraglio. "Inverarity owned that too," Metzger said. "Did you know that?"

87   "Sadist," Oedipa yelled, "say it once more, I'll wrap the TV tube around your head."

88   "You're really mad," he smiled.

89   She wasn't, really. She said, "What the hell didn't he own?"

90   Metzger cocked an eyebrow at her. "You tell me."

91   If she was going to she got no chance, for outside, all in a shuddering deluge of thick guitar chords, the Paranoids had broken into song. Their drummer had set up precariously on the diving board, the others were invisible. Metzger came up behind her with some idea of cupping his hands around her breasts, but couldn't immediately find them because of all the clothes. They stood at the window and heard the Paranoids singing.

Serenade

As I lie and watch the moon
On the lonely sea,
Watch it tug the lonely tide
Like a comforter over me,
The still and faceless moon
Fills the beach tonight
With only a ghost of day,
All shadow gray, and moonbeam white.
And you lie alone tonight,
As alone as I;
Lonely girl in your lonely flat, well, that's where
*   it's at,*
So hush your lonely cry.
How can I come to you, put out the moon, send
*   back the tide?*
The night has gone so gray, I'd lose the way, and
*   it's dark inside.*
No, I must lie alone,
Till it comes for me;
Till it takes the sky, the sand, the moon, and the
*   lonely sea.*
And the lonely sea . . . etc. [Fade out.]

92   "Now then," Oedipa shivered brightly.

93   "First question," Metzger reminded her. From the TV set the St Bernard was barking. Oedipa looked and saw Baby Igor, disguised as a Turkish beggar lad, skulking with the dog around a set she took to be Constantinople.

94   "Another early reel," she said hopefully.

95   "I can't allow that question," Metzger said. On the doorsill the Paranoids, as we leave milk to propitiate[24] the leprechaun, had set a fifth of Jack Daniels.

96   "Oboy," said Oedipa. She poured a drink. "Did Baby Igor get to Constantinople in the good submarine 'Justine'?"

97   "No," said Metzger. Oedipa took off an earring.

---

23. suet: fat from cattle or sheep

24. propitiate: gain the good will of; appease

98 "Did he get there in, what did you call them, in an E Class submarine?"

99 "No," said Metzger. Oedipa took off another earring.

100 "Did he get there overland, maybe through Asia Minor?"

101 "Maybe," said Metzger. Oedipa took off another earring.

102 "Another earring?" said Metzger.

103 "If I answer that, will you take something off?"

104 "I'll do it without an answer," roared Metzger, shucking out of his coat. Oedipa refilled her glass, Metzger had another snort from the bottle. Oedipa then sat five minutes watching the tube, forgetting she was supposed to ask questions. Metzger took his trousers off, earnestly. The father seemed to be up before a court-martial, now.

105 "So," she said, "an early reel. This is where he gets cashiered, ha, ha."

106 "Maybe it's a flashback," Metzger said. "Or maybe he gets it twice." Oedipa removed a bracelet. So it went: the succession of film fragments on the tube, the progressive removal of clothing that seemed to bring her no nearer nudity, the boozing, the tireless shivaree²⁵ of voices and guitars from out by the pool. Now and then a commercial would come in, each time Metzger would say, "Inverarity's," or "Big block of shares," and later settled for nodding and smiling. Oedipa would scowl back, growing more and more certain, while a headache began to flower behind her eyes, that they among all possible combinations of new lovers had found a way to make time itself slow down. Things grew less and less clear. At some point she went into the bathroom, tried to find her image in the mirror and couldn't. She had a moment of nearly pure terror. Then remembered that the mirror had broken and fallen in the sink. "Seven years' bad luck," she said aloud. "I'll be 35." She shut the door behind her and took that occasion to

blunder, almost absently, into another slip and skirt, as well as a long-leg girdle and a couple pairs of knee socks. It struck her that if the sun ever came up Metzger would disappear. She wasn't sure if she wanted him to. She came back in to find Metzger wearing only a pair of boxer shorts and fast asleep with a hardon and his head under the couch. She noticed also a fat stomach the suit had hidden. On the screen New Zealanders and Turks were impaling one another on bayonets. With a cry Oedipa rushed to him, fell on him, began kissing him to wake him up. His radiant eyes flew open, pierced her, as if she could feel the sharpness somewhere vague between her breasts. She sank with an enormous sigh that carried all rigidity like a mythical fluid from her, down next to him; so weak she couldn't help him undress her; it took him 20 minutes, rolling, arranging her this way and that, as if she thought, he were some scaled-up, short-haired, power-faced little girl with a Barbie doll. She may have fallen asleep one or twice. She awoke at last to find herself getting laid; she'd come in on a sexual crescendo in progress, like a cut to a scene where the camera's already moving. Outside a fugue of guitars had begun, and she counted each electronic voice as it came in, till she reached six or so and recalled only three of the Paranoids played guitars; so others must be plugging in.

107 Which indeed they were. Her climax and Metzger's, when it came, coincided with every light in the place, including the TV tube, suddenly going out, dead, black. It was a curious experience. The Paranoids had blown a fuse. When the lights came on again, and she and Metzger lay twined amid a wall-to-wall scatter of clothing and spilled bourbon, the TV tube revealed the father, dog and Baby Igor trapped inside the darkening "Justine," as the water level inexorably²⁶ rose. The dog was first to drown, in a great crowd of bubbles. The camera came in for a

---

25. shivaree: noisy celebration

26. inexorably: persistently

close-up of Baby Igor crying, one hand on the control board. Something short-circuited then and the grounded Baby Igor was electrocuted, thrashing back and forth and screaming horribly. Through one of those Hollywood distortions in probability, the father was spared electrocution so he could make a farewell speech, apologizing to Baby Igor and the dog for getting them into this and regretting that they wouldn't be meeting in heaven: "Your little eyes have seen your daddy for the last time. You are for salvation; I am for the Pit." At the end his suffering eyes filled the screen, the sound of incoming water grew deafening, up swelled that strange '30's movie music with the massive sax section, in faded the legend The End.

108 Oedipa had leaped to her feet and run across to the other wall to turn and glare at Metzger. "They didn't make it!" she yelled. "You bastard, I won."

109 "You won me," Metzger smiled.

110 "What did Inverarity tell you about me," she asked finally.

111 "That you wouldn't be easy."

112 She began to cry.

113 "Come back," said Metzger. "Come on."

114 After awhile she said, "I will." And she did.

Critical Explorations: Reading

This chapter is best appreciated once it is reread. Use these five questions as guides to understand the peculiar motivations of these characters, the role that technology plays, and the satirical tone of the entire chapter. The questions can be used as responses in your reading or dialogic journal.

1. Reread paragraph 2. How does the narrator describe Southern California? Analyze the metaphors and similes that the narrator uses to describe this area.

2. How does the narrator use the hypodermic needle metaphor (paragraph 4) to describe the roads in Southern California? How does this metaphor help you see Southern California highways differently?

3. Reread paragraph 79. What happens to the hair-spray can? How is this can a symbol for the narrator's attitude toward technology?

4. Reread paragraphs 105–114. How is the sexual activity between Oedipa and Metzger described in relation to the technological objects of which they are a part? What do you think this passage says about love and sex in a technological society?

5. Throughout this selection, several peculiar names are introduced: Mucho Maas, Oedipa, Baby Igor (paragraph 16), the Paranoids (paragraph 8), to name a few. Analyze the suggestiveness of these names and others you may find in this selection to explain the tone that these words help create. What do you think is Pynchon's attitude toward his subject—technology in the twentieth century and the people who live within this technology?

Critical Explorations: Writing

The following five questions are topics that you can pursue in formal essay responses. As with the previous essay you have written, share your drafts with peers and your instructor. You will need to be familiar with all the literary terms introduced in this chapter to best respond to each of these questions.

1. In the selection you read from *Being There*, Jerzy Kosinski presents two major influences on Chance's character—television and his experiences as a gardener. Study the evidence in this selection, and infer how gardening and television have shaped Chance's character. What, specifically, has he learned from these experiences? How are these experiences similar? How are they different? Finally, by analyzing the characters who come into contact with Chance, determine what aspects of his character seem so appealing to them.

2. What are the elements of popular culture and technology that DeLillo treats in the first four chapters of *White Noise*? How are these ele-

ments of popular culture perceived by Jack Gladney, his family, and friends? Pay particular attention to the peculiarities of the characters that DeLillo creates—their jobs, their obsessions, the ways they relate to each other. Also consider the language DeLillo uses, especially his metaphors.

3. Helena María Viramontes's "Miss Clairol" relies on the products of popular culture to develop the characters of Arlene and Champ. The description of these products also helps create the story's mood. Describe this mother–daughter relationship. Then show how the products that Arlene admires and uses and that Champ uses help create our understanding of these two characters and our responses to them and to their world.

4. Chapter 2 of *The Crying of Lot 49* is a humorous satire of American popular culture and technology. In another sense, it is a serious indictment of twentieth-century technological America. What, specifically, is Pynchon satirizing in this chapter? Where is the humor? Where is the seriousness? What literary practices does he use to achieve this blending of humor and seriousness, or dark humor? Pay particular attention to the bizarre story line, the peculiarities of the characters, and the metaphorical language that Pynchon uses to describe Southern California—the place and its people.

5. All four of these authors—Kosinski, DeLillo, Viramontes, and Pynchon—use the objects of popular culture as the background to their character development and story line. In analyzing character and story line, one can also determine the particular attitude, or tone, that each author has toward the materials of popular culture. Compare each writer's attitude toward popular culture. How are they similar? How are they different?

Student Writing

Below you will find a student's response to the Kosinski excerpt; it is her second draft.
Read the draft carefully; then answer the questions that follow.
June responded to the following topic:

Analyze Chance's character, paying particular attention to how the garden and television influence his behavior. Then show how Chance's character becomes the vehicle for the satire that Kosinski creates.

The Garden Variety

The Lord God took the man and put him in the garden of Eden. Genesis 2:15

—therefore the Lord God sent him forth from the garden of Eden, to till the ground from which he was taken. He drove out the man; and at the East of the garden of Eden he placed a cherubim. . . . Genesis 3:23–24

1   *Being There* by Jerzy Kosinski is a story of a man, Chance, whose only influences have been the media, specifically television, and the garden he cares for. Those two influences are his parents. They have shaped Chance's behavior and his thinking process. The book revolves around the misadventures of Chance, and how he fumbles through life with a minimum of guidance. Kosinski, through this simple man, presents a fairly

scathing view of American society. He has tackled the issue of television's influence over us by using a simpleton as a benchmark. This is the story of the media's power, and of society's susceptibility to its influence.

2   The garden is Chance's only comfort. It is the only place where he is hands-on with life. The rest of the time he is only a watcher, an observer. He watches television, believing it to be reality. He is seemingly unaware that there is a society going on outside of the garden walls that is not as simple or resolvable as the things on television. Since the garden is Chance's only lived experience, it is the only thing he is able to communicate to other people once he leaves his house. Television is all he thinks about, but he speaks very little about it, except to ask if it's o.k. if he can watch. The garden is the nurturing parent who teaches about growth and change: "Chance felt with his fingers the prickly pine needles and the spawning twigs of the hedge. They seemed to reach toward him" (23). Television is the distant parent who describes situations without explanation. After his appearance on television Chance wonders, "Would there be two Chances after the show: one Chance who watched TV and another who appeared on it?" (51). With television as the parent, the child is forced to figure it out for himself.

3   From the garden Chance has learned all he will ever learn about human interaction. The garden's nurturing ways have given Chance his only sense of linear time. When he is thrust into the "real world," the garden is the only thing he can relate to others. It is the only real thing he has ever known. The garden has taught Chance about abundance; how caring and tending will bring growth: "In a garden . . . growth has its seasons" (45). The garden flourishes under Chance's tender care and attention. When asked his advice on things he always returns to the garden. The garden metaphor is universal, it encompasses many things. Here, Kosinski has created an interesting dualism. The garden *is* a wonderful metaphor to explain the inner workings of the economy. However, the garden is the only thing that Chance has any true knowledge of. The only thing Chance understands happens to be something everyone can relate to.

4   The garden has also given Chance extraordinary patience. He knows the fruits of his labor will eventually pay off. When he meets all other characters, it is his patience that has them all so intrigued. Patience breeds silence; silence breeds mystery. His "charisma" lies partly in his ability to stay quiet and focused. His patient observation of the workings and growing within the garden serve him perfectly when he finds himself outside of it.

5   The television fills Chance's thoughts but it provides little guidance. Everything he watches gives him only a vague outline of human connections. As he leaves his home for the last time he is "surprised . . . so far, everything outside the gate resembled what he had seen on TV. . . . He had the feeling that he had seen it all" (24). Television is how he thinks people behave. Their actual behavior is foreign to him: "Television reflected only people's surfaces. . . . And to him, the viewers existed only as projections of his own thought, as images" (54). He is only alive when the television is on. The television distorts his garden reality. The time that is on television is in total contrast to the linear, seasonal reality of the garden. He seems to see the two entities as totally unrelated. After meeting the President, in person, and then seeing him on television, he is unable to comprehend that those two events are related. The television gives him a practical yet skewed view of life.

6   Chance's parenting is incomplete. He is an innocent in the garden, totally unaware that he is lacking in survival skills. The people he meets are also amazingly unaware of his deficiencies. In fact, they see these lackings as signs of his superiority. Chance is the sponge who sucks up whatever is put before him. He expels it, leaving the person to whom he is speaking with to believe that he understands.

7   The other characters see what they want to see in Chance. Even his name is changed to

Chauncey Gardiner because E.E. doesn't hear him correctly. She hears what she wants to hear. The Russian reacts to Chance in much the same way. He perceives his silence as modest intelligence; believing that Chance is actually a Soviet sympathizer, and learned professional. Mr. Rand bestows on himself the duty of father figure to Chance. He "sees" that Chance has potential. Like any good father, Mr. Rand wants Chance to succeed in business. He also gives Chance E.E.: "And . . . by the way . . . if anything should happen to me, please do take care of her. She needs someone like you . . . very much" (60). This encounter epitomizes the entire Chance illusion. In reality, no one knows who he is, so how could he be someone that E.E. needs? The answer ties directly to Kosinski's point of view.

8   Jerzy Kosinski reveals a world of vapid individuals who find Chance to be irresistible. He creates characters who use Chance's innocence to feed their own inflated egos, and superficial personalities. Kosinski's view of American society is quite damning. He appears to see society as a heartless machine. A group of people that will believe anything they see on television. And since Chance was raised, at least partially, on TV, he becomes the perfect citizen. Chance is the looking-glass, everyone sees what they want to see in him. He is the ultimate media creation.

9   Kosinski has created a microcosm of society: where media is God. Our desires, according to Kosinski, are insatiable, and yet Chance is impotent. The characters force their own desires on them, and when he is unable to respond, they take it as superiority of spirit. It would appear that we crave connection, but it's not a true human connection. The fact that Chance stays unengaged doesn't seem to bother anyone within the book. The technological fix gets us off, but, Kosinski seems to say, it will eventually castrate us.

10   Chance is Everyman. He is whatever people want him to be. Even though he is cast out of the garden, as Adam and Eve were, he is able to survive. In fact, he thrives. Without even trying he achieves the American dream: power, influence, money, and affluence. What is wonderfully ironic is that he cares nothing for it; all he wants is to watch TV. Kosinski paints a world where, of course, Chance would flourish. It is a media saturated place where what looks good, is automatically considered good. There is no regard for the internal workings or connections of humanity. Luckily, Chance's innocence appears to protect him from this dark place. He always can find a garden: "Taut branches laden with fresh shoots, slender stems with tiny sprouting buds shot upward. The garden lay calm. . . . Peace filled his chest" (118).

1. Reread paragraph 1. In your own words, write out June's argument. Is June's argument cogent? If not, how would you want to revise it?

2. Paragraphs 3 and 4 focus on the ways that the garden has educated Chance. List the ways the garden has influenced Chance, according to June. Are these paragraphs focused on this one issue, or is there any extraneous material?

3. In paragraph 5, June concludes: "The television gives him [Chance] a practical yet skewed view of life." What evidence does June present in this paragraph to support this conclusion? Is there any other evidence that you would want her to include here?

4. In paragraph 8, June notes that Chance "is the ultimate media creation." In an editing conference, her peers suggested that June expand this section. How do you think June can further explain what she means by "ultimate media creation"?

5. In her concluding paragraph, June presents an interesting insight: "Luckily, Chance's innocence appears to protect him from this dark place [the media world]." In her final draft, I suggested that she elaborate upon this thought. What inferences can you make from June's statement?

Peer Responses

Use some or all of these questions to respond to your peer's draft. Comment as specifically as you can so that your peer can use your comments to productively revise her draft.

1. How does the draft begin? Do you have a sense for where the draft is going? Does your peer adequately introduce the work, the characters, and the literary practices that help explain the text?

2. Select the section that describes character. Analyze one of these paragraphs. Is the character description clear? Does your peer analyze the character's motivations or merely summarize the character in relationship to the story line? Does your peer relate elements of popular culture to her character analysis?

3. Locate the section of the draft treating literary practices: satire, metaphor, and so on. Study one of these paragraphs. Is your peer's analysis of this literary practice accurate? Does she relate this analysis to the ways that the work portrays popular culture? Are there any other elements in the work that your peer could also analyze to explain this literary practice?

4. Study a section of your peer's draft that comments on quoted material. Are these comments appropriate? Accurate? Do you think more can be said? If so, what?

5. Locate a paragraph in the draft that seems to you to be the best example of literary analysis. Tell your peer why you think this paragraph is so successful.

Chapter 3

Analyzing American Television

Introduction

In America, television is a popular medium with far-reaching effects. Some Americans watch a lot of television and others very little, but television's influence is felt throughout America. Television is often the first witness to significant historical moments, such as the assassination of President Kennedy in 1963 as well as the inauguration of the President every four years. It is there to broadcast the high points of professional sports—the Super Bowl, the World Series, the NBA playoffs, and so on. Television is also the recorder of less-important moments that so many Americans view in situation comedies, game shows, and talk shows.

The questions we will examine in this chapter are these: How does television influence American thought and behavior? What American beliefs are part of television programming?

There are many kinds of television programming in America. During the day, television stations generally broadcast game shows, soap operas, and talk shows; during the evening, news programming; and at night, series, often situation comedies. Sometimes nighttime television includes hour-long dramas and movies made for television. On weekends and Monday nights in the fall, there are sports events of all kinds, particularly football, basketball, and baseball. Cable television has extended the choices that television viewers can make with separate movie, news, and music channels.

What all these programs share in America is that they are privately sponsored. With the exception of public television, whose budget is made up of private donations and some federal money, all programs rely on private sponsors: beer companies, oil corporations, soap, perfume, and jeans manufacturers. These companies and corporations buy commercial time from particular programs, and it is this money that funds the television show in question. Therefore, these commercial sponsors influence the nature and direction of the programs they sponsor. These sponsors' refusal to fund a program can determine whether the network will renew the program for another season, and their dislike for a particular comment made in a program can force the producers to revise the program before its showing.

The ratings systems try to determine who and how many people view each show. These ratings are daily studied by network executives, sponsors, and producers of the various programs. A poor rating can quickly lead to the cancellation of a television program.

What a critical viewer of American television realizes is that programs serve to sell their sponsors' products. It is often the case that a particular sponsor drops its support of a program because a certain character in the show has used profane language or expressed an idea unacceptable to the sponsor. That is, the program does not fit in with the image the sponsor has of its product and its customer.

Therefore, the goal of a critical television viewer is to infer what the program's and sponsor's belief systems are and then to determine whether he agrees with these beliefs. As with the photographs and popular events that you examined in Chapter 1, the beliefs of a particular program are unstated. You may infer them from the story line or from the characters' statements. Analyzed from this semiotic perspective, television viewing can be seen as a critical practice, as thoughtful as the analysis of a novel or short story that you examined in Chapter 2. Television viewing is a passive activity only if you choose not to question a program's beliefs.

In the popular situation comedy *Murphy Brown,* for example, Murphy's decision to become a single parent says much about what her producers see as the possibilities of today's American family. Further, their portrayal of

Murphy as a bright, successful, and opinionated news broadcaster presents their idea of gender in the nineties. Moreover, programs like *Beverly Hills 90210* and *Melrose Place* suggest how the creators of those programs understand American wealth and beauty. Also, the possibilities of technology are seen daily in television science fiction programming. Consider, for example, the huge success of *Star Trek,* which is still aired daily in current shows and in reruns of the original in the United States and abroad. Further, you can see how American sponsors and producers understand equal opportunity by the news broadcasters of color you see each day on news programming. And the belief in patriotism is shown most often in the political speeches you see and the editorials you hear on the various news channels. Finally, all the programs you view—situation comedies, dramas, and even news—present their own version of the American happy ending.

Critical Practices

The same critical practices you investigated in Chapter 1 and some of those you studied in Chapter 2 will apply to your critical viewing of television programs. First, you need to define the kind of popular medium that American television is. Second, you can analyze each television program you watch—its organization, the details you find in setting and character, its overall effect. Like the photographs you analyzed in Chapter 1 and the fiction selections in Chapter 2, you can begin to infer what the beliefs behind a program are by the way a television personality speaks, acts, or dresses.

Two new critical practices emerge in television viewing that ask for careful examination: sequencing and evaluating. Both practices will provide you with additional ways to investigate television programming.

To Sequence

Sequencing is a natural, often overlooked critical practice. Children frequently learn to count before they enter school, and they are often able to tell their parents the sequence of events of their favorite story in great detail before they learn to read. Sequencing can also be a complicated activity. It can involve the intricate procedures that computer programmers apply to writing a program or that scientists rely on as they move through the steps of their experiments.

For the purposes of American popular culture and television, *sequencing* involves the viewers' understanding and prediction of the stages in a narrative: how a drama or situation comedy begins, develops, and concludes. You touched upon the critical practice of sequencing when you examined the American belief in a happy ending in Chapter 1 and when you studied the story lines of the literature selections in Chapter 2. Unlike the selections you read in Chapter 2, however, television life may begin in difficulty, but it most often ends happily.

As children, we effortlessly learn about narrative patterns—how a fairy tale begins with a problem and comes to some sort of resolution, how a television cartoon character completes an action in the time allotted. Before they enter school, children most often know that the narratives they have read to them or watch on television have a beginning, middle, and end.

Television comedy and drama also have the same narrative pattern of beginning, middle, and end. Yet television narratives must place this sequence within the confines of a twenty-two- or forty-four-minute time frame. Eight minutes per half hour are usually reserved for commercials and network announcements.

The critical practice most television viewers use is predicting the outcome of a narrative. *Predicting*—correctly anticipating what will come next in a narrative—is the key critical practice in sequencing. In a murder mystery program such as the popular *Murder, She Wrote*, the pleasure that the viewer finds is solving the crime before Jessica Fletcher reveals her brilliant solution. In fact, the murder mystery show can be seen as the model for how the critical practice of sequencing is used in television viewing. The critical viewer predicts the outcome through inferences she makes from the details in the narrative. She may recall an ashtray present in the first scene but missing in the next or a phrase stated by the victim and repeated by the murderer. The experienced predictor of television narratives knows how the stories are structured. He knows their careful development. He quickly learns how situation comedies unfold a problem, how dramas present their story, how details are used in a murder mystery to lead to only one conclusion.

The television viewer is often interested in a particular show when she cannot easily determine how it will end. Although most situation comedies have a happy ending, the more intelligent ones leave the details of the ending in doubt until their conclusion. A carefully developed television narrative is not easily written because of the time limitations imposed upon television scripts. That is, how can a television writer compose a script of twenty-two minutes that has enough detail to challenge the viewer's predictions until its end? Because of this time constraint, many television programs have predictable conclusions that are not challenging enough for the critical television viewer.

In reading literature, you also predict. But prediction is often not as important as understanding the characters and appreciating the language.

To predict the structure of a narrative, you need to do the following:

1. be familiar with the general pattern of each program: situation comedies, murder mysteries, action, and so on

2. know what details in the narrative are more important to the story line than others

3. formulate possible solutions to the problem presented in the show before the show ends

These sequencing practices are ones that viewers of narratives also use when they read fiction. But fiction can weave more complicated story lines and add greater detail to the characters and setting, and television narratives must simplify the narratives they present. It is for this reason that many careful readers of fiction find most television narratives to be lacking in details and too predictable.

To Evaluate

What usually happens to television viewers is that they quickly express their likes and dislikes about a particular program. Like the child who learns to sequence before formal schooling, the human being evaluates at a very early age. For example, an infant shows his dislike for particular foods by his facial expressions or by spitting these foods out.

What the critical thinker is able to do is to give reasons for her likes and dislikes. That is, she is able to carefully evaluate her experiences. Your goal as a television viewer is to learn to critically evaluate what you see—not simply to say that a particular program is terrible or enjoyable, but *why* it is so.

To evaluate is to judge—determining the worth of something. *To critically evaluate* is to judge based upon carefully defined standards and comparisons that relate to the subject that you examine. *Hasty evaluations* are usually the result of quick, uncritical conclusions. These conclusions are often based upon your personal prejudices. *Prejudices* are beliefs based upon insufficient information; therefore, they are biased beliefs. For example, if you expressed a dislike for a police drama just because you had unpleasant experiences with the police, then you would be making a hasty evaluation. Your evaluation would be based upon a personal prejudice, not upon a set of definitions and standards that you would apply to all television dramas. Often by realizing that you have made a hasty evaluation, you can examine your prejudices, many of which you may not even be aware of. Much will be said about hasty generalizations in the introduction to Chapter 4.

Responsible evaluations of television programming, on the other hand, use accepted definitions and critical practices. These evaluations apply definitions and critical practices to the details of the particular program. These are also the practices that respected television critics use in their publications when they evaluate programs. Let's assume that you are evaluating a situation comedy for *Time* magazine. A responsible way to review the series would be to consider the criteria that define quality situation comedies—socially aware topics, strong characters, unique settings, to name just a few. *Criteria* are the standards that one uses to judge a work. You would also be comparing this particular situation comedy to other respected comedies of the past and present. If you dislike some part of the comedy because of your personal prejudices, you would explain that some of your evaluation is not based upon accepted criteria, but upon your own feelings. Sometimes prejudices influence even the most intelligent reviewers of television, yet the respected reviewers acknowledge their prejudices in their reviews.

To evaluate television effectively, then, you need to use the following critical practices:

1. Responsibly define the terms you are using to evaluate the program.

2. Use criteria for judgment that are commonly accepted. If your criteria are not accepted, say why yours differ from the standards for television reviewing. For example, if you believe that effective situation comedies should not address important social issues, say why.

3. Carefully consider the details of the program in your praise or condemnation of a particular television show.

4. Separate a valid criticism of a program from your prejudices about the program's topics or actors.

The significant criteria that you will be using in evaluating television programming involve character and story line. Although there are other technical issues in television viewing that professional reviewers analyze, such as camera techniques and editing, your first reviews of television shows should concentrate on character and story. You would be asking the following questions about the program's characters. These are some of the same questions you asked of the characters in literature:

1. Are the characters believable? That is, are their actions and statements legitimate? Note that even quality science fiction television scripts create legitimate characters within the fantasy world that they have created.

2. How is the character simplified because of the limiting time frame of television and the censorship of its sponsors?

3. Does the character present what you consider to be an important human problem? Or is the character merely expressing what is popular at the time? For example, does an actor portraying a lifeguard honestly show in her role the type of work lifeguards do, or are her attractive face and body more often serving to model popular beachwear?

4. Is the acting appropriate? Is the actor in character?

There are two types of questions that you would ask about a television story line. Again, you asked similar questions when you analyzed the literary selections:

1. Is the story line too simple or predictable? That is, can you tell how the story will conclude within your first five minutes of viewing?

2. Does the story address what you consider to be an important human question? Or is the story simply an excuse for displaying the actors' physical beauties or charms?

In evaluating news programming, you can apply similar critical questions:

1. What sort of news is reported? Do you consider the reporting newsworthy or sensationalistic? That is, are crimes and accidents reported merely for their horror, and are sexual topics reported more to excite than inform the viewing audience, all in order to achieve a higher audience share in the ratings?

2. Does the news report show several sides of a story? For example, is a war reported from the points of view of both parties?

3. Is the journalist knowledgeable, adding to your understanding of the news report, or is he just an attractive face whose physical beauty improves television ratings?

These are just a few of the ways that you can begin to evaluate television. These questions should begin to show you that to criticize television is an easy matter, but to evaluate a program requires a set of critical practices.

Recapping

Television is a very important medium in American popular culture, whether you are an avid viewer or rarely watch it. To see how important television is in expressing the beliefs of American culture and to understand the ways that television influences American thought and behavior require critical practices.

Along with the activities of defining, analyzing, and inferring, in viewing television, you also must sequence and evaluate. You sequence most often when you follow and predict the story line in situation comedies and dramas, whereas you evaluate whenever you judge a television program—drama, situation comedy, or news program. Critical evaluations of television programs allow you to separate a valid criticism from a prejudice.

Reading Selections   *9–12*

The following four selections will provide you with several, often differing, points of view on American television. These perspectives will expand on what you just learned in the introduc-

tion. The first selection is an interview with the famous communications professor Neil Postman, who discusses his reasons for considering television to be negative in children's learning.

The second selection is written by the popular culture critic Pat Aufderheide. Here she discusses the artistic merits of music videos. This second selection provides an interesting contrast to Postman's ideas.

In Selection 11, Jannette L. Dates carefully examines the history of African Americans in American television comedies. This excerpt is from a full-length study titled *Split Image: African Americans in the Mass Media.* In this selection, you will see how a media excerpt analyzes television characters. In Selection 12, Elayne Rapping carefully studies the unstated beliefs that underlie local television news in a chapter titled "Local News: Reality as Soap Opera." In expert semiotic fashion, Rapping presents what most television news viewers do not see.

All of these selections will provide you with a deeper understanding of how American television interprets popular culture.

Selection 9

"TV's 'Disastrous' Impact on Children"
Neil Postman

Neil Postman, a professor of communications, has written extensively on the media. In this interview, Postman answers many of his concerns about the ways that an uncritical viewing of television negatively affects children's thinking. This interview will provide you with ideas that are both challenged and supported in the other three selections.

Postman will give you the scholar's understanding of television's relationship to learning. He answers various questions: How is television viewing different from reading a book? What do children learn on television that they did not learn before its popular use? How can television be used in the classroom? For the most part, Postman speaks in general terms about television, but his answers to these questions will give you a context so that you can begin to examine television programming that interests you.

As an interview in a popular magazine, this selection should not be too difficult for you to understand the first time through. Postman has one argument, and he hammers away at it: television's influence on children has been disastrous. As you read and reread this interview, list Postman's evidence to support this argument. Next to each piece of evidence, note whether you agree or disagree, and see if you can come up with more supportive evidence or with counterevidence. This commentary will prepare you for Selection 10, which paints a generally favorable picture of MTV.

Reading–Writing Preparation

Before you read this selection, you may want to answer the following questions in writing or discussion:

1. How do you think children's behavior changes after children watch several hours of television a day?

2. What do you think children learn from television?

TV's "Disastrous" Impact on Children

1 Q: Professor Postman, is television a good or bad influence on the way children learn?

2 A: It's turning out to be a disastrous influence, at least as far as we can determine at present. Television appears to be shortening the attention span of the young as well as eroding, to a considerable extent, their linguistic powers and their ability to handle mathematical symbolism.

3 It also causes them to be increasingly impatient with deferred gratification.[1] Even more serious, in my view, is that television is opening up all of society's secrets and taboos, thus erasing the dividing line between childhood and adulthood and leaving a very homogenized[2] culture in its wake.

4 Q: Is television more pervasive in a child's world than school?

5 A: Absolutely. I call television the "first curriculum" because of the amount of attention our children give to it. By now, the basic facts are known by almost everyone: Between the ages of 6 and 18, the average child spends roughly 15,000 to 16,000 hours in front of a television set, whereas school probably consumes no more than 13,000 hours.

6 Moreover, it is becoming obvious that there really is no such thing as "children's" programming. Between midnight and 2 in the morning, there are something like 750,000 children throughout America watching television every day. There's a fantasy people have that after 10 p.m. children are not watching television; that's nonsense.

7 Many parents, as well as educators, also have the mistaken belief that television is an "entertainment medium" in which little of enduring value is either taught by or learned from it. Television has a transforming power at least equal to that of the printing press and possibly as great as that of the alphabet itself.

8 Q: How does TV hurt a child's linguistic ability?

9 A: Television is essentially a visual medium. It shows pictures moving very rapidly and in a very dynamic order. The average length of a shot on a network-TV show is about 3 seconds, and on a commercial about 2½ seconds. Although human speech is heard on television, it is the picture that always contains the most important meanings.

10 Television can never teach what a medium like a book can teach, and yet educators are always trying to pretend that they can use television to promote the cognitive habits and the intellectual discipline that print promotes. In this respect, they will always be doomed to failure. Television is not a suitable medium for conveying ideas, because an idea is essentially language—words and sentences.

11 The code through which television communicates—the visual image—is accessible to everyone. Understanding printed words must be learned; watching pictures does not require any learning. Television has no counterpart to the McGuffey reader.[3] As a result, TV is a medium that becomes intelligible to children beginning at

---

1. deferred gratification: delayed pleasure

2. homogenized: characterized by similarity or the lack of difference

---

Frederick Rissoner and David Birch, eds. *Mass Media and the Popular Arts.* New York: McGraw-Hill, 1983, 273–79. © *U.S. News & World Report,* January 19, 1981.

3. McGuffey reader: reading textbook used by elementary schoolchildren in America in the 1800s and early 1900s

about the age of 36 months. From this very early age on, television continuously exerts influence.

12   For that reason, I think it's fair to say that TV, as a curriculum, molds the intelligence and character of youth far more than formal schooling. Beyond that, evidence is accumulating that TV watching hurts academic performance. A recent California Department of Education survey indicated that the more children sit in front of the television, the worse they do on achievement-test scores.

13   Q: Are you saying that television doesn't allow a person to accumulate knowledge based on past experiences?

14   A: That's right. Language itself tends to be sequential and hierarchical, and it allows complex ideas to be built up in writing through a logical progression. Most of all, language tends to be more abstract: it encourages the use of imagination.

15   It is not true, as many insist, that watching TV is a passive experience. Anyone who has observed children watching television will know how foolish that statement is. In watching TV, children have their emotions fully engaged. It is their capacity for abstraction that is quiescent.[4]

16   I'm not criticizing television for that. I'm saying that's what television does; that is the nature of the medium; that's why the word *vision* is in the word *television*. And there are some wonderful uses of that feature. Television, after all, does have a valuable capacity to involve people emotionally in its pictures. Certainly, there are instances when television presents drama in its fullest and richest and most complex expression.

17   Q: How does television affect interaction in the classroom?

18   A: One of the most obvious implications is that the traditional idea on which almost all schools are based is undermined. Schools assume that there are some things you must know before you can learn other things. They assume that not

---

4. quiescent: quiet, inactive

all things are as immediately accessible as they are on television and that it takes hard work and lengthy periods of study to attain many desirable things that are not immediately visible, such as knowledge.

19   Yet because the attention span of children is contracting, teachers are under terrific pressure to make everything relevant—meaning immediately accessible to the student—because if it is not, teachers report over and over again that the students turn off. Now, no one wants to teach students who are turned off. So the temptation is very great for teachers to substitute for real learning something that's fairly jazzy and that will immediately capture the attention of kids.

20   I'm not saying that's always bad, but it would be a mistake to allow that strategy to dominate one's thinking about teaching. I think teachers have to face up to deferred gratification and to the idea that learning requires prerequisites. There are times when you are going to have to say to kids, "You must understand such and such before we can get on to this next point." And if the kid says, "But this is boring," or "How can I use it?" sometimes you have to say, "I know, but that's the way some things are." Television works against this notion.

21   Q: Should teachers employ audio-visual aids that have a relationship to television to enhance their instruction?

22   A: No. I'm against that for a couple of reasons. The most important is that a high degree of visual stimulation, such as you get with these audio-visual media, tends to distract attention away from language. I recently reviewed some studies on the effects of illustrations in learning-to-read books, and the evidence is that the more illustrations in readers, the less well the students learn the words.

23   I think this "hidden curriculum" runs through all the new media—television, movies, videotape and computerized video games. We become more sensitive to visual representations and less to language. In an environment in which non-linguistic information is moved at the speed of

light, in nonlogical patterns, in vast and probably unassimilable[5] quantities, the word and all it stands for loses prestige, power and relevance.

24 Q: Does this happen with adult programs, too?

25 A: Yes. We recently did some studies on the Public Broadcasting Service series "The Ascent of Man," with Jacob Bronowski. We asked people who liked the programs to recall things that Bronowski said on specific subjects, and over and over again we found that people couldn't remember what he said, because the visual component of the show was so dramatic. I suspect the same thing is happening with Carl Sagan's "Cosmos" series. It's a visually attractive program, and people simply cannot attend to the language.

26 Q: Are Bronowski's or Sagan's books very different from their television presentations?

27 A: Altogether different. As a matter of fact, we used Bronowski's *The Ascent of Man* book in one of our seminars. Students were astonished that the book has a thesis and an argument, both of which were absent from the TV show. A book invites attention to language by its nature. A TV show invites attention to pictures, making Bronowski's thesis and argument invisible. Now, I'm certainly not against shows like this. I want to be clear on that. But we have to understand that they often do not have the lasting educational value that is attributed to them.

28 Q: Does television programming create among youth the impression that all problems can be solved easily?

29 A: Yes, especially the commercials. The best figures I have seen say that in the first 20 years of an American kid's life, he or she will see something approaching 1 million television commercials at the rate of about a thousand a week. This makes the TV commercial the most voluminous information source in the education of youth. These commercials are about products only in the sense that the story of Jonah is about the anatomy of whales.

30 A commercial teaches a child three interesting things. The first is that all problems are resolvable. The second is that all problems are resolvable fast. And the third is that all problems are resolvable fast through the agency of some technology. It may be a drug. It may be a detergent. It may be an airplane or some piece of machinery, like an automobile or computer.

31 The essential message is that the problems that beset people—whether it is lack of self-confidence or boredom or even money problems—are entirely solvable if only we will allow ourselves to be ministered to by a technology.

32 Most of these commercials are little vignettes or stories that have a beginning, a middle and an end. The beginning usually states the problem, as in a mouthwash commercial. But that commercial is not really about bad breath. It's about a person's need to be acceptable to a member of the opposite sex, which is an important issue for most of us.

33 Beer commercials, so far as I can tell, are almost always about what the anthropologists call male bonding. What these commercials are really about is men's need to hug each other and slap each other on the behind and applaud each other for a good hunt.

34 Automobile commercials seem to be about the need for autonomy,[6] the need for independence. Indeed, in American life, the automobile does represent, for the young especially, this sort of break from our dependence on our parents. Once a kid gets a car, he's free.

35 Commercials teach these important themes through parables. Repeatedly, the parable is structured in the same way. The problem is stated; then, in 8 to 10 seconds, the middle part comes, which is the resolution of the problem— through a painkiller or an ointment or a flight to

---

5. unassimilable: closed or unreceptive

6. autonomy: self-government

Hawaii or a new car. Then there's a moral. The moral is nailed down at the end, where we are shown what happens if a person follows this advice. And the actor, of course, is usually ecstatic. One has simply got to wonder what the effects are on a young adult who has seen a million of these little vignettes. One has to ask, "What is being taught?"

36   Q: Do television drama shows and situation comedies also present a simplistic version of life?

37   A: The problem with most of the commercial-network shows is that they've committed themselves to a particular format that really does not portray anything other than caricature.[7] What's interesting about this are the almost automatic assumptions made in these caricatures.

38   For instance, on most of these programs you find a kind of anti-intellectualism—that is, characters who have any sort of education or discernment are almost always depicted as unfeeling snobs. Someone like Fonzie, on the other hand, a "man of the people," would inevitably be depicted as warm and responsive to human feelings. It's very difficult for a youngster to find on these programs any model of someone who is admirable and who is also educated.

39   Of course, there's been a lot written about negative attitudes toward blacks and women and the aged, and to some extent the producers of these programs try to respond to that. But anyone who expects that shows like "Charlie's Angels" and "Happy Days" and "Three's Company" will give a realistic portrayal of people is kidding himself.

40   In addition, many of these shows have 24 minutes to present a problem and then to solve it. And it is very rare to find a commercial program that does not, in the end, resolve everything quite neatly and tie everything up, which again reinforces the idea that every problem is manageable.

41   Q: Do some programs glorify the less admirable side of human nature?

42   A: Yes. Someone ought to take a look at this J. R. Ewing character on "Dallas" to find out what has made him so appealing. There was a time in America when there was a connection in people's minds between some moral code and the law. Now we seem to be in a time when the moral dimension to law has been stripped away and most people think of the law simply as a matter of social control.

43   And in a way, J. R. represents that because he's constantly doing rotten things and illegal things. Yet people just say, "Well, it's a question of whether he'll be caught or how clever he will be in managing the situation." Americans do admire, after all, technique, and J. R. is a good technician. He knows how to manipulate people; he knows how to manipulate money; he knows how to manipulate business; he knows how to get all kinds of people to do his bidding. So in a way, J. R. embodies an American spirit of "If you know how to do something well, that is admirable."

44   Q: Does TV in some way rob youngsters of their childhood?

45   A: Television communicates the same information to everyone simultaneously, regardless of age, sex, level of education or life experience. Therefore, television eliminates many of the important ways that we distinguish between children and adults. For example, one of the main differences between an adult and a child is that the adult knows about certain facets of life—its mysteries, its contradictions, its violence, its tragedies—that are not considered suitable for children to know, or even accessible to children.

46   What television does is to bring the whole culture out of the closet, because programs need a constant supply of novel information. In its quest for new and sensational ventures to hold its audience, TV must tap every existing taboo in the culture. . . . As a consequence, these become as familiar to the young as they are to adults. The new media tend to obliterate classes of people, particularly the difference between what we call adulthood and childhood.

---

7. caricature: humorous and exaggerated description

47   Q: Where do you see this merging of adults and children?

48   A: For openers, some of the highest-paid models in America are now 12 and 13-year-old girls who are presented to us in the guise of sexually enticing adults, so much so that old-timers might yearn for the innocence of Lolita compared to these.

49   If you look at the children as they are depicted on situation comedies, such as "Love Boat" or "Different Strokes," you find that they're really little adults. Their language is the same as adults', their interests the same, their sexuality the same. It's getting harder to find children who are portrayed as children in many prime-time shows.

50   In one hand-lotion commercial, viewers are shown a mother and daughter and challenged to tell which is which. To me, this tells us that it is considered desirable that a mother should not look older than her daughter, or that a daughter should not look younger than her mother. If there is no clear concept of what it means to be an adult, there can be no concept of what it means to be a child.

51   Q: What are the consequences of this trend?

52   A: One result of television's homogenization of adulthood and childhood is that it begins to show up in other facets of society. The language of adults and children tends to merge, as do their interests, their dress, their amusements.

53   For example, there are fewer and fewer distinguishing characteristics in children's clothing or, for that matter, in children's games. Things like Little League baseball or Peewee football are modeled after televised sports in their organization and emotional style. No longer are many games played simply for pleasure. Now you need sophisticated equipment, you need umpires, you need spectators. And kids don't play so much for pleasure as they do to enhance their reputation.

54   The language of children and adults has also been transformed so that, for example, the idea that there may be words that adults ought not to use in the presence of children now seems faintly ridiculous. With TV's relentless revelation of all adult secrets, it is not inconceivable to me that in the near future we shall return to the 13th and 14th-century situation in which no words were unfit for a youthful ear.

55   I would also mention the growing movement to recast the legal rights of children so that they are more or less the same as those of adults. The thrust of this movement—which, by the way, is opposed to compulsory schooling—resides in the claim that what has been thought to be a preferred status for children is instead only an oppression that keeps them from fully participating in the society.

56   Q: Do you think it is important to preserve a concept of childhood?

57   A: Yes. The invention of childhood was one of the most humane inventions of the Renaissance. What it did was to make it a cultural principle that we had to nurture and protect children. It promoted ideas throughout society that are important, such as curiosity and malleability[8] and innocence and a sense of continuity and re-creation. These are the qualities that we've come to associate with childhood that are necessary prerequisites for developing into mature adulthood.

58   Q: What can be done to counter the ways that television is influencing children?

59   A: I have no doubt that television is going to remain the dominant force in the lives of millions of young people. I do think that the school can balance some of the more negative effects of television. For instance, I think the school has to give more stress to language than ever before. Schools also have to concentrate more on history than ever before, because I think the new media tend to be ahistorical.[9] In their classroom rituals, teachers should strive to make a case for tradition and continuity—again, to offset the volatility and novelty of television.

---

8. malleability: adaptability

9. ahistorical: without a sense of history

60 I'm certainly not suggesting censorship, but I do think that some of these movements against pornography and child exploitation are healthy. We have a strong enough tradition of freedom in this country that we can make certain accommodations to combat these worrisome trends.

61 Q: Can parents effectively keep TV away from their children?

62 A: No, but they can try to eliminate as much as possible indiscriminate viewing. They can try to get away from the idea of just turning on the television set to pass time. In a culture that is actively encouraging 9-year-olds to be 29-year-olds, I think parents have to work extra hard to preserve their children's childhood.

Critical Explorations: Reading

Now that you have read the selection once, reread it, answering the following five questions. These questions will help give you a critical perspective on the key questions about television viewing that Postman introduces. You may want to incorporate these answers in your dialogic or reading journal.

1. In paragraph 3, Postman refers to children's impatience with "deferred gratification" that television encourages. What does he mean by this? And what evidence does he give for this argument in the rest of the interview?

2. Postman refers to the transforming power that television has over its viewers. As you reread the interview, determine how television transforms its viewers. How is this transformation different from that caused by reading and writing?

3. Reread paragraphs 29–35—the section on what viewers learn from television commercials. What unstated beliefs do these commercials address? In answering this question, you may want to refer to the seven American beliefs in Chapter 1.

4. In paragraphs 37–40, Postman criticizes television drama and comedy. What are his criti-

cisms? What criteria does Postman seem to be using for his critique?

5. In paragraphs 45–57, Postman expresses his concept of childhood. What qualities of a healthy childhood does Postman consider important? Review this interview to see why television prevents the kind of childhood that Postman describes.

Selection 10

"The Look of the Sound"
Pat Aufderheide

In this selection, from an anthology titled *Watching Television*, Pat Aufderheide examines the music videos of the mid-eighties, particularly those viewed by young people on MTV. Aufderheide sees music videos as unique television statements that need not insult the viewer's intelligence. In many ways, Aufderheide speaks for the artistic merits of music videos. Her analysis of this television medium should provide you with important responses to Postman's commentary on how television negatively influences the young.

This is a long selection in which Aufderheide presents a cogent thesis and a careful analysis of evidence to support this thesis. Aufderheide is writing for a scholarly audience, so some of her terms may be new to you. Look carefully at the footnotes as you read. Your major reading challenge is to identify Aufderheide's argument. Look carefully at paragraphs 4 and 7 to determine her thesis. Then read and reread the selection to see how the following media issues relate to music videos and MTV: (1) commercials, (2) film, (3) narrative television, (4) fashion, and (5) politics. Carefully read the last paragraph to analyze Aufderheide's overall evaluation of music videos and to determine how the viewer and society participate in the creation of this new television medium.

Reading–Writing Preparation

Before reading this selection, you may want to answer the following questions in writing or discussion:

1. In relationship to other kinds of television that you watch, how would you evaluate music videos?

2. What are the common characteristics of the music videos that you have seen?

The Look of the Sound

1   Music videos are more than a fad, or fodder for spare hours and dollars of young consumers. They are pioneers in video expression, and the results of their reshaping of the form extend far beyond the TV set.

2   Music videos have broken through TV's most hallowed boundaries. As commercials in themselves, they have erased the very distinction between the commercial and the program. As nonstop sequences of discontinuous episodes, they have erased the boundaries between programs.

3   Music videos have also set themselves free from the television set, inserting themselves into movie theaters, popping up in shopping malls and department store windows, becoming actors in both live performances and the club scene. As omnivorous[1] as they are pervasive, they draw on and influence the traditional image-shaping fields of fashion and advertising. Even political campaigning is borrowing from these new bite-sized packagers of desire.

4   If it sounds as if music video has a life of its own, this is not accidental. One of music video's distinctive features as a social expression is its open-ended quality, aiming to engulf the viewer in its communication with itself, its fashioning of an alternative world where image is reality. Videos are perhaps the most accessible form of that larger tendency known as postmodern art. That aesthetic-in-formation, signaled variously in the work of such artists as Andy Warhol, Nam June Paik, Thomas Pynchon, Philip Glass, and Keith Haring,[2] is marked by several distinctive features. Among them are the merging of commercial and artistic image production, and an abolition of traditional boundaries between an image and its real-life referent, between past and present, between character and performance, between mannered art and stylized life.

5   When art, even self-consciously lightweight commercial fare, crosses that last boundary, it forces consideration of its social implications. And music videos have triggered plenty of such speculation, especially so since its primary audience is the young. Literary critic Fredric Jameson has suggested that the emerging postmodern aesthetic evokes an intense euphoria, a kind of "high," one that partakes in an experience rather than responding to an artist's statement. It is a provocative, and troubling, observation applied to music videos as they infiltrate the various domains of consumer culture, both on screens and on streets. A euphoric reaction is different in

---

1. omnivorous: eating all kinds of food

From *Watching Television*, Todd Gitlin, ed. New York: Pantheon, 1986, 111–135. © 1986 by Pat Aufderheide. Compilation © 1986 by Todd Gitlin. Reprinted by permission.

---

2. Warhol *et al.*: referring to Andy Warhol and other experimental artists and writers

quality from the kinds of energizing, critical response once called up by rock music, hailed by
Greil Marcus as triggering the critical capacity of
negation, "the act that would make it self-evident
to everyone that the world is not as it seems,"
and enthusiasts of rock culture wonder if music
video heralds a new, more passive era for the
young. Critic Marsha Kinder, for instance, finds
the dreamy structure of videos a disturbing
model for viewers who are stuck in real time. Not
all agree; critic Margaret Morse suggests that the
populist,[3] self-assertive energy of popular culture
may be reclaimed in music video's use of lip-
synching; viewers may make that voice their
own by singing along. Even Jameson, while
positing a new relationship between artwork and
audience, suggests that euphoria may have expressive qualities we cannot yet judge.

6   Whatever one's view, the rapid spread of the
music video look is motive enough to take the
phenomenon seriously. But it is particularly important because it is in the vanguard of reshaping the language of advertising—the dominant
vocabulary of commercial culture—in a society
that depends on an open flow of information to
determine the quality of its political and public
life. And so consideration of its form also implies
questions about the emerging shape of the democratic and capitalist society that creates and receives it.

7   Music video was pioneered on television
with three-to-seven-minute films or tapes whose
visual images were coordinated loosely (or not at
all) with a pop song's lyrics. Until recently, almost all music videos on TV were rock songs
from the dead center of mainstream pop. With
the growing appeal of the form, one sees music
videos of country singers, easy-listening musicians, black rock stars, sometimes even rhythm
and blues groups. If there are no waltz or tango
music videos as yet, they are on their way. When

music video has completed its present phase of
being either acerbically[4] challenged or heralded
by hip pop culture critics (J. Hoberman of the
Village Voice put a music video on his list of top-
ten films of 1984), it will be ready for the easy-
listening, easy-viewing audience. Indeed, VH-1,
a music video channel aimed at adults aged
twenty-five to forty-nine, has launched the process and wobbles toward viability. But long before there is a music video channel for Lawrence
Welk tastes, the format will have pervaded non-
musical features of daily life. Indeed, one of the
striking features of music video is its mutability.[5]

8   This analysis of music video circa 1985 per-
forms an unnatural act on the form, by taking a
kind of photograph of a process defined by constant mutation. Most examples will have disappeared from viewers' memory; performers will
have taken on new personas; and the form may
have relocated itself on the social landscape. But
its energy in this pioneering stage guarantees its
importance in the emerging national pop culture—where the distinctions between public and
private, between social standard and individual
taste, are eroded to a rock beat.

9   Music video's roots are in the mass marketing of popular songs, not only as populist entertainment but as talismans[6] of subcultural autonomy and rebellion in successive generations of
American youth. Top-40-hits radio programs
cemented a pop cultural consciousness in the
1930s. In fact, national mass media were instrumental in shaping a national self-consciousness
stratified by generation—unlike regional and
folk culture, which unified the generations, trans-
mitting legacies while incorporating the new. As
new groups and sounds were created in the image of rebellious self-assertion, they were also
pop-ified, which usually meant whitening them

---

3. populist: referring to the rights of the masses

4. acerbically: sharply, harshly

5. mutability: ability to change

6. talismans: objects that are supposed to bring luck

as well. (English outsiders could market black rhythm and blues to mainstream white audiences as the R & B masters never could.) The 1960s generation celebrated its uniqueness in rock concerts, wore the badges of rock groups, and never moved to communal farms without stereo equipment.

10 Putting together the music with pictures was an early innovation. The Max Fleischer cartoons of the 1930s and 1940s were cut precisely to songs sung by the likes of Cab Calloway and Louis Armstrong. As early as 1943, the Panoram Soundies had brief success. These were jukeboxes placed in nightclubs and diners, where viewers could punch up songs and watch performers on the mini-screen atop the jukebox. A European device called Scopitone brought the gimmick back in the 1960s, though it never caught on, some say because it generally featured mainstream European singers without the oppositional appeal of American pop idols. More influential were commercials borrowing a hip edge from rock sounds, and the commercial-fed work of film artists like Richard Lester, who turned the Beatles into a visual experience. In *A Hard Day's Night,* Lester made the Beatles' screen personae and lifestyle, as well as their performances, the subject of film episodes backed by music cuts. Rock videos were shown in the 1970s in European clubs, and some English underground groups rode them to celebrity. This was a moment in English pop music when the performer's persona had become as important as the sound of the music, and so the form nicely fulfilled its function.

11 The transatlantic success of music video awaited the moment at which cable TV became an option for a substantial number of Americans. Then targeted audiences became commercially attractive. Amid wild talk of whole cable channels devoted to pet care and chess, programmers brainstormed channels that would deliver the same kind of programming—to a big but still targeted audience—around the clock. Movies were a surefire idea, and music seemed an ideal vehi-

cle to attract highly prized consumers: young people. They had value not merely because the young buy records, but because buyable popular culture is central to their lives. Pop culture commodities are now the tools to express personal taste, even talismans of identity and identification with a subculture. No one needs to sell young people on the key role of fad and fashion in designing their identities; indeed, channeling such information to them provides a service welcomed for its news of what's happening.

12 Still, no one foretold the success of music video. At Warner, which gambled on the format in 1980, the prospect of a cable channel wholly dedicated to rock videos, on air twenty-four hours a day, was received with major reservations. Even though the program time was to be filled with free videos given to the channel as promos by record companies, Warner hesitated before backing the concept. Even its strongest in-house advocates only promised record companies that they would see increased sales in two years.

13 But when MTV—Music Television—started up in 1981, its success was almost instantaneous. MTV became a hot media item in itself, and record companies were reporting rising sales within months. Music videos have fueled the current boom in the record industry, a fact reflected in music industry awards for videos. The channel took a little longer to start paying out. MTV stayed in the red for two years before Warner was confident enough of its future to spin it off as a separate company. It showed a profit in 1984, claiming access to 24.2 million viewers, with independent services estimating only slightly less, making it the highest-rated music cable service on the air even after ratings leveled off in 1984.

14 Nielsen ratings for 1985 showed a dramatic 30 percent drop from 1984; the rating was disputed by MTV, which argued with some reason that Nielsen's cable estimates are flawed. But some falloff is indisputable and may reflect the proliferation of similar services in other areas, both

nationally and internationally. And so, mutating again, MTV added rock-oriented nostalgia-laden sitcoms to its nonstop round of para-information,[7] and also changed the faces of its video jockeys. Meanwhile, MTV's signal is being picked up abroad, among other places by TV pirates in Latin America. In Europe, clubs pirate videos on similar services, and in the Soviet Union, illicit music videos are hot tape items.

15   Other music cable channels quickly imitated and improvised on MTV's example, but no cable channel on the scale of MTV has been able to compete, partly because MTV has aggressively attacked rivals legally and with such marketing practices as signing producers to exclusives and paying contracts. Ted Turner accomplished the most spectacular failure, with a service he billed as a more wholesome, family-oriented version of MTV. After abysmal[8] ratings in early weeks, Turner sold his venture to MTV, where it became VH-1. VH-1 is offered free to MTV subscribers, and all cable channels that carry VH-1 carry both. VH-1's most important role may be to hold down space competitors might otherwise occupy.

16   Networks and syndicators also attempted to imitate MTV's success. Some, such as the show *Hot,* which expired after only twelve weeks, collapsed. Others, such as *Night Tracks* and *Friday Night Videos,* became mass-audience successes, and the cable program service Black Entertainment Television began producing its own music video shows. Music video has also made inroads into prime time. Twenty-four-hour-a-day music video channels have proliferated in low-cost and low-reach markets, and at this writing there are currently about eleven such channels on UHF and low-power frequencies. Many broadcasters expect an all-music TV channel to exist in the top hundred markets within the next few years, al-though 1985 was financially rocky for several of the low-power sources.

17   However packaged, the music video format always amounts to wall-to-wall commercials for something. The videos tout particular rock groups and albums. The production "credits" usually include only the name of the group and the record. (This is the viewer's first clue that music videos purvey[9] a peculiar amalgam[10] of celebrity and anonymity; from the outset, they are represented as authorless adventures. The exception comes when a video is made by someone with star status, who has "brand name" recognition.) The videos have become products in themselves, sold in compilation or long-form versions in video stores. Cross-plugging, weaving other products into the atmospherics, is ever more common, and cross-financing goes on too. (RC Cola, for instance, financed a Louise Mandrell video, which then, with its appropriate images of RC-sipping, debuted at the National Soft Drink Association convention in 1985.) When a song cut comes from a movie soundtrack, the video is a virtual movie trailer. Between videos on a program, video jockeys (VJs) tout both the service and, through music industry "news," other music products and tickets for performances. And then there are the commercials.

18   Advertisers have been quick to take a cue from music video's appeal, just as the videos have built in a stylistic base created by commercials. An advertisement for Clairol Heated Rollers, for instance, features close-ups of muscles and aerobically coordinated bodybuilders backed by a strong rock beat. The "bodybuilder" rollers become one of many trigger visuals for a gestalt.[11] A commercial for the Duster car, like the Clairol ad, features the colors black, white, and blue, a color scheme that in its artificiality locates the action

---

7. para-information: auxiliary or substitute information

8. abysmal: extremely disappointing

9. purvey: provide

10. amalgam: combination

11. gestalt: integrated structure or pattern

within television's alternative universe. On an outsized indoor-outdoor jungle gym, the Duster car becomes an actor among a group of peripatetic[12] dancers.

19 It is easy to see why commercials imitate music videos, sometimes even mimicking their opening "credits." It is not merely that advertisers like the pleasure-happy attitude that the videos promote, although Okidata computer software appeals directly to that attitude with a commercial featuring a cartoon character who sits at a terminal muttering "Where's the fun?" It is also that music video never delivers a hard sell, never identifies the record or tape or group as a product. Instead, it equates the product with an experience to be shared, part of a wondrous leisure world.

20 Commercials have always sold the sizzle, not the steak—that is, depended on atmosphere. But they have usually promised consumers that the product will enhance an experience ("adds life," "takes the worry out of being close") or permit one ("don't leave home without it"). But music videos are themselves primary experiences. Music videos give the product a new location on the consumer's landscape, not as messengers of a potential purchase or experience, but as an experience in themselves, a part of living.

21 Two decades ago, science fiction writers imagined a commercial-mad future, where consumers were perpetually dunned with demands to buy. Even the prescient[13] Philip K. Dick, in *The Simulacrum,* imagined roving electronic commercials that attached themselves to beleaguered consumers. But the reality of permanent and pervasive commercials turns out to be quite different. Once commercial reality becomes primary in daily life, the direct appeal to buy can be submerged. Products come to seem "natural." Any product—a record, tape, videocassette, article of clothing, car, perfume—takes its place as an aspect of the gestalt. The raw material for postmodern pastiche[14] art is everywhere.

22 With nary a reference to cash or commodities, music videos cross the consumer's gaze as a series of mood states. They trigger moods such as nostalgia, regret, anxiety, confusion, dread, envy, admiration, pity, titillation—attitudes at one remove from primal expression such as passion, ecstasy, and rage. The moods often express a lack, an incompletion, an instability, a searching for location. In music videos, those feelings are carried on flights of whimsy, extended journeys into the arbitrary.

23 In appealing to and playing on these sensations, music videos have animated and set to music a tension basic to American youth culture. It is that feeling of instability that fuels the search to buy-and-belong, to possess a tangible anchor in a mutable universe while preserving the essence of that universe—its mutability. It allows the viewer to become a piece of the action in a continuous performance.

24 Music videos did not discover the commercial application of anxiety, of course. The manufacturer of Listerine was selling mouthwash on anxiety sixty years ago. Nor did music videos succeed in making themselves widely appealing by somehow duping passive audiences into an addiction to commercial dreams. Music videos are authentic expressions of a populist industrial society. For young people struggling to find a place in communities dotted with shopping malls but with few community centers, in an economy whose major product is information, music videos play to the adolescent's search for identity and an improvised community.

25 The success of MTV has been based on understanding that the channel offers not videos but environment, a context that creates mood. The

---

12. peripatetic: busily walking
13. prescient: seeing into the future

14. pastiche: consisting of items borrowed from several sources

goal of MTV executive Bob Pittman, the man who designed the channel, is simple: his job, he says, is to "amplify the mood and include MTV in the mood." Young Americans, he argues, are "television babies," particularly attracted to appeals to heart rather than head. "If you can get their emotions going," he says, "forget their logic, you've got 'em." Other executives describe MTV as "pure environment," in which not performers but music is the star of the perpetual show.

26   MTV's "pure environment" is expertly crafted. The pace is relentless, set by the music videos, which offer, in the words of one producer, "short bursts of sensual energy." But the image of the program service is casual and carefree. The channel's VJs are chosen for their fresh, offhand delivery and look. They are "themselves," celebrities whose only claim to fame is their projection of a friendly image to youthful viewers. The sets are designed to look like a basement hideaway a fifteen-year-old might dream of, with rock memorabilia and videocassettes adorning walls and shelves. Lighting is intentionally "shitty," instead of the classic no-shadow bright lighting of most TV productions. MTV intends to offer viewers not just a room of their own, but a room that is an alternate world.

27   MTV promotes itself as the populist, even democratic expression of its viewers. Rock stars in promo spots call on viewers to say, "I want my Em Tee Vee!," as if someone were threatening to take it away from them. "Their" MTV, as its own ads portray it, is the insouciant,[15] irreverent rejection of a tedious other world—not the real-life one of work and family, but the world as network news reports it. One commercial spoofs network news promos. Flashing the familiar "Coming at 11" slogan, the ad promises, "MTV provides *reason to live*, despite news of *botched world!*" On a miniature TV set, a logo reads, "Botched World." MTV superimposes its own

version of reality on television's historic moments as well. Space flights—which made history not least for television's live coverage of them—are a favorite subject for MTV's own commercials. One shows astronauts planting an MTV flag on the moon. Another asks, "What if time had never been invented!," showing a space launch countdown without numbers. MTV's promise to remove the viewer from history is succinctly put into the slogan "24 hours every day . . . so you'll be able to live forever!"

28   Viewers are encouraged to play an active role—as consumers, anyway—in MTV's separate world. They can vote for their favorite video by calling a 900 telephone number, which costs fifty cents. They can compete in contests to win visits with rock stars and vacation trips. The contests have a zany spin; as John Sykes, the restless promotion exec at MTV, says, "Our promotions have to reinforce our irreverent image."

29   Music video programs that aren't round-the-clock reach a total number of viewers that is larger than MTV, in part because more people have access to broadcast than to cable. They have had a lower media profile, in part because of MTV's hype machine, in part because they compete with other programs, and in part because they do not have a built-in advantage in styling their own image that MTV has. Unlike that twenty-four-hour service, which like a water faucet is there when you need it, programs must begin and end. Viewers there cannot "live forever," and time is an inescapable reality. Still, some broadcast programs attempt to immerse viewers in an alternative environment, whether it is a studio set rigged to look like a permanent party or disco, or the basement hideaway feature on *Rock 'n' America*.

30   Wherever they appear, music videos are distinctive because they imitate dreams rather than the plot or event structure of bounded programs. Even the usually thin narrative threads in song lyrics rarely provide the basis for a video's look and action. ("If you can hear them, the words

---

15. insouciant: free from worry

help a bit," says video producer Zelda Barron wryly; her videos for Culture Club feature the bizarre, supernatural, and exotic, and use hectic montage rather than narrative logic. Her explanation for her style—that the budgets aren't big enough to produce a coherent story—fails to explain why the features have the heady dream elements they do.) In *Film Quarterly,* Marsha Kinder has noted strong parallels between dreams and music videos. She cites five elements: unlimited access (MTV's continuous format and people's ability to both sleep and daydream); structural discontinuity (for instance, abrupt scene shifts); decentering (a loosely connected flow of action around a theme); structural reliance on memory retrieval (both videos and dreams trigger blocks of associations with pungent images); and the omnipresence[16] of the spectator. In *Fabula,* Margaret Morse notes many of the same features, particularly the absence of reliance on narrative; she focuses on the magical quality of the word, as lip-synched by the performer, who can appear anywhere in the video without being linked with the images or events, as if a dreamer who could create a world.

31   Many videos in fact begin with someone dreaming or daydreaming. For instance, Kool and the Gang's "Misled" begins with a band member in his bedroom, launching into a dream-adventure in which he is both himself and a small Third World boy, threatened by a glamorous white female ghost and engaged in an adventure that imitates *Raiders of the Lost Ark*—significantly, another commercial fantasy. The dream never really ends, since after his band members wake him up, they all turn into ghosts. Thelma Houston's "Heat Medley" shows the performer daydreaming to escape an unpleasant morning conflict with her husband. She daydreams a central role for herself on a *Love Boat*-like episode that turns into a nightmare of disastrous romance.

32   While the fantasies of music videos are open-ended, they do play on classic story lines, such as boy-meets-loses-wins-girl and child-is-menaced-by-monster-and-conquers-it. Some weave fairy tale themes—in which the protagonist is either a preschooler or is infantilized—into the dream. But performers easily switch identities, magical transportations occur, and sets are expressionistically[17] large or small. In Midnight Star's "Operator," giant telephones dwarf performers, and a telephone booth magically pops up and disappears on highways. In Billy Joel's "Keeping the Faith," a judge's bench becomes a giant jukebox on a set featuring commercial talismans of the 1950s. In ABC's "The Look of Love," Central Park becomes a cartoon set (commercial kiddie culture), and Nolan Thomas' "Yo' Little Brother" looks like a Saturday morning cartoon version of *The Cabinet of Dr. Caligari.*[18]

33   Kinder believes that manufactured fantasy may have a much more far-reaching effect on people's subconscious attitudes and expectations than we now imagine, perhaps conditioning not only our expectations today but our dreams tomorrow. Her fears are far-reaching—and unprovable—but her careful analysis of parallels between dream structure and music video structure have fascinating implications for the form. Music videos offer a ready-made alternative to social life. With no beginnings or endings—no history—there may be nightmarish instability, even horror, but no tragedy. Tragedy is rooted in the tension between an individual and society. Likewise, there is no comedy, which provokes laughter with sharp, unexpected shifts of context, making solemnity slip on a banana peel.

---

16. omnipresence: present everywhere at the same time

17. expressionistically: artistic style giving expression to inner experiences

18. *The Cabinet of Dr. Caligari:* Robert Wiene's classic twenties German film portraying evil

Dreams by contrast create gestalts, in which sensations build and dissolve. And so they nicely match the promise and threat of consumer-constructed identity, endlessly flexible, depending on your income and taste. Obsolescence[19] is built in. Like fashion, identity can change with a switch of scene, with a change in the beat. The good news is: you can be anything, anywhere. That is also the bad news—which whets the appetite for more "news," more dreams.

34 The makers of music videos, however, scorn sophisticated analysis and charges of conspiracy to shape the dream world of a generation. From their perspective, the production process imposes stringent limits on fantasy. Music videos are typically made as promotion items for albums, funded by record companies. Almost always, this means performers will appear in the video. (Bruce Springsteen's absence from "Atlantic City" caused a major media uproar.) It also pretty well guarantees they will not be shown performing, although sometimes they seem to. No record company volunteers to use live performance footage, because the sales item is the record on which the musical number in the video appears, and it is difficult to synch the cut to performance shots. Lip-synching does allow the performers to appear as pure celebrities—crooning, resting, acting out fantasies, "performing" without being hooked up to instruments. And, as Morse points out, it allows the viewer to "sing along," participating in the celebrity and the dream, perhaps even claiming ownership of the fantasy.

35 A more abstract constraint on videos is their cost. Until 1984, most videos were made at a loss, for figures on the order of $35,000 to $50,000, as foot-in-the-door opportunities for aspiring filmmakers. Record studios resist expanding their promotional budgets to meet the real production costs, although they have increased budgets as videos have become more popular. The ever

present smoke and mirrors in video are, among other things, cost-cutting measures.

36 Indeed, if you ask a video producer why a certain image, effect, or look was used, the answer is often a list of production problems, rational reasons for arbitrariness. And yet in spite of increasing diversity—more video graphics, less of the thuggish heavy-metal sadism—music videos from different musicians, visual artists, and record companies show disconcerting similarities.

37 Music videos have no heroes, because they do not feature individuals in the sense that plot-driven entertainment does. Music video offers unadulterated celebrity. The living human beings do not play characters, but bold and connotative icons. Frequently, those icons evoke sex roles (not sexuality). In her hit video "Like a Virgin," Madonna alternately takes on the aspect of a whore—in black bad-girl clothes—and a virgin, in white ballroom and wedding-type dresses. In other videos, movie-mafioso types abound; performers strut in white ties and black shirts, projecting macho images of power and money. A bold image is crucial to video and, now, recording-artist celebrity. Bryan Adams, whose hit video "Cuts Like a Knife" was widely criticized for its sadomasochistic elements, was pleased that the video removed a hint of weakness from his pop-rock image. "The most important thing [the video did] for me was establish my look," he said.

38 Just as interesting as the importance of look over character is how quickly the look changes. Several major performers depend on constant innovation and recombination as a defining element of their celebrity. Cyndi Lauper recreates herself with each new video and album in ingenious refashionings of cheap clothes. Her image as an artist with integrity is related to her ability to refashion herself uniquely at each new turn of the product wheel. Many performers hold up as a model the career of David Bowie, who pioneered the concept of the disposable image. In England, a foremost image-manipulator is Malcolm McLaren, the former art student who be-

---

19. obsolescence: process of becoming out of date

came a fashion designer and marketer, and also a music promoter of punk groups such as the Sex Pistols. As punk became passé, McLaren remade Adam Ant's image from punker to swashbuckler, appropriating imagery of the pirate, the highwayman, and the Indian "brave." "Pirates steal everybody's culture and shove it all on their backs," he said, "so you could have this ramshackle mixture of exotic clothes." For such pop culture celebrities, look is at least as important as sound, and rock videos are a mass medium that platforms their latest version of themselves. In fact, with rock videos, personal "identity" has become a central element of commodity production. Music may be only the beginning of the possibilities, as McLaren explained: "In England we don't listen as much as look," he said. "The day comes when somebody turns off the sound and just watches images, maybe focuses on the socks the singer is wearing, then runs out and finds he can't get those. Does he want to buy the record? It doesn't even occur to him. And the industry is beginning to pick up on that, and I think that you'll find that by the end of this decade, the record industry won't be called the record industry. They'll just be selling anything and everything."

[39] The synthesis of television and rock has meant commercial success for people who lack even basic technical skills of musical performance. What was once a scandal, the betrayal of an authentic expression of talent—the sound processing of the Monkees, for instance—is now standard practice, with points given for witty execution. Madonna's own reedy voice is heavily processed on her recordings, and her concerts are notable not for her singing but for her crude gyrations—echoing past pop goddesses of earlier screens such as Marilyn Monroe, in a style that mocks its own referents. Her sultry-sullen, innocent-cynical pose is perfect for labile switches of persona on video. Performers in the video "Yo' Little Brother" do not even pretend to sing. A troupe of four prepubescent children mimic the clothing and stage mannerisms of older rockers, including Bruce Springsteen and Cyndi Lauper—who have thus already been recycled as raw material for pastiche art. The video's producer is now creating a stage act for the four, based on their appearance in the video, in which they will lip-synch on stage.

[40] By contrast, galvanizing rock performers may not produce videos that carry the same charge. The requirements of nonstop video stimulation may work against these performers, for a variety of reasons. Consider Bruce Springsteen, a performer who fiercely maintains a direct connection with his working-class audience as an eye-level hero, who eschews[20] not only glamour but the notion that his image can be altered. He insisted on making a video that used live performance footage for "Born in the U.S.A.," and contracted with independent producer John Sayles. Sayles, a neorealist-style[21] filmmaker, intercut concert footage with scenes of unemployment lines, neighborhood playgrounds, and rustbowl landscapes. Although Springsteen liked the results, his own promotion people were jolted by the video's gritty quality, and it encountered difficulty in gaining time in rotation.

[41] Tina Turner is a distinctive singer, famed for her ability to project raw sexual energy. In videos such as "What's Love Got to Do with It?" exotic fantasies are a weaker evocation of her songs' spirit than her own live performances. Turner changes costumes constantly in her videos, but her persona does not change, and her act fits awkwardly into them as a result. Barbra Streisand also has a distinctive performance style and traditional star status. Her image may be too well defined for the new-age sport of video image permutations. In "Emotion," she engages in a string of unlikely lovers during a dream. But the scene shifts merely look like new locales for

---

20. eschews: avoids

21. neorealist: contemporary artistic movement that is painstakingly realistic

Barbra to show off, and the look is the fatally glamorous Beverly Hills chic rather than the improvisational street glitz of populist celebrity.

42   Music video's lack of a clear subject carries into its constant play with the outward trappings of sex roles. Male images include sailors, thugs, gang members, and gangsters. Female images include prostitutes, nightclub performers, goddesses, temptresses, and servants. Most often, these images are drawn not from life or even myth, but from old movies, ads, and other pop culture clichés.

43   Social critics, especially feminists, have denounced sadomasochistic trappings and stereotypes of exotic women (especially East Asians) in videos. This may indeed be evidence of entrenched prejudice in the culture. For instance, women are often portrayed in videos as outsiders and agents of trouble, which reflects in part the macho traditions of rock. The fetishistic[22] female costumery of many videos probably reflects the role of artifice in shaping feminine sex roles in the culture; there is a fuller cultural grab bag for feminine than for masculine sexual objects.

44   All these sex role stereotypes function differently, however, than stereotypes do in stories—for instance, in pornographic videos and movies. In pornography, doing is everything; it's the act that counts. In music videos, the very act of image manipulation is the action. The sex role, more than a costume, is an identity fashioned from the outside in. While pornographic films feature sexual encounter, in music videos contact is a comparative rarity. The bolder the stereotyping, the more likely it is to turn out that these images are evanescent.[23]

45   You might think that, with romance the theme of most popular songs, videos would feature boy-meets-loses-gets-girl ministories. But love-longing is not the same as a love affair. Soft-focus embraces, memory, and menace make for video visuals, but rarely is there more than a hint of a resolution in the search for bliss. And resolution is more often associated with horror than not. For instance, in a Greg Kihn video, the bride turns into a ghoul on the way to the altar, and becomes a person again when bride and groom escape from the ceremony (an event that marks history, the beginning of something that must have an end), pursued by guests who have turned to ghouls (metaphors for the end of the story they are escaping). In Culture Club's "Mistake Number Three," the bride not only wears black but turns into a robot. The action is an endless transformation of selves, not in what anyone does with or to someone else.

46   Male or female, grotesquerie is the norm. Combine grotesquerie with shifting identities and you get androgyny, as with Culture Club's flamboyant Boy George. Androgyny[24] may be the most daring statement that an entire range of sex roles is fair game for projecting one's own statement of the moment. Gender is no longer fixed; male and female are fractured into a kaleidoscope of images.

47   Fashion's unstable icons also exist in a spooky universe. The landscape on which transient images take shape participates in the self-dramatizing style of the performer-icons. Ordinary sunlight is uncommon; night colors—especially blue and silver—are typical; and neon light, light that designs itself and comes in brilliantly artificial colors, is everywhere. Natural settings are extreme—desert sands, deep tropical forests, oceans. Weather often becomes an actor, buffeting performers and evoking moods. The settings are hermetic[25] and global at the same time, locked into color schemes in which colors complement each other but no longer refer to a natural universe.

---

22. fetishistic: related to objects that elicit a sexual response

23. evanescent: fading away

24. androgyny: the state of having both male and female qualities

25. hermetic: not influenced by external forces

48   It can be a lonely world, but even the loneliness is hypnotically engrossing. One music video visual cliché that provides continuity in the absence of plot is the shot of the performer simply gazing, often at himself or herself in the previous shot. In Roxy Music's "The Main Thing," Bryan Ferry gazes from an armchair at his own just projected image. In Chicago's "You're the Inspiration," members of the group pretend to practice in a nostalgically lit loft. Intercut are scenes of couples in wistful moods and shots of performers brooding individually. It is images like these that provoke Marsha Kinder to call videos solipsistic.[26]

49   Their world, however, is also one of cosmic threat and magical power. The self-transforming figures are menaced by conglomerate figures of authority, which often trigger all-powerful fantasy acts of destruction and salvation. Parents, school principals, teachers, police, and judges provide a cultural iconography of repression. In Heaven's "Rock School," a principal wears a stocking mask, and a school guard menaces students with a Doberman. Bon Jovi's "Runaway" features a girl in miniskirted rebellion against her parents (harking back nostalgically to an era when miniskirts could express rebellion). In retaliation against restrictions, she incinerates them with powers reminiscent of those used in the films *Carrie* and *Firestarter;* we're seeing word magic, the power of dream-song, at work. Sammy Hagar, in "I Can't Drive 55," exercises his "right" to drive as fast as he wants to (desire being asserted as a right); he ends up before a judge whose name is Julius Hangman, from whom he escapes by waking up. Videos often play on the overlapping sexual and political iconography of power in Naziesque sadomasochistic fetishes, with symbols connoting total power without moral or social context. In Billy Idol's "Flesh for Fantasy," as he sings "Face to face and back to back/You see and feel my sex attack," the video shows Idol strutting, preening, performing Nazi-like salutes. Cutting into this one-man parade is a sequence of body parts and geometric forms, some of them drawn from the starkly abstract set. Idol's "sex attack" is not directed; while he sometimes looks directly at the camera, the video's "story" is the construction of a movie-picture portrait of Idol in his stormtrooper/ S & M outfit.

50   The National Coalition on Television Violence, among other groups, has criticized the violence, "especially senseless violence and violence between men and women," in music videos. The criticisms are grounded in a history of objections to violence in TV programs. These violent actions are seen by NCTV analysts (and the middle-class consumers who support the pressure group) as virtual prescriptions to violence in life. But it is hard to assign a prescriptive meaning to random violence that is used not as action but as atmosphere and aestheticizer. Even Central American conflict has been retailed in videos by Don Henley and Mick Jagger, as a backdrop for the dislocated performers making a stand amid rubble and military action in which no side stands for anything. George Gerbner, dean of the Annenberg School of Communications at the University of Pennsylvania, has reassessed the implications of violence in music video, saying, "Many videos express a sense of defiance and basic insensitivity, an unemotional excitement." The sensations evoked by video imagery are disconnected from the realm of social responsibility altogether.

51   In this impulse-driven fantasy world, apocalypse[27] is a recurrent theme. The title of "Purple Rain" refers to nuclear fallout, and Prince's earlier hit song "1999" ends with a child's voice saying, "Mommy, what about the bomb?" Prince's response to the anxiety in the same song is to sing. "If I gotta die I'm gonna listen to my body tonight," and his performance-rich videos offer that spectacle to viewers.

---

26. solipsistic: focusing exclusively on the self

27. apocalypse: the end of the world

52 Postholocaust landscapes frame nightmarish struggles to survive—indeed, to create oneself. The Planet P Project's "Pink World" is an explicit example. A young boy smothered by his mother's attention has a nightmare in which he wakes up in a deserted military dormitory after a world disaster. Groping his way toward "outside," he encounters a desert world inhabited by zombies. Returning to the dorm, he sets immobilized children free; they are reborn in white, all looking like each other.

53 Music videos may be able to give the once-over to the apocalypse, but facing tomorrow or yesterday is something else. In music videos, history has been abolished along with other real-world constraints. In its place is a set of aids to nostalgia. As the Eurogliders, in "Heaven," sing, "I want to find a better place," sepia-toned[28] images of rural life are traced in slow motion. The good old days, the mythic past of music video, is located in the fashion of the 1950s (the early days of pop rock) and in the television and movie images of that period. This was the innocent youth of postwar commodity culture seen from a jaded present, and the closet out of which the recombinant[29] images of celebrity today are drawn. Elton John's "Sad Songs (Say So Much)," like many videos, subscribes to a 1950s dress code, and it echoes *West Side Story* choreography. Ponytails and soda fountains adorn Billy Joel's paean[30] to golden oldies "Keeping the Faith."

54 The use of black and white is the quickest way to evoke TV's mythic golden age. Barry Gibb's "Fine Line" exploits the black-and-white connotation in a typical way. The performer implicitly strikes a parallel between himself and early rockabilly performers, and also between himself and Beatles-era singers, in a black-and-white video featuring cuts between himself on stage and a screaming crowd of adolescent girls. A mythic past can also double as futuristic, as in Don Henley's "The Boys of Summer," where a boy drummer in a black-and-white 1950s household is also the spectator of scenes that evoke the postnuclear future of *On the Beach*.

55 Music video programs rarely take the opportunity to show historical footage of rock performance, as J. Hoberman has pointed out. There is always a danger of invidious[31] comparison between a Bo Diddley, say, and the current video artists. More important, reference to history might rupture the regular delivery of music video's eternal now. Instead, there is a cavalcade of historical references. Music videos incorporate them into the self-reflexive game, giving them an easy, wry, even sardonic tone without social comment or real parody. In David Lee Roth's "California Girls," Roth walks a California boardwalk adorned with pasty manikinlike women in bikinis, while his remake of the 1964 Beach Boys' tune plays. This outdoor body-shopping to a golden oldie tune has ironies ricocheting in every direction: the "California girls" look like bored New York models who never see the sun; Roth aggressively confronts the camera in a way that mocks the Beach Boys' aw-shucks image; girl-watching has become girl-purchasing. But the video itself is neither ironic nor satirical. Roth swaggers through the now kitsch[32] landscape with the confidence of a performer who is above it all, the savvy manipulator of an innocent past.

56 When the past becomes pastiche, no critical distance is possible. As a result, music video's occasional attempts at satire prove feeble. On *Saturday Night Live*, the "Garage Band"'s parody of Michael Jackson's "Beat It" with the chant "Buy It, Buy It, Buy It" looks like a homegrown version of a plausible video. An amateur theatrical group

---

28. sepia-toned: brown-tinted style suggesting a period in the past

29. recombinant: resulting from new combinations

30. paean: song of praise

---

31. invidious: unfair, invalid

32. kitsch: shallow, tasteless art with popular appeal

in Washington, D.C., the Public Interest Follies, included in its 1985 Counter-Inaugural Ball a satirical revue, "Republican TV (RTV)," with songs like "Girls Just Want to Stay Home." Even done well, they became as entertaining as the real thing—but no more so. In fact, they became a version of the real thing.

57   Consider two videos intended to raise social issues—Donna Summers' "She Works Hard for the Money" and David Bowie's "Let's Dance." Trade and gossip magazines report that Summer met a waitress on whom she modeled "She Works Hard." Bowie has been eloquent on the responsibility of music and video to take social positions; he wanted "Let's Dance" to highlight Australian aboriginal rights, and we do see aborigines slipping into an Australian cityscape, but the lyrics give no hint of such an issue. In both cases, any message was lost in the disjunctive images and dreamy fantasy.

58   Videos have been used effectively to raise funds for causes, appealing directly to the viewer's wish to buy-and-belong. "Do They Know It's Christmas?," the most popular song of 1984 in England, was also a hit rock video made by English artists raising money for African famine relief. The video features studio performers looking dolorous, intercut with pitiful scenes of starving African children, who look no more bizarre than most video fantasy characters. This rock relief effort, like the later one by USA for Africa in the United States, allowed consumers to participate in a cause at a distance—charity, but not a connection.

59   It was precisely this distinction that troubled Steve Van Zandt (Little Steven) when he was making his "Sun City" antiapartheid[33] video in mid-1985. In the hour-long making-of-the-video video, he noted that although proceeds of the enterprise would go to the Africa Fund, "this is not a benefit," because South Africans "do not ask us

for charity," but rather give us the chance to see ourselves and realize that their struggle is ours. The video, directed by Hart Perry and Jonathan Demme (both directors with a history of social consciousness), has an unusual structure. It begins with scenes of the South African resort Sun City, a South African voice-over explaining its location and significance. As the song begins, musicians in a series of cameo spots look directly at the viewer, gesturing with clenched fists and pointing as they sing, that they won't play Sun City. Documentary footage is interspersed, not only of South Africa but also of historic moments in American civil rights history, including Martin Luther King saying "I have a dream" (with image but no sound). Dynamic graphics emphasize action rather than attitude; black silhouetted arms rip the screen to reveal marchers carrying coffins, and at one point chanting musicians are superimposed on footage of a massive South African demonstration. Black-edged obituary graphics flash images of South African martyrs in unabashed delivery of "hard" and historical information. The last musical word is had by South African demonstrators.

60   The difference between this and other "cause" videos is not accidental. Van Zandt explains in the documentary that its "look" was intended to "reflect anger and commitment without looking . . . aggressive," and that they wanted musicians to show energy without making it "look like too much fun."

61   Music videos have already had a powerful effect on their context, that of commercial pop culture and its promotion. They are now key to a musical group's success. In 1984, for instance, only three of the top-100 *Billboard* albums did not have a promo video. Groups now write songs with the video in mind, and performers begin careers on tape. Concerts are staged with an eye to expectations raised by the video, as was the case in concerts by the Jacksons and Prince. Rock critic Jon Pareles has noted the change in concert behavior; audiences of performers noted primarily for their videos, he claims, act more passive—

---

33. antiapartheid: against the former South African practice of separating the black and white races

as if they were watching TV—than those of a hot performer like Bruce Springsteen.

62 Some have charged that videos are narrowing the diversity of popular music, whether it's because mass marketing favors blockbusters over the offbeat or because videos "do your dreaming for you." Rocker Joe Jackson, for instance, protested that videos limit the viewer's imagination and devalue musical ability. Certainly, such bland groups as Stray Cats and Men at Work have built success out of their videos. Video is also, however, responsible for creating a lively demand for a band like The Clash in Boise, Idaho. Critic Pareles believes that video could revive flagging energy in rock: "For me, a great rock song is a good tune plus some inspired irritant," he explained. "Rockers are learning to link a radio-smooth audio track to a wild image, an eye irritant." One could just as easily, however, make the opposite argument—the rock videos appropriate shock value into a syncretic[34] stream. The range of sound may not be narrowed as much as the range of meanings.

63 Social pressure on record companies and producers has affected the look and marketing of rock videos. When MTV first began, black performers almost never appeared. When a video by Rick James was rejected, he went public with figures showing that in eighteen months of MTV programming with some 750 videos, only two dozen had featured black performers. In an interview with an MTV video jockey, David Bowie reinforced the complaint, saying, "I'm distraught by the fact that there are so few black artists featured." At the time, MTV executive Pittman had a simple business response: "Cable is in the suburbs." But then Michael Jackson's album *Thriller* took off—even in the suburbs. The success of Prince and Tina Turner brought more color to programming, and now black-oriented music

video programs provide a minimarket for black videos (most of which feature some white performers, showing a careful awareness of a crossover audience). The combination of protest and pop taste has made video programming less overtly racist, but the more black-sounding R & B is still far on the margins.

64 Music video has affected the movie industry as well as the record business. Music video influenced both the formal style and the marketing of the films *Flashdance* and *Footloose*. *Flashdance*'s director Adrian Lyne studied rock videos to get the right "look," and then promoted the film on music video programs. The resulting demand was enough to make this a regular marketing approach. A recent evening of the midnight *ABC Video* program consisted entirely of videos for current commercial films, some incorporating scenes specially shot for video. The crossover from video to the big screen has also spurred a host of films aimed at the youth market and featuring such video action as break dancing and aerobic dancing. The formula is not foolproof, since most films remain chained to the logic of real time and social relations with story lines. *Electric Boogaloo* and *Heavenly Bodies*, two late-1984 offerings, both bogged down when their iconic characters were taken out of dreamland and made to observe the conventions of ordinary living.

65 The rush of music video producers to the wide screen may not dramatically affect the look of movies, which are bounded far more than any TV program, and which cater to audiences who (despite what Jean-Luc Godard[35] once claimed) still expect a beginning, a middle, and an end, and in that order. Studios prize music video producers not for their style, but because they have experience making product fast on low budgets.

66 The film *Purple Rain* is the major exception, a film that delivered at length what music videos do in bits and pieces. It openly exploited the con-

---

34. syncretic: describing the combination of differing beliefs

35. Jean Luc Godard: famous French film director

ventions of music video—especially the search for personal identity through fashion-directed celebrity, and the evocation of nostalgia, a sense of loss, and loneliness. Critics panned *Purple Rain,* arguing that the film lacked dramatic structure and was hopelessly sentimental. In fact, the film was not structured around a plot, but a theme— that of Prince battling his insecurities and adolescent passions. The mawkish quality of its sentiment was matched well to the adolescent's struggle with his out-of-control image. The fact that Prince is an electrifying performer and powerful songwriter gave the film an authenticity rare in any popular art. Prince may have become the royalty of music video's alternative world precisely because he can put tremendous sexual energy and performing ability behind the subject of his own perpetual struggle for expression. In *Purple Rain,* Prince lives in an eternal present under neon lights, swathed in smoke. Resolution means a good gig, a moment of unity between his presence and that of his failed musician-father's. Prince is the authentic child of a society of spectacle, meeting it on its own terms.

67 Narrative television programs have borrowed from music videos as well, most prominently in *Miami Vice.* But music video's fulcrum position may best be revealed in the way it has traveled beyond television, especially in its use by fashion designers. There, the construction of identity through fashion is at the center of the business. Since 1977, when Pierre Cardin began making video recordings of his fashion shows, designers have been incorporating video into their presentations. Videos now run continuously in retail store windows and on floor displays. For many designers, what sells records already sells fashion, and some foresee a fashion channel. The Cooperative Video Network, a television news service, already offers a half-hour program, *Video Fashion News,* with three-minute segments on current designer models. Some designers regard video as a primary mode of expression. Norma Kamali now shows her work only on video, both in stores and on programs.

One of her best-known works is a video called "The Shoulder Pad Song." Another designer, Lloyd Allen, makes videos that sensually evoke his own fashion career. Designer Bill Tice demands that his contracts for personal appearances include showings of his fashion videos. Kamali, saying that her tapes allow her to approach customers "without interpretation," also thinks that video adds a dimension to her work, because it "extends my fantasy," which of course is the reality of her business.

68 The marketing crossover is becoming global, a kind of perpetual feedback system. Michael Jackson has begun to sell fashion licenses for his look, and Christie Brinkley, a supermodel who starred in Billy Joel's "Uptown Girl," recently started her own fashion line. The videos undertaken at Perkins Productions are seen as prospective vehicles for extensive cross-promotion, in which a performer may use a prominently featured soap and a designer fragrance. The video may then circulate freely—in hotel lobbies, stores, and on airplane flights as well as on television programs. Video thrills are moving into all aspects of daily life. McDonald's has installed TV monitors at many cash registers, offering tempting images of food and giving shoppers the sense that fast food is part of a high-tech media world, a piece of the fashion action. "Video wallpaper" is being produced for bars and discos, with commercial products deliberately inserted into the montages in a style called by one producer "bordering on subliminal advertising." In general, the boundary between commercial and noncommercial images is eroding. One Manhattan boutique asked General Electric for a copy of a music videoesque commercial to use in its floor display, "for atmosphere," not for any message but simply for its style.

69 As media image-making comes to dominate electoral politics, music video has invaded that domain too. Consultants to both the Democratic and Republican parties have used music video to explore the mind-set of younger generations. "You can see the tensions among kids rising in

their music," said pollster Patrick Caddell, "as they struggle to figure out what they will become." Or, he might have added, what they are. Republican strategist Lee Atwater decided, "We've got a bunch of very confused kids out there." That hasn't stopped politicians from using music videos as ads; videos were also enlisted (without marked results) in voter registration campaigns in 1984. The collision of music video with traditional political mobilizing brings one world—that of the consumer, concerned with individual choice—smack up against another—that of the citizen, charged with responsibility for public decisions. It is this collision that led fashion analyst Gerri Hirshey, noting the passionate investment of the young in their "look," to write: "If one's strongest commitment is to a pair of red stiletto heel pumps, style has a higher price tag than we'd imagine." In one sense, politics is fully ready for music video, if the success of Ronald Reagan—whose popularity rests on a pleasant media image to which "nothing sticks" while critics search in vain for a corresponding reality—is any guide.

70   The enormous popularity and rapid evolution of music videos give the lie to conspiracy theorists who think commodity culture is force-fed into the gullets of unwilling spectators being fattened for the cultural kill. But it should also chasten free-market apologists who trust that whatever sells is willy-nilly an instrument of democracy. Music videos are powerful, if playful, postmodern art. Their raw materials are aspects of commercial popular culture; their structures those of dreams; their premise the constant permutation of identity in a world without social relationships. These are fascinating and disturbing elements of a form that becomes not only a way of seeing and of hearing but of being. Music videos invent the world they represent. And people whose "natural" universe is that of shopping malls are eager to participate in the process. Watching music videos may be diverting, but the process that music videos embody, echo, and encourage—the constant re-creation of an unstable self—is a full-time job.

Critical Explorations: Reading

Use these questions to reread the Aufderheide selection. These answers should give you a better understanding of the complexity and detail of her argument. They may provide you with material to use in your dialogic or reading journal.

1. Reread paragraph 4. List the most important characteristics that Aufderheide claims define music videos.

2. Paragraphs 17–20 address the relationship between commercials and music videos. How are music videos similar to commercials? How are they different?

3. Reread paragraph 30. How do music videos imitate the dream state?

4. Reread paragraph 66. What aspects of the music video form did *Purple Rain* employ? What does this say about the relationship of music videos to film?

5. Reread the last paragraph. Aufderheide has much to say here. What is her attitude toward the strengths of music videos? How does her assessment relate to her comments about the "commodity culture" and the "free market"?

Selection 11

from *Split Image:*
African Americans in the Mass Media
    Jannette L. Dates

Jannette L. Dates has co-edited a study of the African American in the media, including analyses of African Americans in music, radio, television, film, and advertising. This selection, "Comedies," is excerpted from a longer chapter on television titled "Commercial Television." Critically reading this excerpt will serve two purposes for you. First, it will show you how a communications professor analyzes popular television programming and characters. Her analysis can provide a model for your own analysis of television characters. Second, this selection will give you an accurate chronicle of how African Americans have been portrayed on commercial television from the beginning of television programming in the early fifties to the mid-eighties.

There are two central questions in this selection. First, what social and political influences have shaped the development of the African American character on commercial television? Second, has the television image of the African American changed for the better since Americans began viewing television comedies in the fifties? You will have to infer the answers to these questions from the arguments and evidence that Dates presents throughout the selection.

This long selection is clearly written and moves in a careful chronological sequence beginning in 1950 and ending in 1987. Since Dates's audience is an academic one, her style is exact and carefully documented. Dates also provides a thorough character analysis of several African American television personalities. Read these sections carefully to determine the strengths and weaknesses that she finds in their acting and in their roles. You may want to take notes on Dates's analyses of such actors as Nell Carter and Sherman Hemsley. These notes should help you understand how Dates analyzes television performers.

Reading–Writing Preparation

Before you read this selection, you may want to answer the following questions in writing or discussion:

1. Select a television comedy that focuses on African Americans. What makes this program humorous?

2. How do you think African Americans, Latinos, Asians, and Native Americans should be portrayed on television?

Comedies

1 Televised comedies helped Americans adjust to the social order as transmitted myths and ideologies reinforced society's implicit rules and codes of behavior. In their portrayal of African American images, these comedies picked up threads of the established pattern of white superiority and black servitude, and continued to weave them back into the popular culture. As we have seen in earlier chapters, the pattern had been established by the minstrel shows[1] and con-

---

1. minstrel shows: stage shows in which white performers with blackened faces performed

---

Reprinted by permission of Howard University Press from *Split Image: African Americans in the Mass Media.* Jannette L. Dates and William Barlow, eds. Howard University Press: 1990, 261–80.

tinued by the film, radio, and recording industries. These industries, on the one hand, used African American talents (music, cultural nuances, and jargon), while, on the other hand, they consistently denied those of African heritage opportunities to act as fully respected participants and to reflect their culture in their own way.

2 Researchers such as Matabane, Sklar, Clark, Moore, MacDonald and Signorelli have developed theories that shed light on the reasons television's decision makers allowed very few dramatic programs yet a proliferation of comic ones for framing African American life. These researchers see this phenomenon as indisputably linked with previous eras of racial stereotyping in American popular culture. Moreover, like Althusser and Hall, they suggest that such restriction of racial roles and dimensions was used as a means to reinforce social dominance and control

with respect to preferred social relations between the races. Moreover, they believe that characters in restricted roles had fewer life opportunities, fewer resources, less power, lower status, and a greater likelihood of victimization. In addition, these researchers believe that such predominant reliance on the comedy format for representing African American life patterns also restricted the themes and types of values open to exploration within plot structures. Further, comedic settings coerced viewers into believing that they should not become emotionally involved in the plot on a serious level because it was, after all, just a comedy, supposedly a light-hearted look at life.

3   Television's comic African American characters, unlike their counterparts in some film comedies, failed to illuminate the black experience or speak to African American concerns. Rather, the video medium, with few exceptions, created characters who were black in physical appearance but were most often stereotypical. The characters, stereotypical and otherwise, had views, values, and beliefs that were largely mainstream American. For example, in early television, African Americans who appeared on "The Beulah Show" (1950–53) included seasoned professionals from the film, theater, and radio industries. The Beulah character had originated as a supporting role on radio's "The Fibber McGee and Molly Show" and featured a white male speaking in black dialect. The setting was a "good," white Anglo-Saxon Protestant neighborhood in a middle-class American suburb where the husband-father went to work, and the wife-mother took care of the child at home with the help of her conscientious maid, Beulah. This setting idealized the image of middle-class American life. The solid, comfortable living-room furniture, the knick-knacks carefully placed on tables, the Grant Wood-type[2] picture hanging over the mantel, the clean, well-groomed youngster, were

---

2. Grant Wood: American painter of the early twentieth century known for his midwestern portraits

all symbols of the upwardly mobile, white middle class of the early 1950s. The series usually opened by establishing a problem situation, continued with misunderstandings and confusion that resulted in inappropriate actions on the part of a main character, and ended with the resolution of the initial problem. Beulah was central to the plot in that she guided the family to a safe conclusion, as she alone restored balance and normalcy to the household.

4   This setting and plot structure coincided with life in the real world of that era. It was the time of the silent generation, when President Dwight D. Eisenhower and Vice President Richard Nixon were the chief executives, when blue-collar workers had gradually moved to the suburbs and adopted the ways of the middle class, and when most white Americans believed that life would continue to get better and better for each generation. At this point, African Americans, feeling a liberal momentum that the war against the Nazis had generated, started demanding better conditions for themselves. In keeping with the new, more militant tone heard across the land, the black middle class, in particular, felt compelled to voice firm opposition to Beulah's lower-class origins and her focus on white people's problems. Moreover, they believed that the series reinforced numerous stereotypes for the large number of viewers, who chuckled knowingly, for example, at Beulah's attempts to persuade the consistently lazy, noncommittal Bill to marry her. While some viewers could justifiably note that the "slippery suitor" is typical of most groups of people, in this setting Beulah was the black female servant with little social life of her own. Unable to obtain a commitment from the "significant other" in her life, she seemed destined to nurture and clean up after others. Despite this bleak future, Beulah was content, even happy, about her life and willing to go to great lengths to help others with their problems.

5   As identified in the 1930s by the great black poet and critic, Sterling Brown, two categories of black stereotyping are: the comic Negro and the

contented slave/servant. Beulah, both comic and a contented servant opened the television program, talking directly to the camera about the problem or situation that she and her white family, the Hendersons, were facing that given week. She concluded the opening with a facetious remark such as "Beulah, who spends most of her time in the kitchen but never seems to know what's cookin'." Throughout the thirty minutes of each episode, Beulah conscientiously worked to remedy the family's current problem. She usually enlisted the help of Bill, who was also the handy man for the Hendersons, and her close friend (another maid), Oriole. The Aunt Jemima image discussed in the chapter on the film industry is strongly evident in television as well. Unlike the mammy, who was domineering, strong-willed, and bossy, Aunt Jemima was kind, generous, caring, and sincere. These qualities were typical of the performances of the maids on this show.

6   The maids among these characters were not scripted to question the system that placed them in the servant's role, and they consciously relegated their own lives to secondary status. Viewers could not conceive of Beulah wanting to be anything but what she was or of her fighting for her children to have a life more self-fulfilling than her own. The characters consistently reflected the values and beliefs of mainstream America. For example, in a 1951 show, Beulah orchestrated a ceremony for the Hendersons to renew their wedding vows because she believed they were drifting apart. This was scarcely a concern about others' lives that typically generated energy in real-life African Americans, who were more often totally involved in their own families' basic survival, especially because prejudice and discrimination had often forced these families to the bottom of the nation's socioeconomic scale.

7   From viewing black male television characters as developed by white writers and producers, and using theories suggested by Althusser and Hall, we can decipher the ideological basis for character development. A conclusion can be drawn that white producers of black-oriented comedies carefully crafted the style of leading male characters, hoping to increase their palatability[3] to the dominant culture. For example, in the 1950s series "Amos 'n' Andy," Kingfish had no power: usually he was unemployed, and often he just skirted the edges of the law in some nefarious[4] moneymaking scheme. The humorous plots and appealing characters saved the series from unabashed minstrelsy, but Kingfish's weak power position made him merely an acceptable caricature, and thus acceptable to dominant-culture viewers.

8   "The Amos 'n' Andy Show" was comparable to Jackie Gleason's "The Honeymooners" (1955–71) in story line and theme. Except for Sapphire and Amos, the performers usually spoke in rural black dialect and showed a lack of control over events affecting their lives. They often demonstrated a general lack of knowledge and education, wore unusual clothing such as derbies and flashy suits, and behaved "with exaggerated, hat in hand diffidence[5] and cunning obsequiousness."[6] When a more educated person appeared in the series (Sapphire's, sister, Hortense, in a 1951 program), though she had "book learning," the character lacked common sense. She was odd, sexless, and unable to attract males. Moreover, Kingfish was not in charge in his home as Ralph Kramden was in "The Honeymooners." For example, in the episode "Sapphire's Sister," Kingfish did not want Hortense to come live with them and flatly refused to sleep on the couch so that she could share his wife's bed. He was overruled by his wife on each count. Subsequently, he lost all control of his home. He did not get to use the bathroom for hours in this episode because the women all pushed him

---

3. palatability: acceptability

4. nefarious: very wicked

5. diffidence: showing a lack of confidence or purpose

6. obsequiousness: being overly eager to please

aside. Throughout the series, Sapphire attempted to "refine" Kingfish and his "no-good friends" by making them more like good folks—the good folks of middle-class white America. This was the standard that "good folks" used and against which they measured themselves and others.

9   The rural black dialect, malapropisms,[7] mispronunciations, and misinterpretations found in the "Amos 'n' Andy" radio series are also evident in the television series. For example, in the following excerpt, Kingfish tries to get Andy and his sister-in-law, Hortense, together:

KF: Well Andy lak I tol ya Hortense is a school teacher and she been teachin kids in the 4th grade. Now in order to make an imprint on Hortense I got ta bring ya'up to da intelligence level that she bin accustomed to.

A: Yeah, Dat's da thing ta do all right, but (uh) how we gonna do it?

KF: Well, uh, Hortense is always spoutin' poetry and so I brought a poetry book here. Now Andy, I want ya to mesmerize some of it and when you talk to er I want ya to thow in some a' them, uh, little bits of wisdom. You know, like bon matza and all that stuff.

A: Right.

KF: Well Andy, you better start off on this heah. A-read dat.

A: *The Legend of Hiawatha* by Henry Wadsworth Longfellow. Uh. Took three fellows to write this, huh?

KF: Andy, dat's a long poem. Read that first credenza right dere.

A: Oh, yeah. On the shores of itchy gooma.

10   In this episode it is obvious that Andy cannot read well. Moreover, Hortense, a professional educator, fails to notice that Andy does not know the poem when she talks with him, although it is supposed to be her favorite. This excerpt demonstrates the dialogue that white writers used to draw laughs at the expense of the black "predicament"—implicitly, that black people want to be white or, at the least, to act as they believe white people act. However, blacks are depicted as obviously ill-equipped to achieve that end. The series was seen by middle-class black professionals as a slap in the face. They were furious about being cast in this role. The driving force behind their fury lay in the knowledge that "Amos 'n' Andy" was the only series on network television that focused on African American culture and that it followed the pattern set in minstrelsy, which they feared seemed destined to continue ad infinitum.[8] The NAACP helped to force the series off the air in 1953. Not until fifteen years later was another comedy featuring black leading characters added to a network lineup.

11   Except for African American performers seen on variety shows, who managed on some occasions to infuse some performances with their own interpretations, the African American cultural experience was seldom the focus of network entertainment until the civil rights era of the 1960s heated up. By 1968, the networks felt pressure from within, and from many outside forces, to increase African American participation in the industry. Their new policy was based on and went beyond the 1964 Civil Rights Act. The civil rights movement, coupled with these other pressures, helped push the networks toward producing and airing series that featured African Americans. Thus, the situation comedy "Julia" premiered in 1968. "Julia" was seen by many as an accommodationist[9] program, where the skin color of the lead characters was the only difference between this program and others on the air. It was seen by many critics as too middle-class in orientation, and as a fantasy similar to

---

7. malapropisms: misuses of words with similar sounds

8. ad infinitum: forever

9. accommodationist: trying to please all concerned

the Doris Day-type movies that were then very popular. In "Julia," Diahann Carroll played a widowed nurse with a gruff, but liberal boss. Carroll wore designer clothes and had few problems that were typical of African American women living in that period. In a carryover from early television and in keeping with the trend of shows such as "Ozzie and Harriet," Julia's world focused on "happy problems," such as explaining where babies came from to her insistent seven-year-old son. The program lasted for three seasons.

12 In the 1970s, issue-oriented entertainment was severely snubbed by the vast majority of Americans. The death of relevancy helped to ensure the stifling of television programs or stories treating serious issues affecting African Americans. Ironically, this occurred at a time when blacks, somewhat more than other Americans, placed faith in television as the most credible source of information and as the medium that most effectively reflected African American concerns and issues. As American television moved away from relevant issues, African American participation in television series shifted. The few dramatic roles for black actors that had begun to open up almost totally disappeared, while comedies, purporting to be newly satirical, flourished. Actually, the comedies revived the minstrel stereotypes that had all but disappeared during the 1960s.

13 Flip Wilson dominated network comedy during the 1970s. Though Wilson's comedy/variety show had high ratings and was generally viewed as hilarious, his negative images of black culture (for example, charlatan[10] preacher, female impersonator) caused many African Americans to shudder. Wilson was criticized for his portrayal of "Geraldine Jones," a wise-cracking, hip-swinging woman of the world. For creating this character, Wilson was accused of encouraging ef-

feminacy in young black males who, some believed, would use him as a role model.

14 Les Brown, the television critic, wrote that Flip Wilson was appreciated by all for the originality and distinctiveness of his material, which had "no credible coordinates in white society," and because he did not sentimentalize black culture but mocked it. In the final analysis, however, Brown believed Wilson "substantiated a racist view of blacks," which was a part of his appeal for whites. On the other hand, Wilson was just as popular with African American viewers. His crossover appeal had an antecedent in the early days of minstrelsy. The African American minstrel Billy Kersands had used characters for his routines from African American folklore. He often had animal tricksters ingeniously gain the upper hand over powerful "others," while Wilson had his characters "outsmart" others through verbal exchanges. Both Kersands and Wilson struck a responsive chord among African Americans, who understood each performer's meaning and intent in a different way from those who were uninitiated. Black audiences understood, for example, that Kersands often "poked fun" at whites, just as Wilson did years later.

15 Nevertheless, Flip Wilson's comedy/variety show was different from earlier variety shows in which African Americans had played key roles (for example, "The Billy Daniels Show" in 1952, and "The Nat Cole Show" in 1956), in that Wilson had more control over his image and a larger budget than the earlier performers had had. Like Daniels and Cole, Wilson's show came directly from characters he had developed in his nightclub acts as a stand-up comedian. Moreover, Wilson's Clerow Production Company controlled aspects of the production of the series. At this period in history, American viewers responded to Wilson's vision of the African American experience. It was soon after the height of the civil rights marches and the numerous calls for affirmative action. Because of the tone set by the White House during the administrations of Presidents Kennedy and Johnson, the media decision

---

10. charlatan: one who pretends to have knowledge or skill

makers probably thought the average American believed he was liberal, and that he should be. It appears that "The Flip Wilson Show" was scripted to appeal to this liberal slant among average viewers.

16 In the early 1970s, producers Norman Lear and Bud Yorkin believed that America was at last ready for racial comedy with themes and story lines that sometimes focused on the African American's unique experiences in society. At this point, both Yorkin and Lear had established careers as television writers/producers. Lear, for example, had written material for "The Ford Star Review" and the "Colgate Comedy Hour" and had served as writer/director for "The Martha Raye Show," the "Tennessee Ernie Ford Show," and "The George Gobel Show." As the principal writer/producer of "All in the Family," Lear had solidly established himself as a major force in television comedy. "All in the Family" featured the bigoted, but lovable(?), Archie Bunker, whose wife, daughter, and son-in-law labored, by example and by cajolery and trickery when necessary, to change Bunker into a more tolerant person. From time to time, Lear also included in the cast of characters the owners of a small cleaning establishment in the neighborhood, an African American family: the Jeffersons. Bunker frequently had negative interactions with various members of this family because of his bigotry and racism. Subsequently, the series entitled "The Jeffersons" was a spinoff from "All in the Family." Lear's comedies were very popular, but they sparked controversy during their years on network television. Indeed media critic Michael Arlen saw series such as "The Jeffersons" as a part of the crop of television programs that connected to nothing except the assumption of being connected to something.

17 As readers will recall, television's world of the 1950s and 1960s had featured happy people with happy problems. When "All in the Family" and "The Jeffersons" aired, they generated issues and aroused emotions, often by using racial epi-

thets,[11] that were new to network television and were not fashionable in polite society. In a 1974 research study of reactions to "All in the Family," Vidmar and Rokeach found that prejudiced persons and unprejudiced persons ascribed different meanings to the intent and outcome of episodes in this series. They concluded that unprejudiced and minority viewers perceived and enjoyed the show as satire, while prejudiced viewers perceived and enjoyed the show as one of the few that was "telling it like it is!" Vidmar and Rokeach believed the show reinforced prejudice and racism and that, by making Archie Bunker a lovable bigot, a disservice was done to race relations and social harmony.

18 In any event, Lear's programs were leaders in popular culture, as they brought ethnic humor and wrenching social comment to nationwide television audiences. Lear has said that he felt a strong concern for human values and that he wanted his programs to cause viewers to debate issues, confront problems, and disagree whenever necessary until they were able to work them through. But he also argued that he was not trying to change the world with his television series, noting that "if the Judeo-Christian ethic has had no effect on prejudice over the past 2,000 years, I'd be an awful fool to think we could do it in a half-hour of comedy." With his work, however, Lear created a unique set of television families, which in that decade included more than ten network comedies in which most characters were not afraid to show anger and confusion, and to use earthy language. This set of television families included African Americans as starring characters in "Sanford and Son," and "Good Times," as well as "The Jeffersons." Lear also wrote and produced a pilot for a comedy series about a black congressman entitled "Mr. Dugan." The show never made it to the CBS network as planned. Lear withdrew it as a result of the

---

11. epithets: words used to show contempt

strong negative reaction it received from African Americans, including members of the Congressional Black Caucus, who previewed it. Still, Lear was justifiably called the czar[12] of network television comedies of the 1970s. He set the tone and charted the course that was followed by numerous television comedies for many years after.

19 Lear's "Good Times," particularly, attempted an honest portrayal of the concerns and problems facing black people, which were different from those faced by middle-class white people. Rarely before had viewers seen conscientious, entertaining attempts to portray unique aspects of this part of American life. With encouragement from the producers, black contributors to the candid portrayal of black cultural jargon included the performers, as well as a few black writers, who used their cultural heritage to address issues usually left unaddressed on American television. Conventionally silly television fare, "Good Times" basically was about a family's search for economic stability. At various points, it rose to focus on social/civil rights issues, such as an unemployed father, parents unable to use credit cards because of a poor credit rating, rent parties to raise rent money, racism as it affected various family members' earning power, and the like. The series was essentially an "outsider" creation in that it attempted to tell the majority population about the minority, as opposed to "insider" creations, which are designed for the minority group to contribute to its own culture and identity and to allow it to express its unique worldview.

20 Television viewers' perceptions about African Americans changed during the 1960s as the civil rights story unfolded at dinnertime each day. Moreover, law and order and the "silent majority" were much discussed by those in the Nixon White House of the late 1960s and early 1970s. Then, between 1972 and 1979, Richard Nixon was forced to resign as president of the country, Gerald Ford served out Nixon's term, and Jimmy Carter was elected to a single term in office. When "Good Times" first aired at this point, the civil rights era was drawing to a close. The series was introduced to American viewers by its producers as a sympathetic, "authentic," and realistic portrayal of the black man's plight. The setting in the series established the environment as a lower-class, housing projects apartment, where the frugal, conscientious mother, Florida (played by Esther Rolle, who was formerly the maid on "Maude"), used curtains behind which she hid clothes and household items. One room served this family as the entrance area, living room, and the dining-kitchen area. The three bedrooms were out of most camera shots, as large windows allowed suggestions of daylight or nighttime into the living room-kitchen area. A desk and chair in one corner were surrounded by boxes, probably used to store family belongings. When the series premiered, Esther Rolle was the star. As the scripts developed, however, Jimmie Walker (J.J.), the older son, eclipsed Rolle (Florida) and John Amos (James), as he caught on with teenage viewers who often influenced their parents' viewing patterns.

21 Though the setting was a lower-class, poor neighborhood, the values and beliefs expressed in "Good Times" were from middle America. In the segment "J.J.'s Eighteenth Birthday," for example, the worldly character Willona, with snapping fingers and "I know the score" glances, stated, "When I was twenty-five, I decided to blow out the candles, freeze the cake, and stop the clock," as J.J.'s parents manipulated their plastic money to try to give him a worthy eighteenth-birthday celebration. Willona, established as good-hearted, represented a lower-class figure, but in her the writers created a contradictory image. Viewers were never quite sure whether she was a swinger or a middle-class striver fallen on bad times, who was forced to live in "the projects." The "J.J.'s Eighteenth

---

12. czar: a person in a position of power

Birthday" episode could have evolved into an authentic vignette[13] about black culture at the lower socioeconomic level, but instead the plot developed in the "usual" (white, middle-class) style. For example, for this celebration everyone came in changed clothes, "dressed up" for the occasion, and helped prepare J.J.'s favorite foods. After eating they "moved to the living room," which was two steps from the kitchen table, for coffee and cake. Few people would act this way in this setting.

22   The comedy of "Sanford and Son" was based on the assumption that the characters lacked intelligence. It was a modern version of "Amos 'n' Andy," featuring outlandish (though often funny) plots and one-dimensional clown characters. Redd Foxx was a well-known stand-up comedian from the nightclub circuit. He had built up a strong following among black audiences. His material often featured racy, off-color humor with much profanity. Like Nipsey Russell, a comedian who played minor roles in other television programs and was Foxx's contemporary, and Richard Pryor, another major comedian from television and film, Foxx had used racial incidents as a basis for much of his satirical humor. When he was signed to play Fred on "Sanford and Son," black viewers anticipated and received the type of performances from Foxx that they expected, with some important alterations.

23   Fred Sanford was a stubborn bully who dominated others with his sharp tongue and ever-present anger. Sanford seemed to be angry at anyone who intruded on his turf, from his dead wife's sister to any nonblack who entered his domain, a junkyard where he and his son acquired and recycled society's discards. This series was not original to America, however. The story concept was imported from a popular British series entitled "Steptoe and Son." The American story lines were sometimes infused with African American cultural nuances, but the basic themes were created by white producers and writers, based on the British model. Again, viewers saw African American characters whose values and outlook were shaped and designed by outsiders to their culture.

24   As noted earlier, "The Jeffersons" began as a spinoff from "All in the Family." George Jefferson was cast in the mold of the freed, corrupt, black legislators of the film "Birth of a Nation," who were depicted as arrogant and idiotic. The audience is asked to laugh at Jefferson's antics and his basic insecurity without unconsciously making an association with his blackness. Obviously this is a difficult feat to accomplish. "The Jeffersons" dealt with middle-class strivers who happened to be black. When it was originally broadcast, the theme celebrated the arrival of the nouveau riche[14] black middle class. George Jefferson, characterized by producers as a loudmouthed braggart, spoke a great deal about "honkies" and "whities," while Louise, his wife, tried to appease him and smooth the ruffled feathers of others. Usually, the plots centered on George's attempts to climb the social ladder or make more money, with some note made of how difficult it was for those of African descent to move up in American society. The humor and warmth of the show often came from Louise's methods of controlling George and the problems he caused. Louise Jefferson, though submissive to a degree, exercised great influence over George because, no matter what the conflict, George was never right. Even in the early episodes, though George was recognized as having exceptional business acumen,[15] those skills were never transferred into his personal family relationships. This family was seldom portrayed as engaging in group activities or working toward a collective goal. In a 1983 article in the journal *Channels*, columnist William Henry noted that "The Jeffersons" appealed to white

---

13. vignette: a short tale

14. nouveau riche: referring to persons who have recently become rich

15. acumen: mental abilities

Americans because they represented African Americans who had "made it." "The Jeffersons" was the fulfillment of the American dream. Henry thought that viewers "yearned to believe that a social revolution had been won," and that this somehow freed white Americans from redressing any more grievances which African Americans might have said were due. He went on to argue that though George Jefferson was a counterpart to Archie Bunker, the distinct difference between the two men's situations made George a palatable character to white viewers. He noted that Archie was the master in his own home while George was not ("George's wife outmaneuvered, out foxed and out whoofed him, constantly"). Archie was taken seriously whereas George was not (other characters tried to reason with Archie about his bigotry, while George was ignored or laughed at), and Archie had the respect of his household, while George did not. For example, George constantly battled with his maid over who was really master. In the early years of "The Jeffersons," Lear developed George's character in the manner described above in an attempt to bring to viewers' consciousness some of the same social issues generated by the Archie Bunker character, seen this time through the eyes of a counterpart in the black community—George Jefferson. The Jefferson character, like Bunker, was a flawed person who tried to live life on his own terms, marching to his own drummer and subject to insecurities and human frailties. Lear thus attempted to make viewers empathize and identify with a black person similar in human strengths and failings to themselves. He succeeded with both characters, by touching the pulse of an America that had become jaded by post-Vietnam blues—partially because of ambivalent feelings about the conflict itself and partially because of their loss of faith in the country's leadership. Americans were no longer idealistic about the nation. Thus, Lear's comedies reflected a "tell it like it is" philosophy of life that featured imperfect characters and realistic problems.

25 A 1974 article by Eugenia Collier, a college professor and writer, entitled "Black Shows for White Viewers," compared two of the highly rated television series featuring African Americans in prime time. She concluded that" Sanford and Son" was appealing because viewers could laugh *at* weak people in order to feel good about themselves, whereas viewers of "Good Times" laughed *with* strong survivors. She argued that "Good Times" had appeal because of the universal attractiveness of protagonists pitted against strong outside forces that make courage, resourcefulness, and intelligence essential to survival. She believed that viewers were enriched, made wiser and more humane, by their experiences with "Good Times" but were diminished by their experiences with "Sanford and Son" because the latter program focused on the baser instincts—trickery, ignorance, naïveté, and mental aberration.[16]

26 "Benson" fit the pattern that scripted African American male characters as innocuous true-believers in the system, who supported, defended, and nurtured mainstream, middle-class American values, interests, concerns and even faults. Benson was thus an emasculated, non-threatening, "acceptable" black male. A spinoff from the highly successful series of the seventies, "Soap," the "Benson" series featured Robert Guillaume as Benson Dubois, a witty and quietly subversive but dependable confidant of the governor of some mythical state. Benson began the series as the head housekeeper but was later promoted to a position of Lieutenant Governor. According to sociologist Herman Gray, Robert Guillaume was "attractive and likeable, cool under pressure, and perhaps the quintessential[17] black middle class professional." The Benson character was the apex of all the servant and helping roles that black actors had played

---

16. aberration: deviation from what is normal

17. quintessential: characterized as the most perfect example

historically in television and the movies. There was, however, one major qualification—"Benson was uniquely modern—sophisticated, competent and arrogant! He openly maintained his integrity and his pride week after week [though] . . . the posture of servitude was maintained." In this sense, Gray believed, Benson represented the culmination of a white view of acceptable African American males.

27   The adoption of black male children into middle-class white American homes on television allowed creators opportunities to send conscious and subconscious messages to viewers about molding and controlling the minds and hearts of young African American males, possibly to make them more acceptable to whites. In the situation comedy "Webster," Emmanuel Lewis played the black adopted son of a white couple in a cross between a kid show and a family comedy. Like "Different Strokes," the hit NBC series with a similar theme, the subliminal[18] message the "Webster" series sent out was that black people did not involve themselves with their own people's children when their parents died. This circumstance could be seen as an advantage since white foster parents could then socialize the youngsters into the "real" American way. Even visits from grandparents or cousins, or any evidence of their concern about the youngsters' welfare, were not central to the theme of either of these two series during their first seasons. Beginning with the second season, Ben Vereen was featured as Webster's uncle, who vainly attempted to adopt the youngster and visited with him on occasion. In reality, however, the black extended family often had black women who reared generation after generation of other people's children —grandchildren, cousins, nephews and nieces, and so on—"because their own folks were gone or dead."

28   "The White Shadow," an earlier series that had aired from 1979 to 1981, had featured a white basketball coach/physical education teacher and his predominantly black high-school team. "The White Shadow," "Webster," and "Different Strokes" each treated the issue of race as peripheral, as the frame of reference for addressing other issues where race was simply another individual difference rather than a social or public issue. Race as a central theme of concern in American society was ignored or broken down into simplified components and then resolved with ease. Like early television series such as "East Side, West Side," usually the problems raised on television, even those involving African Americans and particularly evident in these programs, were resolved by a white male problem-solver.

29   The domestic family comedy "Gimme a Break" (1981) seemed to reflect a Reagan-inspired return to the Eisenhower era. The series continued the theme started by the proud but servile, cocky but nurturing, loyal mammies in the many Hollywood film classics and carried into the Eisenhower era by television's "Beulah." The star of "Gimme a Break," Nell Carter, first captured national attention in 1981 when she won four major awards (including a Tony) for her electrifying performance in Broadway's "Ain't Misbehavin'." From there, Carter landed a role as the rambunctious[19] Sergeant Hildy Jones in the television series "Lobo," which was quickly canceled. She had a continuing role in the daytime serial "Ryan's Hope" and played parts in three films—"Hair," "Back Roads," and "Modern Problems."

30   On "Gimme a Break," Carter seemed cognizant of the parallels between her character and other maids' roles black women had played when there were few options open to them if they wanted to practice their craft. She parodied[20] Butterfly McQueen's role in "Gone with the Wind" in one episode and defended her mammy-like role to a visiting friend (Addie, played by Telma

---

18. subliminal: below the conscious level

19. rambunctious: displaying unruly or wild behavior

20. parodied: humorously imitated a serious work

Hopkins) in another episode. Nonetheless, she continued in the role because it was a hit with crossover markets and because roles for African American women, scarce in all forms of mass entertainment, were especially hard to find in network television in the early 1980s. It was an achievement for an African American woman to land the lead role in a hit series, but there were a number of factors that prevented African American viewers from feeling comfortable with Carter's performance in the series. The opening song focused on the show's theme. Its lyrics, sung by the star, included the lines "Gimme a break. I sure could use it. I've finally found where I belong!!" Some asked if these words implied that African American women belonged in someone else's home, caring for other people's children, and neglecting their own lives?

31 In the series, Carter played a dominating mammy to the white children. As she was so ill-tempered and viewers might have been offended by her physical abuse of the white youngsters on the show, it appears that a decision was made to include Addie, as a foil for Nell's temper. Thus, on numerous occasions, Nell insulted Addie, yelled at her, and slapped her around. Addie often ducked when no punch was thrown because she was so used to the abuse. In one program, Nell went to court to beg the judge not to take "her babies" since she had promised their dead mother that she would raise them as her own. The judge decided against the children's aunt and in Carter's favor when Nell fell to her knees, crying and beseeching the judge to let her keep "her" children. For a young African American woman to fall to her knees obsequiously begging to continue in a servant's role on network television in the 1980s was astounding—particularly after the country had experienced the civil rights movement in the 1960s and 1970s, which had engendered much soul-searching about racial issues among thoughtful people, black and white.

32 Nell noted in one episode that Jonathan, Julie's new husband, had broken an irreplaceable knickknack that had been handed down to Nell by her grandmother, who had *immigrated* to this country on a slave ship. One cannot conceive of any thoughtful African American allowing such themes and lines to remain, as they obviously distort historical facts.

33 "Gimme a Break" followed the pattern set by a majority of African American comedies before it: it reflected mainstream beliefs and views, African American culture was not addressed, and the lead character was often irresponsible and childlike. Like "Beulah" from the 1950s, the mammy of "Gimme a Break" lacked the European-oriented sex appeal typical of American television, did not question her role as a servant, put her own life second as she fretted about the problems of her white employers, and could not be viewed as a fighter against the "system," who would want more for African American children than she had.

34 Carter's own strong personality was quite evident in the program, for Nell, the performer and character, was always in control. Even when the children's father, "the chief," was alive and actively involved in the story lines, Nell the character dominated him and everyone else. Loud, bossy, and "in charge" from the moment each episode began, Nell's own ethical code was obvious, but was juxtaposed[21] to a wide amoral streak that allowed her to lie and cheat when it suited her purpose, as the audience roared with laughter. The producers developed Nell as a person who was pragmatic, competitive, and manipulative but likeable and endearing, who was absolutely sure of her values—which were, of course, mainstream America's values. As with the African American comedies of the 1950s and 1960s, the producers did not allow the attention of viewers to stray to events related to racial problems. Nell was made to turn a deaf ear and a blind eye to the biggest issue evident at many turns in the series—the potential social divisiveness of the racial issue. Like most television

---

21. juxtaposed: placed side by side for contrast

programs of the period, this series brought no civil/social rights problems to weekly viewers. Nell nurtured and loved the white youngsters left in her care. The manipulations and domineering attitude were used only to help them in some way.

35 It appears, however, that Nell the performer exerted great influence during the production of the series. Her sense of timing, eye contact with viewers, number of shots focused on her body language, and the camera angles themselves showed a carefully planned and executed delivery of her personality to the audience. It is hard to believe that the producers and writers could have perfected this delivery without Carter's active, detailed involvement. Nell's flawless pacing and pregnant silences, accompanied by a telling glance, allowed viewers to share a secret with her at numerous points in the average show. Thus, although the producers, directors, and writers shaped the Nell character to their mainstream experiences, Nell was able to control aspects of her performances to convey a slightly different message from what was probably written on paper as the original intent. Had she chosen to do so, because of her powerful position, Carter could have infused more African American tradition, experience, and sense of pride and dignity into the series. Not just the star, she also had control over the unconsciously perceived meanings that went beyond the show's dialogue. Carter elected instead to maintain her distance from racial/social issues. Many black viewers were, at best, ill-at-ease with their feelings toward the series, for they viewed Nell Carter as very talented, but misguided. In fact, many middle-class African Americans made it a point never to watch the series.

36 Starring Marla Gibbs (formerly Florence, the maid on "The Jeffersons"), the series "227" of the mid-1980s developed a multi-dimensional, black female television presence. This family comedy had responsible leading characters, despite the trend of the preceding decades that had seen development of irresponsible leads for most African American comedies. Marla played Mary,

an urban apartment house tenant, whose husband and children formed a background for many of the show's plots. Usually Mary and her female neighbors interacted in story lines that followed themes of concern and interest to many women in the 1980's, regardless of race. Like Mary Tyler Moore of the 1970s, the "227" Mary represented everywoman, or what everywoman would like to be. Married to Lester, a construction company supervisor, a steady, reliable husband, and a devoted father, she was the mother of a typical teenage daughter. Mary was slim, well-groomed, and full of the wry wittiness that had endeared her to viewers of "The Jeffersons."

37 In "227" Jackie Haree's character, Sondra, was developed as one-dimensional in most episodes. The one joke surrounding her scenes involved her chasing or being chased by all types of men. However, Mary, Pearl, Rose, and even Sondra, at some point, had some scenes that showed different dimensions of their characters. Various episodes focused on serious concerns that the women addressed within the context of their friendships with each other.

38 Mainstream culture was reflected in most of the plots in the series as the women resolved their problems. For example, Rose and Pearl played supporting roles to Mary and Sondra, who were reminiscent of Mary and Rhoda of the "Mary Tyler Moore" show. Both Marys were straight, middle-class, somewhat do-good types. Sondra and Rhoda were both mavericks. They overtly refused to conform to the straight rules that guided the lives of their respective Marys, though they each recognized the norms and codes of society. In the episode "The Anniversary," for example, Sondra flirted with Mary's father and father-in-law and offered to bring a few extra men to the party as door prizes. She carried such acts off jestingly, suggesting that she was only half-serious and that she recognized how others were responding to her. She obviously enjoyed the attention she received, just as Rhoda enjoyed the responses she received to her unconventional ways of dealing with life. For the most part, although the show featured an all-

black cast, "227" did little to reflect aspects of African American culture. Thus it appealed to both mainstream and African American viewers, who rated it among the top twenty-five shows most weeks.

39 "Amen" premiered during the 1986–87 fall season. Sherman Hemsley (formerly George of "The Jeffersons"), cast as Deacon Ernest Frye of First Community Church, traded barbs with the young, attractive minister, Reverend Rueben Gregory, played by Clifton Davis (formerly the son, Clifton, on "That's My Mama"). Deacon Frye, a practicing attorney who appeared in court to defend clients from time to time, was a softened version of the strutting, posturing, loud-mouthed character Hemsley had played on "The Jeffersons." The main references to black culture were the music played during the opening and at transitional points in the show, the skin color of the characters, and the body language and jargon of some of the characters. Frye, for example, used the ghetto walk typical of many young men in the black inner city when he strutted about. He also bantered frequently with the sisters who served in numerous capacities in the church. On the other hand, the Reverend, often the straight man for Frye's witticisms and caustic remarks, exuded mainstream values. Much of the humor in the series was based on Frye's unconventional interactions with others. His irreverent attitude toward the Reverend and the sisters, for example, caused the audience to roar with laughter.

40 "A Different World" premiered in the fall of 1987. Created and produced by Carsey-Warner Productions, in cooperation with Bill Cosby, it originally featured Lisa Bonet, a young woman who had played one of Cosby's daughters in the series "The Cosby Show." Set in a historically black college atmosphere, the series developed the sparkling, bright-eyed talents of college-age youngsters in an ensemble[22] format. The show was placed on the network schedule to follow the number one–rated Cosby show. Thus, it im-mediately found its way to the list of top ten primetime television programs during the first part of the 1987–88 season. Concerned about Lisa Bonet's willfulness, Cosby brought in Debbie Allen as producer–director. Allen was remem-bered for her pithy,[23] brief role in the movie "Fame." Moreover, she had played roles on tele-vision in shows like "Good Times" and in televi-sion commercials for Excedrin, Nice 'N Easy, and Final Touch. She also had appeared on Broadway in "Purlie" and in road shows of "Raisin," "Guys and Dolls," "The Music Man," and "Sweet Char-ity." Her versatility and skills were demonstrated again and again as she danced and sang on tele-vision programs ("Stompin at the Savoy" with Ben Vereen) and played brilliant dramatic parts, such as her roles in "Roots" on television, and "Ragtime" in film.

41 Debbie Allen burst into American homes in the key role as Lydia in the television series "Fame," American audiences immediately liked her strong-willed, no-nonsense but sensitive, car-ing character. For a change, American television viewers saw a young, attractive, black female professional in the lead role in a continuing series that featured drama as well as music, dance, and comedy. When Cosby and Carsey-Warner tapped Allen as producer–director, it was one of the first times that an African American woman reached the decision-making level in network television, particularly with a primetime top ten–rated se-ries. Allen took "A Different World" in new di-rections. Musical sequences, dancing, dream se-quences, and the like figured in the new twists in the series. Her keen sense of what was authentic to the black collegiate atmosphere and to black culture was used to control plot development. (Allen had graduated from historically black Howard University in 1976.) One episode, for ex-ample, featured a "Step Show," where fraternities and sororities competed before an appreciative audience as they sang and danced in syncopated, African culture-based rhythms. Such events were

---

22. ensemble: a united group of performers

23. pithy: brief and forceful

a regular part of African American undergraduate sorority and fraternity social activities.

Critical Explorations: Reading

Having read the selection once, reread it, and answer the following questions as you do. These questions should provide you with more questions and insights about how television and society influence each other. Also in answering these questions, you will be able to consider the ways that you can effectively analyze and evaluate a television program of your own choosing. You may want to use your answers in your reading or dialogic journal.

1. In paragraphs 3–6, Dates argues that the Beulah character is stereotyped. What evidence does she provide for this point of view?

2. In paragraphs 13–15, Dates analyzes the Flip Wilson comedy show of the seventies. She believes that it provided a racist perspective of the African American. What evidence does she give for this point of view? Yet why does she contend that this program also appealed to African American viewers?

3. Reread paragraph 17. How is it that *All in the Family* was appreciated by both prejudiced and unprejudiced viewers?

4. Dates evaluates Nell Carter's character in the eighties comedy *Gimme a Break* (paragraphs 29–35). What are the positive and negative aspects of the Nell character? What criteria does Dates seem to be relying on in her evaluation of this character?

5. In paragraphs 40–41, Dates gives a positive review of the African American comedy *A Different World*. Infer the criteria that seem to underlie Dates's positive review of *A Different World*. Are these the same criteria that Dates would likely apply to any successful African American television program?

Selection 12

"Local News: Reality as Soap Opera"
Elayne Rapping

This selection is a provocative chapter from Elayne Rapping's book titled *The Looking Glass World of Nonfiction TV*. In her "Local News: Reality as Soap Opera," she carefully looks at the unstated assumptions of local news programming. She focuses on the topics that local news covers, the image that the broadcasters present, and the influence that this American image has on the news items themselves.

In this careful semiotic study, Rapping makes cogent inferences from the statements, gestures, and actions of those who create local news. In analyzing her conclusions, you may want to review the seven American beliefs treated in Chapter 1 and compare them to the beliefs that Rapping finds explain American local news programming.

This is a readable and enjoyable selection. Rapping has a focused thesis, and she provides ample evidence to support it. Determine what Rapping is saying about television news. Then note how she supports this view. Also consider what Rapping has to say about American capitalism. See how her attitude toward capitalism is related to her thesis.

Reading–Writing Preparation

Before you begin reading this selection, you may want to answer the following questions in writing or discussion:

1. What sorts of news topics does your local news station carry?

2. Are there any similarities between the newscasters on local news programs and the television personalities you watch in situation comedies and dramas?

Local News: Reality as Soap Opera

1   Local news was not always the jazzy package we have come to think of as "Happy News," "Eyewitless News" and "Newzak." In fact, local news, until recently, wasn't much of anything. Even national news was, until the early 1960s, a mere fifteen minute segment which affiliates were reluctant to carry because it was not a moneymaker. National news has always been a difficult thing to sell. An FCC[1] ruling requires that it be a regular programming feature, but it doesn't draw viewers well and has never warranted primetime scheduling. Even the special events and reports, which networks carry largely for prestige and to fulfill the "public interest" requirements of the FCC, lose money. Apparently, most people, most of the time, don't like to be educated or informed; after a hard day's work they prefer lighter fare, escapism, something that either numbs or stimulates intense emotions.

2   The expansion of national news to thirty minutes came about because of technical innovations at a time when public life was particularly dramatic. The 1960s were heady days for American news-watchers. The Vietnam War, violent police reactions to massive protests, ghetto riots, public figure assassinations, "all converged to attract nightly viewers in unprecedented numbers." The sophistication of the new TV technologies, especially the portable minicam which allowed live, on-the-spot coverage of breaking news, added to the appeal. So did the highly televisible space flights with their accompanying development of global satellite communications technology. Now major news stories from distant places, as well as the most mundane local fire or car accident, could be brought to audiences as they happened, in full, bold color.

3   Local news was the primary beneficiary of this technology because it enabled stations to turn trivial local events into sensational, colorful dramas. But there was another reason for local news' rise to prominence. By the 1960s, local news had become almost the only original programming produced by affiliates.[2] The networks had become so powerful that they had been able to produce and sell their own shows to affiliates very successfully. They offered an arrangement the locals could not refuse. In exchange for running nationally produced programs, rather than their own, affiliates received "compensation" from the networks. Since the local affiliates could sell their own spots in the network shows, the arrangement was both profitable and efficient. Affiliates no longer had to hire large production staffs and produce elaborate programs. They merely used nationally relayed material, which was slick and popular. Thus, local happenings became the only area which required local production.

4   Another factor in the rise of local news was its growing role in the evening's primetime schedule. Local news is, by default, the program which establishes the personality and tone, the "signature," for each local affiliate. Whatever the quality of the news team and its coverage, that is what viewers come to identify as the quality of

---

1. FCC: Federal Communications Commission

Elayne Rapping. *The Looking Glass World of Nonfiction TV.* Boston: South End Press, 1987, 43–60. Reprinted by permission of the publisher.

---

2. affiliates: local television stations that rely on programming from the network stations

the entire station. And whatever local news show develops the biggest audience is also the show which is most likely to carry its viewers with it through the rest of the evening's shows. Network news as well as the entire schedule of primetime programming for each network thus depend on the ratings of their affiliates' local newscasts. So do the affiliates own revenues for local commercials.

5   As a result of this importance, as early as the 1960s audience research specialists were hired to help in attracting audiences. Paul Klein, a brilliant analyst hired by NBC, came up with the concept of "Least Objectionable Programming." It was based on the insightful idea that audiences did not really "watch a program" so much as they "watched television." The handwriting was on the wall. The move from information to broadly appealing entertainment was a foregone conclusion.

6   The affiliates, sensing the rising appeal of news in general, as well as its pivotal importance in primetime ratings, began to think about the news more carefully. With their eyes fixed on greater profits, commercialization of local news was inevitable. As Ron Powers has said, "the TV newscast was a victim of its own success." Advertisers were quick to zero in on the growing audiences and were willing to pay higher rates for even bigger ones. How to deliver them? The answer came through the services of market research consultants. And when their services paid off more handsomely than anyone had anticipated, the future of TV news was a *fait accompli*. It was to be—in ways more profound and disturbing than anyone imagined—a commodity, a combination of various show business staples packaged and promoted like perfume or pet food.

7   In 1974, local use of media consultants hit the jackpot. NBC's New York affiliate was running a poor third in ratings. Compared to its 333,000 adult viewers, ABC had 697,000 and CBS a whopping 937,000. NBC hired some experts who, using standard marketing techniques, found they could gauge audiences' tastes and their attitudes

toward various news features and styles more effectively than the networks had dreamed possible. Seventeen months later, NBC's "News Center 4" was number one with 708,000 viewers to CBS' 696,000 and ABC's 610,000.

8   At that point "television news had become too important to be left to the newspeople." Marketing whiz kids and TV production experts began determining the content, look and delivery of what was supposed to be important political information and analysis. No expense was spared in what was quickly recognized as a near foolproof investment. Suddenly budgets went sky high. NBC built a $300,000 set, raised anchor Tom Snyder's salary to $500,000 a year and put a staff of 200—"the largest group anywhere putting out a news program, local or national"—to work. Local news had become big business, big show business to be exact.

9   Marketing research is a system developed to determine "what people want," but always within the limits of what the market is prepared to offer. Viewers participating in the research had their past experience to use as a guideline—not some ideal informational universe in which relevant, significant events were offered in a meaningful context. The choices presented by researchers necessarily reflected some variation of selections from within that range. Similarly, once the results of the research are put into practice, and ratings rise accordingly, viewers are not necessarily confirming that their needs have been met. They are merely confirming that as network news goes, they prefer the new arrangement to the old.

10   The researchers discovered that what viewers "chose" to see on local news—and increasingly, over time, on all news—wasn't more in depth reporting on politics or social issues. Far from it. They were dying for something which was not technically news or information at all. They wanted more human interest stories, more personable anchors who would communicate a sense of intimacy and warmth, more sports, more weather, more jazzy graphics and more on-

the-spot coverage of community events—no matter what they were. In a word, audiences wanted local newscasters to create for them a sense of "community."

11 If the results of these findings, in terms of news production, have at times seemed appalling, that is by no means because of "what people wanted," at least not in some absolute sense. The direction of local news reflects two facts about contemporary life and network TV. In the first place, it reconfirms the thesis of this book: the social role of television, in its broadest sense, is to provide that lost sense of community integrity in a fragmented world. That is a legitimate need and, to the extent that local news alone provides it, its popularity is justified. That this society needs to manufacture a synthetic version of community in this way is a reflection of its structural values, not its citizens. It is the economic drive of capitalism, after all, that subverted the homogeneous communities of the past. And it is capitalist economics, more than any human "want," that led to the particularly plastic version of "community" local news came to offer.

12 To provide "what people wanted," local news producers began to revamp their entire newscasts. Everyone needed a "media consultant"—it was not enough to have a general sense of what was wanted. Competition demanded specialists in creating sets, weather maps and other graphic aids. National trends began to emerge, as each station adopted a tried and true format established elsewhere. "Eyewitness News," "News Center 4," and so on, came to represent standardized sets and program formats seen all over the nation. Even some packaged, generic-style news items began to appear. Human interest and other light features are highly transportable in a society which has increasingly given up local color for the modern uniformity of mass-produced shopping malls, fast food chains and eight-screen movie complexes showing the same eight movies from Anchorage to Atlanta.

13 All of this is considered nonfiction. It pretends to present "reality" in the raw. But in truth it could hardly be further from reality. The superficially unique but essentially clonelike communities portrayed on local newscasts everywhere are utopian fantasies. They are Emerald Cities conjured up by the hidden Wizards of marketing research. They construct a false version of reality, a false sense of community and intimacy which, in many lives, must substitute for the real thing. That these Tinker Toy towns are taken at face value by most viewers, are embraced and smiled upon as their own, is a sadder commentary on American life than the much scapegoated media "sex and violence." For the "have schmaltz will travel" anchors that smile out at us from news desks and other cozy local spots are not journalists, strictly speaking, but rather paid performers, impersonating the friends and neighbors we all wish we had.

14 It is all too easy to condemn the audiences whose apparent attitudes and desires brought all this about. That, in fact, is the standard line we get from most educated people and indeed many media workers themselves. It is worth looking at the implications of this position. On the one hand, there is no question that the networks are in the business of manipulation and profiteering. They need to attract and hold audiences and they have found that the best way to do this is with this pseudonews. But if people enjoy and look forward to watching this stuff, it is not because they are stupid; it is because their immediate human needs are not being met elsewhere. What people in this country crave, and increasingly feel the absence of, is human intimacy and a sense of meaning in their lives. They are lonely, confused and increasingly terrified of what the world "out there" might have in store for them.

15 The lack of interest in hard news and analysis is in part attributable to this greater felt need for security and well being. But it is also a function of the educational institutions—of which the media is by now perhaps the most influential—through which we develop our ideas about the world. Functional illiteracy in America is a well known scandal. Even those who are "educated"

are not taught to see events in an historic context or to question the information they receive. When you put together the commercial, show biz style of TV generally, the lack of critical skills in the population at large, and the very real—almost heartbreaking—need for emotional and social gratification, you have a world readymade for the gift of Newzak.

A Day in the Life of Hometown, USA

16   Local news is now quite standardized. It is made up of a series of formulaic features organized in a way which prioritizes things for us. To scan the agenda and time allotments of the items featured on a typical local newscast is to see at a glance what a typical American day is supposed to have been like in Anytown, USA. I have selected, at random, an 11 P.M. Action Newscast from the ABC affiliate in Pittsburgh, on the night of September 26, 1984. First there was a report of a fatal car crash. Then a three year old "was found beaten to death." Then came the death of an eleven month old baby, possibly a result of neglect. A man, we heard next, was sentenced to twenty-five years for arson, followed by a report about a local county's budget problems. All this took four minutes. It was followed by a "teaser" for upcoming stories and a commercial break.

17   At 11:06:50 the national and international news began—with a noticeable local slant. First, and supposedly most important, a local speech by Anwar Sadat's widow was cancelled because of a bomb scare. Then came a quick report on the activities of the President, Secretary of State and Vice President—all of whom had spent their important days delivering speeches. After a quick report on a study of the dangers of tobacco, and another commercial, we were ready, at 11:13, for the sports segment which ran over six minutes—as compared to the seconds-long reports on political and social matters.

18   After the sports came a report on the beginning of the Jewish New Year, a report on the lottery winners, and a commercial break preceded by a teaser for the weather report. The weather itself, second in time-measured importance only to sports, ran for over five minutes. It included footage of the weather reporter's visit to a local grade school that day, complete with pictures of the signs made by the kids—"The Weatherman Cares"—and the refreshment table, jello molds and all. Finally the anchor told cute story about tourists stealing sherry glasses from an English Earl and said good night.

19   With a variety of other similarly earthshaking options, this is what local news does. It sends us off to bed with certain images, ideas and attitudes dancing in our heads. First there is local catastrophe, the more heartrending the better. Kids in need of organ transplants are often featured in the early minutes, along with pleas for money and/or donors. Lately, reports on missing children have also become big news. Any story in which warm feelings combine with dramatic visuals is a shoe-in. Pets stuck in trees, or kids falling into wells are always hot. They allow for sympathy and for a chance to show our local fire fighters and law enforcers on the job, being heroic, making our neighborhoods safe and happy. Whatever national news is shown is usually locally oriented and, if possible, sensational too. Big names are featured doing ceremonial things. If there is a bomb scare, all the better. The local heroes are on the job again.

20   This series of disasters and tragedies may not seem particularly cheering at first glance, but given the realities of modern life, it presents a picture that is in many ways reassuring. In fact, the world it presents to us is remarkably like the fictional world of daytime soap opera. There is a preponderance[3] of trouble and disaster, to be sure; but the trouble and disaster take time-bound, physical forms. The tragedy is always personal, not political, even in the major national news items. It takes the form of illness, natural catastrophe and human failure of a very per-

---

3. preponderance: superior power, force, or number

sonal, immediate kind. The father who beats his child is, by the very fact of his deeds having been reported, already taken into custody. And if the missing child, the child in need of an organ transplant, the victim of fire, are in very bad—even terminally bad—shape, it is not the fault of society or the political system. On the contrary, to the extent that local or national officials enter the picture, they are seen as heroes, good guys—not by dint of any political virtues, but because of their official status. The implication is that given disaster and tragedy in our community, more often than not, there are good professional father figures around inventing new surgical procedures, putting criminals and child abusers where they belong, saving family homes from fire.

21 The very ways in which social leaders are portrayed is reassuringly apolitical and noncontroversial. Speeches, acts of derring do[4] and so on, have no political, social or historic context or implication. Local news, again like soap opera, makes no judgments about issues, except an occasional emotional endorsement of "Democracy" and repudiation of "Communism." It omits any historic or social background information to tie personal events—and even national speeches by individual leaders are personalized—together or make them part of a larger social world. It moves from visually sensational or heart stirring image to image quickly, with each report separated from the other by breaks. Overall, it provides a sense that the average citizen, as victim, patient, frightened worker or homeowner, is important, is cared about and cared for.

22 Local news stations do deal with larger, more ongoing social issues in their own way. But it is not a way which leads to deeper understanding or raises any kind of question about differing policies or strategies for solving such problems. Rather, the ways of solving social problems on local news are wholly in keeping with the ways of solving private problems. From time to time, spe-

cial reports are run on recurring problems. If there has been a rash of rapes, teen suicides or the like, locals will often run a series of brief reports on the topic. Incest, teen sexuality and other sexually titillating topics are particularly popular. Mostly, they are nothing but interviews with victims and local experts in the field. A director of a shelter for battered women may say a few sentences about the number of cases and the gory details of the typical situations. Footage of crying children, bandaged women and—if all else fails—the exteriors of family homes is *de rigueur.*[5]

23 These special reports are usually run during the sweeps seasons to boost ratings at the time when advertising rates are set. When media consultants are brought in, the topics covered can be pretty flimsy. "Bikini fashions" was a hit in one city. A series on "Super Rats" sighted around town actually boosted a Chicago station's audience by 30,000 homes. "We thought it was a joke," said one of the reporters involved. While media experts tend to believe that the popularity of this kind of thing "brings out the worst in human nature," there is more to it than that. This, after all, is just the kind of thing people in a small, close knit community would talk about quite naturally. It is only because of the atomization[6] and impersonality of most cities that we do not normally have these discussions, even when the situation at hand is one that affects an entire community. People often do not know their neighbors anymore, and may even be hostile or fearful of them. Local TV, by acting as neighbor substitute and telling us this kind of story, may not be giving us the news, but it is giving us something we don't get anywhere else and would naturally find interesting or at least useful for small talk.

24 Another feature of local news which is both disheartening and understandable is the increasing use of prepackaged items distributed by

---

4. derring do: daring deeds

5. *de rigueur:* strictly required

6. atomization: reducing into smaller and smaller parts

independent producers or the networks. While the independent items are generally used as fillers on slow nights, the network packages are different. They are produced and distributed so the affiliates can publicize, through popular local newscasts, the network's other programming. As competition from cable and video cassettes impinges on network entertainment audiences, it has become common for the networks to send affiliates whole series of pseudo-promotional clips to be run as news. Most typically, a "report" on a sitcom or soap opera will air, accompanied by guest appearances by stars, or even appearances by newscasters in the shows themselves.

25 This serves two purposes. First it helps boost the shows. But more interestingly, it adds to the personalization of the newscasters, to their transformation from journalists to show business personalities. There they are, acting out a fantasy viewers can only dream of—mingling with popular stars and appearing as actors on television. Never mind that they are already more actors than information gatherers. This ploy intensifies and glamorizes a process which is not consciously understood by most viewers, but which is perhaps the most important ingredient in the success of local news.

26 On another level, of course, there is a great deal of public awareness of much of what I have just described, although not in any coherent, systematic context. And the media itself, in its other forms, often satirizes and criticizes the excesses of news trivialization. Recently, one of the networks aired a very good TV movie about the dangers of sensationalizing the news, and the moral and social issues the practice raises. This is where television acts in its most healthy capacity. The tendency of TV movies to individualize and limit issues is always present, but the process of consciousness raising is nonetheless begun.

27 Late night TV comedy has always been the domain in which social satire flourishes best, and TV news has often been its target. As early as the 1960s, "That Was the Week That Was" began mocking TV news as a genre. HBO's current "Not Necessarily the News" updates the effort. In fact, the best TV comedy today—"Second City TV" and "David Letterman" for instance—takes its humor from its knowing "defrocking" of the hallowed traditions of its own medium. The demise of "Saturday Night Live" was probably in part attributable to its failure to focus on a salient[7] aspect of the social world and mock it. Its best features, in its early days, were its parodies of classic TV genres. That it is now the media itself that most demands satiric comment is a reflection of the "looking glass" hypothesis: that social reality, as we experience it, comes largely through the mediated glass of network convention.

Howdy, Neighbors!

28 If satiric take-offs on TV news have focused mostly on newscasters themselves, it is because the personalities of these people, "the news teams," as they are euphemistically[8] called, are the dominant elements of the genre and the biggest factors in the ratings wars. Most local newscasters have had no experience in print journalism. They were trained and hired to do what local new does: create a sense of "family." So important is this role that local newspeople have become marketable commodities. No longer do they hail from the cities they report on, and pretend to be a part of. They move from town to town in search of the bigger buck, the bigger market, the bigger chance to hit the TV bigtime. "They circulate through the ranks of the farmleague stations on their way to the majors with maximum fanfare." You only need to check the trade paper, *Variety,* to see what has happened. Each week, space is devoted to the moves and salaries of local newscasters. Anyone with appeal will move from Omaha to Denver to Washington

---

7. salient: extremely noticeable

8. euphemistically: using language in a mild and indirect fashion

so fast they will have no time to learn the local landscape, slang or dialect. Newscasters even have agents to negotiate their salaries and career moves.

29   In order to capitalize on, and increase, the sense of family closeness and community solidarity which the news team is supposed to reflect, stations now regularly hire ad agencies to create very elaborate, almost sitcom-like ads for their crews. They are seen doing their shopping, visiting their grandmothers, tending their babies and so on. They are tracked to the bank, the local diner and the Little League in order to promote their local roots and "just folks" personalities. An anchor who has just barely unpacked will say "I love my neighborhood" to attract viewers. And during the sweeps season, when the ratings are monitored, the stations go all out to do more and more of what works best—colorful, emotion-charged stories full of sensational visuals and community spirit.

30   There are anchors who cannot pronounce the English language, much less names and cities of other cultures. There are anchors who cannot read a sentence and make it seem as though they understand their own words. And these people may be the most popular. Grooming, dress and the all-important ability to interact in a chummy way with the other reporters and exude cheeriness and charm are what producers look for. After all, with a script full of half-minute hard news stories stuck between mountains of shocks and tearjerkers, the only reactions really needed are horror, pity and sentimentality.

31   The advancement of women into anchor spots has been heralded as a victory for feminists. Certainly there is truth in this. The change in the newscaster image, from the fatherly authority of Walter Cronkite to the informal sister-brother camaraderie of today's local and national teams is one of the many salutory effects of feminism on the mass media. It is also one of the most dramatic illustrations of the often kinky workings of hegemony. On the one hand, even that bastion of male privilege, "60 Minutes," has

introduced a woman, Jessica Savitch, to the team. And Barbara Walters' position of prominence in the news world would have been unthinkable a decade ago. On the other hand, the image projected by these women is not exactly a model of feminist dignity. And the worst of the negative features foisted[9] upon women newscasters is seen in local news.

32   It is difficult to sort out the convoluted minglings of the demands of feminism and the marketplace in discussing women on the news. For if, on the one hand, women newscasters—like women in every field—must be faster, brighter and more aggressive than their male counterparts, they must also conform to an image of femininity which is saturated with negative stereotypes. Women anchors are invariably young, pretty and ever-smiling. Since they are meant to perform as good neighbors and family members, they mimic the most traditional female versions of those roles. They coo at babies, cluck at naughtiness, sigh emotionally at stories of human tragedy.

33   The case of Christine Craft, the thirty-eight year old local anchor who brought suit against her ex-employer on grounds of sex discrimination, explains it all. Craft was let go because, among other things, she did not take enough care of her appearance and failed to show "deference" to males. The attractive, personable woman won her case, although it was appealed and is still unresolved. But the contradictions in local news shows brought out in the case were enlightening. For it is not only women, but men too, who have been "feminized" by Newszak.[10] Good journalism is in fact a matter of aggressiveness and integrity, not deference or grooming. But since ratings and human interest, not truth, are most valued in local news, show business standards overtake those of journalism. And show business

---

9. foisted: forced upon

10. Newszak: a pun on Muzak, or news that has no character to it

is built on charm and affability. For women, this translates into an image too close to "sweet young thing" for comfort. For men, it comes across as "good old boy." In both cases, it reflects a move from the "watchdog" role of professional, independent journalists to a more entertainment-oriented image of the untroubled Yuppie enjoying his or her lifestyle.

34   In the process of creating the "team," local news has followed another trend set by dramatic series—presenting an image of the family in which authority figures are downplayed, while youth and equality are stressed. Sitcoms have long projected this view of family life. Father has not known best in TV families for a long time now. More often, as in "Family Ties" and "All in the Family," it is the youngsters, more in tune with social reality and often more sophisticated and intelligent, who shine. Bumbling old Dad, with his outdated ideas about life, is the butt of many jokes on TV. (The popularity of "The Bill Cosby Show" may reflect popular discomfort with this trend and a return to patriarchal dignity.)

35   As a trend, the elimination of the strong father figure, and his replacement with a group of palsy-walsy kids who get along fine without him, is at the heart of the news team concept. Expertise and authority are less and less centered in the home, after all. And a family living the good life presented on TV is in fact caught up equally in the concern with youthfulness, fun and being "with it." And so, while Dan Rather and Ted Koppel still affect a patriarchal kind of authoritativeness, the local teams, reflecting personal life and private values, share in the playful, egalitarian[11] image of family life projected by commercials. Sometimes—often, actually—a team will burst into theatrical giggles when a line is flubbed. This collective cracking up emphasizes the childishness of what's going on, the playfulness and the element of leisure activity. Needless

to say, such behavior would be unseemly in a serious analysis of the arms race. But such material is not found on local news.

36   In place of old fashioned journalism, local news inserts interpersonal relations, jokes and teasing. "Where did you get that jacket?" says a woman anchor to the weatherman—who has developed a reputation for slightly out of the ordinary attire. Or perhaps we hear about someone's failure to change her snow tires or stick to his diet. Just like you and me, we think, as we smile warmly to ourselves.

37   The actual coverage of events, and choice of stories, reflects these human, neighborly criteria for news. In fact, the media—especially local news—have become a kind of substitute for all the things a good society is supposed to provide, but which our society dramatically lacks. We live in a world in which social service agencies are underfunded, inefficient and often cruel and insensitive. The police and the courts are filled with corruption and bias in their enforcement of "justice." The sense of community has been replaced by a plastic, nationally uniform series of commercial enterprises. Do you need child care? You won't find much in the way of public assistance and what is available is expensive and corporately owned and managed. Do you worry about the dangers of drugs and violence for your kids? The streets and schools are full of both and there is little being done about it. Government agencies are often as not in on the take or responsible for the violence.

38   But when you turn on the local news, it's a different world entirely. There you see any number of encouraging and reassuring things. The pretty reporter who jokes with the weatherman every day is right there in front of City Hall, or the local prison, keeping us informed of the latest development in a scary situation. The robber is just now being apprehended, she'll assure us. The city council is carefully considering bills to stop drug traffic, to tighten up regulations for child care licenses, to bring more jobs to our city. We ourselves might be frightened to go out and

---

11. egalitarian: characterized by the belief in the equality of all people

observe these things—especially with the media so eager to scare us to death about street violence—but we know if "our Mary" is on-the-spot, it cannot be too bad for too long.

News Teams as Public Servants

39 Serious city council debates on troublesome issues do not in fact bring results very often. So, besides reassuring us that things are being "considered," local newscasters have another, even more important job. As the world and its problems worsen, and the proposed plans to make things better fall by the wayside and are forgotten, the media has become the primary source of its own "good news." It is no exaggeration to say that most of what passes for good news—as opposed to reports that our officials are on the job, working on solutions to social problems—is manufactured by local news stations themselves. More and more, local news stations have been taking their responsibilities as agents of the public interest seriously. News stations and crews are responsible for any number of campaigns and programs to solve community problems.

40 The sign in the grade school lunchroom announcing "The Weatherman Cares" is a symbol of the main role of local TV. It presents an image of an institution—the media itself—that is wholly concerned with us and our needs. Newspeople now traditionally visit schools, lead parades, head charity drives and open malls—all in the name of public interest. In any city you visit you will find that each network affiliate has its own little do-gooder bailiwick. One may focus on collecting food for the unemployed and homeless. One may provide information for returning veterans. One may provide health information.

41 This trend began with the now standard "Action Line" segments in cities everywhere. People, desperate for help in solving everyday problems, took to calling their local TV stations for advice and information. From there it was a quick move to the institutionalization of a special feature in which anyone with a problem calls a certain number and talks to the person in charge of that beat. Say the garbage on your street has been sitting there for weeks, attracting rats and looking generally grotesque. Call "Action Line" and the newscaster will put in a special call on your behalf to the appropriate agency. In a flash your problem is solved. Then you will find yourself on the evening news telling your story to other sufferers of governmental neglect.

42 This is a technique which President Reagan has used with great success. Single out one person, solve her or his problem, and then announce to the world that the system works. Never mind that it took clout to do the job for which every citizen pays taxes. Never mind that one case means nothing in the scheme of things. The point is that help is available, caring and effective. No need to organize, protest or—perish the thought—change any institutional structures or power relations. In fact, one result of this technique is to individualize the whole concept of social problem solving. While giving us a sense of belonging to a cohesive, caring community, it also reinforces the sense that each problem is unique and personal and must be solved on a case by case basis.

43 When this technique took off, stations recognized a real gold mine of viewer loyalty and commercial revenues. And since the world is getting harder and harder to deal with anyway, it was inevitable that bigger problems and bigger media extravaganzas would soon arrive. Following in the tradition of the TV marathon for charity, the stations began running lengthy broadcasts devoted to one particularly serious community issue. Typical issues treated in several-hour long, or even whole day, marathons are those which first speak to local concerns and crises, and second, have great emotional appeal. The plight of Vietnam vets, for example, might be treated as a day long "workshop" in which local news teams and public officials participate.

44 This "group effort" image is one of the most important aspects of this kind of program. It adds to the image of the station as a caring, effective community institution. The hitch is that the

TV crews can do nothing beyond publicizing, and exaggerating, the existing programs and agencies and their effectiveness in "solving problems." In fact, these problems have deep social, historic and political causes. They arise because we live in a society which does not provide needed services and benefits for those on the bottom, those who have the least opportunity and are therefore most often exploited—a perfect description of the Vietnam vets. But the day long attention to their "problems" gives the false impression that this society is functioning in a healthy, just way.

45   One of the most common issues to be treated in this way recently is unemployment. No fewer than sixty cities have in the last few years run lengthy primetime extravaganzas called "Job-a-thons." These shows, sponsored by local stations in areas hard hit by unemployment, are paradigms[12]—almost parodies, really—of what local news is all about. Following the charity marathon format, they pretend to be offering a vital service: a "job exchange." The entire news team is on hand to facilitate the event. Publicity begins early and is relentless, leading anyone with a problem finding work to anticipate the day with great hope. First, every possible employer in need of workers lists openings, complete with job description, requirements and pay. Then everyone seeking work is invited to come on the show and give her or his story and work qualifications. Viewers—both employers and jobseekers—can also call in to offer jobs and request interviews for those listed.

46   This format—part "Queen for a Day," part cattle auction—is both dishonest and exploitative. First of all, the jobs listed are almost invariably minimum wage dead ends that no one else wants. Some are downright Dickensian in their demands. A position as the sole live-in "counselor" at a halfway house for delinquent and addicted teenagers is typical. Most of the opportu-

nities are of the custodial nature, and many are very short term. The "applicants" for these positions are often positively tragic. Most are highly qualified for much more meaningful work. They are people laid off from good jobs, with families to support, and are forced, through sheer desperation, to parade themselves before the TV audience, dressed in their best and nervously trying to make a good impression as they tell their stories. What should elicit outrage brings pity. The always smiling newscasters look dutifully sympathetic and concerned—as they do about everything else they report on. The experience is humiliating and, worse yet, largely useless. In Pittsburgh, one of the hardest hit cities economically, 4,600 people, many with advanced degrees and special skills, applied for about 1,500 jobs. Only 300 fulltime jobs were filled. Almost all were far beneath the talents of their applicants. In Milwaukee, 860 jobs were offered. Of 2,800 applicants, 460 found jobs. Most were with food chains.

47   The sheer number of offerings and ringing phones, seen and heard on the TV screen, give the impression that there is a lot happening, that people are being helped out of seemingly hopeless situations, that a huge social problem is being solved. This impression comes almost entirely from the visual and dramatic format of the programs. The hosts seem to be sweating away, aching hearts in throats, in the interest of the poor souls they exploit as they comfort. Soup kitchens are shown feeding smiling children. Volunteer health care workers describe free health care. Never mind that in reality these institutions are few, understaffed and very limited in the services they are able to provide. It looks impressive on TV. Periodically, local politicians come on or call in to applaud the effort and pledge their support (whatever that means). President Reagan himself called in to the "Virginia Job Day" program. And why not? That is just the sort of "safety net" he loves—one which gets lots of media coverage and almost no meaningful results.

---

12. paradigms: examples or models

48 The society at large is clearly not dealing with the problem of unemployment, or health care, or illiteracy, or any other widescale social crisis affecting the poor, the disabled, the minorities of the country. Nothing vaguely related to the real causes of structural unemployment, or any other social crisis, ever comes up in these shows. There is no analysis of historic causes, no economic analysis, no attempt to look for broad solutions to endemic[13] problems of capitalism. Instead, out of a few bad jokes, crocodile tears and completely misleading images of activity and progress, the viewer is led to believe that no matter what might befall you in these United States, help is just around the corner.

49 So successful have these features become that many stations take on long term commitments to their pet social crises. The station that ran the Job-a-thon in Pittsburgh has continued to collect food for the unemployed on weekends. Each week you see your local favorites—out of their tailored suits and dressed in jeans and parkas—going out to various town centers to personally collect canned goods from viewers and load them onto trucks. Such is the job of a TV reporter. Not only do these people fail to report news, they often collude[14] in increasingly important ways with the corporations and government agencies responsible for the policies that create these problems. This is because they tend to create a false sense that society is in fact working more effectively than is the case to solve problems. Where collective agitation to demand government action might be a more useful response to a crisis, those who might protest are led to believe the issue is being resolved, that no further action is necessary. In this sense, the media have become an indispensable part of the established power structure, ameliorating anxiety and defusing mass anger.

---

13. endemic: peculiar to a particular group or people
14. collude: to act together in a secret understanding

The Real News:
Game Cancelled Because of Rain

50 As dramatic as these special marathons are, they are obviously not what keeps people watching local news every day. What makes up the bulk of the nightly newscasts are sports and weather—issues of no social import at all. Each of these segments runs far longer than any hard news story, no matter how earth shaking. The allocation of time for these segments is based on the findings of market analysts. It was sports and weather, in particular, that viewers were interested in having expanded. Over the years, this has been happening almost on a daily basis. Anyone returning from a trip of any length at all will notice at least minor embellishments to the weather and sports reports. Maps of various aspects of the weather proliferate endlessly. And sports reports are continuously being changed, and changed again, in efforts to make even more attractive what is already the highlight of the broadcast.

51 Sports and weather may be the most vacuous things on the air. They provide little in the way of real information, and what is presented is nearly drowned in glitz. Sports news is the most repetitious and non-analytical thing on TV. There is no sense that economic or social factors come into play in the sports world. On the contrary, the typical sportscast is predictable to the point of self-parody. Athletes are interviewed about a game coming up or just played. The questions and answers are always the same. "How do you think you'll do this season, Bud?" "Well, gee, we're just gonna get out there and give it our best and all," is recognizably typical. (Actually, it is the prototype of most TV interviewing. "How do you feel about your daughter's murder?" "Well, it's hard to put into words. We're just broken up about it." Pointless questions and obvious answers are the stuff of TV "reporting.")

52 The appeal of these reports cannot be understood in terms of news criteria. It is the very desire to escape from "news," from the pressures

of social reality and personal woes, that draws viewers to sports and weather. In that sense, the blurring of entertainment and information creates a situation in which critics, puzzling over entertainment presented as news, may be missing the point. It is because sports is so universal a form of "fun" and relaxation for Americans that it is so talked about and watched. It provides needed "play" after a busy day.

53   That sports seems to be news is related to the role of sports teams in community identity. If football is fun to watch, rooting for a home team is a more significant pastime. It provides one of the strongest forms of community "glue" left to us. There are few activities—none in collective daily life—that provide that sense of belonging and sharing that sports do. In workplaces, where competition and tension rule, the time spent talking about local teams is a welcome respite from the anxiety and hostility of other activities.

54   The weather report plays a similar role. Even those who don't like sports must discuss and concern themselves with the weather. It too binds us together as a community; it too is a common element of our collective daily life. When personal problems—money fears, sexual anxieties—plague us, we often hide them from others. With the weather, we really do share them. That is an important social fact. An interview with Phil McHugh, of the media consultant firm McHugh and Hoffman, explained some of the reasons for emphasizing weather on local news. The interview took place in 1974, at a time when weather was only, on average, about three and one-half minutes of the newscasts. In ten years it has just about doubled. According to McHugh, "People are very much interested in weather. They plan their life around it . . . the mass audience, the people who have to go to work for a living . . . all the mothers want to know how to dress their kids for school."

55   The elaborate, sometimes downright gorgeous graphics used to show us everything we could conceivably want to know about the weather are interesting examples of the way in which television's visual sophistication has improved its ability to provide this kind of shared intimacy and personal advice. Because there are so many different maps and radarscopes available, the weatherperson can stay on screen, saying nothing much, for a very long time. Weather people are usually the homiest, wittiest (actually silliest in most cases) and most informal members of the news team. They are often loved by community members, who will choose a particular news station as much for the weatherperson as anything else. If there is no one at home to commiserate with about the eight days of rain we've just had; no one to complain to about having to cut the grass, miss the softball game; or whatever may happen, we still have good old Bill What's-His-Name to share it with. He understands just how we feel. He too forgot his umbrella, or had to shovel his walk four times in one week.

56   That these weather reporters are in some sense informing us of a phenomenon which has all the trappings of science produces interesting side effects. For one thing, the sexy blondes who reported weather in the 1950s have gone the way of all such blatantly sexist stereotyping on local news. Men do most weather reports, and the women who do it are all business. In that sense, weather and women have made progress toward respectability. But on another level, the pseudo-scientific mystification produced by the sets and charts is excessive. It reflects another trend in media toward taking authority away from us and putting our fates in the hands of scientific experts who are knowledgeable about things beyond our comprehension. Science and pseudoscience are the delights of television, for they justify so much that is done to us and for us. The folklore and finger knowledge that Grandma used often worked after all. She didn't need TV to tell her what nature was up to. While there are positive elements to this trend, it also creates one more area of daily life over which we have lost control and forgotten how to use our common sense.

57   In essence, all these aspects of local news combine to create a feeling of family for those who have none, and for those who have little in common with the one they do have. In so doing they reinforce the corporate definition of family relations too. As one TV station promo promised: "It's not like watching news, it's like watching family!" And it is a family more to your liking than the one you may be stuck with at that. There is a phrase that has gained currency among TV folk lately: "Reality Programming." It is the industry term for the phenomenon signalled by the success of local news—the fact that more and more people seem to prefer nonfiction to fiction on TV. They watch local news in the same spirit that they watch soap operas—in an effort to feel some intense, ongoing human drama in which no matter how bad things may get or seem, there is always a silver lining, an upbeat ending, a hero to solve the problem or at least explain it. They get that from local news. But it is in many ways a more dangerous addiction than the soaps. Soaps after all are—for all but the borderline psychotic—clearly unreal. Local news, on the other hand, is presented and accepted as all too real. What it tells, what it leaves out, how it explains and solves problems, have a lot to do with the way people have come to understand and respond to their daily experience. And yet local news is every bit as much a creation, a fiction, a story as a soap opera. Its characters are playing roles, its stories are distorted and falsified versions of life, and its values are those of the people who make the decisions governing our lives, not our own.

Critical Explorations: Reading

Having read this selection once, read it again with the following five questions in mind. The answers to these questions will help you determine the unstated assumptions that Rapping believes drive local news in America. You may want to use these answers in your reading or dialogic journal.

1. In paragraph 9, Elayne Rapping refers to how marketing research determines "what people want." Why does she place this phrase in quotation marks? Does the viewer really determine what he or she wants to see?

2. Rapping's thesis is that local news provides a sense of community for its viewers. Reread paragraph 13, and describe the sort of community that local news creates. What are Rapping's objections to this television community?

3. Reread paragraph 20. What sorts of tragedies does local news present? What American beliefs underlie these tragic stories? To answer the question, you may want to refer to the seven beliefs examined in Chapter 1.

4. In paragraphs 46–49, Rapping discusses how local news is involved in its community's unemployment problems. Why does she consider this activity dishonest?

5. Comment on the title of Rapping's chapter. How is local news like soap operas?

Critical Explorations: Writing

Choose one of the following five questions to answer in a formal essay. Show drafts of your essay to peers and to your instructor. In drafting your essay, feel free to use any of the material in this chapter and in Chapter 1 or 2—information from the introductions and the twelve reading selections. Each of these questions asks you to apply analysis and inference to the details of the program you choose to write about. You are also asked to use your abilities to sequence a narrative and to evaluate both the story line and the characters in the television program that you select.

1. Choose a television show, either a situation comedy or drama, and analyze it—its story line and characters. Then evaluate it. That is, in what ways is the story line engaging or predictable, and in what ways are the characters believable or stereotyped? You may want

to use parts of the Dates selection as a guide for your treatment of character.

2. Analyze a television program that either focuses entirely on a minority issue or that has one or more minority characters in its cast. Discuss the story line and the characters in this program. Do these characters effectively portray the minority in question, and does the story line accurately depict a social issue or issues that this minority faces? Or do you see problems with the characters and the story lines? You may want to use parts of the Dates selection as a guide to analyze character and to examine the social problems that the program introduces.

3. Analyze a local news program that you normally view on television. Consider the topics that the program covers on a particular night and the personalities who broadcast the news. Does your analysis support Rapping's thesis that local news provides a sentimental sense of community? Or does your news program present a different American belief or beliefs?

4. In the introduction to this chapter, you read about the influence that sponsors have in shaping the character of the shows they sponsor. Choose a prime-time television program, and analyze the story line and characters. Then examine the commercials that sponsor the program to see what American beliefs seem to explain them. Do these beliefs agree or disagree with the beliefs that are represented in this television show?

5. In Selections 9 and 10, the authors present differing points of view on television. Postman assumes that television has a negative effect on a child's learning, whereas Aufderheide suggests that music videos are artistic visual expressions. Summarize the positions each television interpreter takes, and provide the best evidence they give for their positions. Then determine where you stand on this question: Is television an intellectually destructive or an artistic medium? Or is it a bit of both? Provide compelling evidence for your argument, and compare it to Postman's and Aufderheide's.

Student Writing

Below you will find a student's response to a television situation comedy.
It is his second draft. Read the draft carefully; then answer the questions that follow.
Marco responded to the following topic:

Select a television program that you consider successful. List and explain those criteria that seem to characterize successful television characters and story lines. Then apply these criteria to specific moments in the program that you have selected.

Grace Could Save Us All

1   Since the beginning of its popularity in the fifties, television programming has always been ripe with signs pertaining to the American system of beliefs and values. Television serves as a sort of two-way mirror into the social institutions of family, gender, equal opportunity, and the happy ending. On the one hand, it provides us with a set of norms and standards which influence us by our observation of them. On the other hand, it bows to our expectations as a viewing

audience, visually representing ideas that we dictate. This symbolic relationship between life and television creates for the critical viewer a waist deep source of social commentary.

2   The situation comedy, which is perhaps the most formulaic of any programming genre due to its twenty-two minute time constraint, is especially unique in this sort of analysis. The setting, the narrative, and the characters all convey certain messages, and provide excellent criteria for the evaluation of a program. It is important to note that a distinction should be made between a "good" television show and a "relevant" one. A program can be subjectively labeled as "good" simply because it is entertaining, and yet be utterly devoid of strong characters, meaningful dialogue, or unique settings. A "relevant" program is one that possesses all of these things, and in using them, displays a willingness to comment on socially aware topics. The question of whether or not a program is relevant is not usually a matter considered by a casual viewer, but in most cases, the distinction is obvious. Some shows today have taken these considerations and turned them into the core of their programming.

3   One that accomplishes this well is *Grace Under Fire*, a program about a single mother (Grace) with two children and a full-time job. In any given episode, there are evidences of the changes that this country is undergoing in its ideology. The situations that abound in this program present a version of American life that is a far cry from the stuffy patriarchal images of *Father Knows Best* and *Leave It to Beaver*. *Grace Under Fire* provides us instead with more realistic images of family hardships. Grace is employed at an oil refinery, where she is surrounded by men and works as a woman in their world. The job serves as an indication that equal opportunity can be obtained by those who seek it. The Beaver's mother, June Cleaver, rarely left the kitchen from early morning until the dishes were washed after dinner. Her portrayal represented part of the nearly archaic idea that the father and husband is the one who provides for the household, and that

the woman's place is to maintain it. Grace is not only the breadwinner of the family, she cooks, cleans, and cares for her children without a man in the house at all.

4   Many situation comedies that air today derive their angles from families and family situations. This is perhaps the most popular setting because it appeals to a wider range of television audience age demographics. A show such as *Seinfeld* may fail to entertain younger viewers because of its adult oriented content, whereas a show such as *The Simpsons* appeals to an entire family of television viewers on their own level. These shows have members of their families with which each member of a television viewing family can identify. In the recent past, however, some programs have abandoned nuclear families altogether and presented to the public alternative versions of the family. In *Grace Under Fire*, Grace's ex-husband Jimmy is no longer a member of the household, although he does appear as a character in some episodes. He is missing from her television family because he abused her before they were divorced. This format represents a change in our idea of the American family. Much like Murphy Brown, who is now notorious for upsetting Republican Presidential candidates by becoming an unwed television mother, Grace is the sole provider and mainstay of her children's lives. The idea that a family could function without a man at the helm is an idea that would probably never have been breached in a positive light by the programs of the 1950's. This changing view of the portrayal of women is embodied in Grace's crossover of traditional male and female gender roles.

5   The episode that will be focused on here begins with Grace deciding to take her two children camping for the weekend. The camping trip itself, however, is not the focal point of the episode, although the events that take place mostly occur at the campsite. There is another family camped near Grace's, and they have a daughter of approximately the same age as Grace's son, Quentin, who is about eleven or twelve. When

the girl makes fun of Quentin and his younger sister, Libby, he becomes angry and pushes her to the ground. Although this happens off-screen, the girl's mother informs Grace of what happened.

6   Grace's solution to this problem is not a simple one, as most situation comedies allow for. The happy ending is an almost unavoidable facet of the genre. At the end of most programs, the characters have formulated and enacted an all encompassing solution to whatever it was that had troubled them in the episode. In actual life situations, we know that often, no one answer may be right, and that there are usually no quick fixes. Grace confronts her problem by first talking to her son about what happened. She does not offer an immediate solution other than to tell him that hitting people is not an acceptable behavior in any circumstance. He attempts to justify his actions by reminding Grace of the fact that she and his father used to fight frequently. She finds that Jimmy has told Quentin that both parents were responsible for the physical violence of their relationship. Grace insists that she never hit Jimmy, and sends Quentin away without talking about this matter further. This introduction of a second problem, that of her ex-husband lying to their son, presents Grace with a legitimate other concern, which she also must deal with in the episode.

7   The next time Grace talks with Quentin, he is still unaware of the implications of his actions. She makes it clear that she is worried about him having come to the wrong conclusions about how to deal with conflicts from observing what went on in their home before she separated from her husband. At first, Quentin attempts to downplay the importance of his actions, insisting that he didn't hurt the girl. Grace then tells him: "People are going to make you mad your whole life. You've got to come up with some other way of dealing with it. Fighting doesn't help anything, you know that." Here, the program's focus has clearly become domestic violence and its tendency to be initiated by the children of parents

who have abused each other. In this case, Grace is suggesting the idea of nonviolent conflict resolution, which is not an instant fix so much as it is a method that can be used to prevent the problem from arising again in the long-term future.

8   This alone does not resolve the episode, however, and Grace involves Jimmy in the solution. After calling him from the campsite, she visits him upon returning, first bringing up the question of why he lied to Quentin regarding her role in their abuse of each other. He tells Grace that he was trying to balance out all the bad things that she must say about him to their children. This reaction presents Jimmy as a very human character, having a realistic reaction to his own guilt in the eyes of his son. When Grace tells him that Quentin has "hit a little girl," he realizes what her concern had been. The episode ends with Grace asking that he talk with Quentin in order to clear up his previous lie, as well as to discuss the implications of domestic violence.

9   There is no final outcome that leaves all the characters absolved of their dilemmas. Although a resolution has been set into motion, the program does not project any easy outcome to the situation. This willingness to abandon the irrational happy ending prevails throughout every aspect of the show, including its characters' philosophies. This is evidenced in Grace's conversation with the mother of the girl that Quentin had pushed down. In response to the question of where her history with Jimmy ends, Grace says: "It doesn't end. Me and my ex-husband just try to heal, evolve, and make some decent place for the kids." The program offers here realistic pictures of families and relationships, and presents the audience with considerations regarding important social issues.

10   This shift in ideology on the part of the television media from perpetuating stereotypes and inconceivable family relations to addressing social realities is perhaps the most encouraging role that television plays in the country today. The idea that a mother can effectively provide for her household, that a woman can perform favorably

at a "man's" job, and that there are more suitable resolutions to problems than violence are all subjects that probably would have been less likely to surface on television in the past. Perhaps the idea that in some instances mother, not father, knows best, will be one that can produce a more favorable view of women and a more honest one of men. This episode in particular presents a realistic problem and offers it a real solution, not a candy-coated miracle of the half hour family. The issue of domestic violence deserves attention, and its confrontation by script writers attributes relevancy to *Grace Under Fire*.

[11] Socially oriented entertainment could prove to be an excellent vehicle for positive change, and credit should be afforded to those shows that offer it. Programs like *Grace Under Fire* might prove to be among the most beneficial in television if their messages reach the viewing public's consciousness. Television has an undeniable control over most of the images of society we witness in our lifetimes. Its pervasive nature demands that some modicum of awareness be enacted that gives consideration to exactly what it is showing us. *Grace Under Fire* represents an excellent example of this sort of consideration in programming. Obviously, no viewer wants to be blatantly bombarded by the harsh realities of life for an entire set of prime time programs. This is why it is important to note that regardless of my intention in watching *Grace Under Fire*, I still laughed.

1. Reread paragraph 2. What distinction is Marco making between a "good" show and a "relevant" one? Do you think this distinction is an important or useful one in evaluating television programs?

2. Reread the rest of the essay and cite two or three instances where Marco supports this distinction between a good show and a relevant one with evidence from *Grace Under Fire*.

3. In paragraph 6, Marco notes that "Grace's solution to this problem [her son's violent behavior] is not a simple one." Reread this paragraph to determine whether Marco supports

this premise. What evidence does he provide? Is the evidence convincing?

4. Marco concludes his essay with this sentence: "This is why it is important to note that regardless of my intention in watching *Grace Under Fire*, I still laughed." Does Marco anywhere in this draft discuss the humor of this program? If not, where specifically do you think he should include this discussion in his final draft?

5. For the most part, Marco writes in a convincing, clear voice. Yet in a few instances, his sentences are unclear. Revise the following two sentences for clarity:

   - final sentence in paragraph 4: "This changing view of the portrayal of women is embodied in Grace's crossover of traditional male and female gender roles."
   - fourth sentence in paragraph 11: "Its [television's] pervasive nature demands that some modicum of awareness be enacted that gives consideration to exactly what it is showing us."

Peer Responses

Use some or all of these questions to respond to your peer's draft. Comment as specifically as you can so that your peer can use your comments to productively revise her draft.

1. Read the introduction carefully. Does this paragraph effectively introduce the program or television show? Are the major characters or television personalities introduced? Is the general story line or structure of the program mentioned? Is this paragraph too brief? Too lengthy? How can this beginning be improved?

2. Choose one paragraph that analyzes a television character or personality. Is the analysis effective? Do you have a clear picture of the character or personality? Does this paragraph show you how this individual is believable or

stereotyped? What suggestions can you provide to improve this paragraph?

3. Locate the section of the draft that evaluates the show or program. Is the program or show adequately evaluated? Are convincing reasons given for its success or failure? What suggestions can you provide here to improve this part of the draft?

4. Choose one paragraph that is very effective. Say why. Consider how organized the paragraph is, how well it analyzes a particular issue, or how effectively it evaluates the topic in question.

5. What one aspect of the draft do you think needs the most improvement? Say why. Consider ways that your peer can better organize, analyze, or evaluate details from the television program.

Chapter 4

American Advertising and the Subtle Art of Manipulation

Introduction

Advertising has been part of human history ever since humans discovered the possibilities of exchange. Ancient cultures that bartered must have spoken for the value of their particular product in order to get the most benefit from their exchange.

Today, American advertising is a multi-billion-dollar operation, and it expresses itself in several media forms: radio commercials, television commercials, magazine and newspaper ads, and billboards. All of these forms of advertising have certain features in common: (1) they work from a written and/or visual text, (2) they are designed to be short, and (3) their focus is to grab the viewer's attention.

Unlike the text of a television show, which typically fills 22–44 minutes, commercials on television and radio are rarely more than one minute long, usually only 30 seconds in length. Nevertheless, in this short time frame, American advertisers often manage to create a powerful message for the consumer.

Commercials are not only clever verbal statements; they are also very sophisticated visual presentations, using state-of-the-art camera equipment and editing techniques. Very talented and successful cinematographers work on television commercials mainly because they are extremely profitable.

All advertisements on television, on radio, or in magazines have the same goal: to get consumers to buy their product. Advertising companies also believe that retail sales always indicate a country's health. It is no accident that the most successful commercials and the most profitable advertising companies are found in rich societies, such as the United States, that see profit as success. Several of the reading selections in this chapter focus on the ways capitalism is expressed in American advertising. These selections examine the consumer's role within capitalism. They ask a question: Does a capitalist economy reduce the consumer to an object of desire? Some of these scholars of American popular culture use Marxism to evaluate American advertising. Marxist thinkers see the worker in a capitalist society that is controlled by big business. You will find that the last reading selection in this chapter has a response to this premise.

Because of their brevity, all American commercials focus on form, since what the commercial says must be expressed through how the commercial is presented. In the terminology of media theorist Marshall McLuhan, for American advertising, "The medium is the message." What all advertisers want their viewer to come away with is a positive feeling about their product, even though this feeling may have little or nothing to do with the product. For example, an automobile commercial may present a short narrative about a driver scaling the Alps in the advertised automobile. It is this feeling of success in accomplishing this superhuman task that the viewer of the advertisement will want to consider and reconsider. The viewer will then unconsciously transfer this good feeling of accomplishment to the automobile itself. This positive emotion thus creates a desire in him to purchase the automobile. Furthermore, this feeling of confidence often has nothing to do with the automobile's vital statistics: gas mileage, size, durability, and so on.

In addition, many commercials rely on short, memorable slogans that also do little to provide necessary information about the product. Yet a slogan may stay in the viewer's memory long after the thirty-second advertisement is over. As a child growing up in the fifties, I remember that cigarettes were heavily advertised on radio and television. Since then, the Federal Communications Commission has banned their advertising from both radio and television. I still remember the slogan for Winston cigarettes: "Winston tastes good like a cigarette should." The rhyming of *good* and *should* helped make this slogan catchy. Yet what exactly does this slogan say about the cigarette?

That is, what sort of "good" taste does the Winston cigarette provide? The slogan fails to answer this question.

Each generation of television viewers has its own catchy slogans as part of its popular culture, and these slogans are so powerful that even on a preschool playground you can hear two- and three-year-olds reciting these easily remembered sayings.

However, catchy slogans and wish-fulfillment stories are not the only ways advertisers sell their products. The instincts of fear and sex play a major role in American ads as well. Often these elements are suggested, so you must infer what emotion the advertisement is exploiting. Fear is an emotion with no logic attached to it. It is a survival mechanism that all organisms possess. And though sex is not essential to one's survival, it is necessary for the continuation of any species. In this regard, sex is as vital an instinct as fear.

Advertisers understand the power of both of these emotions. Therefore, they can attach one or both of them to their product so that you feel that without this product, you may die or be unable to perform sexually.

Recently, I saw a television advertisement for automobile tires. On this tire a scantily clad infant is joyfully playing while cars are racing by on a heavily traveled highway, and they are within feet of the infant. The inference this advertisement wants you to make is that without these tires, your infant child's life is in danger. Your natural instinct for protecting your child, your fear for her being killed by a fast-moving car on a highway, is behind this apparently innocent scene. Although you may not be able to recognize it immediately, fear drives your response to this commercial. It is only through your inferencing abilities that you can identify the instinct that wants to protect your child.

This advertisement is an example of how commercials speak to you subtly, often subliminally. If you are unable at first to explain your reasons for your often strong responses to commercials, then you are being manipulated by the advertisement. That is, your instincts and desires have silenced your critical practices.

Sex is often similarly employed by advertisers. Some of the sexual suggestions in advertisements have recently become blatant—with skimpily clad, beautiful women and handsome men selling such products as underwear by employing suggestive sexual poses. Yet, more often, the sexual aspect to an advertisement is less obvious. There are frequently ads for soft drinks, suntan lotion, or even coffee that involve a love narrative in which the product serves to make the romance happen. As ludicrous as the connection between sex and coffee or sex and suntan lotion is, these narratives boost sales.

A recent coffee commercial involves a young man who mistakenly knocks on the wrong door in a large urban apartment building. He is attracted to the woman who answers and is even more attracted by the coffee she offers him. Like a soap opera, the commercial spans several episodes of this peculiar courtship.

Another successful technique used by advertising creators is having sports, movie, or television celebrities endorse a product. The creators of these ads assume that the celebrity's fans will buy the product because they want to be like the celebrity in every way they can. But something more subtle is also happening here. In using celebrities, advertising executives are connecting the product with the sport, movie, or television program of which the celebrity is a part. In a sense, these ads are being sold through the playing field, movie, or television program and in the commercial itself. Therefore, advertising happens even when the commercial is not on the air. Thus, when the superstar basketball player Michael Jordan is selling underwear in a television commercial, the viewer remembers the underwear as well when Jordan scores the game-winning basket for his Chicago Bulls.

Seen from this way, advertising is an American medium that saturates our society. Such a perspective gives Marxist scholars of popular culture evidence for their thesis that American consumers are objects of capitalist manipulation. In order to understand the nature of this manipulation and how you are, or are not, one of the manipulated, you need to bring to your viewing of commercials additional critical practices that you have not studied in Chapters 1, 2, and 3.

Critical Practices

As with your examination of American photographs, works of fiction, and television programs, critically viewing commercials requires you to express unstated American beliefs through your abilities to analyze and to make inferences. To more fully appreciate American commercials, you also need to understand how generalizations are formed and the power of connotations in word choice.

To Generalize

To generalize is to summarize from many specific details. Forming generalizations is as natural for the human being as is sequencing and evaluating. Making reasonable generalizations requires some critical skill. For example, if you watch a day's worth of television, you could make the following generalization about television commercials: television commercials are no more than thirty seconds long. Having viewed perhaps fifty commercials and having timed them, you can make a general statement about the duration of commercials that covers all the individual commercials that you have seen. One can never say how much evidence you need in order to determine the soundness of your generalization. What is clear, though, is that seeing only one commercial would not allow you to generalize about the length of television commercials.

Sound generalizations are based upon three criteria:

1. *Accurate* evidence: evidence accepted by those most directly involved in the subject. The type of acceptable evidence varies with the discipline, so social scientists and natural scientists have their own criteria for what makes evidence accurate.

2. *Sufficient* evidence: a large amount of evidence. Again, each discipline determines what constitutes a sufficient amount of evidence. You may have heard the statement on a television or radio commercial for aspirin that "nine out of ten doctors recommend your using this brand." A critical response to this statement would be this: Is the sample sufficient? Were only ten doctors consulted? Or is nine out of ten a percentage of a larger number of doctors questioned?

3. *Representative* evidence: evidence drawn from all aspects of a group. For example, a representative sampling of commercials needs to be drawn from morning, afternoon, evening, and late-evening programming in order to determine a generalization about television commercials. In the social sciences, researchers often conduct a *random sample,* or data selected from a large group in an unpredictable fashion, so that there is little chance of your selecting more data from one sector of this group than from another. In regard to the aspirin commercial mentioned previously, a critical question to the statement that "nine of ten doctors recommend its use" would be as follows: Is this sample of doctors representative? That is, were doctors from several geographic and economic regions of the United States questioned? When a sampling is not representative, it is considered a *biased sample.*

An *unqualified generalization* is one that is true of every specific instance that it explains. These generalizations are difficult to make because one counter-example can make the generalization false. A *counter-example* is evidence that goes against your generalization. An example of an unqualified generalization would be "All humans require oxygen to survive." There is no known case of a human being who has survived for a long period of time without oxygen.

The more common type of general statement is a *qualified generalization:* a statement that is supported by evidence a percentage of the time. One can say this of situation comedies: "Most situation comedies on American television present stereotyped characters." There may well be a few situation comedies that present fully developed characters, but the majority do not. Qualified generalizations require the use of terms of qualification: *many, almost, most always, often, usually, mostly,* and *typically.* Other terms of qualification can show the infrequent cases: *sometimes, occasionally, rarely, infrequently, in a few cases.* Note how the above generalization on situation comedies would be easily questioned if the term of qualification were omitted: "American situation comedies present stereotyped characters."

Your task as a critical reader and writer is to use generalizations responsibly. Critical thinkers are able to distinguish between qualified and unqualified generalizations and know when it is appropriate to use either one. Generalizations in popular culture almost always need to be qualified.

Generalizations fall under the general category of *induction:* making a general statement based upon a body of specific evidence. You were introduced to induction at the very beginning of this textbook in the section titled "Constructing Arguments." Inductive thinking moves from the level of specificity (the individual character in the situation comedy, for example) to the level of generalization (an overarching statement about these situation comedies).

Television commercials tend not to use generalizations—either qualified or unqualified. As mentioned earlier, because of their length, commercials often simplify statements into slogans. What the commercial often expresses are *hasty generalizations*—inductions made from either insufficient or incorrect evidence.

Consider some of the hasty generalizations that you hear on radio and television. In a McDonald's commercial of years past, you heard the slogan "You deserve a break today." As a critical examiner of this generalization, you could ask the following question: "Does everyone deserve a break?" Recent Nike commercials end with a command: "Just do it!" Again, you could ask yourself these critical questions: "Is this commercial saying that we should always 'do'? Aren't there times when one should think before doing?" Finally, a commercial for Coca-Cola noted that "Coke is where the fun is." One could logically question this statement: "Aren't there enjoyable occasions when one is not drinking Coke?" In each case, the advertising slogan simplifies life's experiences.

Another type of questionable generalization that you will find in television commercials is the *false dilemma:* a statement asking you to choose from two extreme positions. How many commercials have you viewed that can be summarized into the following false dilemmas? I either wear the perfume, or I don't get the boyfriend; I either buy the athletic shoes, or I don't get on the team. Advertising creators want to make life's choices simple so that their viewers will be more easily persuaded to purchase their product. By identifying these conclusions as false dilemmas, you will realize that there are many more options open to you somewhere in between the two extreme choices that the commercial presents.

Thus, to successfully analyze any generalization—a statement in a commercial or in any text that you are examining—you need to ask the following questions:

1. Is the evidence correct?
2. Is the evidence drawn from a large sample?
3. Is the evidence representative?
4. Does the generalization accurately interpret what the evidence suggests?

Related to the hasty generalization are two other errors in thought that one finds in American advertising: the bandwagon technique and the appeal to authority. These errors originate in a kind of thinking different from induction: deduction, another term introduced at the beginning of the textbook. *Deduction* uses both parts of induction—the general statement and its details—to come upon a new conclusion. All deductive thinking is made up of three parts: (1) the *major premise,* (2) the *minor premise,* and (3) the *conclusion.* And all three parts of the deduction are known collectively as a *syllogism.* The major premise is the generalization, the minor premise a detail, and the conclusion a synthesis of both the generalization and its detail.

Let's say you are viewing a television commercial for suntan lotion that uses beautiful, sun-tanned models to sell the product. We have already discussed how the models' sexuality is subtly transferred to the suntan lotion. Yet you can also analyze your response to this commercial in the form of a syllogism. The syllogism would say something like the following:

Major Premise: Using this suntan lotion makes one's skin beautifully tanned like the models'.

Minor Premise: I want beautiful skin like the models'.

Conclusion: Therefore, I will purchase this suntan lotion in order to make my skin beautifully tanned like theirs.

The conclusions one comes to in a deduction are only as valid as the premises. If your major premise or minor premise is flawed, the rest of your argument will be flawed as well. Do you see how the major premise in the suntan lotion advertisement is in error? It may not be the case that this particular suntan lotion will make your skin beautiful. Your skin may be allergic to the lotion or to the sun. The major premise can be seen as a hasty generalization. As such, the conclusion is also questionable.

The bandwagon technique is also an example of this error in deductive logic. The *bandwagon* statement asks you to be like, or to join, a particular group. Bandwagon statements make no allowances for individual differences. In the suntan advertisement examined above, the creators did not take into consideration the fact that some people may not be able to have beautifully tanned skin, may not consider tanned skin beautiful, or may not even want to be physically beautiful.

Appeals to authority are also based upon faulty major premises. *To appeal to authority* is to encourage a consumer to buy a product because a famous person uses it. As mentioned earlier in this introduction, celebrities in sports, movies, and television are sometimes called upon to sell products. Viewers who admire these personalities may assume that these celebrities are expert in fields outside their profession. It does not necessarily follow that because Michael Jordan is a great basketball player, he is also an expert on which underwear to buy. Yet we see Michael Jordan advertising briefs and sales of that product going up.

The syllogism upon which this conclusion is drawn goes something like this:

Major Premise: People that I greatly admire are well versed in many fields.

Minor Premise: I greatly admire Michael Jordan.

Conclusion: Being well versed in several fields, Michael Jordan knows what underwear I should buy.

This is not to say that one should never go to authorities for advice. A respected pharmacist may correctly advise you on the best medication to take for your arthritis, or an experienced high school counselor may provide sound suggestions about the college that you would best be suited to attend. In these instances, your syllogism would begin with a sound major premise. Look at how the syllogism about the high school counselor would work:

Major Premise: Authorities may provide helpful advice.

Minor Premise: My high school counselor is an authority on selecting a college.

Conclusion: My high school counselor may provide me with sound advice on what college I should apply to.

Note that the major premise is worded as a qualified generalization (*"may provide"*), so even the counselor's advice may not be the best information that you will get about selecting a college to attend.

To Appreciate the Connotations of Words

Just as commercials successfully use short statements, so do they focus on the power of their words. Because commercials are short experiences, the creators of commercials want their word choice to influence their viewers powerfully.

All words are suggestive. What a word suggests, what other words it brings to mind, is its *connotation*. Words can suggest *positive, negative,* and *neutral* connotations. Words with positive connotations elicit feelings of joy or desire, and words with negative connotations suggest pain and unpleasantness. Words with neutral connotations do not have any strong emotions attached to them. Creators of commercials focus on the positive and negative suggestions of words so that in being introduced to the word, you also reflect on, and respond to, its many associations.

Let's consider the following three words, all referring to an emotional state: *tension, excitement, hysteria. Tension* is defined as the state of being nervous; it can be seen as a neutral term that doctors and psychiatrists refer to when a patient's muscles are not relaxed or when his mind is strained. A positive way of referring to tension is to use the word *excitement. Excitement* suggests feelings of joyful or pleasurable tension. Conversely, tension can be seen negatively as hysteria. *Hysteria* is a state of mind in which the individual is so tense that he is out of control, perhaps psychologically disturbed. Think of your reactions to the following three exclamations: "I'm excited!" "I'm tense!" "I'm hysterical!" Though in terms of body response (heart rate, breathing, blood pressure), these three words describe a similar emotion, your reaction to each word is different. For example, if you wanted to leave a positive impression on a friend you have recently dated, you would likely say "I was excited about our date last night" rather than "I was hysterical about our date last night." Hysteria suggests an image of a person who cannot cope with life, and you would likely not want your date to picture you in this negative way.

When you analyze the connotations of a particular word used in a commercial, you should let your mind freely associate it with other words. As you free associate, jot down the words that come to mind. Then ask yourself some questions:

1. What feelings does this word suggest? Positive? Negative? Neutral?

2. Is this word accurately describing the product? Or do its connotations suggest other associations unrelated to the product?

Let's assume that you are viewing a chocolate bar commercial on television. The advertisers not only refer to its taste as "sweet" but also as "sensual" and "positively sinful." What associations come to mind with such words as *sinful* and *sensual*? Isn't a sensual product one associated with lovemaking? And wouldn't *sinful* suggest going against established rules? It would then be safe to conclude that these two words—*sensual* and *sinful*—together connote illicit lovemaking.

Your next question would be an obvious one: How accurate is the use of such words in the description of a chocolate bar? Unless the chocolate bar has an aphrodisiac in it, the advertisers are irresponsibly equating their chocolate bar with sex and breaking the law. Note how these conclusions come entirely from your analyzing the connotations of these two words in the ad.

The opposite of a word's connotation is its *denotation*, or dictionary meaning. Yet in their contexts—in written texts, in commercials, in everyday speech—words rarely suggest only what a dictionary says they mean. Being an analyst of a word's connotations is an essential critical practice.

Let's see how you can apply these critical practices—making inferences; analyzing generalizations; and examining bandwagon techniques, appeals to authority, and the connotations of words—to a magazine advertisement for Isuzu (next page).

After having studied this ad, you should be able to answer the following questions:

1. What sort of generalization is the title: "The Road Is Paved with Idiots"? What purpose does this generalization serve?

2. What fears does this ad call to mind?

3. What words in the ad connote fear?

4. Who are the "they" and the "we" in this ad?

5. How does the visual material further explain the message of this ad?

THE 58TH UNWRITTEN LAW
OF DRIVING

. . . .

THE ROAD
IS PAVED
WITH
IDIOTS.

. . . .

. . . .
UNLIKE MOST 4WD VEHICLES,
DUAL AIR BAGS COME STANDARD
ON ALL ISUZU TROOPERS.
. . . .

They're out there, those runners of stop signs, those no-signal lane changers.

And while there's little we can do about them, we've gone to great lengths

to make them less of a threat. Case in point: standard dual air bags. You won't

find this on many 4-wheel drives. Are we paranoid? No. Over protective?

Maybe. Then again, who do you trust? Yourself? Or the guy who cut you off

on the freeway? Presenting the Trooper Limited.

For information please call (800) 726-2700.

ISUZU
Practically/Amazing

Courtesy of American Isuzu Motors, Inc.

Recapping

Commercials are subtle forms of persuasion and manipulation. They can be more complicated than television programs. Like television programs, commercials are based upon traditional American beliefs. Yet because commercials are so short, you also need to be aware of the glib slogans and unique word choice that the ad creators use to sell their product.

You can effectively analyze American advertising by examining hasty generalizations, appeals to authority, bandwagon techniques, and the connotations of the words in the ads. By analyzing ads in this way, you also determine the two basic ways of forming arguments: induction and deduction.

Reading Selections   *13–16*

In the following four selections, you will see how scholars who investigate advertising rely on American popular culture to develop their arguments. The first selection is by Elayne Rapping: "Commercials: Television's Ultimate Art Form." This chapter from her *The Looking Glass World of Nonfiction TV* provides a clear introduction to American commercials. She considers in greater depth many of the issues that you read about in the introduction to this chapter. Selection 14 is from Robert Goldman's *Reading Ads Socially*. It is titled "McDonald's 'History of the Family'" and uses the American belief in family to explain a series of McDonald's television ads.

Selection 15, "The Shock(ing) Value at Fashion's Cutting Edge," looks at fashion and fashion advertising to examine the power that fashion has over our society. Richard Martin suggests that fashion and fashion advertising have become the most powerful art of the late twentieth century. Finally, John Fiske, in his selection, "The Jeaning of America," examines the semiotic significance of the tendency of Americans to wear

jeans. In his study, he questions the Marxist perspective that Americans are controlled by capitalistic forces. Selections 15 and 16 work well together because they both carefully examine the ways that popular culture helps explain fashion behavior and how fashion behavior explains popular culture.

Selection 13

"Commercials: Television's Ultimate Art Form"
Elayne Rapping

This chapter excerpt from Elayne Rapping's book *The Looking Glass World of Nonfiction TV* will help answer many of the general questions that you may still have about the effect of television commercials on American thinking. This is a well-organized and clearly written treatment of American television advertising. It examines the nature of this popular art form and explains the motivations of its creators. Rapping also shows how television commercials are similar to the programs they sponsor. Once you complete this selection, you will have a better understanding of the factors that influence American consumers' responses to television commercials.

In this overview chapter, Rapping asks general questions that you should keep in mind as you critically read: What are the essential characteristics of television commercials? How are television commercials structured? How do they relate to the programs they sponsor? As you answer these questions, you will also understand Rapping's attitude toward commercials and how they relate to American capitalism. Since this is a very readable selection, you will not be distracted by difficult vocabulary.

Reading–Writing Preparation

Before you read this selection, you may want to answer the following questions in writing or discussion:

1. How do you respond to television commercials? Do you enjoy watching them? Or do you change to another channel when a commercial comes on?

2. What television commercials are the most memorable to you? Why?

Commercials: Television's Ultimate Art Form

As a teenager, reading both Karl Marx and Honey *magazine,*
I couldn't reconcile what I knew with what I felt. This is the root
of ideology, I believe. I knew that I was being "exploited,"
but it was a fact that I was attracted.
— Judith Williamson

1   It would be inconsistent to end this book without looking at the commercials which have been mentioned so often throughout. If we understand nonfiction television to be made up of forms which partake of elements of entertainment, information and sales, commercials certainly fill the bill. They may be the most perfect form for achieving this neat mixture. Certainly they are emotionally powerful, often fun to watch and filled with information and propaganda urging us to buy the commodities described.

2   It is hard to categorize the commercial as "art" or "information"; it uses elements of both. I have already treated forms which do this to a greater or lesser extent, although with less ambiguity. One withdraws from the label "art" in spite of the esthetic and fictional elements of commercials. They are not entirely informative either, however, since they do invent fictional narratives which serve as homilies, pointing up the commercial message.

3   As with made-for-TV movies, I chose to include commercials because of what they illustrate about TV's method of blurring categories rather than any pure definition of commercials as "nonfiction." They are so much like so many other forms, and in so many ways, that they are an important element in the overview of network

Reprinted by permission of the publisher from Elayne Rapping, *The Looking Glass World of Nonfiction TV.* Boston: South End Press, 1987, 161–71.

TV's evolution in an institutional context. They serve, as no other form does, to illustrate the direct role of the corporate sponsor in influencing TV's esthetic and ideology. Sponsors no longer directly control program content, but they do control the very similar content of commercials. To see the parallels between the style and message of the ads and those of programs is enlightening. It helps to make real the indirect role of sponsors in all TV production.

4   Perhaps because of the uneasiness described by Judith Williamson, so many of us, when confronted by the power, range and appeal of commercial advertising, refuse to acknowledge its significance. We know we are "being exploited," but "it is a fact that [we are] attracted," as Williamson says. "Publicity is the culture of consumer society." But "because we are . . . so accustomed to being addressed by these images, we scarcely notice their total impact." And if we do notice, we feel better couching our perceptions in analytical rather than emotional or esthetic terms.

5   It is far more common to hear admissions of, and arguments for, admiration and even love of such TV series as "Hill Street Blues" and "Cheers" than for the commercials which frame and punctuate them. Yet, in technical skill, creative energy and production costs, most TV commercials are far more elaborate, slick and amusing than the shows they sponsor. Even a decade ago, a thirty second Campbell Soup spot in which Ann Miller danced Busby Berkeley style on the top of a soup can, cost $250,000. At that rate, a ninety minute drama would have cost $45 million—half again what Warren Beatty's film extravaganza, *Reds,* cost years later. As Erik Barnouw has noted, "the commercial is a central element of TV entertainment, outshining most other elements." Media critic Jonathan Price agrees. In his provocatively titled *Commercials: The Best Things on TV,* he lists the many ways "commercials outpace programs" and concludes: "if commercials are artful, the art is objective, not subjective; capitalist, not rebellious; part of a social activity, not a personal means of ex-

pression." Whether "art" or not, it is a fact that 74 percent of viewers admitted, in a recent survey, to finding commercials "fun to watch."

6   It is the power of commercials to entertain and persuade—their artfulness—that makes them a cornerstone of the corporate structure. Multinational corporate conglomerates[1] buy 81 percent of all TV advertising time. Commercials and programs do not conflict with, so much as complement, each other. In technical and stylistic matters, commercials have always set the standards which other programming forms have followed. The use of special effects, fast cutting and montage[2] have been longtime commercial staples which news and dramatic forms have only recently begun to imitate. Even the character types, plots and themes of most fictional programming are determined, far more than most people realize, by the conventions of the commercial message, rather than vice versa.

History: There Really Was a Time When We Had No TV, Dear

7   When, as babies, we are first introduced to the TV screen, it is a permanent, central fixture in our homes, a totem[3] around which the family gathers to "watch the news" or share a favorite drama or comedy. The first words a child utters, the first words she spells, the first songs he sings are, often as not, from TV commercials (as the producers of "Sesame Street" understood) rather than the nursery rhymes of earlier generations.

8   Those of us who remember the post-World War II advent of home TV are now in midlife. Soon there will be no one alive for whom TV's rise to cultural supremacy is lived memory,

---

1. multinational corporate conglomerates: huge businesses that operate in several countries

2. montage: in film, using several shots to form an image

3. totem: an animal or a plant representing a primitive family

rather than an eternal fact of life. It makes sense, then, to trace the development of this institution in terms of the informing role played by commercial advertising in shaping it. For the rise of advertising and home TV are intimately linked.

9   In 1952, the sale of radio time accounted for more than 60 percent of every broadcast advertising dollar. By 1954, TV boasted $500 million in advertising sales, while radio brought in only $44 million. Vance Packard's classic study of the roots of TV advertising, *The Hidden Persuaders,* gives extensive evidence of the ideological aspects of that dramatic development. For a consumer society, real "need" was no longer the impetus for buying. The fact that "most Americans already possessed perfectly usable stoves, cars, TV sets, clothes, etc." made necessary a corps of new "scientists of desire" or "merchants of discontent" whose job it was to "stimulate" consumption artificially among those who "do not yet know what they need." The problems of this new, powerful profession were more esthetic than informational. The industry was eager to hire "gifted artists" whose job it was to "cope with the problem of rapidly diminishing product differences." This they did, using a combination of "fact" and "fiction," imaginative and informational materials which have come to characterize the blurry world of TV in general.

10   By the 1960s, TV advertising had become so expensive that commercials had shifted almost entirely away from one or two minute spots to thirty second spots. This put even greater demands on creative, graphic artists to use highly condensed montages of visual imagery accompanied by the briefest, often-repeated verbal messages. The move from factual information to visual and emotional appeal, based on symbol and image, was complete.

11   The formal and symbolic sophistication of contemporary television commercials, combined with their unabashed mixing of fact and fiction, hype and information, have had profound effects on our national political consciousness. For one thing, TV commercials tend to encourage people to see their identities in terms of what they consume, rather than what they produce. A worker with two cars and a color TV, for example, will gradually begin to see himself or herself as a member of the "middle class" rather than the "working class."

12   According to Erik Barnouw, even the decline of American socialism is in part a result of the success of advertising. As words like "freedom," "love," "success," "fun," even "revolution" became attached to consumer goods rather than social structures, the appeal of socialism, or any radical reform, lost its urgency and meaning. In 1932, notes Barnouw, "the Socialist Party drew 884,781 votes." Such a figure has not been approached since. Of course other factors—particularly McCarthyism—have played major roles in this decline, but the power of television cannot be overlooked in analysing this political trend.

> [If] socialism had promised workers a share in the better things in life . . . television proclaimed it a birthright. The picture window of television showed that everyone could live there . . . Its images were a lesson in living. Soon it was spreading its message in a hundred lands, proclaiming the good life, the age of the consumer.

13   In looking at the role of the commercial on network television, three things must be considered. First, the esthetics and techniques of TV ads have had enormous impact on the way in which programs themselves—both fictional and nonfictional—are visually conceived and executed. Next, the major dramatic and thematic conventions of commercials have had a seminal[4] influence on the very content of both drama and informational programming. And finally, how viewers experience the flow of TV—from news to drama to ads—influences the meaning of every program we watch. This again is primarily attributable to the role of the ads. They can either reinforce or counteract the apparent "message" of any given program.

---

4. seminal: highly original or creative

Marketing as Art

14   The esthetic power of advertising is a crucial component of its political role, because what advertising is meant to do demands the ability to transform mere commodities—through the use of images—into quite other things: objects of human desire, to be exact, which embody qualities impossible for material objects to really possess. Raymond Williams has written about "the system of organized magic which is modern advertising." Far from being a sign of our society's overly materialist bent, says Williams, advertising "is quite evidently not materialist enough." It does not so much sell us material goods to fill material needs as it delivers myths and fantasies. Advertising "is the consequence of a social failure to find means of public information and decision over a wide range of everyday economic life. This failure is the result of allowing control of the means of production to remain in minority hands."

15   In other words, the qualities and values promised us by the rhetoric of democracy are not being delivered. And so we have a huge industry—the advertising industry—whose function it is to fix in our minds the idea that these values can be realized through consumption, that using certain products will bring the fulfillment we all need and seek. Love is sold in ready-to-bake biscuit and cookie mixes. Success comes with a new car. Excitement and adventure, especially of a romantic and sexual nature, is contained in elaborately packaged perfumes and bath products. Progress and human betterment arrive through technology and science. Democracy itself has come to be defined almost entirely in terms of the vast range of product "choices" available to us.

16   Because of the enormous ideological burden placed on advertising in a world where things are generally getting worse and worse for more and more of us, it is reasonable to consider ads as paradigms of the worst TV messages about politics, human relationships and the good life. This is where esthetics plays its most subtle and powerful role. The impact of the visual image, especially when it is juxtaposed in rapid succession with many other images, is both compelling and emotionally affecting.

17   One of the most powerful and misunderstood features of TV commercials—and programs—is the way in which form itself, rather than mere content, communicates meaning. Most analysts of advertising are content to point out the absurdities of the overt messages. Of course the use of a new toothpaste or shampoo is not going to lead directly to true love. Of course the purchase of the proper breakfast cereal or fabric softener will not make husbands and children suddenly appreciate and express adoration for their wives and mothers. But advertisements are not linear or rational in method. They create meaning through juxtaposition of like and unlike, real and fictional elements. They take "certain elements, things or people from the ordinary world" and rearrange and alter them "in terms of a product's myth to create a new world, the world of the advertisement." They function much as dreams and poetry do. They combine elements of reality with wish fulfillment fantasies in a way which touches us where our desires are deepest, and most unfulfilled. If, as Althusser says, "Ideology represents the imaginary relationship of individuals to their real conditions of existence," then TV commercials are ideology of the first order.

18   Examples of typical TV commercials bear this out. Everyone has a favorite example of a "really good" commercial. Usually it is visually startling. The series of Chanel perfume ads, run regularly during the Christmas season, are as good as any. There's the sexually suggestive one in which a physically beautiful man dives into a luxurious pool and comes up between the legs of a physically beautiful woman. The images of luxury and sensual perfection combine with pure eroticism to connect the product with an ideal of sensual pleasure and luxury unavailable to all but a few jetsetters. There's the more romantic ad in which a montage of sophisticated urban images—ultramodern glass highrises, soaring airplanes, and such—are intercut with brief scenes between a man and woman, dressed in sophisticated

elegance, mouthing the "John," "Mary," romantic cliches of 1930s Hollywood. In the background, the Ink Spots sing "I Don't Want to Set the World on Fire," from the same romantic era. In all, it makes no linear sense. But the feeling and the promise are crystal clear. Older viewers, most likely to be buying Chanel for Christmas, will be reminded of the romance and glamour of their youths, as interpreted and remembered by Hollywood.

19 For younger viewers, the most effective ads are equally suggestive, but in a different way. The 501 Levi commercials are as artistically impressive as anything they sponsor, including most of the music videos they so strongly resemble. Street scenes of hip kids—having fun, being cool, hanging out—are shot in a funky "video *verite*"[5] style that contrasts with the sophistication of the Chanel ads. The text reinforces the visual message: if you buy 501 jeans, you'll be as cool and laid back as most teenagers dream of being. "And now my hard to please woman's havin' a hard time pleasin' me," sings the proud but ever so casual owner of the 501s.

20 It is amazing that most of these ads last a mere thirty seconds. They manage to put together a range of images and emotions with a minimum of verbal explanation. Slogans are simple and often repeated and spelled out graphically. All the advertiser wants you to remember is the feeling you got from the ad, and the name and look of the product. They literally "promise you anything but give you Arpege." Advertising "is never a celebration of a pleasure-in-itself. [It] is always about the future buyer. It offers him an image of himself made glamorous by the product it is trying to sell. It makes him envious of himself as he might be." But that "might be" is a fantasy, since the goods offered, in and of themselves, never embody the values that commercial art attaches to them.

---

5. video *verite:* videos that attempt to represent "real" life, or as it is lived on the streets

21 From another angle, advertising is "an elaborate social and cultural form" which responds to "the gap between expectation and control"—in an economic system in which there is "a controlling minority and a widely expectant majority"—by creating a "kind of organized fantasy" which

> . . . operates to project the production decisions of the major corporations as "your choice," the consumers' selection of priorities . . . [and] pretends to a linkage of values between quite mundane products and the now generally unattached values of love, respect, significance or fulfillment.

It does this primarily with visual arts.

Marketing as Melodrama

22 Most commercials include elaborate dramatic situations and characters. They are miniature melodramas where narrative and imagery combine to promise fulfillment—whether emotional, social or economic. The typical forms taken by ads, the people shown, their problems and the solutions offered are all in keeping with the larger messages of TV programming. Just as perfume ads promise us a life of luxury, *a la* "Lifestyles of the Rich and Famous" or "Dynasty," and car ads promise the excitement of the Indianapolis 500, "Knight Rider" or "That's Incredible," most narrative ads promise us things we desire, things we have every right to enjoy, but which most of us will never experience.

23 Among the most common kinds of ads are those for over-the-counter medications, household and business supplies, appliances, and processed or prepared foods. Ron Rosenbaum reports that in the first week of September, 1977, "close to 50 percent of the spots on the CBS and NBC nightly news shows, and nearly a third on ABC" were for medications. He lists nearly forty different product ads—from Dentucreme to Ex-Lax to Geritol to Pepto-Bismol—all of which were meant to inform us that the many ominous signs of the inevitable "debilitation of the body" could be quickly and easily eradicated with a

pill, a cream, a suppository. We all know the way these ads go. First someone agonizingly tries to hide from loved ones the physical condition that is robbing her of her ability to have fun with them. Sometimes it's a middle-aged woman whose arthritis or constipation interferes with her plans to enjoy her husband or grandchildren. Sometimes the same woman agonizes over her husband's ailments. Lately, there has even been an ad in which a young wife's "headache" interferes with her sexual pleasure. In each case, someone suggests a cure. In each case, the results are miraculous. No more pain or "irregularity" to interfere with the joys of family life. No more ailing husband or child to worry over. No more headache to impede the sexual revolution. And it is all done through the marvels of chemistry and modern medical science.

24   The most elaborate versions of this theme are probably the ads for coffee and telephone services. Again and again, we are shown little dramas in which breakdowns in relationships are healed through brewing a cup of coffee or dialing a long distance phone number. The drama is symbolic of course. Coffee, after all, in our culture, suggests human beings cozily getting together in intimate situations. The husband who blows up and apologizes is forgiven and the damage healed with a cup of coffee. Sisters bridge the gaps that separate siblings in nuclear families by sharing coffee. So do employees and bosses. And every possible emotional trauma that comes with the endless mobility, the breakdown of family and community ties that characterize modern life, is healed through the simple slogan, "Reach Out and Touch Someone" via AT&T.

25   What makes the best of these ads—the "Reach Out and Touch" campaign, the Brim and Taster's Choice series—so memorable is characterization and situation. It is hard to miss the fact that every situation assumes a prototypical[6] formula for happiness which is based on the nuclear family,

and each ad addresses familiar issues facing that institution today. Like soap opera, these ads dramatize the current circumstances we have been in and felt awful about. Then they suggest a fool proof answer. Even the ads for Visa credit cards exploit interpersonal problems common in a world of changing sex roles, in which "true love" followed by babies is still the ideal. For career women who "travel a lot," Visa can be the ticket to meeting a new man. "I just got my new card in the mail," says the female executive to her male counterpart, in the mailroom of their urban apartment building. "Want to try it out?"

26   All these "plots" and "characters" are unmistakably identical to the "plots" and "characters" that make up most of network TV programming, whether nonfiction or drama. On TV, all problems are presented as unique and individual, with no relation to history or other social forces. They are solved through the intercession of expert "heroes," often scientists, law enforcement officials, or representatives of other commercial or government institutions. Cures are rapid and complete. Health problems, for example, whether on the nightly news, "St. Elsewhere," or "The Guiding Light" are personal tragedies which only the most eminent doctor, using the most up-to-date equipment and drugs, can solve. There is never a question of using less expensive techniques and so, perhaps, solving the real health problems of this nation—the lack of affordable care for most people. The very idea that there are alternative ways of viewing these problems, much less that we as citizens might participate in debates and decisions about them, is denied.

27   It is no accident that TV celebrities are often chosen to promote these products. "I'm not a doctor, but I play one on TV," says a spokesman for some instant cure. Again we are faced with the blurring of fact and fantasy, the confusion about who and what are "real" on TV. It is quite common to see a soap opera star advertise a household cleaning product on the very show in which she portrays a housewife. This does not confuse or irritate viewers. On the contrary, it adds to the sense of television as all of a piece.

---

6. prototypical: referring to the model on which others are patterned

The associations viewers have with these media personae are what make them effective spokespersons for products guaranteed to solve our life problems. Again, commercials are the prototypes for "real" programs, plots and characters.

28   Most commercials take place in the kinds of homes, recreational facilities or workplaces that are models of everything commercial TV presents as the good life. These settings are the most blatant and powerful forms of propaganda for the consumerist lifestyle. Every beleaguered housewife fighting ring around the collar or waxy, yellow buildup lives in a sparkling clean, brand new, fashionably appointed home. The envy and guilt felt by many women watching these ads is a spur to consumerism that goes beyond the mere buying of the advertised product. You may in fact try Oxydol. But whether you do or not, the vision of a spotless, beautiful home will stick with you. It will subtly lead you to buy a variety of products not even mentioned: furniture polish, floor wax, new appliances and furniture, kitchen canisters and draperies.

29   Multinational corporate sponsors are often the most concerned about pushing capitalist values as equivalent to the good life. Since many do not sell individual consumer goods, they see advertising as a way of bolstering the corporate image in a general way, in an effort to counteract bad publicity about corporate responsibility for widespread social evils. These advertisers sponsor "prestige" programming—TV movies and specials. "People who watch television that they think is exceptional in quality tend to remember advertisers," notes David Poltrack, CBS vice president for research. These ads typically show industry itself as the source of human progress. They often feature workers testifying to the joys of sharing in this good work.

The Flow Is the Message

30   The overall effect of this juxtaposition of ads and programs is interesting to analyze. In a typical hour of soap opera, for example, the problems of characters and commercials blend almost perfectly. Domestic crises such as adultery, rebellious teenagers, accidents and natural disasters, and weddings and funerals are standard fare on soaps. It takes the characters far too long—in most viewers' minds—to straighten things out and get to the happy ending. The ads tell a different tale. Just as the viewer is feeling frustrated and distraught over a favorite character's blindness to some human truth, or refusal to seek help for some problem, the show will cut to a commercial where the very same actors, wearing the same kind of clothes and living in the same kind of houses, will give us the quick answer, the fool proof cure.

31   Children's shows are the most extreme examples of the merging of content and commercial. There are now entire half hour programs featuring as heroes the very toys that sponsor the shows. First we see the Smurfs as heroes; then we are told where we can buy our very own set. The adventure shows are punctuated with ads for games and gadgets which will bring the same kind of adventure into your child's life. The cereal and snack ads play on the child's need to fit in, be part of the crowd. Everyone is eating Sugar Snaps, kids are told.

32   There is no way to appreciate the impact of TV—fiction and nonfiction—without understanding the sheer ideological impact of hearing and seeing different versions of the same propagandistic messages over and over again. What seems like a lot of fast cutting from form to form is in fact a very clever format by which messages are reinforced through the rapidly shifting but constant replaying of key images and ideas. Cultural analysts Michelle and Armand Mattelart have referred to "the syndrome of repetition" as a major factor in the power of "the American image industry" and the global popularity of such American cultural products as "Dallas" and *Raiders of the Lost Ark*. The meaning of an image emerges from the relationship between this image and others that the audience has already seen. This process . . . constantly nour-

ishes the memory of the American image industry.

In the same way, the juxtaposition of various familiar images in the flow of TV programming tends to reinforce their ideological power.

33 The effect of the flow on viewers is even more subtle and powerful in those cases where shows and ads seem to be delivering very different messages. In fact, advertising is one of the most important ways in which network TV manages to present some alternative views and values without undermining its ultimate consumerist, jingoist thrust. When a downbeat theme is presented, dramatically or informatively, the ads will invariably undercut the negative implications and send the viewers off to bed feeling confident and safe. We saw this in our discussions of TV movies like the "The Day After" and "The Burning Bed." The intent of the producer or director to make a socially critical point will be independently undermined by the upbeat, consumerist message of the ads with which it is punctuated.

34 As cable television moves in on network turf, the problem of getting people to watch commercials, rather than zapping the keypad or leaving the room, has begun to worry ad agencies. But those concerned with this problem have a lot of things going for them. For one thing, like all popular TV products, ads are the stuff of our common social communication: the small talk of a society filled with strangers and loners; the jokes of a nation eager to forget the many aspects of their lives that are not at all funny, and over which they feel no control. How else explain the fact that Walter Mondale's only real media points during the 1984 presidential campaign came from his use of a Wendy's slogan: "Where's the Beef?" And who in this country doesn't know about the sexy Jordache ads, the hilarious Express Mail commercials, the arty series of Anacin ads featuring dramatic monologues by serious actors impersonating workers?

35 In a recent *TV Guide* article, a CBS executive worried that zapping was becoming a big problem for advertisers. "We all have this gut feeling that something dreadful is taking place," she said. But no sooner is the problem named than it is easily solved. "The answer is simple. . . . We have to create a zap-proof commercial: a commercial so good that viewers won't want to change the channel." Judging from past performances and from the enormous creative and financial resources available to ad agencies, that is certainly not the impossible dream.

Critical Explorations: Reading

Use these five questions to further examine the Rapping selection as you reread it. In answering these questions, you will be able to express more clearly the semiotics of American television commercials. You may incorporate your answers in your reading or dialogic journal.

1. What does Rapping mean when she says this in paragraph 11: "TV commercials tend to encourage people to see their identities in terms of what they consume, rather than what they produce"? What sort of identity is this? What types of emotional problems can this identity create for the viewer?

2. Reread paragraph 12. How has American advertising led to the decline of American socialism?

3. Reread paragraph 17. Comment on what you think Rapping is suggesting when she says that commercials "function much as dreams and poetry do."

4. Reread paragraph 20. What is the conflict between goods and human values that Rapping sees in American advertising? Specifically, what does she mean when she says that "goods offered, in and of themselves, never embody the values that commercial art attaches to them"?

5. In paragraph 28, Rapping examines the envy and guilt that the viewer of American commercials feels. How does this guilt lead to further purchasing? What sort of desire do this envy and guilt create in the viewer?

Selection 14

"McDonald's 'History of the Family'"
   Robert Goldman

In this selection, Robert Goldman carefully considers how the traditional American belief in the family is used by *McDonald's* advertisers to boost sales of their products. Goldman chooses several popular commercials that *McDonald's* has shown on television over the years, and he analyzes how camera movements, lighting, character, and dialogue all work together to suggest that in the *McDonald's* chain, you can find the best of what the American family stands for. In painting this American family portrait, *McDonald's* is also creating in its viewers a desire for this ideal American family.

Goldman's selection, which comes from his full-length study *Reading Ads Socially,* will provide you with intelligent ways to analyze television commercials that you can then apply to the formal essay you write on commercials.

Since this selection comes from a scholarly sociology book, you may find some of the terms difficult. Look over the footnoted words as you read. Focus on Goldman's analyses of the *McDonald's* narratives. These sections are the most important parts of his argument. See how Goldman weaves American beliefs into his study of the details in these narratives. Finally, determine what all these *McDonald's* commercials have in common. Answer these two questions in your second reading: What American beliefs are found in the commercials that Goldman analyzes? How are these beliefs used in the ads to sell the product?

Reading–Writing Preparation

Before you read this selection, you may want to answer the following questions in writing or discussion:

1. If you can, describe a *McDonald's* television commercial that you have recently seen. How does this commercial help sell *McDonald's* products?

2. Why do you think *McDonald's* relies on the family to sell its products?

McDonald's "History of the Family"

1   The first half of this 1978 *McDonald's* ad tells the 'history' of the American family. Sepia-tinted[1] still photographs are edited together to establish a sense of historical chronology. Combined with contextualizing lyrics, the sepia tinting manufactures an artificial tradition of historical meaning. Counterfeit historical meaning is created by packaging static images of events ripped out of organic, historical context. Linking otherwise discontinuous photographic images as an apparently chronological series of events, this *McDonald's* ad exemplifies historiography[2] in the 'society of the spectacle.' Several decades ago Henri Lefebvre observed that

---

1. sepia-tinted: brown-tinted style suggesting an event in the past

Robert Goldman. *Reading Ads Socially.* New York: Routledge, 1992, 92–100. Reprinted by permission of the publisher.

---

2. historiography: the techniques and principles used to study history

publicity acquires the significance of an ideology, the ideology of trade, and it replaces what was once philosophy, ethics, religion, and aesthetics. (1971: 107)

Now we can add history to the list. By abstracting and separating photographic records of unspecified actors and actions from their lived, organic context, these photographs become signifiers in search of a signified. And the new unity of signifier and signified is imposed by *McDonald's*, which has selected the value of family integrity and stability as the signified.

2   The ad begins by scanning across a drawing of Pilgrim-like figures. This camera movement is repeated with the following photographs: a pioneer family standing in front of a covered wagon; sturdy farm laborers (a woman and two men) standing in a plains hayfield; a late nineteenth-century middle-class family portrait (parents and five children); a group of children on Flag Day circa 1900; and two scenes of southern and eastern European immigrant families. Drawing on an already existent—albeit simplistic—referent system of 'American history' (pilgrims, pioneers, farmers and immigrants), each photograph has been selected for its appearance and mood of authenticity and age. The photos' sepia texture encourages a sense of these images as an authentic recording of an earlier epoch. The arrangement of photographs and lyrics functions as a set of instructions guiding interpretation, positioning viewers to see these otherwise isolated and decontextualized images as a chronologically continuous and coherent sequence of events.

3   Coupled with cues about chronology, careful attention to details of dress (e.g., suspenders, shoes, pants) and milieu[3] in the next scene situates it near the beginning of the twentieth century. But, unlike the preceding images, this scene of youth playing leap frog is presented in film

---

3. milieu: place or surroundings

format and is obviously a manufactured replica. Why does the advertiser risk contradicting and annulling the appearance of authenticity cultivated via the selection of 'real' photos? While the transition to film introduces potentially discrepant interpretive procedures, it is undertaken to create a bridge between the imagery of recorded history and a theme of 'living history.' To minimize the discrepancy and accentuate the theme of continuity the advertiser maintains a strong sepia overtone to the action film. The film gradually brightens as the ad progresses in its movement toward modernity, but remains dominated by browns and then reds. The ad also briefly oscillates between 'original' photographs and the filmed depictions of the transition to modernity. The first film sequence is immediately followed by another original photo of five black women—standing proud, erect and independent—with two children. This photo, in turn, gives way to the ad's most elaborate scenic reproduction: a mock-up of 'G. Watson & Son' family grocery store circa 1920. No detail has been spared: a period car is parked in front, a sign on the window reads 'Fruits & Vegetables: Farm to you,' and produce is arranged on open sidewalk stands. A young boy in knickers runs past. Watson beckons him back and tosses him an apple. The next scene shows three middle-aged women exchanging warm greetings at a family reunion in the 1930s, followed by a scene of a young woman holding a child as she welcomes home her soldier/husband at World War II's close. Lyrics and images have been integrated to spell out the relationship between the family and America's development as a nation-state.

You, you're the one
So loving, strong, and patient.
Families like yours
made all the states a nation.
Our families are our past,
our future and our pride.
Whatever roots we come from,
we're growing side by side.

This version of history presents the family as the major force in the development of US society. This resembles a 'New Right' ideology of the nuclear family fostering the strength and love that make for a free and democratic society. As Jimmy Stewart said in his mini-address before the 1980 Republican Convention, the family is 'the core of the country . . . that's where it all begins.'

4   The ad's narrative appellates[4] viewers, 'You, you're the one': this is 'your' family and 'our' history. The pronouns are not only inclusive, they become the means of joining *McDonald's* with US history; joining *McDonald's* with us—sharing our interests. The lyrics picture the family in terms of the melting-pot ideology—tolerance, diversity, pluralism[5] and consensus. Synchronized to the first scene of an immigrant family at a railing preparing to disembark from a ship is the lyric 'families like . . .' Although the lyric is completed by 'yours,' the image has shifted to a more prominent white middle-class family. While promoting its manifestly non-racist imagery of the melting pot, *McDonald's* latently identifies 'your' family as white and middle class. Still, as a nation, we are really one big happy family—'Whatever roots we come from, we're growing side by side.' Apparently speaking for all of us, *McDonald's* not only makes itself 'our' historian, it also implicates itself in its narrative of history. This is accomplished via a process of pronoun substitution, as the lyrics move from 'you' the subject to 'your' family to 'our' nation-state and history, until we = *McDonald's* + us (subject, family, state).

5   The stress is on continuity—the families that contributed to American ascendancy within the modern world-system were no different from our families. Responding to uncertainty about declining US influence and power throughout the world and the 'traditional' nuclear family in functional disarray, *McDonald's* propounds the counter-thesis that national integrity and the strength of the family as an institution remain, as ever, tied together. But *McDonald's* history of the family conceals 'all evidence of the upheaval and displacement in capitalism's transition from small businesses to multinational conglomerates' (Madison Social Text Group, 1979: 179). Because this excludes conflicts and contradictions to which family life has been exposed with the rise of corporate capitalism, it conveniently denies the ways in which capitalist development has imperiled existing forms of family life even as it has burdened the family with providing privatized emotional support. *McDonald's* nostalgic evocation of personal relations associated with the family-owned grocery store obscures the fact that such relations were negated by the development of corporate capitalism.

6   The ad's second part consists of nine tightly packaged (2–3 seconds each) *scenes* of contemporary families in ideal-typical form. In contrast to the prior sequence, these scenes appear contemporary and timeless. Chronology evaporates following the scene at the end of World War II: the entire history of *McDonald's* in post-war America appears as if cut from a single piece of cultural fabric. Sequencing this series of scenes in relation to the preceding narrative of family history, *McDonald's* superimposes its mythology of the past over the present. These scenes display the following social relations: 1) a mom, dad, brother and sister playfully pillow fight and wrestle on the bed on Sunday morning (the Sunday cartoons lie open on the bed); 2) a brother and sister in baseball uniforms walk home through a park; 3) a pregnant woman and husband stroll in a park-like setting; 4) a black father and young son share a warm embrace; 5) a modern middle-class portrait of a closely knit mother, father and two daughters in front of their home; 6) an elderly black couple rock on the porch as she peels apples and he playfully teases her; 7) a Chicano family—mom, dad, daughter and grandmother —collectively beam as they walk from church where they've celebrated the child's first commu-

---

4. appellates: names

5. pluralism: belief that the world is made up of different people with different values

nion; 8) an elderly couple celebrate an anniversary as they toast each other and blow out the candles on a cake; 9) an attractive all-American couple stand together as the father lifts their infant child over his head.

7   Each scene frames the meaning of the nuclear family, addressing experiences that correspond to genuine needs in the family life cycle: expecting a child, having children, parents and children sharing affection, growing old together. These scenes uniformly locate the experience of harmonious familial relations in a context of leisure and home. Synchronized to the flow of the lyrics, the meaning of these framed photos seems immediately apparent.

> *You, you're the one.*
> *You moms and dads and brothers, sisters and sons.*
> *We're stronger for each other.*
> *A family is a feeling that together is more fun.*
> *Looking out for one another*
> *That's the way our families run.*

The family is defined as an *affective state*. These lyrics depict the family as a support group, a source of nourishment and security, and the means of securing commitment, stability and continuity. When the modern middle-class family portrait fuses with the lyric, 'A family is a feeling . . . ,' the mock-up family photo places all members in physical contiguity, thus signifying the packed ('together') family unit as the natural site for intimacy and trust.

8   Viewers are steered to presume that each scene in the sequence stands for the universal concept of 'the family.' Each scene is structured around the mobilization of paleosymbols.

> Paleosymbols are tied to particular scenes charged with drama and emotion. The paleosymbol does not provide or integrate holistic constructs such as the cross, the hammer and sickle, or aesthetic images that crystallize a wealth of meaning and significance; rather the paleosymbolic requires a whole scene where a positive or negative situation occurs. (Kellner, 1979: 16)

Manipulating paleosymbolic content in these scenes is designed to trigger *positive emotional valences.*[6] *McDonald's* ad turns our subjectivity into their sign by connecting the effect generated by these paleosymbolic scenes with an ideological portrait of *the* American nuclear family that has already been converted into a second-order signifier of *McDonald's*.

9   How do paleosymbols, and the memories they spark, merchandise an ideological defense of the 'American way of life'? An appealing scene in the *McDonald's* ad centers on two children walking along a tree-shaded path through a sunlit park. The camera positions us so the children are seen from behind as they move away from us. A small girl scurries to catch up with a slightly older and bigger brother. They are dressed in oversized baseball uniforms bearing the insignia 'Tigers' across the back, and they wear baseball caps with the bill turned backwards. The younger child half carries, half drags a bat almost as tall as she, while a catcher's mask is draped over her other arm. She is coded as adorable and idolizing of her brother. As she runs to catch up, her brother halts momentarily, turns to face her and waits impatiently but obligingly with his baseball glove perched on his hip. When she reaches him, she grabs hold of his shirt-tail, and still trailing him they start again down the path (away from the viewer and presumably toward home). The scene's visual structure is situated by keying it to the rhythmic strains of 'You, you're the one. You moms and dads and brothers, *sisters and sons*. We're stronger for each other.' The scene, which lasts less than three seconds, proposes an idealized vision of childhood that prompts viewers to compare their own experiences with this memorable image. The scene's structure invites viewers to interpret the ad in terms of the past (nostalgia) and the future (how you would like to see your children).

---

6. valences: forces

10 This type of scene can elicit an empathetic recollection of similar experiences. Warm feelings tapped by this scenic image spark a remembrance immediately appropriated by *McDonald's*, thereby cementing the emotional valence (and the meanings it triggers for any given viewer) to themselves and a broader notion of well-being. Advertisers consider the formulaic construction of such paleosymbolic scenes an efficient means of selling. A noted advertising strategist describes the technique:

> The total amount of information imprinted or coded within our brains is huge, and the associations that can be generated by *evoked recall* are very deep. Information available for recall includes everything we have experienced, whether we consciously remember it or not. The total body of stored material is always with us, and it surrounds and absorbs each new learning experience. Furthermore, it is instantly recallable when cued by the appropriate stimulus. (Schwartz, 1979: 325)

In *McDonald's* ad, post-war American society is a world of harmony and pluralism where stability, security and happiness are rooted in the American family. There is no tension and apparently no divorce in the world of the *McDonald's* family. Everyone smiles and nobody works. The family, it seems, consists only of affective relations conducted in the absence of all mediating relations—with the exception of *McDonald's*.

11 *McDonald's* affirms its faith in the strength and importance of the family as an institution by associating itself with the ideal American family they have decorated. This is confirmed by the yellow *McDonald's* frame that encloses the final photographic representation of the ideal-typical American family at the ad's end. An image of a radiant young couple holding their infant child is suddenly surrounded by the *McDonald's* frame, making it literally a picture in the family album—the *McDonald's* family album. *McDonald's* logo (the yellow-arched M) appears beneath the picture along with the slogan 'We do it all for you.' This frames the positive emotional valence as the experience of family life *brought to you by McDonald's* presence in our lives: 'We do it all for you.'

McDonald's Revisited

12 Another *McDonald's* television ad (1982) celebrated the meaning of continuity in American life by presenting *McDonald's* story of family and community in contemporary urban America. An ideal-typical family has returned to Dad's 'Hometown' so he can show them the world he knew as a child. His memory hunting takes place in the family station-wagon Dad drives. With son and daughter in the back seat and Mom in the front, they cruise the old neighborhood streets. Anticipating his big moment, Dad informs the family his old house is 'just up the street here.' But a soprano voice in the background (functioning as *McDonald's* muse) warns that 'things have changed a bit since you've been around.' And, sure enough, the old homestead has been replaced by condominium apartments. From the back seat the son innocently inquires, 'What floor did you live on, Dad?' Disappointment washes across Dad's face as he realizes 'It's not there any more.' But he quickly reassures both himself and the family as he announces 'Well, wait a minute. I'll show you where my old friend Shorty lived. 'Wait till you see the flower garden in the front yard. It was just . . .' Dad's excited account of what once was ends abruptly as we discover his old friend's house is now a carwash. 'I don't believe it,' Dad sighs and the music sags. Now the daughter has had enough of Dad's fruitless search for his past, and from the back seat she asserts her needs, 'Dad, I hope that the place where you used to eat is still there, 'cause it's late and I'm hungry.' Without a word, Dad immediately responds by looking for his old eating haunt. Mom casts a faintly empathetic glance in Dad's direction, then turns her head toward the window and quietly looks away. Searching for the as-yet-unnamed eating place, Dad drives while

McDonald's singing voice soothes, 'In the night, the welcome sight of an old friend.' Suddenly Dad's eyes widen, he breaks into a satisfied smile and points, 'There it is.' The camera cuts to their car pulling into *McDonald's* parking lot and the muse[7] soothingly frames the experience, 'Feels so right here tonight at *McDonald's again.'*

13   This small dramatic sequence subtly unfolds a set of meaningful relations. The child expresses a want that conflicts with her father's desire to locate his 'roots.' However, the father responds by dutifully deferring/abandoning his wants and acting to meet hers. Mom reacts to the conflict-tinged interaction in silence: she mediates conflict between other family members through silence. Her action acknowledges pre-eminence of the child's need *vis-à-vis* the father's while mutely expressing momentary sympathy for the necessity of Dad's parental sacrifice. This conflict is, however, fully resolved through consumption activities. Dad lights up when he spies *McDonald's*, and when the family enters *McDonald's* restaurant area in the next scene, they are all cheerful and aglow. Everyone's needs are satisfied at *McDonald's*.

14   The family is pictured in this scene as the 'symbolization of the family's social structure.'

> Turning to mocked-up families in advertisements, one finds that the allocation of at least one girl and at least one boy ensures that a symbolization of the full set of interfamily relations can be effected. (Goffman, 1976: 37)

As this portrait of the middle-class nuclear family nears the counter Dad explains to the countergirl (and to us) the personal significance of the occasion. 'I (uh) had my first Big Mac here,' he gestures. The countergirl—young, cute and effusive—asks, 'May get you another one?' 'All around,' replies Dad, as the singer draws out the last phrase of the previous lyric—'again'—to cover (and meaningfully situate for viewers) the salience of this interaction. Nothing changes at *McDonald's*, it's like being home again. A quick cut turns our attention to a close-up of a bespectacled man's face. Something across the room catches his eye. Surprise and disbelief register on his face. Rising from his table, he wonders aloud, 'Curly?' The camera pulls back to show him approaching the family's table, where Dad is animatedly recounting a story about growing up. As the man nears the table Dad interrupts his story, turning his head to see who it is. Dad does a double take, then stands to meet the smaller man, and peering intently at the man he ventures in a quizzical voice, 'Shorty?' ['Is that you?']. The question confirms what we have already suspected, and Shorty opens his arms and affirmatively exclaims 'Curly!' The old friends laugh delightedly, reunited in a joyful embrace punctuated by the lyrics, 'To *McDonald's*, tonight at *McDonald's*.' An image of *McDonald's* golden arches seen through the window, immediately adjacent to the image of old friends embracing, frames the feelings of reunion as being available at *McDonald's*, derivative of *McDonald's* presence.

15   The final scene is a close-up of son and daughter, literally set within a yellow *McDonald's* frame, across which is written the slogan, 'You deserve a break today.' Having absorbed the reunion scene, the girl leans toward her brother and inquires with suggestive irony, 'Curly?' Her brother responds with a passive shrug and roll of the eyes. As a joke about their father's balding condition, this sequence is premised on schisms[8] in generational experiences. The generational distinction is amplified by the structure of this scene. For the first time in this ad the children are presented in their relationship to each other as siblings. And, situated between and in front of their faces is the only prominent display of a hamburger in the ad. The children neither share in, nor care about, their father's reunion. Their needs are more immediate, and what connects

---

7. muse: poet, in this sense

8. schisms: breakups into opposing groups

them together is that *McDonald's* hamburger sitting between them. *McDonald's* curiously acknowledges here that the family unit they have idealized is actually bound together by serialized consumption relations. Or, to put it in advertisers' terms, this family is composed of market segments. Sound marketing strategy dictates that *McDonald's* offer each market segment—parents and children—an appealing incentive for coming to *McDonald's*. But to actualize this strategy, *McDonald's* ends up tacitly subverting their claim that *family* is defined by the rich and empathetic sharing of common experiences.

16   What is being sold here? The viewer knows—and is presumed to know by the advertiser—because of prior acquaintance with *McDonald's* that fast food service is being sold. Yet there is only one mention of a 'Big Mac' (and that, to connote the idea of *McDonald's* as an old friend), and only one conspicuous visual display of a hamburger (deployed to anchor another social relation between the children). In fact, this ad is a sustained attempt *to sell social relations.* In a world characterized by instability, upheaval and the impoverishment of conditions favorable to primary social relations, *McDonald's* depicts itself as a 'haven in a heartless world.' Against the backdrop of commercial urban upheaval, *McDonald's* endures, there to repair the splits in our lives. *Angst*[9] prompted by the absence of stable communities and friends is supposedly healed by *McDonald's*. *McDonald's* is the 'old friend' that remains, solid and reliable, to soothe our wounds and bring us together with 'lost' friends. Although the moment and need the ad taps are authentic, the resolution it provides is false.

17   Is *McDonald's* really a countervailing[10] force against privatized rootlessness and continual social and geographic separation from family and significant others? In fact, the injury they claim to heal is fostered by corporate capitalist institu-

tions that exhibit a greater concern for maintaining internal labor market requirements and corporate balance sheets than for the well-being of local communities (Bluestone and Harrison, 1982). In the late 1970s, one out of four persons in the working population was fired, laid off or transferred every year. When they compel constant geographic mobility that is antithetical[11] to forming stable networks of friends, relatives and neighbors, labor market practices promote social instability and fragmentation in individuals' lives. Thus

> the expectation that one will live in a stable neighborhood with a stable group of friends becomes increasingly unrealistic. Plans are made, futures are decided, and identities and relationships are established on the narrowest of social bases. Nothing else can be counted on. (Smith, 1981: 282)

McDonald's seizes upon anxieties stimulated by separation and isolation, and implies these can be annulled and overcome through consumption of *McDonald's* as a commodity-sign (*McDonald's* = community of kinship and friends). This ideological resolution is possible only by separating consumption relations from production relations. This fiction is compounded when considered in the light of ads' unspoken premise—that a product and its sign are available in exchange for a monetary equivalent. And how is that monetary equivalent obtained?—for the vast majority of the population it is gained through the sale of labor.

18   *McDonald's* offers a resolution consisting of commodifying family and community. When they assert that dissolution of family and community can be countered through consumption at *McDonald's*, the experience of a convivial[12] family life is transformed into a ready-made sign. For this to be so, the fiction must be established that experiences of family life are the same across

---

9. *angst*: dread or anxiety

10. countervailing: opposing

11. antithetical: directly contrasting

12. convivial: festive, jovial

all family units. *McDonald's* resolution to the crisis of personal life is only possible if the family is abstracted from the complex contextual features of daily life. And the only place where that is possible is in the *McDonald's* ad.

Critical Explorations: Reading

The following five questions will test your understanding and use of the critical practices that you have been introduced to thus far, particularly identifying and analyzing generalizations, forming definitions, and analyzing the connotations of words. Answer these questions as you reread this selection. They may provide material for your reading or dialogic journal.

1. Reread the McDonald's slogans displayed in paragraph 3. Rewrite them as generalizations. Are they hasty or valid?

2. In paragraph 5, Goldman examines the nostalgic image of small-town America that McDonald's advertisers use to sell their products. How does this image contradict the type of corporation that McDonald's, in reality, is?

3. In paragraph 8, Goldman introduces the term "paleosymbol" and in paragraph 15 "market segments." Reread these two paragraphs, and, from the details that Goldman presents, define these two terms as completely as you can.

4. In paragraph 11, Goldman concludes that the famous McDonald's golden arches frame the picture in the commercial he analyzes. What inferences can you draw from these arches framing the commercial's final shot? Also, what connotations come to your mind when you consider golden arches?

5. In paragraph 18, Goldman examines the conclusion that the McDonald's commercial in question makes: *"McDonald's* resolution to the crisis of personal life is only possible if the family is abstracted from the complex contextual features of daily life." Rephrase this unqualified generalization. Do you think it is valid?

Selection 15

"The Shock(ing) Value at Fashion's Cutting Edge"
Richard Martin

This selection introduces the interesting relationship among advertising, fashion, and popular culture. Richard Martin is a museum curator, and his expertise is costume and fashion. In this article, Martin poses several thought-provoking questions concerning the ways that fashion both interprets and shapes American popular culture. He also considers the ways that fashion and fashion advertising are both commercial ventures and artistic statements. In the second half of his essay, Martin focuses on the following question: How are fashion and fashion advertising like and unlike art?

This selection is a helpful preparation for this chapter's final reading, "The Jeaning of America," in which John Fiske examines how the consistently popular American blue jean is influenced by and influences American popular culture.

The Martin essay is straightforward, and for the most part it is clearly written and specific. Some sentences are long, but you can generally determine what they mean once you reread them. You may not understand all of Martin's allusions to art, literature, and film, so the footnotes for this selection will provide you with the necessary information. Martin presents one argument and uses evidence from the fashion world to support it. As you read, write out Martin's argument and list the evidence that seems to best support it. After you finish reading and rereading this selection, you will be able to form your own opinions on the roles of fashion and fashion ads in American popular culture. Is fashion commercial gain or artistic statement? Does fashion direct the trends and discussion of popular culture? Or is fashion a reflection of popular culture?

Reading–Writing Preparation

Before you read this selection, you may want to answer the following questions in writing or discussion:

1. What statements do you think people make by the clothes they wear? Choose a particular form of dress, and analyze the statement it seems to be making.

2. What is the most shocking fashion commercial you have seen lately? Why do you think this fashion commercial is so bold?

The Shock(ing) Value at Fashion's Cutting Edge

1   Fashion claimed more victims this season. Six million. The European Jewish Congress rebuked fashion designer Rei Kawakubo of Comme des Garcons for showing striped gray pajamas in her menswear collection last month—on the 50th anniversary of the liberation of Auschwitz.[1] They called the clothing "deeply disturbing" and the runway presentation, on a thin model with a shaved head, "particularly shocking."

2   Ten days later, Comme des Garcons, acting on the entreaty of the Jewish group, withdrew the pajamas and their fabric from the collection and from sale, stating "Comme des Garcons acknowledges now that, however unwittingly, it has caused some people to remember the terrible events of World War II. This misinterpretation has caused Rei Kawakubo much sadness and she has expressed her sincere regret."

3   Thus, an incident passes. All concerned pull back from the brink of hysteria and name-calling. But fashion remains on the edge. While Kawakubo's avowal is that she had no idea anyone would read Auschwitz into striped pajamas—which had numbers printed above the breast

pockets and boot prints painted on them—shown on an emaciated model with cropped hair, it is hard not to associate the clothing with the concentration camps. If no "witting" allusion was being made, fashion nonetheless proceeded to walk its provocative, culturally combustible walk on the runway.

4   Serge Cwajgenbaum of the European Jewish Congress lamented that the clothing might be a "banalization"[2] of Holocaust sufferings. He was mistaken. Fashion, as this incident reveals, is seldom banal. Rather, the representation of cultural politics on the living body is always a matter of fierce feelings and often of vehement denials contending that fashion is meaningless or otherwise so meaningful that it cannot be taken at face value.

5   In 1994, designer Karl Lagerfeld included in his dresses for Chanel Arabic words from the Koran.[3] Not only were the inscriptions embroidered on clothing, but they appeared on one notably low-cut bodice, worn on the runway by buxom model Claudia Schiffer. On Muslim protest, Chanel apologized and destroyed the dresses. One wonders if the fashion gambit is not to offend—and then to offer an apology: dress and redress.

---

1. Auschwitz: World War II Nazi death camp

Los Angeles Times Opinion Section, February 19, 1995. Reprinted by permission of the author.

2. banalization: trivialization

3. Koran: Moslem holy book

Concept: O. Toscani. Courtesy of United Colors of Benetton.

6   Fashion seems to vacillate between outrage and decorum—but the outrage is too frequent to go ignored, either by fashion's advocates or its censors. The politics of the runway are unabashedly confrontational, whether Jean-Paul Gaultier's faux Hasidim[4] or men in skirts or Lagerfeld's audacious and up-front (literally) Koran. The Futurists[5] may have had their manifestoes and the Surrealists[6] their symposiums, but fashion designers have the media of the world in attendance for their declarations.

7   Just days ago, menswear designer John Bartlett gave each guest at his fashion show a pamphlet, "What is the ultimate definition of masculinity?" with the designer's thoughts on the subject. Among other things, he wrote, "In a 'cut-'n'-paste' culture that celebrates John Wayne Bobbitt[7] as a symbol of male heroism, where does the self-aware, expressive, comfortably insane individual find a fit?" Even so, Bartlett's most persuasive statement was his 40 minutes of clothing on the runway, with all media observing.

8   Fashion and fashion advertising have long been on the knife's edge of cultural challenge. Are Oliviero Toscani's AIDS-sensitive images, multicultural children, and strife of war the instruments for enchanting the fashion imagination to buy Benetton sportswear? Recently, a number of Benetton franchises in Germany seceded, expelling Benetton merchandise in protest against the company's social advertizing and shocking images.[8]

---

4. faux Hasidim: a false representation of a Jewish mystical group's dress

5. Futurists: artists in the early twentieth century who depicted the violence and speed of technology

6. Surrealists: artists in the early twentieth century who focused on what the unconscious mind sees

---

7. John Wayne Bobbitt: American made famous in the early nineties by his wife, who severed his penis

8. Benetton won their court case against these former retailers, ensuring that they pay their debt toward the company.

L. M. Otreo / AP Wide World

9   Ever since Brooke Shields averred that nothing came between her and her Calvins in 1980, Calvin Klein has pushed jeans, underwear and fragrance advertising to the limits of body and sexuality in public places and in magazine advertising. Propriety and provocation are carefully, even deliberately, balanced in an image of excitement. Klein piques and perturbs—but seldom does he alienate. Gianni Versace presses the liberal cultural agenda, as if a contract for Kennedy Democrats the world over, in bondage-inspired clothing (1992) and advanced advertising with Madonna and Sylvester Stallone. It is as if he were representing the ACLU[9]—not the other way round. In a time when funding for the arts is uncertain, art may be timorous,[10] whereas commercial fashion—which pays its own bills— is bold.

10   Ironically, fashion is maintaining a myth of the avant-garde[11] long after it has waned in the other arts. In clothing and its advertising, shock remains a value, even while art has subsided into postmodern adjudication[12] with memory and with a median. The outrage that swirled around Vaslav Nijinsky, James Joyce, Paul Poiret, Igor Stravinsky and Marcel Duchamp[13] was specific to each, but the culture of the early 20th Century was attuned to art's surprise, scandal and disturbance. In a more tranquil world for art—if an equally troubled one socially—only fashion insists on acting out dissonance and stirring up the kinds of social ruckus that art once lived by.

11   Is fashion, then, the last gritty, gutsy avant-garde or is it merely the crass and commercial imitator of what used to be the introductory principles of great art?

12   Shockingly, fashion is our abiding connection to the cultures of stimulation and shock. Fashion's motives may not be pure but its aesthetic

9. ACLU: American Civil Liberties Union (liberal legal defense group)

10. timorous: fearfully timid

11. avant-garde: leaders of new and unconventional movements

12. postmodern adjudication: judgments made since World War II

13. Vaslav Nijinsky, James Joyce, Paul Poiret, Igor Stravinsky, Marcel Duchamp: early-twentieth-century artists and writers whose works are now considered great but were considered shocking at the time

position is certain. Fashion is the visual art that has inherited and is striving to maintain—perhaps along with its fellow popular visual art, film—the defining role of cultural pacesetter. Incapable of being rarefied[14]—everyone wears clothes—fashion is the popular visual medium most connected to the cultural issues of gender and sexuality that drive the secular century that Sigmund Freud invented for us.

13   Filmmaker Robert Altman may have made a terrible movie about fashion, but Altman's intuition that fashion was a significant subject was correct. His error was to think he could be more outrageous than fashion itself. The Kawakubo controversy proves this. Altman's naked runway cannot measure up to the Holocaust shadow on the Comme des Garcons runway and the ever-present possibility that fashion will go even farther. Fashion's relentless vanguard has moved beyond titillation[15] and counterculture[16] to probe what really makes us think and what really makes us hurt.

14   How can fashion—those frocks, that frippery—be entrusted with such an important cultural mission and purpose? As Oscar Wilde[17] said, "It is only shallow people who do not judge by appearance. The true mystery of the world is the visible, not the invisible."

15   Perhaps fashion advertising has to challenge our conscience in a time when so little provokes and so little in art really matters. Perhaps fashion, wittingly or unwittingly, impels us to fear, anxiety and the horrific because every other art has chosen the safe course. Our cozy, comfortable relationship to clothes can make us complacent about an art that still has the power to confront and disturb.

---

14. rarefied: rare, extraordinary

15. titillation: superficial excitement

16. counterculture: culture of the young that rejects established values

17. Oscar Wilde: flamboyant late-nineteenth-century Irish playwright and novelist

16   Is fashion political? Ask anyone who has seen a uniform in a time of war or who has reacted to the sexuality of attire.

17   Can a garment mean so much? Ask any Holocaust survivor who once clung to the inexpressible dignity of clothing remnants, the tatters of personal and social decency.

Critical Explorations: Reading

Answer the following five questions as you reread the Martin selection. Responding to these questions will help you understand the more subtle suggestions that Martin is making about fashion and popular culture and the details of his argument. You may want to use some of your answers to these questions in your reading or dialogic journal.

1.   What does Martin mean in paragraph 4 when he says that "the representation of cultural politics on the living body is always a matter of fierce feelings and often of vehement denials contending that fashion is meaningless or otherwise so meaningful that it cannot be taken at face value"? How does this statement relate to Martin's argument about the place of fashion in culture, politics, and art?

2.   Reread paragraph 10. What is Martin's argument here about fashion and art? What inference can you make regarding Martin's attitude toward fashion?

3.   Reread paragraph 12. What does Martin mean when he says that "fashion is our abiding connection to the cultures of stimulation and shock"? What evidence does he provide for this statement in paragraph 12?

4.   Reconsider the Oscar Wilde quotation in paragraph 14: "It is only shallow people who do not judge by appearance. The true mystery of the world is the visible, not the invisible." What do you think Wilde means, and how does this statement relate to fashion and fashion advertising?

5. Reread paragraphs 15–17. From the evidence presented here, infer the attitude that Martin has toward fashion. Be detailed in stating his position. Do you agree with his attitude?

Selection 16

"The Jeaning of America"
John Fiske

John Fiske is a famous scholar of popular culture. "The Jeaning of America" is the first chapter of his book titled *Understanding Popular Culture*. In this selection, Fiske examines the semiotic significance of wearing jeans—the popularity of jeans, the various brands one can choose from, and how the wearers see themselves in this product.

Fiske also uses the wearing of jeans and the commercials used to sell them in order to answer a larger question: In buying jeans, is the consumer controlled by a capitalist economy, or does she help direct this capitalist economy?

"The Jeaning of America" is the most challenging selection in this chapter. Fiske uses several terms that you may not be familiar with. Yet many are defined within the contexts of the paragraphs in which you find these words. Look for clues in these paragraphs to assist you in understanding unfamiliar terminology. Fiske is writing for a scholarly audience, so some of his sentences are hard to follow the first time through. Because this is the introductory chapter of his book, Fiske is also presenting the arguments that he will develop in the rest of his study. Unlike the previous Martin selection, there are several arguments here, and they all somehow relate to semiotics, American culture, and American capitalism.

As you read and reread Fiske, keep the following questions in mind: Why do Americans buy jeans? How are American beliefs related to jeans buying? Who determines the kinds of jeans that the American consumer buys? How is buying jeans a good example of what popular culture means? The answers to these questions will be clearer to you in your second reading.

Reading–Writing Preparation

Before you read this selection, you may want to answer the following questions in writing or discussion:

1. What kinds of jeans do you wear? Why do you think you wear these particular jeans?

2. Have jeans commercials helped determine the kinds of jeans you buy? If so, how?

The Jeaning of America

1   Of the 125 students of mine, 118 were, on the day that I asked, wearing jeans. The deviant 7, also possessed jeans, but did not happen to be wearing them. I wonder if any other cultural product—movie, TV program, record, lipstick—

John Fiske. *Understanding Popular Culture*. Boston: Unwin Hyman, 1989, 1–21. Reprinted by permission of Routledge.

would be so *popular*? (T-shirts were as widely owned, but much less regularly worn.) Students may not be typical of the population as a whole, though jeans *are* widely popular among non-students in the same age group, and only slightly less widespread among older age groups. So thinking about jeans is as good a way as any to begin a book on popular culture.

2   Let's dismiss their functionality first, for this has little to do with culture, which is concerned

with meanings, pleasures, and identities rather than efficiency. Of course jeans are a supremely functional garment, comfortable, tough, sometimes cheap, and requiring "low maintenance"—but so, too, are army fatigues. The functionality of jeans is the precondition of their popularity, but does not explain it. In particular, it does not explain the unique ability of jeans to transect almost every social category we can think of: we cannot define a jeans wearer by any of the major social category systems—gender, class, race, age, nation, religion, education. We might argue that jeans have two main social foci, those of youth and the blue-collar or working class, but these foci[1] should be seen as semiotic rather than sociological, that is, as centers of meaning rather than as social categories. So a middle-aged executive wearing jeans as he mows his lawn on a suburban Sunday is, among other things, aligning himself with youthful vigor and activity (in opposition to the distinctly middle-aged office desk) and with the mythic dignity of labor—the belief that physical labor is in some way more honest than wheeling and dealing is deeply imbued in a nation whose pioneers are only a few generations in the past, and is, significantly, particularly widespread among the wheelers and dealers themselves.

3   My students, largely white, middle-class, young, and well educated, are not a representative sample of the whole population, and so the meanings they made of their jeans cannot be extended to other groups, but the process of making and communicating meanings is representative even though the meanings made by it are not.

4   I asked my class to write briefly what jeans meant to each of them: these notes were then discussed generally. The discussions produced, unsurprisingly from such a homogeneous group, a fairly coherent network of meanings that grouped themselves around a few foci. These meaning clusters related to each other sometimes

coherently, sometimes contradictorily, and they allowed different students to inflect[2] the semiotic network differently, to make their own meanings within the shared grid.

5   There was one cluster of meanings that were essentially community integrative, that denied social differences. Jeans were seen as informal, classless, unisex, and appropriate to city or country; wearing them was a sign of freedom from the constraints on behavior and identity that social categories impose. *Free* was the single most common adjective used, frequently with the meaning of "free to be myself."

6   An article in the *New York Times* (20 March 1988) quotes a psychologist who suggests that jeans' lack of differentiation results not in a freedom to be oneself, but the freedom to hide oneself. Jeans provide a facade of ordinariness that enables the wearer to avoid any expression of mood or personal emotion—they are, psychologically at least, repressive. This flip-side of "freedom" was not evident among my students, and it appears to be a typical psychoanalyst's explanation in that it emphasizes the individual over the social and the pathological over the normal. Clothes are more normally used to convey social meanings than to express personal emotion or mood.

7   The lack of social differentiation in jeans gives one the freedom to "be oneself" (and, I suppose, in abnormal cases, to hide oneself), which, of course, points to a telling paradox that the desire to be oneself leads one to wear the same garment as everyone else, which is only a concrete instance of the paradox deeply structured into American (and Western) ideology that the most widely held communal value is that of individualism. The desire to be oneself does not mean the desire to be fundamentally different from everyone else, but rather to situate individual differences within communal allegiance. There were, as we shall see below, signs of social differences

---

1. foci: plural of *focus*

2. inflect: to alter

between jeans wearers, but while these may contradict, they do not invalidate the set of communally integrative meanings of jeans.

8   Another cluster of meanings centered on physical labor, ruggedness, activity, physicality. These meanings, again, were attempts to deny class differences: the physical toughness connoted by jeans allowed these middle-class students to align themselves with a highly selective set of meanings of physical labor (its dignity and its productivity, but certainly not its subordination and exploitedness). Jeans were able to bear class-specific meanings of the American work ethic.

9   Their physicality and ruggedness were not just inflected toward work, they also bore meanings of naturalness and sexuality. *Natural* was an adjective used almost as frequently as *free*. The informality of jeans in contrast with the formality of other clothes was a concrete instance, or transformation, of the deeply structured opposition between nature and culture, the natural and the artificial, the country and the city. The body is where we are most natural, so there was an easy cluster of meanings around the physicality of jeans, the vigor of the adolescent body, and "naturalness." This meaning cluster could be inflected toward strength, physical labor, and sports performance (for sport allows the middle-class body the recognition of physical prowess that labor allows the working class) for the men, and toward sexuality for the women. Of course, such gender differences are not essential, but they are sites of struggle for control over the meanings of masculinity and femininity. Many women participated in the more "masculine" meanings of jeans' physicality, as did many men in their more "feminine" ones, of sexual display.

10   These natural/artificial and physical/nonphysical meanings joined with others in a set clustered around the American West. The association of jeans with the cowboy and the mythology of the Western is still strong. The meanings that helped to make the West significant for these 1980s students were not only the familiar ones of freedom, naturalness, toughness, and hard work

(and hard leisure), but also progress and development and, above all, Americanness. As the opening of the western frontier was a unique and definitive moment in American history, so jeans were seen as a unique and definitive American garment, possibly America's only contribution to the international fashion industry. Despite the easy exportability of the Western myth and its ready incorporability[3] into the popular culture of other nations, it always retains its Americanness: it thus admits the forging of links between American values and the popular consciousness of other nationalities. Similarly, jeans have been taken into the popular culture of practically every country in the world, and, whatever their local meanings, they always bear traces of their Americanness. So in Moscow, for example, they can be made sense of by the authorities as bearers of Western decadence, and they can be worn by the young as an act of defiance, as a sign of their opposition to social conformity—a set of meanings quite different from those of contemporary American youth, though more consonant[4] with those of the 1960s, when jeans could carry much more oppositional meanings than they do today.

11   If today's jeans are to express oppositional meanings, or even to gesture toward such social resistance, they need to be disfigured in some way—tie-dyed, irregularly bleached, or, particularly, torn. If "whole" jeans connote shared meanings of contemporary America, then disfiguring them becomes a way of distancing oneself from those values. But such a distancing is not a complete rejection. The wearer of torn jeans is, after all, wearing jeans and not, for instance, the Buddhist-derived robes of the "orange people": wearing torn jeans is an example of the contradictions that are so typical of popular culture, where what is to be resisted is necessarily present in the resistance to it. Popular culture is deeply contradictory in societies where power is unequally dis-

---

3. incorporability: ability to blend

4. consonant: in agreement

tributed along axes of class, gender, race, and the other categories that we use to make sense of our social differences. Popular culture is the culture of the subordinated and disempowered and thus always bears within it signs of power relations, traces of the forces of domination and subordination that are central to our social system and therefore to our social experience. Equally, it shows signs of resisting or evading these forces: popular culture contradicts itself.

12   The importance of contradiction within popular culture is elaborated throughout this book, but for the moment we can turn to a discussion of two of its characteristics: the first I have noted, that contradiction can entail the expression of both domination and subordination, of both power and resistance. So torn jeans signify both a set of dominant American values and a degree of resistance to them. The second is that contradiction entails semiotic richness and polysemy.[5] It enables the readers of a text, or the wearers of jeans, to partake of both of its forces simultaneously and devolves to them the power to situate themselves within this play of forces at a point that meets their particular cultural interests. So jeans can bear meanings of both community and individualism, of unisexuality and masculinity or femininity. This semiotic richness of jeans means that they cannot have a single defined meaning, but they are a resource bank of potential meanings.

13   Of course, the manufacturers of jeans are aware of all this and attempt to exploit it for their commercial interests. In their marketing and advertising strategies they attempt to target specific social groups and thus to give their product subculturally specific inflections of the more communal meanings. Thus a TV commercial for Levi's 501s shows three youths, obviously poor and of subordinate class and/or race, in a rundown city street. The impression given is one of the sharing of hard living and toughness: the picture is tinted blue-gray to connote the blueness of jeans, of blue-collar life, and of "the blues" as a cultural form that expresses the hardships of the socially deprived. The sound track plays a blues-influenced jingle. Yet, contradicting these pessimistic meanings are traces of cowboyness, of living rough but succeeding, of making a little personal freedom or space within a constrained environment, and of finding a masculine identity and community within the hard living. The ad bears distinct traces of the ideology of meritocratic[6] capitalism that one can, should, make one's success and identity out of hard conditions; one should not be born to them.

14   This image of jeans may seem very different from that promoted by an ad for Levi's 505s that show a girl wearing them looking up at the sky, where a skein[7] of wild geese is flying in a formation that spells out "Levi's." This foregrounds meanings of freedom and naturalness, and then links feminine sexuality to them. In the two ads freedom, nature, and femininity are directly opposed to deprivation, the city, and masculinity, and Levi's jeans cross the opposition and bring to each side of it meanings of the other. So the inner-city youths can participate in the meanings of nature and freedom in their jeans, as the young woman can take these meanings with her into an urban environment, confident that they will fit easily. All meanings are ultimately intertextual[8]— no one text, no one advertisement can ever bear the full meanings of jeans, for this can exist only in that ill-defined cultural space between texts that precedes the texts that both draw upon it and contribute to it, which exists only in its constant circulation among texts and society. The 501 and 505 ads specify quite different inflections of this intertextuality of jeans, but they necessarily draw

---

5. polysemy: multiple meanings

6. meritocratic: describing equality based upon merit

7. skein: flock

8. intertextual: meaning derived from several texts

upon it. For all their surface difference, their deep semiotic structure is shared, and thus the wearer of one bears, to a greater or lesser degree, the meanings of the other.

15   Jeans are no longer, if they ever were, a generic denim garment. Like all commodities, they are given brand names that compete among each other for specific segments of the market. Manufacturers try to identify social differences and then to construct equivalent differences in the product so that social differentiation and product differentiation become mapped onto each other. Advertising is used in an attempt to give meanings to these product differences that will enable people in the targeted social formation to recognize that they are being spoken to, or even to recognize their own social identity and values in the product. The different meanings (and therefore market segments) of 501s and 505s are created at least as much by the advertising as by any differences in the jeans themselves.

16   Designer jeans, then, speak to market segmentation and social differences: they move away from the shared values, away from nature, toward culture and its complexities. Wearing designer jeans is an act of distinction, of using a socially locatable accent to speak a common language. It is a move upscale socially, to the city and its sophistication, to the trendy and the socially distinctive. The oppositions between generic jeans and designer jeans can be summarized like this:

generic jeans	designer jeans
classless	upscale
country	city
communal	socially distinctive
unisex	feminine (or more rarely, masculine)
work	leisure
traditional	contemporary
unchanging	transient
THE WEST	THE EAST
NATURE	CULTURE

17   Jeans' semiotic shift from the left to the right is partly a way in which grass-roots myths of America can be incorporated into a contemporary, urbanized, commodified society, one where the pressures of mass living and the homogenizing forces that attempt to massify us have produced a deep need for a sense of individuality and social difference. So the ads for designer jeans consistently stress how they will fit YOU; the physicality of the body is more than a sign of nature, vigor, and sexuality, it becomes a sign of individuality. Our bodies are, after all, where we are most ourselves and where our individual differences are most apparent: "Get into great shape, . . . your shape. With Wrangler. The jeans that give you the shape you want in the size you want . . . *A Fit for Every-Body*" or "Your exact waist size, you've got it. Exact length? It's yours" (Chic jeans). The increasing individualism, of course, goes with a rise up the social ladder. So Zena jeans are instrumental in enabling their owner (who, in the ad, has just stepped out of them for purposes left to our imaginations) to meet a hunk with a law degree from Yale who's into downhill skiing but hates French films. Jeans have moved into a world where class difference and fine social distinctions within class are all-important.

18   Along with class difference goes gender difference. It is significant how many of the ads for designer jeans are aimed at women, for, in our patriarchal[9] society, women have been trained more than men to invest their social identity, self-esteem, and sexuality in the appearance of their bodies.

19   Underlying these manifest differences are the more fundamental ones of the differences between East and West, and between culture and nature. The East was where the continent was first civilized (which means colonized by whites), and from this base of culture, nature was gradually pushed back westward until the pioneers

---

9. patriarchal: male dominated

reached the West Coast. Still, today, it is common to think of the East as sophisticated (i.e., belonging to culture), whereas the West is relaxed or cool (i.e., closer to nature). The development of "Silicon Valley"[10] introduces a note of contradiction, but does not yet, I think, invalidate the cultural meaning of the difference between the two sides of the continent.

20 Robert McKinley (1982), in an essay called "Culture Meets Nature on the Six O'Clock News," suggests that the East will always stand for culture for geographical reasons. The time zones mean that news (accounts of the activities of culture) occurs first in the East, which helps to establish the East as the center of culture. The rotation of the earth, which gives the East its temporal advantage, also has another effect: it makes most of our weather come from the west, so the news (culture) moves East to West, and weather (nature) moves from West to East.

The Commercial and the Popular

21 The relationship between popular culture and the forces of commerce and profit is highly problematic, and it is one of the themes that runs throughout this book. We can begin to examine some of the issues by looking in more detail at the example of torn jeans.

22 At the simplest level, this is an example of a user not simply consuming a commodity but reworking it, treating it not as a completed object to be accepted passively, but as a cultural resource to be used. A number of important theoretical issues underlie the differences between a user of a cultural resource and a consumer of a commodity (which are not different activities, but different ways of theorizing, and therefore of understanding, the same activity).

23 Late capitalism, with its market economy, is characterized by commodities—it is awash with

them, it would be impossible to escape them, even if one wanted to. There are a number of ways of understanding commodities and their role in our society: in the economic sphere they ensure the generation and circulation of wealth, and they can vary from the basic necessities of life to inessential luxuries, and, by extension, can include non-material objects such as television programs, a woman's appearance, or a star's name. They also serve two types of function, the material and the cultural. The material function of jeans is to meet the needs of warmth, decency, comfort, and so on. The cultural function is concerned with meanings and values: All commodities can be used by the consumer to construct meanings of self, of social identity and social relations. Describing a pair of jeans, or a TV program, as a commodity emphasizes its role in the circulation of wealth and tends to play down its separate, but related, role in the circulation of meaning.

24 This difference of emphasis (on money or meanings) carries with it a corresponding difference in conceptualizing the balance of power within the exchange. The commodity-consumer approach puts the power with the producers of the commodity. It is they who make a profit out of its manufacture and sale, and the consumer who is exploited insofar as the price he or she pays is inflated beyond the material cost to include as much profit as the producer is able to make. This exploitation, in the case of jeans, often takes on a second dimension, in that the consumer may well be a member of the industrial proletariat[11] whose labor is exploited to contribute to the same profit (the principle remains even if the commodity produced by the worker is not the actual jeans bought in his or her role as consumer).

25 When this approach tackles the question of meaning, it does so through a theory of ideology that again situates power with the owners of the

---

10. Silicon Valley: Northern California area known for its work in computer technology

11. proletariat: working class

means of production. Here, the theory would explain that jeans are so deeply imbued with the ideology of white capitalism that no one wearing them can avoid participating in it and therefore extending it. By wearing jeans we adopt the position of subjects within that ideology, become complicit with it, and therefore give it material expression; we "live" capitalism through its commodities, and, by living it, we validate and invigorate it.

26 The producers and distributors of jeans do not *intend* to promote capitalist ideology with their product: they are not deliberate propagandists. Rather, the economic system, which determines mass production and mass consumption, reproduces itself ideologically in its commodities. Every commodity reproduces the ideology of the system that produced it: a commodity is ideology made material. This ideology works to produce in the subordinate a false consciousness of their position in society, false for two reasons: first because it blinds them to the conflict of interest between the bourgeoisie and proletariat (they may well be aware of the difference, but will understand this difference as contributing to a final social consensus, a liberal pluralism in which social differences are seen finally as harmonious, not as conflictual), and second because it blinds them to their common interests with their fellow workers—it prevents the development of a sense of class solidarity or class consciousness. Ideology works in the sphere of culture as economics does in its own sphere, to naturalize the capitalist system so that it appears to be the only one possible.

27 So how much of a resistance to this is wearing torn jeans? In the economic sphere there is a trace of resistance in that for jeans to become naturally ragged they need to be worn long past the time when they would normally be considered worn out and thus need replacing with another pair. Reducing one's purchase of commodities can be a tiny gesture against a high-consumption society, but its more important work is performed in the cultural sphere rather than the

economic. One possible set of meanings here is of a display of poverty—which is a contradictory sign, for those who *are* poor do not make poverty into a fashion statement. Such a signified rejection of affluence does not necessarily forge a cultural allegiance with the economically poor, for this "poverty" is a matter of choice, although it may, in some cases, signify a sympathy toward the situation of the poor. Its main power is in the negative, a resuscitation of jeans' ability in the 1960s to act as a marker of alternative, and at times oppositional, social values. But more significant than any other possible meaning of ragged jeans is the fact that the raggedness is the production and choice of the user, it is an ex-corporation of the commodity into a subordinate subculture and a transfer of at least some of the power inherent in the commodification process. It is a refusal of commodification and an assertion of one's right to make one's own culture out of the resources provided by the commodity system.

28 Such "tearing" or disfigurement of a commodity in order to assert one's right and ability to remake it into one's own culture need not be literal. The gay community made a heroine out of Judy Garland by "tearing" or disfiguring her image of the all-American, all-gingham girl-next-door, and reworked her as a sign of the masquerade necessary to fit this image, a masquerade equivalent to that which, in the days before sexual liberation permeated the whole of the social experience of gays.

29 Excorporation is the process by which the subordinate make their own culture out of the resources and commodities provided by the dominant system, and this is central to popular culture, for in an industrial society the only resources from which the subordinate can make their own subcultures are those provided by the system that subordinates them. There is no "authentic" folk culture to provide an alternative, and so popular culture is necessarily the art of making do with what is available. This means that the study of popular culture requires the

study not only of the cultural commodities out of which it is made, but also of the ways that people use them. The latter are far more creative and varied than the former.

30 The vitality of the subordinated groups that, in various shifting social allegiances, constitute the people is to be found in the ways of using, not in what is used. This results in the producers having to resort to the processes of incorporation or containment. Manufacturers quickly exploited the popularity of ragged (or old and faded) jeans by producing factory-made tears, or by "washing" or fading jeans in the factory before sale. This process of adopting the signs of resistance incorporates them into the dominant system and thus attempts to rob them of any oppositional meanings.

31 This approach claims that incorporation robs subordinate groups of any oppositional language they may produce: it deprives them of the means to speak their opposition and thus, ultimately, of their opposition itself. It can also be understood as a form of containment—a permitted and controlled gesture of dissent that acts as a safety valve and thus strengthens the dominant social order by demonstrating its ability to cope with dissenters or protesters by allowing them enough freedom to keep them relatively content, but not enough to threaten the stability of the system against which they are protesting.

32 So Macy's advertises "Expressions—Faded attraction . . . the worn out jean from Calvin Klein Sport." "Worn out in all the right places," the copy continues, "brand new jeans slip on with the look and feel of old favorites. And when Calvin's cool white crew neck is added (a soon-to-be new favorite) you're set for a totally relaxed mood." Any possible oppositional meanings are incorporated and tamed into the unthreatening "old favorites." The producers exert their control over the signs of wear by ensuring that they occur only in the "right places," and then use this incorporated and thus defused language of opposition to sell more commodities (the white crew neck) to the people they have stolen it from.

In such ways, the theory of incorporation tells us, signs of opposition are turned to the advantage of that which they oppose and fashionably worn-torn garments become another range of commodities: the raggedness of worn-out jeans, far from opposing consumerism, is turned into a way of extending and enhancing it.

33 Such explanations of popular culture tell us only part of the story; they concentrate almost exclusively on the power of dominant groups to maintain the system that advantages them and thus they assume, rather than question, the success of the strategy. They fail to recognize the social differentiation that still exists between the wearers of "really" old, torn jeans and Macy's customers, and thus overlook any resistances to incorporation that ensure that its victories are never more than partial. Consequently, they paradoxically align themselves with the forces of domination, for, by ignoring the complexity and creativity by which the subordinate cope with the commodity system and its ideology in their everyday lives, the dominant underestimate and thus devalue the conflict and struggle entailed in constructing popular culture within a capitalist society.

34 De Certeau uses a military metaphor to explain this struggle; he talks about the strategy of the powerful, deploying their huge, well-organized forces, which are met by the fleeting tactics of the weak. These tactics involve spotting the weak points in the forces of the powerful and raiding them as guerrilla fighters constantly harry and attack an invading army. Guerrilla tactics are the art of the weak: they never challenge the powerful in open warfare, for that would be to invite defeat, but maintain their own opposition within and against the social order dominated by the powerful. Eco (1986), too, speaks of "semiotic guerrilla warfare" as being the key to understanding popular culture and its ability to resist the dominant ideology. This, in its turn, I would argue, helps to maintain the sense of social differences and the conflict of interest within those differences that is essential if the

heterogeneity[12] of our society is to be productive and not static, progressive and not reactionary.

35   Change can come only from below: the interests of those with power are best served by maintaining the status quo. The motor for social change can come only from a sense of social difference that is based on a conflict of interest, not a liberal pluralism in which differences are finally subordinated to a consensus whose function is to maintain those differences essentially as they are.

36   Popular culture always is part of power relations; it always bears traces of the constant struggle between domination and subordination, between power and various forms of resistance to it or evasions of it, between military strategy and guerrilla tactics. Evaluating the balance of power within this struggle is never easy: Who can say, at any one point, who is "winning" a guerrilla war? The essence of guerrilla warfare, as of popular culture, lies in not being defeatable. Despite nearly two centuries of capitalism, subordinated subcultures exist and intransigently refuse finally to be incorporated—people in these subcultures keep devising new ways of tearing their jeans. Despite many more centuries of patriarchy, women have produced and maintained a feminist movement, and individual women, in their everyday lives, constantly make guerrilla raids upon patriarchy, win small, fleeting victories, keep the enemy constantly on the alert, and gain, and sometimes hold, pieces of territory (however small) for themselves. And gradually, reluctantly, patriarchy has to change in response. Structural changes at the level of the system itself, in whatever domain—that of law, of politics, of industry, of the family—occur only after the system has been eroded and weakened by the tactics of everyday life.

37   Until recently, the study of popular culture has taken two main directions. The less productive has been that which has celebrated popular

culture without situating it in a model of power. It has been a consensual model, which viewed popular culture as a form of the ritual management of social differences out of which it produced a final harmony. It is a democratic version of elite humanism, which merely resituates the cultural life of a nation in the popular rather than the highbrow.[13]

38   The other direction has been to situate popular culture firmly within a model of power, but to emphasize so strongly the forces of domination as to make it appear impossible for a genuine popular culture to exist at all. What replaced it was a mass culture imposed upon a powerless and passive people by a culture industry whose interests were in direct opposition to theirs. A mass culture produces a quiescent,[14] passive mass of people, an agglomeration[15] of atomized individuals separated from their position in the social structure, detached from and unaware of their class consciousness, of their various social and cultural allegiances, and thus totally disempowered and helpless.

39   Recently, however, a third direction has begun to emerge, one to which I hope this book will contribute. It, too, sees popular culture as a site of struggle, but, while accepting the power of the forces of dominance, it focuses rather upon the popular tactics by which these forces are coped with, are evaded or are resisted. Instead of tracing exclusively the processes of incorporation, it investigates rather that popular vitality and creativity that makes incorporation such a constant necessity. Instead of concentrating on the omnipresent,[16] insidious practices of the dominant ideology, it attempts to understand the everyday resistances and evasions that make that ideology

---

12. heterogeneity: differences within a group of people

13. highbrow: highly cultivated intellectual tastes
14. quiescent: resting
15. agglomeration: state of being gathered together
16. omnipresent: present in all places at the same time

work so hard and insistently to maintain itself and its values. This approach sees popular culture as potentially, and often actually, progressive (though not radical), and it is essentially optimistic, for it finds in the vigor and vitality of the people evidence both of the possibility of social change and of the motivation to drive it.

Critical Explorations: Reading

Use these questions to help you understand this selection as you reread it. "The Jeaning of America" is a challenge because it not only discusses the semiotics of jeans advertising and wearing but also places this practice into a larger theoretical discussion. Answering these questions should assist you in sorting out these two issues. You may want to use your answers to these questions in your reading or dialogic journal.

1. In paragraph 7, Fiske claims that jeans provide the wearer with a "desire to be oneself." What sort of individualism does the jeans wearer represent? You may need to consider evidence from various parts of this selection.

2. In paragraph 11, Fiske introduces his own definition of popular culture. Reread this paragraph and list the essential characteristics of his definition.

3. In paragraphs 25–26, Fiske explains why "a commodity is ideology made material." What does he mean by this statement?

4. In paragraph 27, Fiske treats the "raggedness" of jeans. Why does he think jeans wearers choose this ragged look? How does this look relate to Fiske's understanding of "excorporation" (paragraph 29)?

5. Reread paragraphs 36–39. Identify the three perspectives on popular culture that Fiske examines. Which perspective does he seem to favor? What language can you locate as evidence to show that Fiske supports this particular perspective?

Critical Explorations: Writing

The following are four formal essay assignments that will test your critical ability to analyze American commercials. To respond successfully to each of them, you will need to reconsider the American beliefs discussed in Chapter 1 as well as all of the critical practices that you have studied so far. Pay particular attention to the material on hasty generalizations, appeals to authority, and the bandwagon technique discussed in this chapter.

As with your other essay assignments, share your drafts with your peers and instructor.

1. Watch a television commercial. Videotape it if you can. Study both its visual and textual presentation. Then analyze it for its unstated American beliefs, the fears or sexual desires that it may create in you, and any errors in hasty generalizations that it may present. Begin by discussing the story line carefully. Use the Goldman selection as a model.

2. Analyze the following magazine advertisement (page 214). Study all of its aspects: both its written and visual text. Identify the American beliefs that explain it as well as any desires that it seems to be relying on. Further, analyze the generalizations that are part of its written text. Are there hasty generalizations? Appeals to authority? Bandwagon appeals?

3. Select a particularly provocative advertisement, either on television or in a magazine. Some of the more suggestive ads today are done by Calvin Klein, Benetton, and Diesel, to name a few. Analyze this ad carefully for its statement and overall effect. That is, what is the ad saying? How is it saying it? Focus particularly on the provocative nature of the ad. Is the ad merely relying on fear or desire to sell its product, or it is asking the viewer to reconsider a particular American belief or beliefs? You may want to refer to the Martin article as a guide as you complete your analysis.

The 4WD Isuzu Rodeo makes it real easy for you to spend more time on the slopes. It's got a butt-kicking 175-hp, fuel injected engine. And it features winter start mode,* which keeps the wheels from slipping with the push of a button, so you won't have to wait around for the plows to shave the road. And the Rodeo is incredibly affordable, so you'll have money left over for important stuff like neon gloves and lift tickets. And crutches. Hey, we won't leave you hanging.

For more information   please call (800) 726-2700.

ISUZU
Practically/Amazing

Courtesy of American Isuzu Motors, Inc.

4. Study several recent advertisements for jeans seen on television and in magazines. Apply to one or more of these jeans ads John Fiske's argument that jeans styles both reflect the desires of advertising executives and the desires of the consumer. In what specific ways does your ad(s) show the consumer's freedom or lack of freedom? Analyze your ad(s) carefully: examine the details of the narrative, identify the unstated beliefs and desires, determine the audience of jeans wearers that is being spoken to, and show how the consumer of these jeans is ultimately seen.

Student Writing

Below you will find a student's analysis of "The Road Is Paved with Idiots" car advertisement. (You can find this ad on page 182 of this chapter.) It is his first draft. Read the draft carefully; then answer the questions that follow. Cristo responded to the following topic:

This essay topic has two parts. In the beginning of your essay, comment briefly on the several logical practices that ads generally rely on. Then select an advertisement. Analyze it in terms of the American beliefs that seem to inform it, the language it uses to sell the product, and the logical practices that the ad employs.

Idiots on the Road

1   The American media, which fills us with messages that mirror or contradict our social views, is the primary tool that is used by corporations to sell their products. In the daily interaction between the consumer and the advertiser(s), a two-way dialogue occurs with both parties influencing each other. The consumer influences the media by voicing and displaying their attitudes, while the media manipulates the consumer by using the consumer's social views and attitudes to sell products. In reaction to this manipulation, many consumers begin to act like mindless zombies that buy products on the basis of the media's message. In their ads, the media incorporates our views on sex and beauty, many of which are gender biased. These advertisements use unqualified generalizations and invoke certain aspects of society that we fear. These ads may evoke an emotional and/or intellectual response in the consumer that he/she will associate with the product or with the need for the product. In the Isuzu Trooper ad in *Time* magazine, the advertiser places the Trooper on a dry grass hillside area. The vehicle is surrounded with bumper cars and is under a bluish sky with patchy clouds. In this ad, the advertiser(s) clearly uses an eye-catching generalization, views on beauty and leisure, and certain fears concerning the lack of safety in vehicles.

2   In many ads, the advertiser will generally use our views on sex and beauty to sell a product. Since we live in a visual culture, advertisers will relay a visual message that directly enters our subconscious. These views on sex and beauty include the use of women as sex objects, the use of a natural rural setting instead of an urban setting, and the use of images of the rich and

powerful in order to invoke an image of prestige and glamour.

3   Advertisers also use our fears in their ads. Most often the advertiser will address our fears about the lack of safety, the lack of beauty, lack of money, lack of acceptance from peers, and the lack of control in our lives. It is interesting to note that it is these same fears that are present in our television and movie programming. These fears are then supported by a visual and/or written confirmation that are present in the ad.

4   Advertisers then set about trying to grab the consumer's attention quickly. Basically, there are two ways of achieving this goal. An advertiser may use written text and/or an eye-catching visual barrage. When the advertiser decides to use the prior, he will usually utilize a generalization. Generalizations are statements that summarize from specific details. There are various types of generalizations that the advertiser may employ. He may use a generalization that is either qualified or unqualified. In the case of the unqualified generalization, the advertiser will make a claim that is true in all instances. Most of the time, an advertiser wilfully commits this fallacy in order to attract attention. An advertiser may also use the fallacy of the false dilemma. In this scenario, the consumer is presented with an "either or proposition" that has untrue choices or consequences. In most cases, an inaccurate, insufficient or unrepresentative induction or hasty generalization is used.

5   In the Trooper ad, some aspect of the view of beauty is used. The Trooper is positioned in what appears to be a rural setting of a dry-grass hillside that is under a blue-sky filled with patches of clouds. This background represents a view of beauty found in nature. During the time of the Westward Expansion, pioneers often described the beauty they witnessed in their journeys. They described vast forests, enchanting sunsets, grassy hills, majestic lakes, rivers and rocky pathways. During these times of massive migration, people believed that beauty was found when man communed with nature. Thus, the background in the

ad represents this mystical view that beauty may be present in a natural, rural setting. It may be inferred that the advertiser has placed the Trooper in this setting to imply that the Trooper is not just a sports/utility vehicle, but it is also a "naturally beautiful" vehicle. I may go as far as to state that the advertiser is implying that the occupants of such a vehicle will become more beautiful. This goes hand in hand with the fear of being considered as not beautiful.

6   In the ad, the advertiser also uses the generalization that "the road is paved with idiots." This unqualified and hasty generalization is used to attract attention and invoke fear. This generalization assumes that many of the other motorists on the freeways and byways of American pose a great danger to the observer of the ad. As seen on the caption, it describes those "idiots" who don't signal and run stop signs. The generalization is humorously supported by the presence of the bumper cars. The generalization and the bumper cars relay the message that some "idiot" may bump you and that the Trooper is one way of protecting yourself.

7   The most obvious technique used in the ad is the invocation of fear. The bumper cars and the generalization summon childhood memories of being bumped in every direction while riding bumper cars. Once these memories are evoked, horrible thoughts of a terrible accident is triggered in our subconscious. Then we react naturally by trying to find ways of securing ourselves. The ad nonchalantly provides this security by discussing and displaying the Trooper's safety features. The air bags, impact protecting structure, and four-wheel disc brakes then promotes a safe, secure, and comforting image that contradicts the vision of the accident. This fear is then casually contradicted by the statement in the caption that states that the Trooper reduces the threat of accidents.

8   In careful analysis, this ad targets males who are quite affluent. The everyday Joe can't afford to visit a beautiful, secluded, rural area like the one presented in the ad. *Time* magazine also

tends to have educated readers who are involve with the economy, politics, and many other facets of society. In order to make the Trooper more attractive to this specific audience, the ad preys on the American belief in technology. The brief but sufficient and effective discussion of the Trooper's features support the notion that we believe that technology solves everything. I will go so far as to say that the advertiser is relaying the message that the Trooper will provide for a happy ending, another one of our popular beliefs. This can be inferred from the peaceful setting of the hillside and the playful images of the bumper cars.

9   Most Americans tend to share the attitude that most matters should be solved with efficiency and practicality. But most Americans also believe that "all work and no play" makes anyone a dull person. The dilemma between work and fun is addressed in the Isuzu motto, "Practically/*Amazing*." The motto and the images in the add suggests that not only is the Trooper a safe and conservative vehicle, but it is also a vehicle used for fun and leisure. The safety features, in conjunction with the word "Amazing" in the motto, suggests that the vehicle's occupants will also be safe while having fun.

10   Overall, this ad is very convincing and yet interesting. It uses an irrational generalization to achieve certain goals that are necessary in selling the Trooper. It provides an unusual visual image that invokes fear and certain American beliefs. All these components are then packaged together to sell the Trooper. The Isuzu motto also specifically targets individuals who seek certain conservative qualities in a vehicle but also want to be able to have fun with the vehicle. The serene calmness in the background and the bumper cars represent the interesting duality in the motto and in society. The generalization makes the observer of the ad feel smarter than the "idiots" on the road. The invocation of certain fears and the utilization of the other parts of the ad subconsciously invoke the idea that smart yet careful individuals drive the Isuzu Trooper.

1. Reread paragraph 5, in which Cristo discusses the rural setting of the ad. He concludes that this setting suggests that "the occupants of such a vehicle will become more beautiful." Are there any other inferences that you think Cristo can make from the placing of the Trooper in a rural setting?

2. Cristo discusses the title of the ad: "The road is paved with idiots." He rightly calls this statement a hasty generalization, yet he proceeds to analyze this statement with such qualifiers as *many* and *some*. How would you suggest that Cristo revise paragraph 6 so that his analysis of this hasty generalization is clearer?

3. In paragraph 7, Cristo refers to the fear that is evoked in this ad. Cristo notes that "horrible thoughts of a terrible accident is [are] triggered." Yet he fails to describe how a bumper car can cause a horrible accident. Why do you think the ad uses bumper cars instead of real cars? How does this type of car make the fear less real? How can Cristo revise this paragraph, given the playful associations of bumper cars?

4. Reread paragraph 8. What is the topic of this paragraph? Does Cristo focus on this one topic in this paragraph? What other topics does he introduce? How would you suggest that Cristo revise this paragraph?

5. Reread paragraph 9. Summarize Cristo's analysis of the Isuzu motto "Practically/*Amazing*." In what ways is his analysis cogent and his paragraph well organized?

Peer Responses

Use some or all of these questions to respond to your peer's draft. Comment as specifically as you can so that your peer can use your comments to productively revise his draft.

1. Study the beginning of the draft. Does your peer introduce the advertisement adequately?

Does he generally describe the purpose of the ad and introduce those elements of the ad that he intends to analyze? Is there anything here that you would like your peer to omit or to include?

2. Analyze the section of the draft that treats the American beliefs that the ad seems to rely upon. Does your peer show how the ad is using these beliefs to sell its product? Does your peer clearly present the relationship between the ad and these beliefs? Would you suggest that your peer include additional beliefs?

3. Determine if your peer analyzes the logical practices the ad uses. If so, select one logical practice and determine if your peer has correctly identified this error in the ad. Does your peer show how this practice is misused? Does your peer rely on details from the ad in his analysis? Are these appropriate details? Or would you suggest any other details that could show this error more clearly?

4. Choose one paragraph in the draft that is particularly persuasive. Show why it is so effectively written. What details does your peer use? How do they logically support the argument of the paragraph?

5. Does your peer use visual evidence from the ad to support his argument? Is he effectively using this evidence? Would you consider suggesting that your peer use additional visual evidence?

Chapter 5

Popular Culture in Speeches

Introduction

On first analysis, one would not consider speeches as texts that form part of American popular culture. But if one sees how American politicians are at the center of so much of the news we hear on radio, watch on television, and read in newspapers and magazines, then we see how politicians, like sports and television celebrities, help shape our daily thoughts and actions. Also, popular culture is so pervasive that important people may use it as the subject of their talks.

In this chapter, you will read four speeches. Two are political speeches. The first is President Bill Clinton's 1993 Inaugural

Address, the second Jesse Jackson's 1988 presidential nomination speech at the Democratic National Convention. In the third selection, a television executive presents his thoughts on our future use of the media. The final speech was given to a college audience by an English professor. He considers how reality is represented differently on a college campus and on television.

Political speeches, like television shows and television and radio commercials, are media events often seen by millions of Americans. We watch or hear the speech. Only afterwards, if we are interested, do we reread the text of the speech in the newspaper. Presidential addresses on television are the most significant political media events that we experience. This chapter addresses what American political speeches and speeches about the media share with the popular culture texts that we have examined thus far, and also how these speeches differ from television shows and commercials.

To understand the power of speech making, one needs to examine the three aspects of oral addresses that the ancient Greek philosopher Aristotle treated in his *Art of Rhetoric* almost 2,300 years ago. In this work, Aristotle analyzes three necessary features to any speech: its ethos, its pathos, and its logos. *Ethos* is the sense of character that the speaker creates for her audience. Aristotle believed that an audience will not enthusiastically listen to a speaker they do not trust. Very quickly in the course of the speaker's address, a listener decides whether he can trust what the speaker is saying. All effective speakers want to build a trustworthy persona, or character, in their speech. In Aristotelian terms, their intent is to create an ethos that their listeners can trust, because speakers realize that without a respected ethos, their audience will ignore the content of their speech.

Moreover, the speaker wants to create a desired emotion in her listeners. The kind of emotion the listeners get from the speech is its *pathos*. A speaker may want her country to go to war; therefore, she instills a sense of fear in her listeners. Or she may want to emphasize that a group of people in her country is in great need of federal aid that only increased taxes can provide. In this sense, the speaker wants to create sympathy for the group that she would like to help. Thus, uppermost in any effective speaker's mind is the desired emotion, the targeted pathos, that she is seeking to make real in her audience.

Aristotle then asks a practical question: How can a speaker create this desired ethos and pathos? What are his materials? Here is where Aristotle makes logos a necessary part of this triangle. *Logos* is the set of reasoning practices that the speaker uses to make his ethos and pathos effective. Logos includes both the logical practices that the speaker uses as well as the kinds of evidence that he selects.

What is powerful about these concepts of ethos, pathos, and logos is that Aristotle never thought of them as separate parts in a speech. Rather, all three are interwoven—creating and changing one another. For example, a speaker whose ethos you admire will have a greater chance of making you feel a certain way, or of influencing your pathos, while a speaker with sharp reasoning practices will also affect your pathos and your understanding of his ethos.

This ethos–pathos–logos triangle is one that you will consider in several of the speeches that you study in this chapter.

Furthermore, Aristotle describes three types of speeches, and his distinctions are still important for American speech making today. The first type of speech Aristotle examines is *deliberative:* the oratory of the lawmaker. The deliberative speech is most like the presidential and congressional addresses you witness today. The purpose of a deliberative speech is to persuade an audience to agree to a political decision that the speaker has made or wants to make: Should the United States go to war with Iraq? Should there be health insurance for everyone in the United States?

The second type of oral address Aristotle refers to is *judicial:* the speech of lawyers. The purpose of a lawyer's speech making, both in ancient Greece and in the United States today, is to find ways to prove her client's innocence or her adversary's guilt. The intent of an attorney in a murder trial is no different than that of an ancient Athenian lawyer: to persuade the jury of the guilt or innocence of the person being tried. Unlike the essays that you have been reading and writing that explain and analyze, deliberative and judicial oratory tries to persuade its listeners to change their position.

The final oral text that Aristotle analyzes is the *epideictic:* the speech of praise or blame, often given at a funeral. Similar to the epideictic speech today is the eulogy, which praises a recently deceased individual. The epideictic is also used in parts of deliberative and judicial speeches when a lawmaker or attorney wants to praise or condemn an individual. Although the epideictic text is not as persuasive as deliberative and judicial speeches, it is still a more persuasive piece of writing than it is an analytic one. The epideictic speech is not asking the listener to act on a political issue or to decide the guilt or innocence of a defendant, but its speaker wants to persuade the audience of the strengths or weaknesses of the person in question.

For Aristotle, all these forms of speech making use specific means to persuade their audience. Today the political speech also has its means of persuasion, in many ways like the means of persuasion that advertisers use. Both political speeches and ads encourage you to act in a certain way—to vote in a manner that conforms to the speaker's position or to buy a certain product. Moreover, political speeches and radio and television ads are oral media, and both the speech maker and the advertising creator need to persuade subtly. One finds slogans both in speeches and commercials. In a televised address to the nation on April 30, 1973, Richard Nixon is quoted as saying "There will be no whitewash in the White House." This use of *white* serves as a memory tool, much as commercials rely on catchy phrases in order for you to remember, then buy, their product.

Moreover, the language of commercials and the language of speeches use words with strong connotations. Commercials often employ a language with sexual connotations, but political speeches frequently rely on a language that creates a sense of patriotism and duty. You will often find phrases in presidential addresses like "the integrity of the Presidential Office" or "our

Founding Fathers" that are used to apply a sense of importance and patriotism to American politics as well as to give to the speaker an ethos of dignity. As with commercials, much of what you hear in speeches has an unstated emotional appeal, winning you over to the speaker's side and creating a positive pathos in you and other listeners.

Finally, commercials, political speeches, and some speeches about popular culture use basic American beliefs to convince their audiences. They may call up images of the nurturing American family and the American individualist. These emotive images do much to influence the listeners to agree with the speaker.

As with the advertisements you analyzed, you need to find ways to uncover these unstated images to see if they responsibly support the logic, or logos, of the speech or if the speaker is using them to flatter the audience as a way of gaining its sympathy and support.

Critical Practices

Because speeches are longer texts than commercials, their speakers can use more-complex reasoning practices—some to further their argument and others to move their audience away from undesirable positions. Texts in popular culture rely on three basic types of reasoning that you will need to be alert to: (1) the argument of causation, (2) the argument of analogy and comparison, and (3) the argument directed against the individual. Political speeches and other speeches on popular culture also use stylistic devices to enhance their logos, including (1) nominalized language, (2) pronoun choice, and (3) repetition.

The Argument of Causation

Understanding causes is an essential step by which we put our world together. We are always considering the reasons that events occur in our lives. For example, "I woke up with a headache today. Is it because I slept only four hours last night?" "I did well on my history exam. Is it because I studied my notes carefully?" But causation is very difficult to be precise about. We can never know for sure whether a lack of sleep caused our headache or whether other factors were involved in our high grade on the history test.

Political speakers frequently use causal arguments to explain why the country is operating smoothly or poorly: "Our economic problems stem from our four-trillion-dollar debt." "Our inflation is down because of the new tax law on capital gains." To understand how speakers use and misuse causal arguments, you need to analyze the kinds of causes that explain our experiences. There are four: (1) the necessary cause, (2) the sufficient cause, (3) the necessary and sufficient cause, and (4) the contributory cause.

A *necessary cause* is one in which the cause must always be present in order for the effect to occur. For example, oxygen must always be present for fire to occur. So you can say that oxygen is the necessary cause for fire. You most often identify necessary causes to explain events in the natural world. Very rarely can you locate a necessary cause to explain a human event, because human events are complicated.

A *sufficient cause* is not as binding as a necessary cause. It is simply a cause that, on its own, may lead to an effect. A trip switch is a sufficient cause for lights to go off in a house. Unlike a necessary cause, a sufficient cause does not always accompany its effect. An electric short, rather than the trip switch, can also cause lights to go off in your home. That is, a sufficient cause is one that may have caused your lights to go off, whereas a necessary cause is one that always occurs with the effect. In another sense, when you are wondering why your lights went off—because of trip switch, electrical short, power failure—you are considering some of the sufficient causes for lights to go off in your home.

A *necessary and sufficient cause* is the rarest of all the causes, and again it usually describes a physical or biological activity rather than a social or historical event. A necessary and sufficient cause both requires that the agent be present (as with a necessary cause) but that it is the *only one* present. Oxygen is necessary for fire to occur, but oxygen also needs some form of heat to start the fire. Conversely, in the health fields, epidemiologists can locate a specific flu virus that is responsible for the outbreak of a particular set of symptoms: the Type A virus, the Type B virus, and so on. These viruses can be seen as the necessary and sufficient causes for the specific flu symptoms of an individual. No other organism can cause this particular physical condition. More often it is the case that several factors work together to create a particular effect. Collectively, they can be seen as the necessary and sufficient cause. For example, in order for an electric light bulb to function properly, the following agents must work together: adequate current, a light bulb that is not defective, and satisfactory electrical wiring.*

By far the most common type of cause you will come across in analyzing speeches is the *contributory cause*, or one cause among many that affects a particular condition. You often hear people using contributory causes when they examine human actions: historical events such as wars or economic crises. For example, your governor may attribute your state's economic decline to (1) fewer housing constructions, (2) a 12 percent unemployment rate, and (3) an unbalanced budget. These conditions may have contributed to the state's economic problems, but one cannot pinpoint which cause was the most significant the way one can with a necessary and sufficient cause.

---

*Adapted from Vincent Barry, *Good Reason for Writing* (Belmont, CA: Wadsworth, 1983), 170.

Sometimes political speakers want to make matters easy for their audience or choose to point a finger at the opposing political party, so they attribute the lagging economy to one cause—the national debt, let's say. This is an error in causal thinking because it makes a contributory cause a sufficient cause. This is known as a *causal oversimplification.*

At other times, a political speaker may want to simplify a complex issue and thus chooses the most recent cause to be the sufficient cause of a particular historical event. Let's say auto workers go on strike in December. In November, the month before, Bill Clinton had been elected President. A Republican congressman in Michigan could say that Clinton's election was the cause of the auto workers' strike. Yet it is more likely that these same workers had decided to strike over a salary dispute whether or not Clinton became President. This error in causation is called *post hoc* (actually *post hoc ergo propter hoc:* "after this, therefore because of this"). In analyzing a major economic or political event, you need to suspect a speaker who attributes the latest cause to the political situation in question.

Another error in causation is called the *slippery slope:* the assumption that one event becomes the cause of a chain reaction of events. This was the kind of causal thinking used by some Americans who supported the United States' involvement in South Vietnam. The argument went as follows: if South Vietnam falls to the North Vietnamese Communists, then all non-Communist Asia will quickly fall to the Communists. Rather than looking at a simple cause, as do the post hoc or causal oversimplification errors, the slippery slope argument emphasizes a single effect. In this instance, the effect of Communism in South Vietnam becomes the case for all of non-Communist Asia. As a critical analyst of this argument, you could ask how the fate of one country can predict that of another.

Analogies and Comparisons

In political speeches, you will find comparisons to other political and historical figures as well as analogies to previous historical and political events. Speakers in the media often compare one television show or movie to another or make analogies between one period in media history and an earlier period. As in the use of causal arguments, you need to see how responsibly comparisons and analogies are used in the political and media speeches that you examine. To be accurate, *comparisons* need to show how objects, people, or ideas *from the same class* are similar. It would be accurate for Bill Clinton (as he does in his Inaugural Address) to compare himself to Franklin Roosevelt, because both became President. That is, they are part of the same class, called the American presidency. However, it would be an inaccurate comparison for an American senator to compare his position to that of Bill Clinton or Franklin Roosevelt. That is, a senator is not part of the class called presidency. As you critically examine a speech, see what types of comparisons the speaker is making and whether the comparisons that the speaker makes fall into the same class.

Analogies are more complicated types of comparisons. An *analogy* links two different items in an attempt to show what these two items have in common. You can consider an analogy successful if it presents more similar characteristics than dissimilar ones. An analogy is called a *false analogy* if the opposite is true: there are more dissimilar characteristics in the comparison than there are similarities.

Analogies are frequently used in political and media speeches. A political leader may talk about a great moment in American history and compare it to a contemporary event. A speaker in the media may compare a period in moviemaking to the present. For example, a few years ago politicians often compared the financial downturn of the early nineties to the Great Depression of the thirties. In analyzing this analogy, you need to examine how the Great Depression is like the economic moment of the early nineties. If you find that there are more dissimilarities than similarities, you could refer to this association as a false analogy.

Historical analogies are never exact comparisons, so you cannot predict what will happen today from past events. Rather, effective analogies serve to help you understand today's event better by considering a similar event in the past. In regard to the analogy of the Great Depression to the economic problems of the early nineties, you first need to make a list of problems from the Depression that you think are similar to or different from those of the early nineties. You could make a list like this one:

Economic Problems in Great Depression	Economic Problems of Early Nineties
unemployment	unemployment
national debt	national debt
drop in construction	drop in construction

After compiling such a list, you would need to carefully research the evidence from both moments in history. If you find similar statistics, then you could consider the analogy a valid one. If you find more differences than similarities, though, you would have to consider the analogy false.

The Argument Ad Hominem

Speakers like to show themselves in a favorable light. One easy way to make themselves look good is to criticize their opponent. A responsible way to criticize a political opponent is to cite credible evidence from the opponent's political record that shows his inability to serve. An irresponsible way to criticize an opponent is to name call—the *argument ad hominem:* literally, the argument addressed "to the man." Insulting your opponent is irrelevant; it has nothing to do with her strengths and weaknesses. Just as you have been shown how to evaluate popular culture with evidence and arguments, so you should ask of any speaker reasons for criticizing her opponent. If the reasons are not there, if all you hear in the speech is simply a series of empty accusations, then you would be correct in criticizing the speech.

For example, if a presidential candidate accuses his opponent of being a liar, he is resorting to the argument ad hominem. But if he shows where in his opponent's campaign statements there are discrepancies, then this accusation would be more acceptable. Sometimes calling an opponent a liar is appropriate, but only if the accuser provides evidence from the opponent's statements and actions.

As you listen to political and media speeches, see if the speaker resorts to name calling; then determine if the accusation is justified by the evidence he presents. Be leery of speakers who make an accusation without providing credible support for it.

Similar to the argument ad hominem is the *circumstantial argument ad hominem*. In this type of faulty argumentation, the individual is not called a name directly, but the circumstances of her life are called into question. An example of the circumstantial argument ad hominem often occurred in discussions surrounding Ronald Reagan, whose competence as President was called into question because he was once an actor. Many critics of the President asked "How can an actor run a country?" Yet the argument is flawed because there is no professional diploma required to become President of the United States the way there is for a teacher, doctor, lawyer, or other field requiring licensing or examination. By reminding their listeners of his former profession, the opponents of President Reagan wanted to question his competence as President. In this instance, you would be correct to examine President Reagan's record as President, not his acting career, if you wanted to evaluate his performance as President.

The Style of Speeches

Like commercials, speeches also use their form to make their points—that is, how they say what they say. Although speakers choose from a variety of styles, there are three stylistic approaches that can help you analyze speeches: (1) nominalized language, (2) repetition, and (3) the shift in pronoun case from *I* to *we*.

A *nominalization* is a verb form that has become a noun. For example, *to investigate* is a verb; *investigation* is a noun or nominalized form of the verb. Nominalizations can be used when a speaker wants to hide the agent, or doer, of the action; they usually end in *tion, ation,* or *ment*. Let's say that a movie executive does not want his company to know that a private detective agency is investigating the actions of some of his employees, so he uses the nominalization *investigation* in this way: "I have asked for an investigation of our staff." By using the nominalization *investigation,* this executive can avoid telling his employees who the agent of the investigation is.

Passive voice structures can also be used to delete important information about the doer. An active voice sentence would read "The detective agency is investigating the case." Its passive voice construction would be "The case is being investigated by the detective agency." Note that in the passive voice structure, the agent, or subject of the sentence, is placed at the end of the sentence rather than at the beginning. From this passive voice structure, it is easy to take out the agent and simply say "The case is being investigated."

As a critical evaluator of speeches, you need to ask yourself how a nominalization or deleted form of the passive voice is being used. Examine the text to see if there is a need to know the agent and if this agent is being subtly deleted so that the listener is not given all of the information. If needed information is being kept from the audience, then you can conclude that the passive voice or the nominalization is being used irresponsibly.

Repetition, another stylistic device, is the continued use of a word or phrase in a text. Repetition is often used by speakers as a mnemonic. As a listener, you tend to remember a word or phrase that is repeated. In a section of Clinton's Inaugural Address (Selection 17), Clinton repeats *change* three times in the following phrase: "Not change for change's sake, but change to preserve America's ideals." Since change is one of the key issues in Clinton's address, this repetition is used to bring out a central theme of his speech. In the Jesse Jackson speech, note how many times the term *common ground* is used; it is the focus of his speech.

Sometimes a grammatical structure is repeated. This is called *parallelism.* In his Inaugural Address, Clinton uses the parallel structure of the preposition *in . . . :* "We must invest more in our own people, in their jobs and in their future." Here, parallelism gives an acoustical order to the phrases. It allows the listener to more easily remember the key nouns, or objects of the preposition: *people, jobs,* and *future.* For these three issues—people, jobs, and future—are key elements in Clinton's address. Repetition also gives to the listener a sense of unity. Just as the sentence structure is carefully organized, so, Clinton may be suggesting, is the state of affairs that he proposes for his country.

As a critical listener of repetition and parallelism, you need to ask these questions: What word, phrase, or structure is being repeated? Why is it being repeated? Are these important moments in the speech?

Sometimes repetition and parallelism can be used irresponsibly by a speaker to move the listener away from what is said to how it is said. Repetition can become an incantation that the audience is lured to mindlessly repeat. At times, this sort of repetition can be dangerous because it almost hypnotizes the audience so that they forfeit their critical listening of the speech for an emotional response to it. Repetition of this kind is what demagogues use, for their intent is mindless control of their audience, not dialogue.

Finally, you need to see how pronoun cases are used and changed during the course of a speech. *I* refers to the speaker, whereas *we* refers to the speaker and the audience together.

This move is often made by a speaker to flatter his audience—to encourage a sympathetic pathos. The speaker is almost saying "I'm not working alone to make this change, but we, together, will make this change happen."

You need to be careful to note when these changes in pronoun case occur in a speech to verify that, at this point in the speech, the speaker is speaking for you.

In analyzing pronoun changes in a speech, you need to ask two questions:

1. By including *me*, is the speaker speaking for me, or flattering me?
2. Do I feel that I am a part of the "we" that the speaker describes?

Recapping

Speeches on popular culture are complicated texts. They require the listener to determine their ethos (the speaker's character), their pathos (the emotion created in the audience), and their logos (their logical and rhetorical practices). These three aspects of speeches are carefully interrelated, informing and transforming one another.

The logical errors that you as a critical listener and reader of speeches on popular culture need to analyze include (1) errors in causation—post hoc and slippery slope, (2) faulty comparisons and false analogies, and (3) the argument ad hominem as well as the circumstantial argument ad hominem.

Furthermore, the stylistic issues that often describe American speeches on popular culture include (1) nominalizations, (2) repetition and parallelism, and (3) the change in pronoun case and number.

Knowing how these aspects of speech making are used will allow you to evaluate whether a speech is responsible or irresponsible, effective or ineffective.

Reading Selections   17–20

The following texts include two political speeches and two speeches about the media. The first speech is Bill Clinton's Inaugural Address—his first official statement as President, in January of 1993. The second address was given by Jesse Jackson in 1988 in his bid for the Democratic nomination for President.

The third selection is by television executive Shelly Schwab, who describes the media of the twenty-first century to the School of Business of New York University. The final selection is by Michael J. Kobre, an English professor addressing his college's undergraduates on academic reality versus media reality.

All four speeches have a different audience and occasion, so you will see each speaker relying on various rhetorical and logical practices to present his argument. Your knowledge of the terms introduced in this chapter will help you greatly in critically examining these texts. You will see how each speaker employs varying logical practices and rhetorical techniques to effectively create an ethical character that speaks to his audience.

Finally, the first two speeches will show you how political issues are tied closely to the American beliefs you have studied throughout this text. The last two speeches will help you reflect on what you have learned so far about the media and popular culture. The third selection will allow you to consider how the media will change in your lifetime, and the last speech will ask a central question: How do you see the world differently as a student in college and as a viewer of popular movies and television?

These four speeches are a fitting conclusion to the twenty selections you will have examined in this textbook.

Selection 17

"Inaugural Address, 1993"
Bill Clinton

This is Bill Clinton's first address to the nation as President of the United States. His audience is an inclusive one since he is speaking to the entire world. American politicians, American citizens, as well as foreign politicians and citizens listened intently to what this new American President had to say.

This is not the typical political speech Clinton had previously given. His purpose is not to list the specifics of his program, but to speak in generalities about his vision of America and about his role in this vision. Furthermore, Clinton is speaking with a sense of American presidential history in mind: How is he going to be like the predecessors he mentions: George Washington, Thomas Jefferson, and Franklin Roosevelt?

Clinton's speech is a straightforward address. The sentence structure is simple, and the vocabulary is not academic. Your challenge in reading this speech is to make appropriate inferences about the American beliefs that drive it. Make marginal comments about these beliefs as you read and reread. Then study those words that Clinton repeats: *change, sacrifice, responsibility.* Ask yourself how these words reinforce the American beliefs that Clinton is relying on. Finally, see how Clinton's use of repetition and parallelism brings out his key points.

Reading–Writing Preparation

Before you read this selection, you may want to answer the following questions in writing or discussion:

1. In a President's first speech to the American public, what issues do you think he should discuss?

2. What are the elements that you think make a presidential speech memorable?

Inaugural Address, 1993

1 My fellow citizens.

2 Today, we celebrate the mystery of American renewal.

President Clinton's Inaugural Address, January 20, 1993. Associated Press

3 This ceremony is held in the depth of winter. But, by the words we speak and the faces we show the world, we force the spring.

4 A spring reborn in the world's oldest democracy, that brings forth the vision and courage to reinvent America.

Change Necessary

5   When our founders boldly declared America's independence to the world and our purposes to the Almighty, they knew that America, to endure, would have to change.

6   Not change for change's sake, but change to preserve America's ideals—life, liberty, the pursuit of happiness. Though we march to the music of our time, our mission is timeless.

7   Each generation of Americans must define what it means to be an American.

8   On behalf of our nation, I salute my predecessor, President Bush, for his half-century of service to America, and I thank the millions of men and women whose steadfastness and sacrifice triumphed over Depression, fascism and communism.

9   Today, a generation raised in the shadows of the Cold War assumes new responsibilities in a world warmed by the sunshine of freedom but threatened still by ancient hatreds and new plagues.

10   Raised in unrivaled prosperity, we inherit an economy that is still the world's strongest, but is weakened by business failures, stagnant wages, increasing inequality and deep divisions among our own people.

11   When George Washington first took the oath I have just sworn to uphold, news traveled slowly across the land by horseback and across the ocean by boat. Now, the sights and sounds of this ceremony are broadcast instantaneously to billions around the world.

A Peaceful Competition

12   Communications and commerce are global; investment is mobile; technology is almost magical; and ambition for a better life is now universal. We earn our livelihood in America today in peaceful competition with people all across the Earth.

13   Profound and powerful forces are shaking and remaking our world, and the urgent question of our time is whether we can make change our friend and not our enemy.

14   This new world has already enriched the lives of millions of Americans who are able to compete and win in it. But when most people are working harder for less, when others cannot work at all, when the cost of health care devastates families and threatens to bankrupt our enterprises, great and small, when fear of crime robs law-abiding citizens of their freedom and when millions of poor children cannot even imagine the lives we are calling them to lead—we have not made change our friend.

15   We know we have to face hard truths and take strong steps. But we have not done so. Instead, we have drifted, and that drifting has eroded our resources, fractured our economy and shaken our confidence.

16   Though our challenges are fearsome, so are our strengths. Americans have ever been a restless, questing, hopeful people. And we must bring to our task today the vision and will of those who came before us.

Muster Determination

17   From our revolution to the Civil War, to the Great Depression to the civil rights movement, our people have always mustered the determination to construct from these crises the pillars of our history.

18   Thomas Jefferson believed that to preserve the very foundations of our nation, we would need dramatic change from time to time. Well, my fellow Americans, this is our time. Let us embrace it.

19   Our democracy must be not only the envy of the world but the engine of our own renewal. There is nothing wrong with America that cannot be cured by what is right with America.

20   So today, we pledge an end to the era of deadlock and drift—and a new season of American renewal has begun.

21   To renew America, we must be bold.

22   We must do what no generation has had to do before. We must invest more in our own people, in their jobs and in their future, and at the same time cut our massive debt. And we must do

so in a world in which we must compete for every opportunity.

23 It will not be easy; it will require sacrifice. But it can be done, and done fairly, not choosing sacrifice for its own sake, but for our own sake. We must provide for our nation the way a family provides for its children.

24 Our founders saw themselves in the light of posterity. We can do no less. Anyone who has ever watched a child's eyes wander into sleep knows what posterity is. Posterity is the world to come—the world for whom we hold our ideals, from whom we have borrowed our planet and to whom we bear sacred responsibility.

Offer More Opportunity

25 We must do what America does best: offer more opportunity to all and demand more responsibility from all.

26 It is time to break the bad habit of expecting something for nothing, from our government or from each other. Let us all take more responsibility, not only for ourselves and our families but for our communities and our country.

27 To renew America, we must revitalize our democracy.

28 This beautiful capital, like every capital since the dawn of civilization, is often a place of intrigue and calculation. Powerful people maneuver for position and worry endlessly about who is in and who is out, who is up and who is down, forgetting those people whose toil and sweat sends us here and pays our way.

29 Americans deserve better. And in this city today, there are people who want to do better. So I say to all of you here, let us resolve to reform our politics, so that power and privilege no longer shout down the voice of the people. Let us put aside personal advantage so that we can feel the pain and see the promise of America.

30 Let us resolve to make our government a place for what Franklin Roosevelt called "bold, persistent experimentation," a government for our tomorrows, not our yesterdays.

31 Let us give this capital back to the people to whom it belongs.

32 To renew America, we must meet challenges abroad as well as at home. There is no longer clear division between what is foreign and what is domestic—the world economy, the world environment, the world AIDS crisis, the world arms race—they affect us all.

33 Today, as an old order passes, the new world is more free but less stable. Communism's collapse has called forth old animosities and new dangers. Clearly America must continue to lead the world we did so much to make.

34 While America rebuilds at home, we will not shrink from the challenges, nor fail to seize the opportunities, of this new world. Together with our friends and allies, we will work to shape change, lest it engulf us.

35 When our vital interests are challenged, or the will and conscience of the international community is defied, we will act—with peaceful diplomacy whenever possible, with force when necessary. The brave Americans serving our nation today in the Persian Gulf, in Somalia and wherever else they stand are testament to our resolve.

36 But our greatest strength is the power of our ideas, which are still new in many lands. Across the world, we see them embraced—and we rejoice. Our hopes, our hearts, our hands are with those on every continent who are building democracy and freedom. Their cause is America's cause.

37 The American people have summoned the change we celebrate today. You have raised your voices in an unmistakable chorus. You have cast your votes in historic numbers. And you have changed the face of the Congress, the presidency and the political process itself.

38 Yes, you, my fellow Americans, have forced the spring.

39 Now, we must do the work the season demands.

40 To that work I now turn, with all the authority of my office. I ask the Congress to join with

me. But no President, no Congress, no government, can undertake this mission alone.

41   My fellow Americans, you, too, must play your part in our renewal.

42   I challenge a new generation of young Americans to a season of service—to act on your idealism by helping troubled children, keeping company with those in need, reconnecting our torn communities. There is so much to be done—enough, indeed, for millions of others who are still young in spirit to give of themselves in service, too.

We Need Each Other

43   In serving, we recognize a simple but powerful truth: We need each other. And we must care for one another.

44   Today, we do more than celebrate America; we rededicate ourselves to the very idea of America:

- An idea born in revolution and renewed through two centuries of challenge;

- An idea tempered by the knowledge that, but for fate, we—the fortunate and the unfortunate—might have been each other;

- An idea ennobled by the faith that our nation can summon from its myriad[1] diversities the deepest measure of unity;

- An idea infused with the conviction that America's long heroic journey must go forever upward.

Work Until Work Done

45   And so, my fellow Americans, as we stand at the edge of the 21st Century, let us begin with energy and hope, with faith and discipline, and let us work until our work is done. The Scripture

---

1. myriad: an indefinitely great number

says, "And let us not be weary in well-doing, for in due season, we shall reap, if we faint not."

46   From this joyful mountaintop of celebration, we hear a call to service in the valley.

47   We have heard the trumpets. We have changed the guard. And now—each in our own way, and with God's help—we must answer the call.

Critical Explorations: Reading

As you reread the Clinton address, let these five questions help you examine the kinds of logical and stylistic moves that the President makes. After completing all the questions, ask yourself what overall effect the text seems to have on you: Does it create a sense of confidence? Do you feel that the United States has a new vision under this new President? You may want to use the answers to these questions in your reading or dialogic journal.

1.   Clinton makes several references to renewal and change—particularly in paragraphs 2, 19, and 27. Why do you think these issues are important to the subject of his speech?

2.   Clinton makes comparisons to previous Presidents—Washington (paragraph 11), Jefferson (paragraph 18), and Franklin Roosevelt (paragraph 30). Do you think that these comparisons are accurate? What is the effect of these comparisons on the entire text?

3.   Clinton makes an analogy between children and family and the citizens of the United States and its leaders (paragraph 23). Is the analogy a fair or false one? What is the effect?

4.   In paragraphs 37–38, Clinton changes pronoun case and number. Why? What is the effect on the pathos that Clinton is attempting to create here?

5.   For the development of his ethos and for the pathos he creates, what is the purpose of Clinton's use of scripture in paragraph 45?

Selection 18

"Common Ground and Common Sense"
Jesse Jackson

The Reverend Jesse Jackson, an influential African American civil rights leader, ran for President as a Democrat in 1988. This speech, titled "Common Ground and Common Sense," was given to a worldwide television audience at the Democratic National Convention in Atlanta, Georgia, on July 20, 1988. Michael Dukakis was finally nominated as the Democratic presidential candidate but was soundly defeated by George Bush in November of that year. Jackson represented a political organization made up of Americans from all walks of life: a coalition of various ethnic groups, races, and social classes that he named the Rainbow Coalition.

This speech, like so many of Jackson's addresses, is an inspired text that focuses on the social problems that Jackson believes America must correct. Jackson relies largely and effectively on repetition and parallelism to explain his political goals.

Jackson introduces three names that you may be unfamiliar with. Rosa Parks (paragraph 1), who was in the audience that evening, was an African American woman who refused to sit in the back of a bus in 1955 in Montgomery, Alabama, encouraging Martin Luther King, Jr. to begin a boycott of the city's segregated bus system. Lee Iacocca (paragraph 78) was the president of Chrysler Corporation at the time of Jackson's speech, and CETA (paragraph 89), standing for the Comprehensive Employment Training Act, was a federal job-training program for the poor. The other allusions that may be unfamiliar to you are explained in the context of Jackson's speech.

Like the Clinton address, this speech is clearly written in simple sentences and uses an easy-to-understand vocabulary. Infer the American beliefs that underlie Jackson's address. List these beliefs in marginal notes. Also, determine what specific political changes Jackson would make if he were President. Place these specifics in the margins as well. Finally, see how Jackson artfully uses repetition and parallelism to bring out his most important points.

Reading–Writing Preparation

Before you read this selection, you may want to answer the following questions in writing or discussion:

1. What issues do you think an African American presidential candidate should discuss in his speech?

2. In what ways do you think the speeches of African American politicians are different from those of white politicians?

Common Ground and Common Sense

By Jesse Jackson, *Candidate for Democratic Presidential Nomination*
Delivered at the Democratic National Convention, Atlanta, Georgia, July 20, 1988

1   Tonight we pause and give praise and honor to God for being good enough to allow us to be at this place at this time. When I look out at this convention, I see the face of America, red, yellow, brown, black and white, we're all precious in God's sight—the real rainbow coalition. All of us, all of us who are here and think that we are seated. But we're really standing on someone's

shoulders. Ladies and gentlemen, Mrs. Rosa Parks.

2   The mother of the civil rights movement.

3   I want to express my deep love and appreciation for the support my family has given me over these past months.

4   They have endured pain, anxiety, threat and fear.

5   But they have been strengthened and made secure by a faith in God, in America and in you.

6   Your love has protected us and made us strong.

7   To my wife Jackie, the foundation of our family; to our five children whom you met tonight; to my mother Mrs. Helen Jackson, who is present tonight; and to my grandmother, Mrs. Maltilda Burns; my brother Chuck and his family; my mother-in-law, Mrs. Gertrude Brown, who just last month at age 61 graduated from Hampton Institute, a marvelous achievement; I offer my appreciation to Mayor Andrew Young who has provided such gracious hospitality to all of us this week.

8   And a special salute to President Jimmy Carter.

9   President Carter restored honor to the White House after Watergate. He gave many of us a special opportunity to grow. For his kind words, for his unwavering commitment to peace in the world and the voters that came from his family, every member of his family, led by Billy and Amy, I offer him my special thanks, special thanks to the Carter family.

10   My right and my privilege to stand here before you has been won—in my lifetime—by the blood and the sweat of the innocent.

11   Twenty-four years ago, the late Fanny Lou Hamer and Aaron Henry—who sits here tonight from Mississippi—were locked out on the streets of Atlantic City, the head of the Mississippi Freedom Democratic Party.

12   But tonight, a black and white delegation from Mississippi is headed by Ed Cole, a black man, from Mississippi, 24 years later.

13   Many were lost in the struggle for the right to vote. Jimmy Lee Jackson, a young student, gave his life. Viola Luizzo, a white mother from Detroit, called nigger lover, and brains blown out at point blank range.

14   Schwerner, Goodman and Chaney—two Jews and a black—found in a common grave, bodies riddled with bullets in Mississippi. The four darling little girls in the church in Birmingham, Ala. They died that we might have a right to live.

15   Dr. Martin Luther King Jr. lies only a few miles from us tonight.

16   Tonight he must feel good as he looks down upon us. We sit here together, a rainbow, a coalition—the sons and daughters of slave masters and the sons and daughters of slaves sitting together around a common table, to decide the direction of our party and our country. His heart would be full tonight.

17   As a testament to the struggles of those who have gone before; as a legacy for those who will come after; as a tribute to the endurance, the patience, the courage of our forefathers and mothers; as an assurance that their prayers are being answered, their work has not been in vain, and hope is eternal; tomorrow night my name will go into nomination for the presidency of the United States of America.

18   We meet tonight at a crossroads, a point of decision.

19   Shall we expand, be inclusive, find unity and power; or suffer division and impotence.

20   We come to Atlanta, the cradle of the old south, the crucible of the new South.

21   Tonight there is a sense of celebration because we are moved, fundamentally moved, from racial battlegrounds by law, to economic common ground, tomorrow we will challenge to move to higher ground.

22   Common ground!

23   Think of Jerusalem—the intersection where many trails met. A small village that became the birthplace for three great religions—Judaism, Christianity and Islam.

24   Why was this village so blessed? Because it provided a crossroads where different people met, different cultures, and different civilizations could meet and find common ground.

25   When people come together, flowers always nourish and the air is rich with the aroma of a new spring.

26   Take New York, the dynamic metropolis. What makes New York so special?

27   It is the invitation of the Statue of Liberty— give me your tired, your poor, your huddled masses who yearn to breathe free.

28   Not restricted to English only.

29   Many people, many cultures, many languages —with one thing in common, they yearn to breathe free.

30   Common ground!

31   Tonight in Atlanta, for the first time in this century we convene in the South.

32   A state where governors once stood in school house doors. Where Julian Bond was denied his seat in the state legislature because of his conscientious objection to the Vietnam War.

33   A city that, through its five black universities, has graduated more black students than any city in the world.

34   Atlanta, now a modern intersection of the new South.

35   Common ground!

36   That is the challenge to our party tonight.

37   Left wing. Right wing. Progress will not come through boundless liberalism nor static conservatism, but at the critical mass of mutual survival. It takes two wings to fly.

38   Whether you're a hawk or a dove, you're just a bird living in the same environment, in the same world.

39   The Bible teaches that when lions and lambs lie down together, none will be afraid and there will be peace in the valley. It sounds impossible. Lions eat lambs. Lambs sensibly flee from lions. But even lions and lambs find common ground. Why?

40   Because neither lions nor lambs want the forest to catch on fire. Neither lions nor lambs want acid rain to fall. Neither lions nor lambs can survive nuclear war. If lions and lambs can find common ground, surely, we can as well, as civilized people.

41   The only time that we win is when we come together. In 1960, John Kennedy, the late John Kennedy, beat Richard Nixon by only 112,000 votes—less than one vote per precinct. He won by the margin of our hope. He brought us together. He reached out. He had the courage to defy his advisors and inquire about Dr. King's jailing in Albany, Georgia. We won by the margin of our hope, inspired by courageous leadership.

42   In 1964, Lyndon Johnson brought both wings together. The thesis, the antithesis and to create a synthesis and together we won.

43   In 1976, Jimmy Carter unified us again and we won. When we do not come together, we never win.

44   In 1968, division and despair in July led to our defeat in November.

45   In 1980, rancor in the spring and the summer led to Reagan in the fall. When we divide, we cannot win. We must find common ground as a basis for survival and development and change and growth.

46   Today when we debated, differed, deliberated, agreed to agree, agreed to disagree, when we had the good judgment to argue our case and then not self-destruct, George Bush was just a little further away from the White House and a little closer to private life.

47   Tonight, I salute Governor Michael Dukakis.

48   He has run a well-managed and a dignified campaign. No matter how tired or how tried, he always resisted the temptation to stoop to demagoguery.[1]

---

1. demagoguery: using emotion and prejudice to arouse an audience

49   I've watched a good mind fast at work, with steel nerves, guiding his campaign out of the crowded field without appeal to the worst in us. I've watched his perspective grow as his environment has expanded. I've seen his toughness and tenacity close up. I know his commitment to public service.

50   Mike Dukakis' parents were a doctor and a teacher; my parents, a maid, a beautician and a janitor.

51   There's a great gap between Brookline, Massachusetts and Haney Street, the Fieldcrest Village housing projects in Greenville, South Carolina.

52   He studied law; I studied theology. There are differences of religion, region, and race; differences in experiences and perspectives. But the genius of America is that out of the many, we become one.

53   Providence has enabled our paths to intersect. His foreparents came to America on immigrant ships; my foreparents came to America on slave ships. But whatever the original ships, we're in the same boat tonight.

54   Our ships could pass in the night if we have a false sense of independence, or they could collide and crash. We would lose our passengers. But we can seek a higher reality and a greater good apart. We can drift on the broken pieces of Reaganomics,[2] satisfy our baser instincts, and exploit the fears of our people. At our highest, we can call upon noble instincts and navigate this vessel to safety. The greater good is the common good.

55   As Jesus said, "Not my will, but thine be done." It was his way of saying there's a higher good beyond personal comfort or position.

56   The good of our nation is at stake—its commitment to working men and women, to the poor and the vulnerable, to the many in the world. With so many guided missiles, and so much misguided leadership, the stakes are exceedingly high. Our choice, full participation in a Democratic government, or more abandonment and neglect. And so this night, we choose not a false sense of independence, not our capacity to survive and endure.

57   Tonight we choose interdependency in our capacity to act and unite for the greater good. The common good is finding commitment to new priorities, to expansion and inclusion. A commitment to expanded participation in the Democratic Party at every level. A commitment to a shared national campaign strategy and involvement at every level. A commitment to new priorities that ensure that hope will be kept alive. A common ground commitment for a legislative agenda by empowerment for the John Conyers bill, universal, on-site, same-day registration everywhere—and commitment to D.C. statehood and empowerment—D.C. deserves statehood. A commitment to economic set-asides, a commitment to the Dellums bill for comprehensive sanctions against South Africa, a shared commitment to a common direction.

58   Common ground. Easier said than done. Where do you find common ground at the point of challenge? This campaign has shown that politics need not be marketed by politicians, packaged by pollsters and pundits. Politics can be a marvel arena where people come together, define common ground.

59   We find common ground at the plant gate that closes on workers without notice. We find common ground at the farm auction where a good farmer loses his or her land to bad loans or diminishing markets. Common ground at the schoolyard where teachers cannot get adequate pay, and students cannot get a scholarship and can't make a loan. Common ground, at the hospital admitting room where somebody tonight is dying because they cannot afford to go upstairs to a bed that's empty, waiting for someone with insurance to get sick. We are a better nation than that. We must do better.

60   Common ground. What is leadership if not present help in a time of crisis? And so I met you at the point of challenge in Jay, Maine, where

---

2. Reaganomics: economic belief during the Reagan presidency that tax benefits to the wealthy would trickle down to profits for the middle class and poor

paper workers were striking for fair wages; in Greenfield, Iowa, where family farmers struggle for a fair price; in Cleveland, Ohio, where working women seek comparable worth; in McFarland, Calif., where the children of Hispanic farm workers may be dying from poison land, dying in clusters with Cancer; in the AIDS hospice in Houston, Texas, where the sick support one another, 12 are rejected by their own parents and friends.

61 Common ground.

62 America's not a blanket woven from one thread, one color, one cloth. When I was a child growing up in Greenville, S.C., and grandmother could not afford a blanket, she didn't complain and we did not freeze. Instead, she took pieces of old cloth—patches, wool, silk, gabardine, crockersack on the patches—barely good enough to wipe off your shoes with.

63 But they didn't stay that way very long. With sturdy hands and a strong cord, she sewed them together into a quilt, a thing of beauty and power and culture.

64 Now, Democrats, we must build such a quilt. Farmers, you seek fair prices and you are right, but you cannot stand alone. Your patch is not big enough. Workers, you fight for fair wages. You are right. But your patch labor is not big enough. Women, you seek comparable worth and pay equity. You are right. But your patch is not big enough. Women, mothers, who seek Head Start and day care and pre-natal care on the front side of life, rather than jail care and welfare on the back side of life, you're right, but your patch is not big enough.

65 Students, you seek scholarships. You are right. But your patch is not big enough. Blacks and Hispanics, when we fight for civil rights, we are right, but our patch is not big enough. Gays and lesbians, when you fight against discrimination and a cure for AIDS, you are right, but your patch is not big enough. Conservatives and progressives, when you fight for what you believe, right-wing, left-wing, hawk, dove—you are right, from your point of view, but your point of view is not enough.

66 But don't despair. Be as wise as my grandmama. Pool the patches and the pieces together, bound by a common thread. When we form a great quilt of unity and common ground we'll have the power to bring about health care and housing and jobs and education and hope to our nation.

67 We the people can win. We stand at the end of a long dark night of reaction. We stand tonight united in a commitment to a new direction. For almost eight years, we've been led by those who view social good coming from private interest, who viewed public life as a means to increase private wealth. They have been prepared to sacrifice the common good of the many to satisfy the private interest and the wealth of a few. We believe in a government that's a tool of our democracy in service to the public, not an instrument of the aristocracy in search of private wealth.

68 We believe in government with the consent of the governed of, for, and by the people. We must not emerge into a new day with a new direction. Reaganomics, based on the belief that the rich had too much money—too little money, and the poor had too much.

69 That's classic Reaganomics. It believes that the poor had too much money and the rich had too little money.

70 So, they engaged in reverse Robin Hood—took from the poor, gave to the rich, paid for by the middle class. We cannot stand four more years of Reaganomics in any version, in any disguise.

71 How do I document that case? Seven years later, the richest 1 percent of our society pays 20 percent less in taxes; the poorest 10 percent pay 20 percent more. Reaganomics.

72 Reagan gave the rich and the powerful a multibillion-dollar party. Now, the party is over. He expects the people to pay for the damage. I take this principled position—convention, let us not raise taxes on the poor and the middle class, but those who had the party, the rich and the powerful, must pay for the party!

73 I just want to take common sense to high places. We're spending $150 billion a year

defending Europe and Japan 43 years after the war is over. We have more troops in Europe tonight than we had seven years ago, yet the threat of war is ever more remote. Germany and Japan are now creditor nations—that means they've got a surplus. We are a debtor nation—it means we are in debt.

74 Let them share more of the burden of their own defense—use some of that money to build decent housing!

75 Use some of that money to educate our children!

76 Use some of that money for long-term health care!

77 Use some of that money to wipe out these slums and put America back to work!

78 I just want to take common sense to high places. If we can bail out Europe and Japan, if we can bail out Continental Bank and Chrysler—and Mr. Iacocca makes $8,000 an hour, we can bail out the family farmer.

79 I just want to make common sense. It does not make sense to close down 650,000 family farms in this country while importing food from abroad subsidized by the U.S. government.

80 Let's make sense. It does not make sense to be escorting oil tankers up and down the Persian Gulf paying $2.50 for every $1.00 worth of oil we bring out while oil wells are capped in Texas, Oklahoma and Louisiana. I just want to make sense.

81 Leadership must meet the moral challenge of its day. What's the moral challenge of our day? We have public accommodations. We have the right to vote. We have open housing.

82 What's the fundamental challenge of our day? It is to end economic violence. Plant closing without notice, economic violence. Even the greedy do not profit long from greed. Economic violence. Most poor people are not lazy. They're not black. They're not brown. They're mostly white, and female and young.

83 But whether white, black or brown, the hungry baby's belly turned inside out is the same color. Call it pain. Call it hurt. Call it agony. Most poor people are not on welfare.

84 Some of them are illiterate and can't read the want-ad sections. And when they can, they can't find a job that matches their address. They work hard every day. I know. I live amongst them. I'm one of them.

85 I know they work. I'm a witness. They catch the early bus. They work every day. They raise other people's children. They work every day. They clean the streets. They work every day. They drive vans with cabs. They work every day. They change the beds you slept in these hotels last night and can't get a union contract. They work every day.

86 No more. They're not lazy. Someone must defend them because it's right, and they cannot speak for themselves. They work in hospitals. I know they do. They wipe the bodies of those who are sick with fever and pain. They empty their bedpans. They clean out their commode. No job is beneath them, and yet when they get sick, they cannot lie in the bed they made up every day. America, that is not right. We are a better nation than that. We are a better nation than that.

87 We need a real war on drugs. You can't just say no. It's deeper than that. You can't just get a palm reader or an astrologer; it's more profound than that. We're spending $150 billion on drugs a year. We've gone from ignoring it to focusing on the children. Children cannot buy $150 billion worth of drugs a year. A few high profile athletes—athletes are not laundering $150 billion a year—bankers are.

88 I met the children in Watts who are unfortunate in their despair. Their grapes of hope have become raisins of despair, and they're turning to each other and they're self-destructing—but I stayed with them all night long. I wanted to hear their case. They said, "Jesse Jackson, as you challenge us to say no to drugs, you're right. And to not sell them, you're right. And to not use these guns, you're right."

89 And, by the way, the promise of CETA—they displaced CETA. They did not replace CETA. We have neither jobs nor houses nor services nor training—no way out. Some of us take drugs as

anesthesia[3] for our pain. Some take drugs as a way of pleasure—both short-term pleasure and long-term pain. Some sell drugs to make money. It's wrong, we know. But you need to know that we know. We can go and buy the drugs by the boxes at the port. If we can buy the drugs at the port, don't you believe the federal government can stop it if they want to?

90 They say, "We don't have Saturday night specials any more." They say, "We buy AK-47s and Uzis, the latest lethal weapons. We buy them across the counter on Long Beach Boulevard." You cannot fight a war on drugs unless and until you are going to challenge the bankers and the gun sellers and those who grow them. Don't just focus on the children, let's stop drugs at the level of supply and demand. We must end the scourge[4] on the American culture.

91 Leadership. What difference will we make? Leadership cannot just go along to get along. We must do more than change presidents. We must change direction. Leadership must face the moral challenge of our day. The nuclear war build-up is irrational. Strong leadership cannot desire to look tough, and let that stand in the way of the pursuit of peace. Leadership must reverse the arms race.

92 At least we should pledge no first use. Why? Because first use begat first retaliation, and that's mutual annihilation. That's not a rational way out. No use at all—let's think it out, and not fight it out, because it's an unwinnable fight. Why hold a card that you can never drop? Let's give peace a chance.

93 Leadership—we now have this marvelous opportunity to have a breakthrough with the Soviets. Last year, 200,000 Americans visited the Soviet Union. There's a chance for joint ventures into space, not Star Wars and the war arms escalation, but a space defense initiative. Let's build in space together, and demilitarize the heavens. There's a way out.

94 America, let us expand. When Mr. Reagan and Mr. Gorbachev met, there was a big meeting. They represented together one-eighth of the human race. Seven-eighths of the human race was locked out of that room. Most people in the world tonight—half are Asian, one-half of them are Chinese. There are 22 nations in the Middle East. There's Europe; 40 million Latin Americans next door to us; the Caribbean; Africa—a half-billion people. Most people in the world today are yellow or brown or black, non-Christian, poor, female, young, and don't speak English—in the real world.

95 This generation must offer leadership to the real world. We're losing ground in Latin America, the Middle East, South Africa, because we're not focusing on the real world, that real world. We must use basic principles, support international law. We stand the most to gain from it. Support human rights; we believe in that. Support self-determination; we'll build on that. Support economic development; you know it's right. Be consistent, and gain our moral authority in the world.

96 I challenge you tonight, my friends, let's be bigger and better as a nation and as a party. We have basic challenges. Freedom in South Africa—we've already agreed as Democrats to declare South Africa to be a terrorist state. But don't just stop there. Get South Africa out of Angola.[5] Free Namibia.[6] Support the front-line states. We must have a new, humane human rights assistance policy in Africa.

97 I'm often asked, "Jesse, why do you take on these tough issues? They're not very political. We can't win that way."

98 If an issue is morally right, it will eventually be political. It may be political and never be right. Fannie Lou Hamer didn't have the most votes in Atlantic City, but her principles have outlasted every delegate who voted to lock her out. Rosa Parks did not have the most votes, but

---

3. anesthesia: drugs causing insensitivity to pain

4. scourge: person or thing that destroys

---

5. Angola: a country in Southwest Africa

6. Namibia: a country in Southwest Africa, just south of Angola

she was morally right. Dr. King didn't have the most votes about the Vietnam war, but he was morally right. If we're principled first, our politics will fall in place.

99 Jesse, why did you take these big bold initiatives? A poem by an unknown author went something like this: We mastered the air, we've conquered the sea, and annihilated distance and prolonged life, we were not wise enough to live on this earth without war and without hate.

100 As for Jesse Jackson, I'm tired of sailing by little boat, far inside the harbor bar. I want to go out where the big ships float, out on the deep where the great ones are. And should my frail craft prove too slight, the waves that sweep those billows o'er, I'd rather go down in a stirring fight than drown to death in the sheltered shore.

101 We've got to go out, my friends, where the big boats are.

102 And then, for our children, young America, hold your head high now. We can win. We must not lose you to drugs and violence, premature pregnancy, suicide, cynicism, pessimism and despair. We can win.

103 Wherever you are tonight, I challenge you to hope and to dream. Don't submerge your dreams. Exercise above all else, even on drugs, dream of the day you're drug-free. Even in the gutter, dream of the day that you'll be up on your feet again. You must never stop dreaming. Face reality, yes. But don't stop with the way things are; dream of things as they ought to be. Dream. Face pain, but love, hope, faith, and dreams will help you rise above the pain.

104 Use hope and imagination as weapons of survival and progress, but you keep on dreaming, young America. Dream of peace. Peace is rational and reasonable. War is irrational in this age and unwinnable.

105 Dream of teachers who teach for life and not for living. Dream of doctors who are concerned more about public health than private wealth. Dream of lawyers more concerned about justice than a judgeship. Dream of preachers who are

concerned more about prophecy than profiteering. Dream on the high road of sound values.

106 And in America, as we go forth to September, October and November and then beyond, America must never surrender to a high moral challenge.

107 Do not surrender to drugs. The best drug policy is a no first use. Don't surrender with needles and cynicism. Let's have no first use on the one hand, or clinics on the other. Never surrender, young America.

108 Go forward. America must never surrender to malnutrition. We can feed the hungry and clothe the naked. We must never surrender. We must go forward. We must never surrender to illiteracy. Invest in our children. Never surrender; and go forward.

109 We must never surrender to inequality. Women cannot compromise ERA[7] or comparable worth. Women are making 60 cents on the dollar to what a man makes. Women cannot buy meat cheaper. Women cannot buy bread cheaper. Women cannot buy milk cheaper. Women deserve to get paid for the work that they do. It's right and it's fair.

110 Don't surrender, my friends. Those who have AIDS tonight, you deserve our compassion. Even with AIDS you must not surrender in your wheelchairs. I see you sitting here tonight in those wheelchairs. I've stayed with you. I've reached out to you across our nation. Don't you give up. I know it's tough sometimes. People look down on you. It took you a little more effort to get here tonight.

111 And no one should look down on you, but sometimes mean people do. The only justification we have for looking down on someone is that we're going to stop and pick them up. But even in your wheelchairs, don't give up. We can-

---

7. ERA: Equal Rights Amendment, a proposed amendment to the Constitution that would have made it illegal to discriminate against an individual because of gender; it failed to be ratified by three-fourths of the states.

not forget 50 years ago when our backs were against the wall, Roosevelt was in a wheelchair. I would rather have Roosevelt in a wheelchair than Reagan and Bush on a horse. Don't you surrender and don't you give up.

112 Don't surrender and don't give up. Why can I challenge you this way? Jesse Jackson, you don't understand my situation. You be on television. You don't understand. I see you with the big people. You don't understand my situation. I understand. You're seeing me on TV but you don't know the me that makes me, me. They wonder why does Jesse run, because they see me running for the White House. They don't see the house I'm running from.

113 I have a story. I wasn't always on television. Writers were not always outside my door. When I was born late one afternoon, October 8th, in Greenville, S.C., no writers asked my mother her name. Nobody chose to write down our address. My mama was not supposed to make it. And I was not supposed to make it. You see, I was born to a teen-age mother who was born to a teen-age mother.

114 I understand. I know abandonment and people being mean to you, and saying you're nothing and nobody, and can never be anything. I understand. Jesse Jackson is my third name. I'm adopted. When I had no name, my grandmother gave me her name. My name was Jesse Burns until I was 12. So I wouldn't have a blank space, she gave me a name to hold me over. I understand when nobody knows your name. I understand when you have no name. I understand.

115 I wasn't born in the hospital. Mama didn't have insurance. I was born in the bed at home. I really do understand. Born in a three-room house, bathroom in the backyard, slop jar by the bed, no hot and cold running water. I understand. Wallpaper used for decoration? No. For a windbreaker. I understand. I'm a working person's person, that's why I understand you whether you're black or white.

116 I understand work. I was not born with a silver spoon in my mouth. I had a shovel pro-

grammed for my hand. My mother, a working woman. So many days she went to work early with runs in her stockings. She knew better, but she wore runs in her stockings so that my brother and I could have matching socks and not be laughed at at school.

117 I understand. At 3 o'clock on Thanksgiving Day we couldn't eat turkey because mama was preparing someone else's turkey at 3 o'clock. We had to play football to entertain ourselves and then around 6 o'clock she would get off the Alta Vista bus; then we would bring up the leftovers and eat our turkey—leftovers, the carcass, the cranberries around 8 o'clock at night. I really do understand.

118 Every one of these funny labels they put on you, those of you who are watching this broadcast tonight in the projects, on the corners, I understand. Call you outcast, low down, you can't make it, you're nothing, you're from nobody, subclass, underclass—when you see Jesse Jackson, when my name goes in nomination, your name goes in nomination.

119 I was born in the slum, but the slum was not born in me. And it wasn't born in you, and you can make it. Wherever you are tonight you can make it. Hold your head high, stick your chest out. You can make it. It gets dark sometimes, but the morning comes. Don't you surrender. Suffering breeds character. Character breeds faith. In the end faith will not disappoint.

120 You must not surrender. You may or may not get there, but just know that you're qualified and you hold on and hold out. We must never surrender. America will get better and better. Keep hope alive. Keep hope alive. Keep hope alive. On tomorrow night and beyond, keep hope alive.

121 I love you very much. I love you very much.

Critical Explorations: Reading

As you read and reread the Jackson speech, let these five questions help you examine the key points of Jackson's argument as well as the rhetorical devices that he uses to support his argument. After answering all of the questions, ask yourself how this address has made you reconsider the social issues that Jackson introduces. You may want to consider using the answers to these questions in your reading or dialogic journal.

1. In paragraphs 19 and 67, Jackson relies on either–or propositions, or false dilemmas, to support his argument. Locate these propositions and analyze their logic. In paragraphs 91–92, Jackson examines the use of atomic warfare. What cause–effect relationship does he set up here? Is it a valid relationship, or could you show that it is a slippery slope argument?

2. Reread paragraphs 59–60. Jackson begins paragraph 59 with this statement: "We find common ground. . . ." Who, along with Jackson, make up the "we"? By examining the evidence in these two paragraphs, how would you describe these people? What effect do these two paragraphs have on your understanding of the ethos that Jackson creates?

3. This speech is titled "Common Ground and Common Sense." Review paragraphs 59–61 to analyze Jackson's use of the term *common ground,* and examine paragraphs 79–80 to determine how he uses the terms *common sense* and *sense.* Does this title accurately summarize Jackson's overall argument?

4. Reread paragraph 84. With whom does Jackson want to be part of here? What evidence does Jackson later use to further show that he is in fact "one of them"?

5. In paragraph 98, Jackson concludes that "if an issue is morally right, it will eventually be political." What cause–effect relationship is he establishing here? Do you agree? Or can you construct an argument that would question this relationship?

Selection 19

"Television in the Nineties"
Shelly Schwab

Shelly Schwab is a television executive who gave this address to the School of Business at New York University in 1994. Schwab was chosen to present a lecture that is given each year by a prominent businessperson. Unlike the previous two political speeches, Schwab's purpose is more educational than political: he wants to inform his audience about the current status and future of television. Since Schwab is a major figure in the American television industry, he presents a generally positive picture of his business. This speech adds additional information to the selections on American television that you analyzed in Chapter 3.

This is a straightforward text. Schwab relies on a direct, factual business voice to discuss television's direction. You may want to examine the ethos that Schwab creates as you study this text. Examine especially paragraphs 1 and 57. Also pay careful attention to the language that Schwab uses to describe the television industry: Is it generally positive? Does his language suggest that television is a powerful force in American culture? You may want to carefully read paragraphs 5, 6, 8, and 9. Finally, consider the predictions that Schwab makes about television in the twenty-first century. What is your attitude toward these new media possibilities?

Reading–Writing Preparation

Before you read this selection, you may want to answer the following questions in writing or discussion:

1. In what ways do you think television is going to change in the future?

2. Do you think the addition of cable stations has improved the quality of television?

Television in the Nineties

Revolution or Confusion?

By Shelly Schwab, *President of MCATV Universal Studios*

Delivered at the Stern School of Business, Undergraduate College, New York University,
Joseph I. Lubin Memorial Lecture, New York, New York, March 1, 1994

1   In 1958, I came to NYU not full of confidence. I thought it was a long shot that I would be accepted, and, if I were, I wasn't confident I could get through and graduate. It was here that I learned a most important lesson: If you dedicate yourself to a goal, develop a discipline to succeed, have the desire to sacrifice for that success, and put passion into your work, you will achieve your goal. It's a lesson that has served me well throughout my life. I will always be indebted to NYU for setting that tone.

2   I appreciate Dean Diamond's invitation to deliver the Lubin Lecture this year and consider it an honor and a privilege to be here this evening.

3   Now let's talk television.

Television in the Nineties: What Does the Future Hold for It?

- Where do the real opportunities lie?

- With dozens of cable channels now available to the average home, and hundreds more on the way, how many do we actually watch?

4   What is signal compression? Multiplexing? Video on demand? Interactivity? What are the underlying questions and challenges posed by the coming electronic or information "superhigh-

---

Vital Speeches, October 1994. Reprinted by permission of the author and the publisher.

way?" Beyond entertainment, what bearing will it have on our lifestyles?

Television in the Nineties: Revolution or Confusion?

5   Although most of us in this room have spent our entire lives with television, it's still really a medium in its infancy. Yet, even in just four short decades, it's remarkable how many moments have touched, molded, and reshaped our lives.

6   However, even with its rich and colorful history, in terms of real practical potential television hasn't even scratched the surface.

7   Once upon a time it was a medium of limited options on limited channels. For the three networks—ABC, CBS, and NBC—the underlying strategy was not so much to "entice the viewer" as to schedule the "least objectionable programming." But the day of targeting the passive viewer is over, no longer is a family of four sitting down to watch *Bewitched* considered making optimum use of the medium.

8   We're entering an age of audience fragmentation where programmers will find that their success depends on the aggressive pursuit of an individual viewer, with almost limitless options— 500, 600, even 1,000 channels.

9   When I was growing up, I thought I had a big choice—seven channels to choose from! But it was television, and it was new, and it was exciting. But today's viewers aren't as easily wooed. For broadcasters, the coming electronic age is the technological equivalent of Columbus setting sail for the

New World: It's uncharted territory, but where there's great danger, there's also great opportunity—opportunity best realized by understanding the dynamics that brought us to this point.

Let's Look Back for a Few Moments at the Growth of Television by Decade

10   I can remember in the fifties when television watching was considered an "event." Milton Berle was the talk of the country, but for my family to watch it, we had to go to a neighbor's house—we didn't own a TV. And we weren't alone: the same was true all over the country. But in just a five-year span, television penetration in terms of households went from almost nothing to two-thirds of the country.

11   In the sixties, the television terrain became more colorful, literally, with network schedules being converted to all-color lineups, and many of us getting our first color sets. The sixties were also the decade of the "demographic"[1]—as ratings analysis turned from being strictly quantitative to qualitative as well. Advertisers began looking past raw numbers of households to find just who were their viewers—by age, sex, income.

12   By the seventies, the networks were aggressively programming for young, urban viewers. Gone were such longtime favorites as Jackie Gleason, Ed Sullivan, Red Skelton, even Lassie, and the silly rural sitcoms of the sixties such as *Green Acres* and *The Beverly Hillbillies*. Instead, they were replaced by such landmark series as *All in the Family, M*A*S*H, Mary Tyler Moore Show,* starting a new era in television comedy featuring story lines more sophisticated and relevant than anything that preceded it.

13   The question as we entered the eighties was: Where are the audiences going? The terrain of television began shifting. Instead of having the three major networks, with all other options almost an afterthought, the television landscape began taking on the look it has today . . . with the networks being just one of the viewers' alternatives.

14   First, there was the phenomenal growth of the independent stations (stations not affiliated with any of the big three networks). In 1975, there were only 102 of these so-called "indies" throughout the country. By 1985, there were 300, and there are now more than 430. This not only provided a major new alternative for viewers but, in effect, created a gold rush among program producers. Fulfilling the need of these independent stations is what transformed syndication[2] into what it is today . . . now a major competition to the networks. Today many of the most popular and watched series are not on the networks but in syndication, i.e., *Oprah, Donahue, Star Trek, A Current Affair, Wheel of Fortune, Jeopardy,* and *Baywatch.* As a result, the amount of advertising expenditures for non-network or syndicated programs has gone from $25 million annually in 1980 to $1.5 billion today.

15   A second new programming front was cable. In 1980 (and remember, this was only 14 years ago) cable penetration stood at just 18 percent of all households. CNN and MTV were launched and are now staples of daily life, and by 1985 cable penetration had jumped to 43 percent. It now stands at over 60 percent.

16   But, in addition to these changes from without, the eighties also brought the networks change from within: All three networks were sold—ABC to Capital Cities, NBC to General Electric, and CBS to Laurence A. Tisch of the Loews Corporation. And television's founding fathers, William Paley, David Sarnoff, Leonard Goldenson, visionaries who shaped each net-

---

1. demographic: relating to population, in this case to the number of viewers

2. syndication: the selling of a program to a number of independent stations

work's philosophy, were replaced by corporate entities run by bottom-line investors.

17   Meanwhile, another visionary and entrepreneur on global scale, Rupert Murdoch, was buying both 20th Century Fox and the Metromedia stations and forming the Fox Broadcasting Company (later to become the fourth network). Ted Turner was adding to his Turner broadcasting empire by starting up additional cable channels and, more recently, acquiring Hollywood production companies.

18   Another critical change facing television, and Madison Avenue in particular, was the skyrocketing number of "VCRs." Viewers were increasingly zapping through commercials when playing back tapes. With 55 percent of all homes having remotes by 1988, "grazing" or "channel hopping" during commercials became the advertisers' other big nightmare. (And a woman's nightmare as well, as men more than women are usually the zapping "culprits.")

19   This brings us to the nineties: With so many new entertainment alternatives coming into the field, what are the ramifications for the networks, the program suppliers, the advertisers, the viewers?

20   For the three major networks, their diminishing share of the audience pie is down to 60 percent and on any given night as low as 50 percent. Ten years ago it was 80 percent.

21   Fox, for example, as the upstart network, has already siphoned off a significant number of the big three networks' most demographically desirable viewers—the 18- to 34-year-olds—by aggressively programming for them with such series as *In Living Color, Beverly Hills 90210,* and *The Simpsons.*

22   In addition, more competition is on the way from Paramount and Warners, who are now engaged in a race to sign up as many affiliates as possible for their proposed fifth and sixth networks. It prompted one network insider to wonder, "If networks are a dying business, how come everyone is in such a rush to start one?"

23   The answer is, of course, that the networks may not necessarily be dying, but to survive they may have to reconfigure[3] significantly. Based on new FCC[4] regulations, there is now a strong possibility that one or two of the networks could be bought by film studios, or vise versa. Networks that were until recently pure buyers of programs will increasingly become suppliers, producing not only their own programming but, in select instances, that of their competition. For example, Fox, which has its own network, is now producing the Emmy Award-winning series *Picket Fences* for CBS. The old definition of mixed emotions was "watching your mother-in-law drive off a cliff in your new Cadillac." The new equivalent may be producing the number one series in prime time—for your competition.

24   Other changes facing the networks? The news and sports divisions may not survive on all three. Networks will continue to buy stakes in more and more advertiser-supported cable channels such as ESPN, Lifetime, and A&E; again, under the theory that as long as someone has to be in competition with me, why not let it be me?

25   What are the programming trends of the nineties? Or to be more pragmatic, I suppose, in which directions are the economic realities of the business forcing network programmers to turn?

26   Sitcoms and dramas will continue to be staples of the networks' lineup. On the other hand, "action-hours" series such as the *A-Team* and *Magnum P.I.* that once accounted for 21 percent of the networks' lineups will continue to be conspicuous by their absence. With only the occasional exception, they just don't make 'em like they used to. Why? Strictly economics—the dollars involved don't make any sense. Exploding buildings and crashing car scenes are just too expensive to produce.

---

3. reconfigure: reorganize

4. FCC: Federal Communications Commission

27   Action-hours cost between $1.3 to $2 million per episode to produce versus $1 million for dramas and $700,000 for reality programming. Incidentally, if big-budget action series are endangered, conversely, do you know what the fastest-growing form of programming on television is? Infomercials! As a start-up business, it's gone from grossing nothing to $1 billion a year, virtually overnight (and growing).

So Where Do We Stand in 1994 and Beyond?

- There are now 94 million TV homes, reaching 98 percent of the country (1950: 4 million TV homes/10 percent of the country).

- Sixty-five percent of TV homes have two or more sets.

- Sixty-one percent of TV homes have cable.

- The average home receives 35 channels (1950s = 2.9). Of those 35 channels, does anyone know how many the typical adult-viewer watches in any given week? 7.5. How many will you watch when there are 500 channels?

- The average household views over 7 hours a day/51 hours a week.

- VCR penetration is 83 percent. That's a lot of taping.

- But only half of all home-recorded tapes are ever played back.

- Thirty percent of all households have "PCs."

- Advertising is still the lifeblood of television: in 1950, $171 million was spent on total TV advertising. Now it's at $33 billion!

28   But beyond over-the-air broadcasting and cable, what are the alternate technologies being developed as means of delivering television?

29   There's "DBS," direct broadcasting satellite. This system will beam a package of channels directly to homes that have small dish antennae. This service is scheduled to launch nationally this year. Another new competing delivery system is microwave technology. This simultaneously transmits dozens of channels for television, telephone, and data. Homes are reached by bouncing the signal off buildings or other objects until it reaches its destination.

30   But everything we've been discussing so far—the evolution of television, the new technologies—while dramatic and exciting, pales[5] in comparison to the changes at hand.

31   A radically changed medium lies just around the corner, and the key to it is the coming electronic or information superhighway, which will use fiber-optic wires to compress and deliver 500, 600, or even 1,000 channels!

But Will This Lead to Revolution— or Total Confusion?

32   Here's where the real opportunities lie. John Sculley, former chief executive of Apple Computer, estimated that the formation of a single interactive information industry could generate revenue of $3.5 trillion by the year 2001.

33   The potential is enormous, but so is the massive outlay of capital required to finance this superhighway: over $400 billion (that's more than the gross national product of Canada). That's also why cable companies that until now have enjoyed virtual monopolies in their service areas are suddenly rushing into a series of mergers and partnerships with the one industry they most feared as future competition: the telephone companies. The Baby Bells are cash cows and they have the capital and resources to build and deliver the infrastructure[6] to the information superhighway. Of course, a great deal of the direction and growth in this area is tied to government regulations. One of the greatest fears caused by all the recent megamergers[7] is access, the ability

---

5. pales: becomes seen as smaller or less significant

6. infrastructure: underlying foundation

7. megamergers: the joinings of huge corporations

of everyone—companies, consumers, institutions —to tap into the superhighway. Will a small number of "gatekeepers" be able to cause a "bottleneck?" How do Congress and the courts plan to enforce access?

34 There will be a lot of new words in our vocabulary—"multiplexing," "CD-ROM," "access" —that's the new language of the superhighway. Other buzzwords include fiber optics, infrastructure, signal compression, high definition, servers, interactive programming, multimedia, video dial tones, network time shifting, video on demand, bulletin board services, and virtual reality, with more and more coming on-line every day. But none of this is speculation. It isn't Buck Rogers fantasizing. It's what we are now capable of achieving.

35 What shape will the superhighway take? One senior cable executive offered this example: one of a 600-channel universe.

- First, a 100-channel "grazing zone" that would be similar to current traditional cable television.

- Next, there would be a 200-channel "quality zone" providing two additional channels for each channel in the "grazing zone" on which their best programming would· be repeated.

- Beyond that, a 50-channel "event TV zone" for live pay-per-view events such as boxing—and finally

- A 250-channel "video store" that would be reserved for movies, and these movies won't necessarily be previously released theatricals; they may be big-budget spectaculars running concurrently with or prior to their theatrical runs.

36 What about programming on the superhighway? As a viewer, what would I find in the proposed grazing zone? Programming not meant as a mass viewing experience but designed for the individual: What I or you want, when we want it. For instance, movies that can now be ordered at

several specific times during the day will be available at any time at all—virtually "on demand."

37 Incidentally, another example of "video on demand" is a system developed by a company called U.S.A. Video, which will digitize and compress full libraries of movie studios. Those compressed signals will be sent over telephone lines and stored in a box attached to a user's set, where they can keep the movie or event for up to 24 hours with the ability to rewind, fast forward, or pause it—just like a rented video.

38 But as a programmer, competing with hundreds of other channels, how will I effectively reach as many viewers as possible?

39 One of the strategies prominently mentioned by the broadcast networks and their cable counterparts is "multiplexing"—expanding their lineup to more than one channel at a time. For instance, it's Monday at 8 p.m. and HBO-One will be running a movie, while HBO-Two has a concert, and HBO-Three carries the series *Dream-On*.

40 What about the enormous potential of pay-per-view? Theatrical premieres and special events notwithstanding, the greatest example of a built-in pay-per-view audience is in sports. Thus far, only boxing, wrestling, and Howard Stern have managed to take full advantage of this technology; but the day of the pay-per-view "season ticket" will soon be at hand. It's speculated that the NFL could soon be offering a weekly tray of "pay-per-view" games if you want to watch a game other than the one carried in your market. And there will be special plans offered, if you wish to follow one particular out-of-town team for an entire season.

41 What about "interactive programming?" Forget the image of the couch potato who sits before his set going from channel to channel in a semivegetative state, the way my generation watches television. We're going to be replaced by a new generation of viewers raised on interacting with their sets. I can just hear an incredulous child saying to a parent, "You mean you used to watch movies without being able to decide what happens next?" Imagine reaching the

last scene in *Casablanca* and then getting to choose who Ingrid Bergman goes off with at the end? Humphrey Bogart or Paul Heinreid? Heinreid wouldn't stand a chance!

42 But is this really what viewers want? To pick the end of their favorite television shows or films? Or does that somehow diminish the viewing experience? As a novelty, it might work, but on a regular basis?

43 At the recent superhighway summit at UCLA, opinion was split—Jeffrey Katzenberg, the chairman of the Walt Disney Studios, said that as a viewer he wouldn't want to sit home and determine the outcome of films. On the other hand, Lucie Salhany, the Fox Broadcasting Corporation chairman, says that this is something they are interested in and want to explore. Two major studios with opposite views.

Again, Revolution or Total Confusion?

44 "Virtual reality," the sexiest of the new buzz-words, is another form of interactivity. The user is able to interact in what is usually a computer-driven environment. For example, batting against a major league pitcher while sitting in your living room. This experience is enhanced with video, audio, and graphics and gives the senses a full three-dimensional effect.

45 But "interactive programming" goes far beyond just playing simulated games or having your kids interact with *Beavis and Butthead*. By the way, that thought alone is enough to make me want to rethink the entire technology. But it's about interacting with other people. Interactive television will revolutionize education, politics, lifestyles.

46 Vice President Gore, the Clinton Administration's point man on the information superhighway, told CEOs[8] at the UCLA summit that providing every school, library, and hospital with access to the superhighway's educational and informational tools was the highest priority and targeted

the end of the decade for them to meet that challenge, which the CEOs in turn pledged to do.

47 Interactive television will change politics, careers, communication. Interest groups, scattered by geography, will be able to "link up," becoming much more effective, much more demanding. For those looking for a different quality of life, it will be much easier to run a business in a remote area, without leaving your home.

48 And you won't have to go out to do your marketing either. Instead of a trip to the supermarket, you'll be able to call up a market's entire inventory—by price, by brand, by size—and place your order by touching your screen. From foods, to fashion, to furnishing your home, to any aspect of your life—you'll soon be able to satisfy your shopping needs via video malls. In fact, *Joan Rivers Shopping Show* aside, the whole concept of home shopping has an enormous upside that has barely been scratched.

49 Also, let me mention briefly "high definition" television. It's important to realize that the quality of the images you'll be seeing on-screen, in the high-definition universe, will be taking a quantum leap.[9] Not only will we have greater options regarding what to watch, but it will be provided in a wide-screen format with unprecedented clarity. The audio will also be beyond anything previously available, and you'll be able to hang it on your wall. Today's sets will seem as primitive and outmoded as the black-and-white sets of the fifties.

50 Yet, even with all the terms used to describe the future of the superhighway—enormous, gargantuan,[10] unlimited—the bottom line is that no one agrees regarding what form it will finally take. With companies investing hundreds of millions, even billions of dollars, there's still no consensus on how it will pay off. Mistakes will be made. There won't be a magic switch that you turn on and it will suddenly be there.

---

8. CEOs: chief executive officers of corporations

9. quantum leap: a sudden or extreme change

10. gargantuan: of enormous size

51 Again, returning to my earlier analogy about Columbus setting sail for the New World: Where there are great opportunities, there are also great dangers. Will too much emphasis be placed on technologies and not enough on services being designed and how they impact people?

52 In fact, we can go down an entire list of questions posed by the advent of the superhighway:

- How long will it take to construct? Five years or fifteen?

- How much will it cost?

- How much are consumers willing to pay for it?

- Will the superhighway mean the end of privacy? With everything one watches or orders being logged, where are the safeguards?

- What is the role of government?

- What is the future of over-the-air broadcasting?

- What kind of balance will be reached between interactive and passive programming?

- With so many specialized cable channels already here or on the horizon, are you ready for the cowboy channel and the mystery channel; the senior citizen, video game, talk show, and game show channels? What is the future of the mass-viewing experience?

- How will advertisers get their messages to viewers with itchy fingers on their remotes?

- What do television home shopping malls mean for local businesses?

The List Goes On . . .

- Will newspapers and magazines become obsolete?

- Is a computer-literate society necessarily a literate society?

- Will the superhighway create a generation able to cocoon itself by never leaving the house? Will interactive programming in a sense replace social interactivity?

53 Obviously, if the future of television is a superhighway, we're only now approaching the on-ramp. We stand on the threshold of a convergence of technologies: cable, computers, VCRs, satellites, and fiber-optic networks.

54 The forthcoming explosion is the technological equivalent of the big bang,[11] creating a new universe of almost limitless possibilities. We will be able to move information on a massive scale. For example, fax machines are currently capable of moving 14,000 bytes per second. By the turn of the century and with the new technology, it will be 1-billion bytes per second.

55 Well, for the last 30 minutes we covered just the headlines of what television was and what it will be. So, in closing, we ask the question again. Television in the nineties: is it revolution or confusion? Obviously from my remarks tonight, you know that I feel that the answer is: it's both.

56 In fact, your future home entertainment equipment will be so sophisticated that it's probably going to take either Einstein or a seven-year-old to work it.

57 I'll end by quoting one of the industry's giants and futurists, Ted Turner. He recently said,

> "Even with all these great technological breakthroughs and advances, most of my friends still can't program their VCRs and get the 12 to stop blinking."

58 Thank you.

Critical Explorations: Reading

Answer the following questions as you reread the Schwab speech. In answering these questions, you will better appreciate the rhetorical practices that Schwab relies on to persuade and inform his audience. These answers may serve as material for your reading or dialogic journal.

---

11. big bang: theory that the universe was created from a gigantic explosion

1. Reread paragraphs 1 and 57 to determine the ethos that Schwab establishes. Describe the character that Schwab creates in these two paragraphs. How would this character likely please, or win over, his New York University business audience?

2. In his speech, Schwab sometimes refers to significant events in American history to describe the achievements of television. He mentions Christopher Columbus in paragraph 9 and the California gold rush in paragraph 14. What effect do these historical allusions have on the audience's understanding of American television?

3. Reread paragraph 16. Summarize the changes that have been made in network ownership. Who replaced the previous owners? What do these new owners seem to have in common?

4. Schwab refers to discoveries in physics to describe television's future technology. He refers to a "quantum leap" in paragraph 49 and to the "big bang" in paragraph 54. How do these allusions from physics shape the audience's attitude toward television technology?

5. In paragraph 55, Schwab concludes that television in the nineties is both revolution and confusion. Read through the address quickly to determine the sorts of evidence he uses for both positions. Do you think that Schwab presents more evidence for television in the nineties as a revolutionary medium or as a confusing medium?

Selection 20

"The Real World: Things Are Not as Simple as They Seem"
Michael J. Kobre

In this speech, given at Queens College in North Carolina, Professor Michael J. Kobre speaks to the class of 1995 as they begin their senior year. His focus is on what these students will face in the "real" world once they graduate. In interesting ways, Kobre ties his understanding of the "real" world into a discussion of the media and politics. Three recurring questions organize Kobre's speech: How do the media influence the viewer's understanding of the world? How do the media influence the behavior of politicians? How does a college experience differ from this media reality?

In many ways, these are fitting questions for the final selection of this textbook because in the previous selections that you have read, you have been asked the first two questions or questions like them. Furthermore, as a college student, it is important for you to consider this last question: to reflect on how your college education has provided you with ways to examine your culture.

Like the previous speech on television, the Kobre address is straightforward: clearly organized and written. As you read and reread this speech, you may want to determine the various ways that Kobre defines reality, particularly as he considers this term in paragraphs 4, 6, and 21. Further, you may want to examine what Kobre means when he refers in paragraph 14 to the media as creating "the illusion of intimacy." This concept is central to Kobre's understanding of the difference between media and academic reality.

Reading–Writing Preparation

Before you read this selection, you may want to answer the following questions in writing or discussion:

1. What sort of education do you receive from the media? How does this education differ from the one you're getting in college?

2. What factors do you think shape your understanding of reality?

The Real World: Things Are Not as Simple as They Seem

Critical Issues Facing Young People Today

By Michael J. Kobre, *Assistant Professor of English, Queens College*

Delivered at the Fall Convocation of Queens College,
Charlotte, North Carolina, September 6, 1994

1   This is a funny place for me to be today. It's not only that I've *never* spoken in front of an audience this large before, but this is also the first day of *Rosh Hoshanah,* the Jewish New Year, and it feels a little strange to be in a chapel rather than a temple. Still, in many ways, it's fitting to be here. Because in Judaism anything having to do with education is considered a *mitzvah,* a blessing. And because we are here to celebrate the beginning of a new year too, a new academic year.

2   Of course, for some of you in the audience—and by this I mean the class of '95—this is not only a beginning but an end as well. You've begun the *last* year of your education at Queens. You're about to leave the familiar confines of the academic world to enter what we routinely call "the real world." It's an important time in your lives—and not an easy one either.

3   But today I would like to think a little bit about those terms. The real world. The academic world. We're used to thinking of them as opposites, as if what we do here in a place like Queens is somehow cut off from the hard-edged reality of the world of commerce and industry. And in a way that's true. Here, in the academic world, on our very *best* days, we have the luxury of contemplation, of time to read and, think and talk about the most important issues of human life. We're not pummeled[1] by the relentless demand to produce and to maximize profits. We have the time—and, indeed, the responsibility—to admire the beauty of a line from Shakespeare or to consider the ethical questions that are unavoidable in a fiercely competitive society like ours.

4   And yet, I have to admit that the notion that what we do here is somehow less "real" than what goes on outside the campus is troubling to me. For one thing, the academic world is not really a safe haven from practical concerns. A college or university, like any other large institution, still has to pay its bills. Nor is it some refuge for naive idealists. In the academic world, like the real world, idealism inevitably struggles with pragmatism and compromise—and it doesn't always win.

5   For another thing, I think what we do here is real because I've seen the faces of our students. I've watched them change over four years. And I'm reluctant to dismiss what happens to them as some artificial experience that will fade in importance once they leave the enclosed world of the campus. Let me ask the class of '95 to help me with this point. I want all of you to think for a moment about everything you've learned in the past three years, everything you've experienced.

Vital Speeches, November 1994. Reprinted by permission of the author and the publisher.

1. pummeled: beaten with fists

The books you've read, the friends you've made, what you've learned about yourself. Can anyone *actually* say that all of that was *not* real? At one time or another, some of you may even look back and think that these years were the *most* real part of your life. That they were the time when you lived most openly, most freely.

6   In fact, not only is the academic world *real*, but in my opinion the real world is becoming more and more artificial. Of course, it's always been difficult to tell what's real and what's not. Because we live in a complex world, ambiguity is an inevitable part of it. Is this what I really want to do with my life? Does the other person really love me? Do I love in return? I remember Lee Stoffel, our distinguished professor of religion, once saying in a panel discussion in Liberal Learning that faith is always tempered by doubt. How true. Whether we mean faith in God, in another person, or in ourselves, few beliefs are so strong that they are never questioned. For all of us, there are times in our lives when reality is shifting and elusive.

7   But I think, also, that at this moment in the life of our culture reality is under siege in a way that it's never been before. Why is this? It is a consequence, I believe, of what Neil Postman in his landmark book *Amusing Ourselves to Death* calls

> "The most significant American cultural fact of the second half of the twentieth century: the decline of the Age of Typography [the age of the written word, that is] and the ascendancy of the Age of Television."

Postman suggests that in an age of television—when the average American spends seven hours a day passively watching TV and more homes have television sets than indoor plumbing—entertainment becomes the greatest value of all. And consequently the line between truth and illusion, between reality and artifice[2] gets a little thin.

8   As Postman writes,

> "No matter what is depicted [on television] or from what point of view, the overarching presumption is that it is there for our amusement and pleasure. That is why even on news shows which provide us daily with fragments of tragedy and barbarism, we are urged by the newscasters to 'join them tomorrow.' What for? One would think that several minutes of murder and mayhem would suffice as material for a month of sleepless nights. We accept the newscasters' invitation because we know that the 'news' is not to be taken seriously. . . . Everything about a news show tells us this—the good looks and amiability of the cast, their pleasant banter, the exciting music that opens and closes the show, the vivid film footage, the attractive commercials—all these and more suggest that what we have just seen is no cause for weeping. A news show, to put it plainly, is a format for entertainment, not for education, reflection or catharsis."[3]

9   Indeed, it seems to me that in "the real world" reality and entertainment are becoming increasingly indistinguishable. Consider, for instance, our most recent war. When America and its United Nations allies drove Saddam Hussein and his troops out of Kuwait, all of us at home could tune in daily as if we were watching a mini-series. Each network provided its own title and theme music for its coverage, and, as the critic Neil Gabler noted in *The New York Times*,

> "The casting was impeccable. Articulate, brilliant, rugged, sensitive, heroic H. Norman Swarzkopf was a figure of Herculean[4] proportions"

while

> "Saddam Hussein resembled the evil mastermind from a Saturday afternoon serial."

---

2. artifice: cunning or craftiness

3. catharsis: emotional cleansing

4. Herculean: having extraordinary strength or size

It was a perfect little war, just made for television, with clearly defined good guys and bad guys, breathtaking footage of smart bombs dropping down chimneys with pinpoint accuracy, and a whole array of souvenir videos after it was over so you could watch it again and again.

10   Or, as another example of the way in which reality and entertainment are becoming increasingly mixed up, let's consider the most recent mini-series that has gripped America. You know, O.J. Even before his life turned into an episode of *Columbo,* he was one of those people who live on the cusp between reality and fantasy, who enjoy that vague status of being "a television personality." Sometimes he would appear on television playing himself, whether as a pitchman for Hertz or as a sportscaster for one of the networks or a guest on *The Tonight Show.* Sometimes he would turn up pretending to be someone else. But in either case what we were seeing was at least in part a fantasy. We know now, as the layers of his life are increasingly peeled away and exposed to the public, that the private man was in some ways very different from the one we saw running through airports in commercials or trading quips[5] with talk show hosts.

11   Perhaps years from now people will talk about where they were the night of the famous car chase on the Santa Monica freeway in the same way that an earlier generation would never forget where they were when they heard that President Kennedy was shot. That was, I think, a quintessential[6] moment in modern American culture when reality and fantasy fused together in one surreal[7] mix. There we were, all around the nation, glued to our television sets, watching the little white Bronco drive and drive with its accompanying phalanx[8] of police cars as helicopters circled overhead and the usual cast of experts intoned gravely about O.J.'s psychological state. What were we all waiting to see? Did we expect O.J. to stop the car and shoot it out with the cops? Was Keanu Reeves going to drop down from a helicopter on to the hood of the Bronco and then reenact a scene from *Speed?* Or were we waiting for something else, something less glamorous but equally lurid?[9] A flash of blood across the windshield, the car spinning out of control, while a doomed man takes his own life in front of millions of viewers.

12   Maybe the weirdest part of the night, though, was the people who were gathered on the overpasses or by the side of the road cheering him on. What were they there for? When reporters asked some of the crowd later, they responded in vague terms. "I just had to be there," said one man. "I wanted to be a part of history," said another woman. Indeed, it seems that all across L.A. people spontaneously got up from what they were doing and hurried to the freeway to catch a glimpse of the white Bronco. In a way, these people were a little like medieval peasants who would see religious visions and suddenly leave their homes and families to make a pilgrimage on foot to the holy land.

13   Why were they there that night in L.A.? Perhaps it was the presence of the television cameras all around them. The novelist John Updike once said that you feel more real if you've been on television. Maybe this is why the crowd on the overpass would wave to the cameras whenever a news helicopter passed overhead. Maybe they just wanted to be part of that world that they watched every night on TV, that larger-than-life world on the other side of the camera that O.J. himself existed in.

14   Or maybe it was because they genuinely loved him, the Juice, and they thought they knew him. After all they saw him—we all saw him—all the time on television, and the glare of the media creates the illusion of intimacy. After a while in

_____

5. quips: clever or witty remarks

6. quintessential: the most perfect

7. surreal: depicting the thoughts of the unconscious

8. phalanx: a closely massed group

_____

9. lurid: gruesome and revolting

the spotlight, public figures become so familiar to us that we become as involved in their personal lives as their professional achievements. Just think for a minute of some of the famous couples whose domestic dramas have played out across our TV screens in the last few years. Roseanne and Tom, Donald and Marla (and sometimes Ivana), Charles and Di, Lyle and Julia, Michael and Lisa-Marie, Bill and Hillary, Oprah and Steadman. We think we know them so well that we're on a first-name basis.

15 *But we don't.* This presumption of familiarity is, as the O.J. Simpson case has tragically reminded us, only the *illusion* of intimacy. The handsome, genial man we saw on television was at the least an abusive husband who terrorized his wife. And this particular case is only one example of the way in which reality and artifice mingle together in the television age.

16 Perhaps the most extreme and troubling form of all this confusion over what's real and what's not can be found in the political world. In the television age, politics has become a kind of performance art in which appearance *is* reality. Consider, for instance, this scene from the 1980 campaign. Ronald Reagan, the presumptive favorite for the Republican nomination for president, has been stunned by a loss to George Bush in the Iowa Caucuses. Bush, eager to capitalize on his success, challenges Reagan to a one on one debate just before the crucial New Hampshire primary. But when Reagan shows up at the debate with the other Republican hopefuls in tow, the sponsors of the debate try to pull the plug on the event. They expected a *mano a mano*[10] showdown between Bush and Reagan. No showdown, they say, no debate. Yet just at the moment when they're about to turn off the microphones and the cameras, Reagan explodes in a rage. "I paid for this microphone," he says, pounding the lectern with his fist, while Bush sits idly beside him, looking uncomfortable. It is a triumphant moment for Reagan, as all the commentators duly note later, a

demonstration of strength that made Bush look weak and indecisive in comparison and contributed to Reagan winning the New Hampshire primary and ultimately the nomination. But what no one realized at the time was that Reagan's words and gestures were copied from the climactic moment of a 1949 Spencer Tracy and Katherine Hepburn film *State of the Union* in which Tracy played a candidate for the Republican nomination for president. Reagan, the ex-movie star turned candidate, won a real election by imitating Tracy, the movie star *playing* a candidate.

17 In the years since then, of course, all of Reagan's successors and would-be successors learned from his mastery of political imagery. Fourteen years later, for instance, Bill Clinton walking the Normandy Beach to commemorate the 50th anniversary of the D-Day invasion bends down in silent meditation and makes a small cross from a pile of stones at his feet. It is a touching moment, as our Commander in Chief silently ponders the sacrifices of the men who died on this beach 50 years before. But what are the press doing there, huddled a few yards away, with their cameras trained on the President? Is it an accident that as Clinton kneels on the beach he is perfectly framed for the cameras between a pair of old battleships anchored off shore? What is real and what is artifice?

18 Ultimately, politics in America at the end of the 20th century has become a war of images contrived for the television screen rather than an exchange of ideas. Our politicians have become performers desperate for airtime. Consequently, a crucial debate on a measure aimed at curbing the violence and despair that is tearing apart our cities disintegrates into a battle of slogans, and what we see on television is Al D'Amato, the Republican Senator from New York, holding up a drawing of a pig and singing, "Old MacDonald had some pork, ei ei o."

19 As you can see, then, "the real world" is not what it used to be. Transformed by the glare of the cameras and, indeed, by our own relentless demand to be entertained—for *we* are at fault here too—reality in all its complexity slips

---

10. mano a mano: hand to hand

through our grasp. At our worst, we accept illusion for truth. We mistake the simple answers that we want to hear for the difficult choices that we have to make. Indeed, in the coming years, as this nation confronts many seemingly intractable problems, we will all be tested. Can we learn to distinguish between reality and artifice? Can we see through the cleverly staged advertisements and events? Can we hear beyond the simplistic slogans like "socialized medicine" and "tough on crime" and "tax and spend"?

20 And that, in conclusion, is why I believe that what we do here *in the academic world* is at least as real and important as what goes on outside our walls. For it is here, in our classrooms, that we try to develop the skills in critical thinking and interpretation that are so necessary in the late 20th century when the problems that face us are becoming more complex and the line between truth and illusion is becoming harder to see. If we do nothing else, we remind our students and ourselves of the great truth that the Czech writer Milan Kundera identifies as the recurring message or all great novels:

"Things are not as simple as they seem."

21 Let me end with those words, because they are as good a beginning to another year in the academic world as any. For as we grapple with all of the complexity of the new ideas and new experiences of the year to come, we would do well to remember that this complexity should not be feared. Because it is the very condition of life in a *real world*. So remember, remember. Things are not as simple as they seem.

Critical Explorations: Reading

Answer these five questions as you reread the Kobre speech. In responding to these questions, you will better understand the differences that Kobre establishes between the reality of popular culture and that of academic life. They may serve as material for your reading or dialogic journal.

1. Reread paragraph 1. Why does Kobre refer to the Jewish New Year? And why does he focus on education as a blessing? How does this information help shape Kobre's ethos for his audience?

2. In paragraph 10, Kobre analyzes O. J. Simpson as a television personality who lives "on the cusp between reality and fantasy." What does Kobre mean by this phrase, and how does it relate to the evidence that he presents about Simpson in this paragraph?

3. Occasionally, Kobre presents generalizations about how Americans experience their culture. Study the following two statements and determine if they are hasty or reasoned: (1) "But I think, also, that at this moment in the life of our culture reality is under siege in a way that it's never been before" (paragraph 7). (2) "Ultimately, politics in America at the end of the 20th century has become a war of images contrived for the television screen rather than an exchange of ideas" (paragraph 18).

4. Reread paragraph 16. Summarize this incident between Presidents Bush and Reagan. Why do you think that Kobre included this anecdote? How does it support his argument about media reality?

5. Throughout this speech, Kobre hints at what he means by reality. Reread paragraphs 4, 6, and 21. With the comments made in these paragraphs, write two definitions: a definition of media reality and a definition of academic reality. How do these definitions help explain Kobre's final conclusion: "Things are not as simple as they seem"? (paragraph 21).

Critical Explorations: Writing

The following writing topics can be answered as formal essay responses. As with the other essays you have written, share your drafts with your peers and instructor. To effectively respond to all of these questions, you will need to know the terminology presented in the introduction to this chapter and be familiar with the American beliefs examined in Chapter 1.

1. In his Inaugural Address, President Clinton uses change and renewal as the principal issues to organize the major theme of his speech. What is this theme, and how does he develop it? In discussing the ways that he develops this theme, consider the following aspects of Clinton's address: (1) its ethos and pathos, (2) the comparisons Clinton makes, and (3) Clinton's stylistic choices, especially his use of repetition and pronoun shift.

2. Jesse Jackson's "Common Ground and Common Sense" is based upon the careful use of the rhetorical devices of repetition and parallelism. Much of the passion of this speech comes from Jackson's artful use of these two rhetorical techniques. Begin by discussing the arguments that Jackson presents in his address. Then analyze the following paragraphs for their use of repetition and parallelism: 65, 74–77, 79–80, 81–82, 85, 95, and 108. What is Jackson saying in these paragraphs, and how do repetition and parallelism complement what he is saying? Finally, how do these devices contribute to the ethos and pathos created in Jackson's address?

3. In the last part of "Television in the Nineties," Shelly Schwab presents the technological future of television. Much of this discussion is in paragraphs 33–54. Select several of these new technologies. First, carefully summarize what Schwab says about them. Then analyze what you think their impact will be on the television viewer of the near future. Do you believe these technologies will be beneficial, harmful, or a bit of both?

4. In Selections 19 and 20, Shelly Schwab and Michael J. Kobre present different ideas about television. Using relevant evidence from both speeches, determine how these two speakers see television differently. In the Schwab speech, you may want to focus on the ways that he uses language and historical allusions to present his image of television. In the Kobre speech, you may want to analyze his argument that television "creates the illusion of intimacy" (paragraph 14). Finally, after analyzing the arguments made in these two speeches, express your own position concerning television's influence on American culture.

5. In these four addresses, a different ethos is presented in each speech. Compare the various ethical characters that are created in the Clinton, Jackson, Schwab, and Kobre addresses. Which ethical characters are similar? Which are different? How does each speaker create his particular ethos? Which of these four ways of creating ethos are similar? Which are different?

Student Writing

Below you will find a student's response to President Clinton's first Inaugural Address; it is her first draft. Read the draft carefully; then answer the questions that follow. Carmela responded to the following topic:

Analyze the Clinton address from the following perspectives:
the American myths it evokes, its ethos, and its pathos.

The New President Inspires the Nation

1   The inaugural address of a newly installed Head of State must necessarily be inspirational. Not persuasive (which is less lofty in its theme) because he has already persuaded the electorate his time has come to lead the nation. Not self-congratulatory and certainly not manipulative, because his mission is just starting: there is nothing yet to crow about. Rather, inspirational because the tasks at hand are usually enormous; hence, the Head of State needs everyone to share both his vision and the responsibility for carrying out his mission.

2   President Bill Clinton's inaugural address on January 22, 1993 needed to be inspirational. The U.S.A. was in the depths of winter—literally and figuratively—from which the citizenry needed rescue. The American economy was "weakened by business failures, stagnant wages, increasing inequality, and deep divisions among our people" (par. 10). The President had to sow the seeds of renewal and recovery and thereby reap the rebirth of spring (par. 3).

3   As an inspirational speech, President Clinton's inaugural address is replete with reference to America's fundamental myths: the American people's belief in and desire to preserve the time-worn ideals of life, liberty, and the pursuit of happiness; likewise, of democracy, economic justice, and racial equality. President Clinton himself acknowledges that these ideals are far from having been achieved in America. He mentions, for instance, that rampant criminality has deprived the law-abiding citizens of their freedom (of mobility, from fear, etc.); that the high "cost of health care devastates families and threatens to bankrupt our enterprises" (par. 14); that politicians and power brokers continue to maneuver for position and influence, "forgetting these people whose toil and sweat . . . pays our way" (par. 28).

4   Additionally, the myths discussed by Jack Solomon in *The Signs of Our Time* may be gleaned by the President's inaugural speech: the myth of childhood, in the President's reference to "our troubled children" (par. 42) and how "millions of poor children cannot even imagine the lives we are calling them to lead" (par. 14); the myths of science and technology and of progress in his description of technology as being magical (par. 12)—despite which, ironically, our communities are torn and need to be reconnected (par. 42); and the myth of the American dream, which he spoke of our "universal ambition for a better life" (par. 12).

5   Precisely because of these weaknesses in the American political and socio-economic system, the President's call for change to preserve America's ideals and values—which our forefathers shed blood and sacrificed their life to—in his inaugural speech was timely and imperative. The country's problems are severe, yet not insurmountable. If the American people can be bold enough to effect dramatic changes in the system and in themselves, and undertake great sacrifice

in the process, then, from the depths of winter, spring can indeed be reborn.

6   The President referred to America's basic myths to appeal to all segments of American society. Unlike some of his predecessors, his was a policy of inclusion. (Thus, in his subsequent pronouncements, the public is made aware of his greater sensitivity to the needs of the youth—which he treats as a new political constituency—and of heretofore discriminated segments of society: people of color, gays and lesbians, the urban poor, the unemployed and underemployed, and the homeless.)

7   But these are not his only audiences in his inaugural speech. He was addressing the rest of the world as well—"a world warmed by the sunshine of freedom [following the collapse of communism] but threatened still by ancient hatreds and new plagues" (par. 9). After all, "there is no longer any clear division between what is foreign and what is domestic" (par. 32). What happens to the world economy and world environment affects Americans. Conversely, what happens to the U.S.A. affects the rest of the world, this country being the world's last remaining superpower, and its economy, despite its ills, is "still the world's strongest" (par. 10). Hence, America must continue to lead the world it "did so much to make" (par. 33); this world America "will defend in peaceful diplomacy whenever possible and with force when necessary" (par. 35). (As an aside, this seems no different from President Clinton's predecessors; this has always been the U.S. government's foreign as well as military policy.)

8   But a speech cannot be inspiring unless the speaker commands respect and inspiration himself. What kind of leader is President Bill Clinton, and why are Americans inspired by his compelling rhetoric of reinventing America? Aside from his youthful vitality and restless energy, the ethos he shows is that of a trustworthy leader with a genuine affection for an identification with his people. Note how he never used the pro-

noun "I" in his inaugural speech, using instead "we" and "us," thus involving everyone—appealing to his people's pathos—in his vision and his mission.

9   Indeed, what America's new Chief of State calls forth is a renaissance of vision and a mission-sharing throughout America. It is too early to say if this can be achieved, but the American people are inspired and enthused: for they know, as the new President does, that there's strength in numbers and in shared commitment, and that these can cure what's now ailing America.

1.   Reread Carmela's first paragraph. What distinctions is she making among speeches that are persuasive, self-congratulatory, manipulative, or inspirational? Are these distinctions elaborated upon in the rest of her draft?

2.   In paragraph 4, Carmela introduces some of the American myths that Clinton considers important for the success of his country, citing excerpts from his address. In conference, it was suggested that Carmela expand her analysis here. What sort of additional commentary on these excerpts can Carmela include in order to better analyze Clinton's use of these myths?

3.   In conference, Carmela was encouraged to delete paragraph 6. Reread this paragraph to determine if it should be present. Give your reasons for deleting or retaining it.

4.   In paragraph 8, Carmela responds to one of the issues of the essay topic: ethos. Her peers suggested that she needed more evidence from the address to support her claim that Clinton is "a trustworthy leader." What additional evidence from Clinton's address could you provide Carmela to support the ethos of a trustworthy individual that Clinton creates?

5.   Carmela's peers suggested that she needed to say more in paragraph 8, or in a separate paragraph, about the pathos that Clinton cre-

ates in his audience. If you were to provide suggestions on how to revise this section of Carmela's essay, what evidence from the address would you want her to include about the pathos that this speech creates?

Peer Responses

Use some or all of these questions to respond to your peer's draft. Comment as specifically as you can so that your peer can use your comments to productively revise her draft.

1. Consider the introduction to your peer's draft. Does it adequately prepare you for what the draft discusses? Or does this introduction need revision?

2. Locate a paragraph in your peer's draft that is particularly well organized. Analyze those elements that make it a successfully organized paragraph.

3. Trace the argument made in a particular paragraph or section of your peer's draft. Is the argument clearly presented? Or are there elements in the argument that are unclear or illogical? If there are unclear or illogical elements, how would you revise them?

4. Locate the section of the draft in which your peer analyzes ethos. Is this section of the draft complete? Or are there topics here that you would like your peer to include or revise? (This question does not apply to topics 3 and 4, page 256.)

5. Locate the section of the draft in which your peer analyzes pathos. Is this part of the draft complete? Or are there additional topics in this section that you would want to see included or topics that you would want to see revised? (This question does not apply to topics 3, 4, and 5, page 256.)

Chapter 6

The Research Paper on Popular Culture

Introduction

The research paper is frequently the assignment that students in a composition course dread the most, with students often waiting until the end of the semester to complete it. Sometimes they are dissatisfied with the topic they have chosen, and the research assignment becomes more a task demonstrating the student's correct use of research format than one that culminates in a carefully researched essay.

At times, instructors refer to the research paper as the term paper in order to show that it is an essay assignment that has developed during the entire term. This is the sort of writing assignment that you will be introduced to here. In Chapters 1–5, you explored various aspects of popular culture in America. At this point, you are more familiar with this topic than you were in Chapter 1, and you have examined and applied the critical practices that students and scholars use to effectively investigate texts in popular culture. In this chapter, you will select and analyze a specific issue in popular culture. You will explore it in greater detail, using the texts that you have examined so far as well as those texts that you will find in your research of the subject. Seen in this way, the research paper will more likely be the culmination of what you have accomplished this term rather than a dreaded, mechanical exercise.

Critical Practices

Since the research paper is a culminating writing assignment, you will be applying most of the critical practices that you have learned, particularly analyzing, making inferences, evaluating, and forming valid inductions. You will be analyzing the various texts for their arguments, you will be making inferences about what the writers in these texts are suggesting, you will be evaluating the various texts you have read by choosing those works that best explain your topic, and, finally, you will be constructing generalizations from the details that you read concerning your topic.

What is new about the critical practices that you will employ in the research paper is that you will be reading several sources and putting the ideas from these sources together. This ability to put together is a sophisticated critical practice known as *synthesizing*. In fact, synthesizing is the significant new critical practice that you will need in order to complete your research paper. A related critical practice is *creating:* developing a new idea from your synthesis.

To Synthesize

To synthesize is to combine several ideas into your own argument. In this way, synthesizing transforms what you have learned into something new. When you synthesize material from various texts, you apply two critical practices that you are already familiar with: comparing and contrasting. But in the case of the research paper, you may be comparing eight, nine, ten, or more texts as opposed to two or three. At first, the process of synthesizing ideas from several texts may seem overwhelming. You will be a successful synthesizer if you focus on a few texts at a time at first. You should ask two simple questions: How does the first text differ from the second? How is the first similar to the second?

Let's say you are examining the topic of the history of television commercials in American television from 1980 to the present, and you have read ten articles on this topic. All but one have suggested that television commercials in this time span have introduced very sophisticated camera techniques and have provided several examples of the kinds of experimental visual effects that commercials lend to television. You would be able to synthesize this evidence into the valid generalization that television commercials are at the forefront of television technique and experimentation. You would not have been able to make this generalization, or formed this induction, had you merely studied two articles. In this sense, your research on these ten articles has provided you with more authority to make this generalization.

To Create

The research you do now and later in your educational career may allow you to come upon a new insight or even an original idea. Creating new ideas, of course, is not what your instructor is expecting of you in your research paper, but it is important to realize that *creation* is the culminating critical practice that has defined all important contributions to a discipline. Creation is the result of synthesis: a scholar or student analyzes all the literature in his field. By synthesizing this material, he moves to a new level of understanding. For example, in studying the contributions of Albert Einstein to the field of nuclear physics or Charles Darwin to the study of biology, you will find that both examined the research of their predecessors and contemporaries. A large part of their new theories rested on their ability to synthesize the ideas of their predecessors and peers before they came to their own conclusions.

Ask these questions as you move in your research from one text to another. These questions are at the heart of synthesis and creation:

1. How is this text like others I have read on this topic?
2. How is this text different from the others I have read on this topic?
3. Can I combine the ideas from previous texts with the ideas in this one to come upon a valid generalization or a new idea about my topic?
4. Which generalizations that I have made concerning my reading would apply to all the texts? Which generalizations would apply to only some of my reading?

Necessary Steps in Completing a Term Paper

The following procedures are the ones that most students follow when they work to complete the final draft of their term paper:

1. Selecting a topic
2. Locating relevant materials
3. Taking notes

4. Evaluating and organizing the notes
5. Drafting the paper

Selecting a Topic

As you realize by now, the field of popular culture is a wide one. It studies several kinds of media and is researched in many academic disciplines. At this point, you should be clearer what areas of popular culture interest you— for example, television, political speeches, advertising, or literature on popular culture.

Your first important task in the research paper assignment is to select a topic that genuinely interests you. You will have enormous trouble writing a meaningful essay on a topic that you do not personally want to research. Once you have selected a topic, write down the most important questions that you would like to have answered on this topic. Let's assume that you are interested in American television commercials. Some of the questions you might ask of this topic could include the following:

1. What were the first television commercials?
2. How have commercials changed over the past forty years?
3. How have the American beliefs that explain these commercials changed over this time frame? Or have these beliefs stayed the same?
4. How have television advertisements influenced television programming?

Once you have written these questions down, consider your time frame in writing the paper and the maximum length of the assignment—ten typed pages? Fifteen? Given these constraints, ask yourself what you can reasonably accomplish. Most often, students choose a topic that is too broad. So begin small. That is, limit your topic. You may want to focus on just one of the questions you generated about your topic: the first television commercials or commercials by decade.

Finally, write out your topic in a phrase or sentence. Share this topic with your peers and your instructor, and listen to their input. See if your topic is "doable" given the time and page constraints.

Let's say you decide on the following topic: American television commercials in the fifties (1950–1959).

Locating Relevant Materials

Your next step is to see how much material is available on the topic. Again, ask your instructor and peers to see what sources they may already be aware of. Then go to your college library, local community library, or local university library to begin searching for material.

Bring your topic and the titles of sources you may already have to your reference librarian. Reference librarians tend to be extremely helpful, and they will save you much time in tracking down sources and in not looking for sources in the wrong places. Reference librarians will also provide you with the names of appropriate encyclopedias to consider. Encyclopedias are helpful starting points because they give you a general picture of your topic and usually a bibliography of the most important material concerning it.

Your reference librarian will also show you which popular periodical, newspaper, or scholarly journal indexes to use. These references will provide you with titles of both popular and scholarly articles on your topic. The most common index for researching popular culture is *The Reader's Guide to Periodical Literature,* which contains titles of articles appearing in magazines of general interest. You will find more scholarly material on your topic in the *Humanities Index* or the *Social Science Index.* Since many of the selections you have read in this text are from scholarly journals, you should not find the academic material you research too difficult. Here are what two typical entries from *The Reader's Guide to Periodical Literature* look like:

> Letterman lets his guard down [cover story] B. Zehme.
>   il pors *Esquire* v122 p96-102 D '94
> Making a killing on talk TV [guest on Jenny Jones show
>   murdered] M. Peyser. il pors *Newsweek* v125 p30
>   Mr 20 '95

Note that for a complex topic like television, the material is divided into subdivisions, such as "Talk shows." Note also the order that the bibliographic information follows: title of article, bracketed summary of the material, author, magazine, volume, pages, and date. (*Il* is an abbreviation for *illustration,* and *pors* is an abbreviation for *portraits.*)

You will also need to locate entire studies and anthologies for the topic you research. Here, it is wise to begin your search of these materials in the card catalog. Most libraries now have this material online—that is, on computers. You can retrieve this information either by author or by title. Here is how an entry by author looks:

SHELF LOC	301.16
AUTHOR	Read, William H.
TITLE	America's mass media merchants/ William H. Read
PUB/DATE	Baltimore: Johns Hopkins University Press, c 1976. 209 p.
DESCRIPT.	
BIB NOTE	Includes bibliographic references and index.
SUBJECT	Intercultural communication
SUBJECT	Mass media

Note that this library uses the Dewey Decimal System (301.16) to catalogue its material. Other libraries use the Library of Congress System to classify their material.

In searching through the periodical indexes and the card catalogs, you need to use your organizing and categorizing abilities in order to locate useful materials. Let this question go through your mind if you have difficulty locating a particular title: Under what other subjects could my topic be catalogued? Let's say you are looking for material on American commercials in the fifties. Of course, the following topics come to mind at first: commercials, advertisements, popular culture, and the fifties. But as you examine this topic to see where else it could be found, you could likely find additional information in the following areas: the history of American advertising, American television, and the history of American television.

Computers are now revolutionizing access to information, and libraries are continually upgrading their computer capabilities. As well as providing their titles online, many libraries allow you to browse the holdings of other, often larger, city and university libraries. This technology is known as computer networking. Libraries can also provide you with CD-ROM information, which comes in the form of computer disks containing extensive bibliographic information on various topics. Encyclopedias with ample video material are also on CD-ROM. Your reference librarian can apprise you of the computer technology that exists in your library.

A further computer technology reshaping library research is information access via the Internet. Some libraries and homes now pay a monthly fee to subscribe to online carriers such as Prodigy and CompuServe. The "information highway" allows you to access up-to-date information on nearly any topic you are researching—from encyclopedia material to recently given speeches. Often you can use these information services to easily access current magazine articles and difficult-to-locate essays from periodicals, information that used to take days to track down using conventional library methods. You can download, or print, any of this information and use it in your research. What you will find by using computer information services is that you will have at your fingertips a wealth of information, sometimes most of the information available, on the topic that you are researching. Again, your research librarian can help you access information on these information services if they are available at your library.

By the end of your library and computer search, you should have from fifteen to twenty sources—both articles and books. Now you are ready to sort through the material.

Taking Notes

As you read through the material, you need to ask the same critical questions that you have asked of the selections in this text:

1. What is the writer saying?
2. Is the argument valid?
3. How is the material organized?

4. What is the evidence?
5. Is this evidence valid?

A new question that you need to begin asking as you read through this material is one of comparison and synthesis:

6. How does the material I'm studying relate to the other material I have read? That is, how does one article or excerpt agree or disagree with another?

You can write your notes in various ways, on 4-inch by 6-inch cards or on note paper. Just be sure that you have all the necessary bibliographic material written down: author, title, place of publication, publisher, copyright date, and pages read. You may have to return the library material before you complete your research paper, and you will need all of this bibliographic information for your final draft. Look at the following examples of notes taken on 4-inch by 6-inch cards:

Elayne Rapping. The Looking Glass World of Nonfiction TV. Boston: South Press, 1987. p. 163
1952—60% of ad money spent on radio
1954—TV spent $500 million on ads, radio $44 million—big increase from 1952 commercials in the fifties "using a combination of 'fact' and 'fiction,' imaginative and informational materials . . ."

What types of notes do you write? There are three:

1. Notes of summary: you rephrase the material accurately in your own words, as in the material from the previous note card: "1952—60% of ad money spent on radio."
2. Notes of evaluation: you comment on the importance of the material—whether it agrees or disagrees with the other material you have read and the quality of its conclusions and research. Consider the following example, again from the previous note card: "big increase from 1952."
3. Direct quotations: you sometimes come across material that is worded so well or is so important to your argument that you copy a sentence or sentences directly, as you found in the previous note card on television advertising: "using a combination of 'fact' and 'fiction,' imaginative and informational materials. . . ."

As you are taking your notes, consider your topic. Ask the following questions: Is my topic too broad? Is it too specific? How can I rephrase my topic? This note-taking stage is the ideal time for you to reconsider your topic. Also, begin asking yourself more questions: What does the research say about my topic? For example, were commercials in the fifties exploitative? Simple-minded? Did these commercials present several or a few underlying

American beliefs? Are these commercials different from those of today? Or does there seem to be disagreement in the material I have considered?

As you consider these questions, you can start formulating your argument, or thesis. By the end of your note taking, you should have a sense of the argument that you intend to present. Remember that your research paper does not simply introduce a series of facts, but synthesizes them into a particular argument. Your term paper, like the others you have written, wants both to inform and persuade.

Evaluating and Organizing the Notes

You should now have enough material to use for your research paper. In the best of cases, you will have more than you can use. Now is the time to write out your argument in a sentence or two. Have your peers and instructor respond to it. If they question your argument, show them the evidence that you have found for making it.

Once your argument is clear in your mind and accepted by your instructor and peers, you are now ready to organize the rest of your paper in a rough outline. Let's say you want to show how commercials in the fifties are structured on three basic beliefs: the nuclear family, patriotism, and distinct male and female roles. You now want to analyze your evidence: Does your research include an analysis of specific commercials? Studies of several commercials? Creators' personal recollections of commercials produced in the fifties? A combination of these?

At this time you may still not be certain how best to organize your research paper. You may want to brainstorm as a prewriting activity before you compose a final outline. Brainstorming, as you learned at the beginning of this textbook, involves listing ideas in any fashion, not being concerned with which ideas are general and which are more specific. From this disordered list, you can more easily formulate an organized outline that moves from general to specific points of information by picking and choosing material that seems to be related. Consider the following brainstorming list on TV commercials in the fifties:

TV Commercials in the Fifties

1. Focus on stay-home mother and working father.
2. A nuclear family.
3. Consider toothpaste commercials.
4. 1956 presidential commercials important.
5. Focus on patriotism.
6. I've gathered a lot of information.

A rough outline on TV commercials in the fifties could look like this, using some of the material gotten from the brainstorming list:

Argument: American TV commercials in the fifties are based on three basic American values: nuclear family, working father and homemaker mother, and patriotism. All three of these beliefs created a conservative American picture.

- nuclear family in fifties commercials

   working father

   housewife mother

   respectful children

   See analyses of television commercials in *Reading Television.* Consider fifties commercials on toothpaste, automobiles, and kitchenware.

- working father and homemaker mother in fifties commercials

   Father made important decisions and was looked to as the center of the family.

   Mother concerned with keeping home and children clean and neat; deferred to father's decisions.

   See analyses of fifties television commercials in *Television Culture;* analyze the two toothpaste commercials and three automobile commercials for how parents are portrayed (Buick, Chevrolet, and Ford).

- patriotism in fifties commercials

   See election commercials for 1956, particularly the ads for Eisenhower and Stevenson in newspapers and magazines.

- conclusion

   (tentative) should restate thesis and show how the bulk of the evidence supports the thesis.

Or you may want to present these notes in a visual way, sometimes known as a map, as shown in Figure 6.1 on the following page.

At this time, do not concern yourself with the number of paragraphs or pages that you plan to devote to each section. Just be sure that the sections you intend to cover relate in a logical way and that all of them speak to your thesis. Let your peers and instructor see this general outline or cluster. Have them evaluate your evidence. Before you begin writing, jot down next to each subtopic the sources you plan to use. You may refer either to page numbers from your sources or to the number of the note card or page of notes that you intend to include in your draft. Numbering all of your note cards or pages of notes is an efficient way to refer to your research as you draft your paper. See how this numbering system is used on a part of the previous outline:

- patriotism in fifties commercials

   See election commercials for 1956, particularly the ads for Eisenhower and Stevenson in newspapers and magazines.
   Eisenhower: 7, 9, 11–12; Stevenson: 24–25, 31–36.

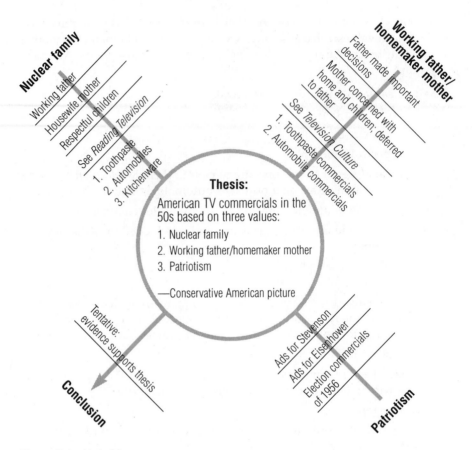

Figure 6.1   Note Map

Now with an argument, an outline or cluster, and selected notes, you are ready to begin drafting your essay.

Drafting the Paper

Some instructors may ask you to present a more thorough outline before you begin drafting. There is an argument to be made that a too-detailed outline may stifle your writing because, as you write, you will be revising your argument, your evidence, and your overall organization. What you should have in mind during this drafting stage is a general sense of the direction of your argument and most of the evidence that you plan to use.

Move through the writing of your draft at a fairly fast pace. Remember that you can always revise anything you have written. You may even want to set writing benchmarks, depending on the amount of time you have. A benchmark schedule could look like this:

1. Finish introductory remarks by 4/25.
2. Complete section on family by 4/30.
3. Complete section on gender by 5/4.
4. Complete section on patriotism by 5/7.
5. Complete concluding remarks by 5/9.

You cannot compose a ten-typed-page research paper in one sitting, unlike a short writing assignment, in which you may be able to complete a draft without a break. Note that the drafting of this term paper is projected to take fourteen days.

As you draft your research paper, keep in mind that this particular essay is different from the analytical essays that you have previously written. For one, in a research paper you need to demonstrate that you have read widely on your topic, so you must cite from several of the sources that you have researched, and you need to compare the various sources to one another.

Also, you must cite your quotations in ways different from your approach in the short, analytical papers you are used to writing. There are two citation formats—MLA and APA—that you will learn about in this chapter.

As you are working on the middle of your essay, consider how you would like to conclude your research paper. Ask the following questions as you draft the body of your essay:

1. What has the research suggested so far?
2. Has it supported the argument I'm presenting?
3. Is there conflict in the research?
4. In my synthesis of the research, have I come upon conclusions that are new—not mentioned in any of the sources?

Your conclusion needs to be both summative and synthetic. That is, you need to refer to the major points you made in your research and explain what all your research suggests.

At various stages in the drafting of your essay, you should share your work with your peers and your instructor. Listen to their commentary and include the suggestions that you think are correct. As with the shorter papers you have written, revise for ideas and organization.

And as with your shorter essays, edit your paper only after you are comfortable with your revisions. Editing a research paper is more complicated than editing a shorter essay. Along with editing for surface errors in grammar and usage, you also need to see if your MLA or APA documentation adheres to correct format. If you focus on questions of surface errors and documentation format too soon in the writing process, you may interfere with the organization and developing ideas of your essay.

MLA Documentation

Essays in the humanities use the MLA (Modern Language Association) format. Your instructor may ask you to use this format in your research paper. Here are the major conventions and rules of the MLA style:

Quoting.   There are two important ways that quotations are used in research papers—either as part of the paragraph itself or as a longer, indented quotation, called a block quotation. Prose of four lines or fewer (in terms of your writing, not the source's text) should be part of the paragraph itself, and quotations of more than four lines should be indented.

This is what a short quotation looks like in the MLA format:

> *As Frith notes, "Liverpool groups saw themselves similarly as romantic artists" (174).*

This quotation comes from a Simon Frith essay, "The Cultural Study of Popular Music," in an anthology titled *Cultural Studies* (Lawrence Grossberg, Cary Nelson, and Paula Treichler. *Cultural Studies*. New York: Routledge, 1992, 174–82). Note that a comma is used to introduce the quotation and that the page number where the quoted text is to be found comes after the closing quotation mark, with the period coming at the very end of the sentence—after the page number. There is no added punctuation inside the quotation. You place a punctuation mark inside the quotation only if the quotation itself uses a question mark or an exclamation point, as in the following citation from the same Frith selection:

> *As Kobena Mercer asks, "What is it about white people that makes them want to be black?" (177).*

Note, though, that a period still ends the entire sentence.

In some cases you may want to quote a phrase instead of a sentence. Normally, you do not introduce this material with a comma, as you see in the following example:

> *Frith talks about how rock music "is an expression and celebration of sociability" (177).*

Although a comma does not come after *music,* a period still ends the sentence after the page number.

If you have not previously identified the author, you need to do so in parentheses before the page number. Let's say you are referring to the Frith selection, but you do not mention the author in your introductory text. Your documentation would look like this:

> *In regard to popular song writing, it is important to note that "guitarists, drummers, and some producers have to work out for themselves how to sound like their models" (Frith 175).*

Note that commas do not separate the author and the page number of the citation. Whenever you can, however, mention the author as you introduce the quotation. If you are citing two or more works by the same author, include a shortened version of the title of each work that you cite:

> *In regard to popular song writing, it is important to note that "guitarists, drummers, and some producers have to work out for themselves how to sound like their models" (Frith, "Cultural Study" 175).*

Note the use of the comma to separate author and shortened title.

The MLA format is much more streamlined than the footnote procedure formerly used, which listed every quoted source at the bottom of each page or at the end of the essay with Latinate phrasing such as *Ibid.* and *Op cit.* With this new format, readers do not have to stop reading the text to determine where a particular source originates. If a reader does want to track down a source as she reads, a complete list of sources is found at the end of the essay in a section titled "Works Cited." More will be said about the Works Cited page in the following section.

When you introduce a block quotation, you use a colon at the end of your text. Then you indent the quoted material *ten spaces from the left-hand margin and double space the entire quotation.* You do not indent on the right. Here is an example of a block quotation using the MLA format:

> *The next point Frith makes is an important one:*
> > *Second, the tension in this world is less than between amateurs and professionals (labels which describe positions in the continuity in a performing career) than between local and national reference groups. Finnegan and Cohen both show that almost all young rock musicians do fantasize about "making it" nationally and becoming rich and famous. (176)*
> *The key difference that Frith emphasizes is with the terms "local" and "national."*

Note that there are no quotation marks around a block as there are around the shorter quotations that are within the paragraph proper. Also, remember that if you want to comment on a block quotation, you can make it part of the original paragraph by placing this commentary after the block quotation and ten spaces to the left of the quotation, as in the example above.

If you study this same block, you find that quotation marks are placed around *making it.* Those quotation marks were used by Frith. If you were to introduce this quotation as a sentence or phrase, and not block it, you would place single quotation marks around it and double quotation marks around the entire quotation:

> *Frith notes that "almost all young rock musicians do fantasize about 'making it' nationally and becoming rich and famous" (176).*

The single quotation marks around *making it* indicate that your citation also includes quoted material.

At times, you may want to eliminate quoted material that is not pertinent to your research purposes. You can delete material from a quotation by using *ellipsis points,* or three consecutive points (. . .). See how the three ellipsis points are used in the following example:

As Frith notes, "Pubs . . . prefer live groups" (177).

What has been deleted is the transition *on the other hand,* which is not important to the quotation that this writer has selected.

Be sure, though, that you do not delete material that distorts the quotation in any way. For example, you would be doing injustice to the Frith selection if you eliminated the *almost* in the following sentence:

Frith emphasizes that both "Finnegan and Cohen both show that . . . all young rock musicians do fantasize about 'making it' nationally and becoming rich and famous" (176).

Frith evidently wants to show that this generalization about rock groups does have exceptions. Removing the *almost* makes his statement unqualified when in reality it is qualified.

Works Cited Page   Your bibliographic listing, called the *Works Cited* in the MLA format, comes at the very end of your research paper.* This is a list of all the references you have used: periodicals, books, interviews, recordings, and so on. All the sources are placed in alphabetical order, last name first. If the work has no author, it is alphabetized by the first word in its title (except *a, an,* or *the*).

There are a few rules that apply to all bibliographic entries. All bits of information (author, title, place of publication, publisher, and copyright date) are separated by periods and two spaces. If you list two or more sources by the same author, the second and ensuing titles are introduced by three hyphens followed by a period (---.). Also, all entries are double spaced, and if the information for an entry goes beyond one line, you indent the rest of the entry *five spaces* from the left.

In the event that your material does not provide a place of publication, write *N.p.* where you would normally write the city; if it does not provide a publisher, write *n.p.* And if there is no copyright date, write *n.d.* at the end of the bibliographic entry.

For the place of publication, refer to the city alone. Naming the state is not necessary. Also, just use the first word or two of the publishing house's name (*Wadsworth* instead of *Wadsworth Publishing Company*). Further, refer to university presses by the initials "UP," as in *Chicago UP* instead of *University of*

---

*For a complete discussion of MLA bibliographic style, see Joseph Gibaldi, *MLA Handbook for Writers of Research Papers,* 4th ed. (New York: Modern Library Association, 1995).

Chicago Press. Finally, if a publisher is known by an abbreviation, use it rather than the full name—for example, *NCTE* rather than *National Council of Teachers of English.*

The following shows how references should be presented. Refer to this format for the bibliographic entries that you list in Works Cited:

1. Book by One Author
   Berger, John. *Ways of Seeing.* New York: Penguin, 1972.

Note that a colon separates the place of publication from the publishing house and that a comma separates the publishing house from the copyright date.

2. Book by Two or Three Authors
   Fiske, John, and John Hartley. *Reading Television.* London: Methuen, 1978.

Note that the author listed first is written last name first; the second and following are written first name first.

3. Book by Four or More Authors
   Fiske, John, et al.

Note that *et al.* is a Latin abbreviation for *and others.* If there are more than three authors, simply list the first name mentioned and write *et al.* after this first entry.

4. Edited Book
   Wright, John W., ed. *The Commercial Connection.* New York: Delta, 1979.

If there are more than one but fewer than four editors, list their names followed by *eds.* If there are four or more, list the first name followed by *et al., eds.*

5. Article or Chapter in an Anthology
   Henkoff, Ronald. "Ads for Advertisers: How Advertisers See Their Audiences." *The Commercial Connection.* Ed. John W. Wright. New York: Delta, 1979. 192–98.

Note that the article title is placed in quotation marks, *Ed.* comes before the editor's name, and it is capitalized.

6. Work in Multiple Volumes
   Abrams, M. H., ed. *The Norton Anthology of English Literature.* 5th ed. 2 vols. New York: Norton, 1986.

7. Edition of a Book
   Abrams, M. H., ed. *The Norton Anthology of English Literature.* 5th ed. 2 vols. New York: Norton, 1986.

Never use the abbreviation *ed.* to identify a book's first edition. You would simply use *The Norton Anthology of English Literature* if you were listing the first edition of this work.

8. Article in a Reference Book with a Known Author
   Optonsky, Stan. "Television." *Collier's Encyclopedia*. 1991 ed.

9. Article in a Reference Book with No Known Author
   "Telecommunications Systems." *Britannica*. 1990 ed.

10. Magazine or Newspaper Article with a Known Author
    Ellenthal, Ira. "Vogue: The Ultimate Authority." *Product Marketing* Apr. 1980: 19.

If the magazine includes the day of publication, write the day this way: 10 Apr. 1980. Note that months—except May, June, and July—are abbreviated. Also note that the last entry gives the page number(s) where the article is to be found.

11. Magazine or Newspaper Article with No Known Author
    "Despite Less Blatant Sexism, Ads Still Insult Most Women." *Wall Street Journal* 1 Aug. 1985: 19.

This article would be alphabetized with the "D" listings.

12. Article in a Scholarly Journal
    Herskovitz, Richard. "The Shell Answer Man and the Spectator." *Social Text* 1 (1979): 182–85.

Note that the "1" refers to the volume number of the journal and that the year of publication is in parentheses.

13. Pamphlet with a Known Author
    Thomas, William V. *Trends in Advertising*. Washington, DC: Congressional Quarterly Inc., 1981.

14. Pamphlet with an Unknown Author
    Advertising Packaging, & Labeling. National Association of Consumer Agency Administrators. Washington, DC: GPO, 1990.

Note that *GPO* is the abbreviation of *U.S. Government Printing Office*.

15. Government Publication
    U.S. Commission on Civil Rights, *Window Dressing on the Set: Women and Minorities in Television*. Washington, DC: GPO, Aug. 1977.

16. Interview in a Magazine, Newspaper, or Other Periodical
    Hawn, Goldie. Interview. With Lawrence Grobel. *Playboy* Jan. 1985: 71+.

Note that if the interview is not titled, indicate that it is an interview, but do not place quotation marks around your title. If you use an interview found in a book, treat the interview as if it were a chapter of the book, and begin with the name of the person being interviewed. Then include the bibliographic information regarding the book. If the interview is in a newspaper, begin with the name of the person being interviewed and follow the normal procedure for citing a newspaper article.

17. Interview on Radio, Television, or Record
     Berry, Chuck. Interview. *Hail! Hail! Rock 'n' Roll!* 1987.

Note that *Hail! Hail Rock 'n' Roll!* is a documentary in which Berry was interviewed. If the interview was on television or radio, you mention the station, the city, and the date—for example, *KNBC, Los Angeles. 30 Apr. 1994.*

18. Speech or Lecture That Is Recorded
     King, Martin Luther. *The Great March to Freedom.* Motown Record
     Corp., 1963.

This is a title of an album containing several of Dr. King's speeches. Titles of specific speeches would be put in quotation marks.

19. Radio or Television Program
     Doogie Howser, M.D. Created by Stephen Boccho and David E. Kelley.
     KTLA, Los Angeles. 5 Jan. 1995.

You can mention the director or writer instead of the creator. If the television show has a title, place it before the name of the program and put it in quotation marks.

20. Record, Audiotape, or Music CD
     Public Enemy. *What Kind of Power We Got?* Def Jam Recordings, 1994.

21. Material Downloaded from a Computer Service
     Kazan, Elia. "On What Makes a Director." *Working with Kazan.* 1973.
     Online. Internet. 30 Dec. 1996.

The first date is the original publication date of the print source; the second is the date of online access.

Heading and Title.   Your heading information needs to be placed on the first page of your research paper. At the top left margin, include your first and last name, your instructor's name, the name of the course, and the date. Centered just below your heading should be the title of your research paper. Capitalize all but little connecting words such as *and, but, or, to, on, a, an* unless these words begin your title or subtitle. Let your title be specific enough so that your reader has some sense of what your research entails. Here is an example of a correct heading and focused title for a research paper using MLA format:

```
Elsa Barrueta
Professor Sotiriou
English 103
25 Mar. 1997

Gender Roles in American Advertising: 1980-Present
```

Pagination.   Your pages should be numbered consecutively from the first page to the end at the top right corner of the paper. Starting with page 1, write your last name before you list the page, as in the following:

Barrueta   1

(You may want to study the student research paper on pp. 290–296.)

APA Documentation

Essays in the social sciences use the APA (American Psychological Association) format. You likely came upon social science material in your research, and you may have already seen how the APA format works. You might choose to use this format for the final draft of your research paper. Following are the major conventions and rules that APA* asks you to follow.

Quoting and Citing Sources.   MLA and APA share certain quoting conventions. For one, short quotations are placed in quotation marks in both systems, and quotations within quotations are indicated by single quotation marks. Short quotations are generally introduced with commas, long ones with colons. In both systems, sentence punctuation comes at the end of the citation, not in the quotation, unless the punctuation is a question mark or exclamation point. Finally, in both systems, you may use ellipsis points to delete material not important to your research.

Unlike MLA, which asks you to indent longer quotations ten spaces from the left, APA asks you to indent this material *five* spaces from the left. In both systems, long quotations are flushed right. MLA asks that you indent quotations of more than four lines of text, APA of passages of *more than forty words.*

The quoting procedures for the APA format differ in certain ways from MLA. MLA and APA both require the author and page number, but APA asks for the date of publication as well. If the author is given in the sentence, the date and page number should come right after the quotation, as in the following example from a chapter in George Lipsitz's study *Time Passages: Collective Memory and Popular Culture.* (Minneapolis: Minnesota UP, 1990, 133–48):

> *As Lipsitz notes, "Mexican-Americans have faced unique problems of cultural identity and assimilation" (1990, p. 133).*

Or you can refer to the date of publication and the page number right after you mention the author:

> *Lipsitz (1990, p. 133) notes that "Mexican-Americans have faced unique problems of cultural identity and assimilation."*

---

*For a complete discussion of APA editorial style, see *Publication Manual of the American Psychological Association*, 4th ed. (Washington, DC: American Psychological Association, 1994).

If you do not mention the author in the sentence, then you also include the name in parentheses in this fashion: (Lipsitz, 1990, p. 133). Unlike MLA documentation, the APA format requires that you separate author, date, and page number with commas, and asks that you use the abbreviation *p.* or *pp.* before the page number(s).

If your source has two or more authors, you need to include both or all of the names the first time you introduce the work. After that, you must cite both names, using an ampersand (&), in the case of a co-authored book. If the book has more than two authors, in subsequent references you need to cite the first author and the Latin abbreviation *et al.*

Even if you do not quote directly, but cite an author for the first time, you must place your source's date of publication right after the author's name or title in this fashion:

Lipsitz (1990) focuses on Chicano music in East Los Angeles.

If there is no author of your source, then you refer to the title and date of publication the first time you introduce your material:

The article "Panting for Bruce's Jeans" (1985) is a good place to start a discussion of advertising and jeans.

References.   When you use APA conventions, your bibliographic list at the end of your paper follows several procedures that are different from MLA format. Instead of *Works Cited*, use the word *References* centered at the top of the page. But like MLA, double space all bibliographic information, and alphabetize each entry by last name or the first word of the title, if there is no author. Indent each entry five spaces, but succeeding lines of an entry are not indented. If you introduce two or more works by the same author, list them in order of their publication date from earliest to latest. Do not use the three hyphens and a period (---.) as you would in MLA.

Like MLA, APA introduces four units of information: author, title, date of publication, and place of publication. Yet the order differs, as you will see in the examples that follow. Also, rather than writing out the author's given name or names, use just initials. Further, do not capitalize all important words in the title of a book or article, *just proper nouns and the first word of the title and the first word of the subtitle, if there is one.* But capitalize all the important words in newspaper and magazine titles. Also, do not place the titles of articles in newspapers, magazines, or journals in quotation marks, yet italicize or underline book, magazine, and newspaper titles, as you would in MLA format. As with your page references in your paper proper, use the abbreviations *p.* and *pp.* when you provide bibliographic information for an article in a magazine, newspaper, or journal.

As in MLA, use shortened names of publishing companies. But unlike MLA, which lists just the city of publication for all publishing companies, with APA list only the city of publication if it is a large, well-known one, but list the city and the state abbreviation if the city is small or obscure.

The following is a sample list of references using the APA format. Use these examples as you compile the entries for your References page:

1. Book by One Author
    Berger, J. (1972). *Ways of seeing.* New York: Penguin.

Note that the publication date is always in parentheses.

2. Book by Two or More Authors
    Fiske, J., & Hartley, J. (1978). *Reading television.* London: Methuen.

Note the use of the ampersand and that each author's last name is printed first.

3. Book Edited by One Individual
    Wright, J. W. (Ed.). (1979). *The commercial connection.* New York: Delta.

Note that *Ed.* is capitalized and placed in parentheses after the editor's name.

4. Book Edited by Two or More Individuals
    Grossberg, L., Nelson, C., & Treichler, P. (Eds.). (1992). *Cultural studies.* New York: Routledge.

5. Article or Chapter in an Anthology
    Henkoff, R. (1979). Ads for advertisers: How advertisers see their audiences. In J. W. Wright (Ed.), *The commercial connection* (pp. 192–198). New York: Delta.

Note that the page numbers of the article are in parentheses.

6. Edition of a Book
    Abrams, M. H. (1986). *The Norton anthology of English literature* (Vols. 1–2). (5th ed.). New York: Norton.

7. Article in a Scholarly Journal
    Herskovitz, R. (1979). The Shell Answer Man and the spectator. *Social Text, 1,* 182–185.

Note that the volume number is set off with a comma and underlined or in italics and that *pp.* is not used to introduce page numbers, as it is in newspaper articles.

8. Magazine or Newspaper Article with Known Author
    Ellenthal, I. (1980, April). Vogue: The ultimate authority. *Product Marketing, 9,* 19.

Note that the date of publication comes after the year.

9. Magazine or Newspaper Article with No Known Author
    Despite less blatant sexism, ads still insult most women. (1985, 1 August). *Wall Street Journal,* p. 19.

```
                                    Gender Roles
                                         1



                        Gender Roles in
                        American Advertising:
                        1980-Present

                        Elsa Barrueta




                                    English 103
                                    Professor Sotiriou
                                    November 25, 1998
```

Figure 6.2   A Sample Title Page

10. Audio Recording
    Public Enemy. (1994). What Kind of Power We Got? [CD]. New York: Def Jam Recordings.

11. Material Downloaded from a Computer Service
    Kazan, E. (1973). On what makes a director. In Working with Kazan [On-line]. Available: http://www.leonardo.net/dga/newsletter/page html

Title Page.   The title page under APA procedures is a separate page. Your title goes in the center of the page. Under the title and centered, place your first and last name. Two-thirds down the page and to the right, include these pieces of information, one under the other: course name and number, professor's name, due date.

On the top right-hand corner of the page, include your running head, and directly underneath identify the first page number. A running head is simply an abbreviated title of your paper. See Figure 6.2 for a sample APA title page.

Pagination.   Paginate consecutively from the title page to the References page. The page number goes directly under the running head and to the end of the margin, as shown on the title page in Figure 6.2.

Recapping

The research paper incorporates all the critical practices that you have learned in this text. It is a longer paper that relies heavily on the critical activity of synthesis. In reading and writing from several sources, you need to compare and contrast ideas and to join ideas. This activity of synthesizing research material may lead to creation: coming upon a new idea. Although your research paper may not come upon new ideas, your completed research paper will show you how most scholarship in the humanities and the social sciences works and how new ideas in these fields are created.

Two frequently used formats for documentation are the Modern Language Association system (MLA) and the American Psychological Association system (APA). MLA is used in humanities research, and APA is used in research in the social sciences.

Critical Explorations: Writing

Below you will find ten research paper topics that deal with aspects of American popular culture. Read through these questions and select one that particularly interests you. When you choose your topic, be sure that you follow the steps listed in this introduction on pages 264–271 to complete the research paper. As you move through these steps, get feedback from your peers and your instructor.

When you begin your final draft, determine which research format you plan to use: MLA or APA. Use the rules and procedures introduced in this chapter to apply a research format to your final draft.

1. Select a particular period of American television advertising, and analyze both the beliefs and logical practices that informed it. Select specific commercials of the period. Analyze story line, word choice, and generalizations. You may want to investigate a decade: the fifties, sixties, seventies, eighties, or nineties.

2. Choose a particular television genre (detective, mystery, situation comedy, and so on), and trace its development from 1950 to the present. In what ways has this genre changed? How does this genre represent any changes in the basic beliefs of Americans? Focus on characters and story line.

3. Analyze how men or women have been portrayed in a particular American program (situation comedy, mystery, and so on) or in American commercials from 1950 to the present. Carefully analyze the beliefs that explain the story lines and characters of the programs that you choose. How have these programs or commercials shown a change in the American attitudes toward being male or female?

4. Analyze a particular ten-year period in American television broadcasting. What

news topics were emphasized? How was the news reported in this period? What American beliefs helped explain the news coverage? You may want to use Elayne Rapping's Selection 12 (Chapter 3) as a model for your analysis of the news.

5. Select a particular ethnic minority, and analyze how this group has been portrayed on American television. How does the programming that you examine reflect American attitudes toward this minority? By analyzing character and story line, determine if these attitudes have changed or remained the same. You may want to use Jannette L. Dates's Selection 11 (Chapter 3) as your guide.

6. Select five speeches from an American President and analyze the rhetorical practices the President employs. Consider the ethos, pathos, and logos of these speeches. Also, analyze the style of these speeches. In what ways are the speeches similar? How are they different?

7. Choose five speeches from Martin Luther King, Jr., Malcolm X, or Jesse Jackson, and analyze the rhetorical practices used in these speeches. Consider the ethos, pathos, and logos of each speech, as well as its style. What do all five speeches have in common? In what ways are they different?

8. Select a specific ten-year period in America and analyze one or more dress styles popular during those years. Describe in detail the dress style(s) that you choose to analyze. Then consider the following questions: What social statements did this style(s) in dress make? In what ways did this style(s) support or call into question traditional American beliefs? Consider several magazine or newspaper advertisements that presented this particular dress style. You might refer to John Fiske's "The Jeaning of America" (Selection 16 in Chapter 4) as a guide to analyzing the dress style(s) you select.

9. Read two novels by an American author who has examined American popular culture: Thomas Pynchon, Jerzy Kosinski, Don DeLillo, or any other writer you have found who has depicted American popular culture. What do these two novels, together, suggest about the author's attitudes toward popular culture in America? In what literary ways are these attitudes expressed? Focus especially on the works' tone, character development, story line, point of view, word choice, and metaphorical language. You may refer to critical studies of the author and novels that you examine.

10. Choose any aspect of American popular culture not treated in the above essay questions and analyze it. Focus on how this practice interprets traditional American beliefs. Carefully describe the practice you choose, and thoroughly comment on the unstated assumptions that seem to explain it. Then determine what this practice in popular culture seems to say about the people who embrace it. Some of the cultural practices that you can consider include comic books, rock music, MTV, rock concerts, attending a popular American sports event, or playing a particular American sport. If you choose to examine MTV, use Pat Aufderheide's Selection 10 (Chapter 3) as your model.

Bibliography of Popular Culture Texts

Below you will find a list of references from the Robert Goldman study *Reading Ads Socially*. These sources refer both to the world of advertising and to various aspects of popular culture. Most of this material is written from an academic's perspective, similar to many of the selections that you have read in this textbook. Read through these sources to locate those that may apply to the topic you have chosen to research. See if you can find these titles in your library. They may provide you with some of the material you need to do your research, or they may lead you to other sources that apply to your topic. Note that these entries follow a British bibliographic format rather than MLA or APA.

References

Abrams, Bill (1982) 'Why Revlon's Charlie seems to be ready to settle down.' *Wall Street Journal,* December 23: 9.

Achen, Sven T. (1981) *Symbols Around Us.* New York: Van Nostrand Reinhold.

Adorno, Theodor (1941) 'On popular music.' *Studies in Philosophy and Social Science,* 9: 117–48.

Advertising Age, March 7, 1988: 30–1, S-7.

'ARF's Object: Out to improve advertising's image.' (1983) *Broadcasting,* March 14: 158.

Arlen, Michael (1980) *Thirty Seconds.* New York: Penguin.

Atlas, James (1984) 'Beyond demographics.' *Atlantic Monthly,* 254 (October): 49–58.

Balbus, Isaac (1977) 'Commodity form and legal form: an essay on relative autonomy.' *Law and Society Review,* 11: 571–88.

Barnouw, Erik (1978) *The Sponsor,* New York: Oxford University Press.

Barthes, Roland (1972) *Mythologies.* New York: Hill & Wang.

—— (1977) *Image—Music—Text.* New York: Hill & Wang.

Bateson, Gregory (1972) *Steps to an Ecology of the Mind.* New York: Ballantine.

Baudrillard, Jean (1981) *For a Critique of the Political Economy of the Sign* (trans. Charles Levin). St Louis: Telos Press.

—— (1983a) *Simulations.* New York: Semiotext(e).

—— (1983b) *In the Shadow of the Silent Majorities . . . Or the End of the Social.* New York: Semiotext(e).

Benjamin, Walter (1969) 'The work of art in the age of mechanical reproduction,' in Hannah Arendt (ed.) *Illuminations.* New York: Schocken Books, pp. 217–52.

Berger, John (1972) *Ways of Seeing.* New York: Penguin.

—— (1974) *The Look of Things.* New York: Viking.

Berger, John and Mohr, Jean (1982) *Another Way of Telling.* New York: Pantheon.

Reprinted by permission of the publisher from Robert Goldman, *Reading Ads Socially.* New York: Routledge, 1992. 233–39.

Bernstein, Peter W. (1979) 'Psychographics is still an issue on Madison Avenue,' John W. Wright (ed.) *The Commercial Connection*. New York: Delta, pp. 135–40.

Best, Steve (1986) 'The commodification of reality and the reality of commodification.' *Chicago Literary Review,* September 26: 14–15, 17.

Birnbaum, Jeffrey (1979) 'The squeeze is on: snug designer jeans capture a market.' *Wall Street Journal*, March 13: 1.

Bluestone, Barry and Harrison, Bennett (1982) *The Deindustrialization of America*. New York: Basic Books.

Boiko, Karen (1977) 'Jontue: Revlon does it.' *Product Marketing*, March: 26–30.

Bologh, Roslyn (1979) *Dialectical Phenomenology: Marx's Method*. Boston: Routledge & Kegan Paul.

Boorstin, Daniel (1961) *The Image: A Guide to Pseudo-Events in America*. New York: Atheneum.

Braverman, Harry (1974) *Labour & Monthly Capital*. New York: Monthly Review Press.

Brenkman, John (1979) 'Mass media from collective experience to the culture of privatization.' *Social Text*, 1: 94–109.

Britton, Andrew (1988) 'The myth of postmodernism: the bourgeois intelligentsia in the age of Reagan.' *CineAction!*, Summer: 3–17.

Buck-Morss, Susan (1977) *The Origin of Negative Dialectics*. New York: Free Press.

Busacca, Richard and Ryan, Mary P. (1982) 'Beyond the family crisis.' *Democracy*, 2, 4(Fall): 79–91.

Byrne, David (1986) *True Stories*. New York: Penguin.

Campbell, Colin (1987) *The Romantic Ethic and the Spirit of Modern Consumerism*. Oxford: Basil Blackwell.

Carton, Barbara (1988) 'Reebok opens $20 million drive.' *Boston Globe*, June 17.

'C-E's O'Connor Critiques Ad Biz "Client"' (1980) *Advertising Age*, November 10: 475.

Christon, Dean (1987) Interview with Director of Product Publicity, Levi Strauss & Co., 1 July.

'Consumer Magazine Ad Linage' (1987) *Advertising Age*, November 16: 81–2.

Cook, Louise (1983) 'Lessons of the recession may stick, analyst says.' *Lexington Herald Leader*, May 21: D-8.

'Cosmetics: Kiss and Sell' (1978) *Time*, December 11: 86–96.

Cott, Nancy (1987) *The Grounding of Modern Feminism*. New Haven: Yale University Press.

Cox, Meg (1981) 'McDonald's ad account won by Leo Burnett.' *Wall Street Journal*, October 12: 44.

Czitrom, Daniel J. (1982) *Mass Media and the American Mind*. Chapel Hill: University of North Carolina Press.

D'Amico, Robert (1978) 'Desire and the commodity form.' *Telos*, 35: 88–123.

Davidson, C. (1988) 'Reebok et al.: ad-stract art!' *Adweek*, June 20: 1,4.

Davis, Mike (1978) '"Fordism" in crisis.' *Review*, 2: 207–69.

—— (1988) 'Urban renaissance and the spirit of postmodernism,' in E. Ann Kaplan (ed.) *Postmodernism and its Discontents*. London: Verso, pp. 79–87.

Debord, Guy (1977) *Society of the Spectacle*. Detroit: Black & Red Press.

'Despite Less Blatant Sexism, Ads Still Insult Most Women' (1985) *Wall Street Journal*, August 1: 19.

Dews, Peter (1986) 'Adorno, post-structuralism and the critique of identity.' *New Left Review*, 157: 28–44.

Douglas, Susan (1988) 'Flex appeal, buns of steel and the body in question.' *In These Times*, September 7–13: 19.

Ears on Politics and Economics at CTFA Meeting' (1980) *Product Marketing*, April: 1, 27, 40.

Ellenthal, Ira (1979) 'Vogue: 'the ultimate authority.' *Product Marketing*, March: 19.

Ellis-Simms, Pam (1984) 'Ailing Levi's stitches together a new strategy.' *Marketing & Media Decisions*, 19 (August): 58ff.

Ennis, F. Beavin (1982) 'Positioning revisited.' *Advertising Age*, March 15: M-43, 46.

Enzensberger, Hans M. (1974) *The Consciousness Industry*. New York: Seabury Press.

Ewen, Stuart (1976) *Captains of Consciousness*. New York: McGraw-Hill.

Featherstone, Mike (1983a) 'The body in consumer culture.' *Theory, Culture & Society*, 1(2): 18–33.

—— (1983b) 'Consumer culture: an introduction.' *Theory, Culture & Society*, 1(3): 4–9.

—— (1987) 'Lifestyle and consumer culture.' *Theory, Culture & Society*, 4: 55–70.

Fish, Stanley (1982) *Is There a Text in this Class? The Authority of Interpretive Communities*. Cambridge: Harvard University Press.

Fiske, John and Hartley, John (1978) *Reading Television*. London: Methuen.

Foster, Hal (1986) 'Signs taken for wonder.' *Art in America*, June: 86.

Frith, Simon (1981) *Sound Effects. Youth, Leisure, and the Politics of Rock 'n' Roll*. New York: Pantheon.

Frith, Simon and Horne, Howard (1987) *Art into Pop*. London: Methuen.

Fromm, Erich (1955) *The Sane Society*. New York: Fawcett.

Garfield, Bob (1988) '"U.B.U." Takes shots at nonconformity.' *Advertising Age*, October 3: 70.

Gendron, Bernard (1986) 'Theodor Adorno meets the Cadillacs,' in Tania Modleski (ed.) *Studies in Entertainment*. Bloomington: Indiana University Press, pp. 18–36.

Gitlin, Todd (1980) *The Whole World is Watching*. Berkeley: University of California Press.

—— (1981a) 'Review essay.' *Theory and Society*, 10: 139–59.

—— (1981b) 'The new video technology: pluralism or banality?' *Democracy*, 4: 60–76.

—— (1989) 'Postmodernism: roots and politics.' *Dissent*, Winter: 100–8.

Goffman, Erving (1959) *The Presentation of Self in Everyday Life*. New York: Anchor Books.

—— (1976) *Gender Advertisements*. New York: Harper.

Goldman, Robert and Dickens, David (1983) 'The selling of rural America.' *Rural Sociology*, 48, 4: 585–606.

Goldman, Robert and Wilson, John (1977) 'The rationalization of leisure.' *Politics and Society*, 7: 157–88.

Goode, W. J. (1970) *World Revolution and Family Patterns*. New York: Free Press.

Gottdiener, Mark (1985) 'Hegemony and mass culture: a semiotic approach.' *American Journal of Sociology* 90, 5: 979–1001.

Gouldner, Alvin (1982) *The Dialectic of Ideology and Technology*. New York: Oxford University Press.

Gramsci, Antonio (1971) *Selections from the Prison Notebooks*. New York: International Publishers.

Greenberger, E. and Steinberg, L. (1986) *When Teenagers Work: The Psychological and Social Costs of Adolescent Employment*, New York: Basic Books.

Habermas, Jürgen (1970) *Toward a Rational Society*. Boston: Beacon Press.

Hall, Stuart (1972) 'The determinations of news photographs,' in S. Cohen and J. Young (eds) *The Manufacture of News*. Beverly Hills: Sage.

—— (1977) 'Culture, the media, and the "ideological effect,"' in James Curran *et al.* (eds) *Mass Communication and Society*. London: Arnold, pp. 315–48.

—— (1980) 'Encoding/decoding,' in Stuart Hall *et al.* (eds) *Culture Media and Language*. London: Hutchinson, pp. 128–38.

Haug, Wolfgang F. (1986) *Critique of Commodity Aesthetics: Appearance, Sexuality and Advertising in Capitalist Society*. Minneapolis: University of Minnesota Press.

Hebdige, Dick (1979) *Subculture: The Meaning of Style*. New York: Methuen.

—— (1988) *Hiding in the Light*. London: Routledge.

Henkoff, Ronald (1979) 'Ads for advertisers: how advertisers see their audiences,' in John W. Wright (ed.) *The Commercial Connection*, New York: Delta, pp. 192–8.

Herskovitz, Richard (1979) 'The Shell answer man and the spectator.' *Social Text*, 1 (Winter): 182–5.

Hodge, Robert and Kress, Gunther (1988) *Social Semiotics*. Ithaca: Cornell University Press.

Hohendahl, Peter (1979) 'Cultural theory, public sphere and culture: Jürgen Habermas and his critics.' *New German Critique*, 16: 89–118.

Horkheimer, Max (1947) *Eclipse of Reason.* New York: Oxford University Press.

Horkheimer, Max and Adorno, Theodor (1972) *Dialectic of Enlightenment.* New York: Herder & Herder.

Houghton, Jay C. (1987) 'Semiotics on the assembly line.' *Advertising Age,* March 16: 18.

Hyde, Jack (1981) 'Following the scent.' *Sky,* December: 68–75.

Jakobson, Roman (1961) 'Linguistics and poetics,' in Thomas A. Sebeok (ed.) *Style in Language.* Cambridge: MIT Press.

Jameson, Fredric (1983) 'Postmodernism and consumer society,' in Hal Foster (ed.) *The Anti-Aesthetic Essays on Postmodern Culture.* Port Townsend, WA: Bay Press, pp. 111–25.

—— (1984) 'Postmodernism, or the cultural logic of late capitalism.' *New Left Review,* 146: 53–92.

'The Jeans Industry: Fashioning a New Look' (1984) *Financial World,* September 19–October 2: 30–1.

Kaplan, E. Ann (1987) *Rocking Around The Clock: MTV, Postmodernism & Consumer Culture,* London: Methuen.

Kellner, Douglas (1979) 'TV, ideology, and emancipatory popular culture.' *Socialist Review,* 45 (May–June): 13–54.

—— (1983) 'Critical theory, commodities and the consumer society.' *Theory, Culture & Society,* 1(3): 66–83.

—— (1987) 'Baudrillard, semiurgy and death.' *Theory, Culture & Society,* 4: 125–46.

—— (1988) 'Postmodernism as social theory: some challenges and problems.' *Theory, Culture & Society,* 5: 239–70.

Kerouac, Jack (1955) *On the Road.* New York: Signet.

'A Kick in the Pants for Levi's' (1984) *Business Week,* June 11: 47–8.

Kline, Steven and Leiss, William (1978) 'Advertising, needs, and "Commodity Fetishism."' *Canadian Journal of Political & Social Theory,* 2: 5–30.

Koten, John (1984) 'Coca-Cola turns to Pavlov.' *Wall Street Journal,* January 19: 31.

Kovel, Joel (1978) 'Rationalization and the family.' *Telos,* 37(Fall): 5–21.

—— (1981) 'Desire and the family.' *The Age of Desire.* New York: Pantheon.

Kroeber-Riel, Werner and Barton, Beate (1980) 'Scanning ads—effects of position and arousal potential of ad elements,' in James H. Leigh and Claude R. Martin, Jr. (eds) *Current Issues and Research in Advertising 1980.* Ann Arbor: University of Michigan, pp. 147–64.

Kuhn, Annette (1985) *The Power of the Image: Essays on Representation & Sexuality.* London: Routledge & Kegan Paul.

Lakoff, Robin T. and Scherr, Raquel L. (1984) *Face Value: The Politics of Beauty.* Boston: Routledge & Kegan Paul.

Landis, Dylan (1981) 'Disengaging the engaged.' *Advertising Age,* March 2: S-2, 4.

Lasch, Christopher (1979a) *Haven in a Heartless World.* New York: Harper.

—— (1979b) *The Culture of Narcissism.* New York: Warner Books.

Lash, Scott (1988) 'Discourse or figure? Postmodernism as a regime of signification.' *Theory, Culture & Society,* 5: 331–6.

Lauerman, Connie (1980) 'Does your perfume make you feel like a star?' *Lexington Herald Leader,* December, 18: B-1.

'Lawsuits Filed over Polo Symbol' (1984) *Lexington Herald Leader,* February 24: A2.

Lears, T. J. Jackson (1983) 'From salvation to self-realization,' in Richard Fox and Jackson Lears (eds) *The Culture of Consumption: Critical Essays in American History, 1880–1980.* New York: Pantheon, pp. 3–38.

Lebowitz, Glenn (1979) '"Liberated woman" replaces "sex" as emphasis for fragrance ads.' *Product Marketing,* October: 10.

Lefebvre, Henri (1969) *The Sociology of Marx.* New York: Vintage.

—— (1971) *Everyday Life in the Modern World.* New York: Harper.

Leiss, William (1976) *The Limits of Satisfaction.* Toronto: University of Toronto Press.

Levi Strauss Press Release (1987) 'Music celebrities happy to sing the blues,' July.

Lukács, Georg (1971) *History and Class Consciousness.* Cambridge: MIT Press.

McGill, Douglas (1989) 'Nike is bounding past Reebok.' *New York Times,* July 11: C1,3.

McLuhan, Marshall (1967) *The Medium is the Massage.* New York: Bantam.

McWilliams, Michael (1985) 'Levi's highlights low-life setting.' *Advertising Age,* October 21: 51.

Madison Social Text Group (1979) 'The new right and media.' *Social Text,* 1: 169–80.

Marchand, Roland (1985) *Advertising and the American Dream: Making Way for Modernity, 1920–1940.* Berkeley: University of California Press.

Marcuse, Herbert (1960) *Reason and Revolution.* Boston: Beacon Press.

—— (1964) *One-Dimensional Man.* Boston: Beacon Press.

Marshall, Christy (1980) 'PRIZM adds zip to consumer research.' *Advertising Age,* November, 10: 22.

Marx, Karl (1967) *Capital.* Volumes 1 & 2. New York: International Publishers.

—— (1973) *The Grundrisse.* Baltimore: Penguin Books.

Mayer, Martin (1958) *Madison Avenue, U.S.A.* New York: Harper.

'Men's Scents on Trial: What Sells Them Best?' (1979) *Product Marketing,* April: 48.

Miller, Mark Crispin (1988) *Box In: The Culture of TV.* Evanston: Northwestern University Press.

Mills, C. Wright (1951) *White Collar.* New York: Oxford University Press.

—— (1967) 'Situated actions and vocabularies of motive,' in I. L Horowitz (ed.) *Power, Politics and People.* New York: Oxford.

Moog, Carol (1989) *Are They Selling Her Lips?* New York: William Morrow.

Morris, William (ed.) (1976) *American Heritage Dictionary of the English Language.* Boston: Houghton Mifflin.

Mowen, John C. (1980) 'On product endorser effectiveness: a balance model approach,' in James H. Leigh and Claude R. Martin (eds) *Current Issues and Research in Advertising 1980.* Ann Arbor: University of Michigan, pp. 41–57.

Murray, Sir James A. H. (ed.) (1962) *A New English Dictionary on Historical Principles.* Oxford: Oxford University Press.

Nichols, Bill (1979) 'Sanger Harris profits from fantasies.' *Advertising Age,* February 26: S-2, 4.

O'Connor, James (1987) *The Meaning of Crisis.* New York: Basil Blackwell.

Ogilvy, David (1983) 'Ogilvy on advertising.' *Advertising Age,* August 1: M-4, M-5, M-48, M-52.

'Panting for Bruce's Jeans' (1985) *Time,* September 2: 40.

Papson, Steve (1990) 'The IBM tramp,' *Jump Cut,* 35 (April): 66–72.

Parker, Richard and Churchill, Lindsey (1986) 'Positioning by opening the consumer's mind.' *International Journal of Advertising,* 5: 1–13.

Pashukanis, Evgenii (1978) *Law and Marxism: A General Theory,* London: Ink Links.

Patterns (1985) 'Big ad campaign comes up winners: a business success, an artistic triumph.' January, 2, 1: 1, 3.

Plummer, Joseph T. (1979) 'Life-style patterns,' in John W. Wright (ed.) *The Commercial Connection,* New York: Delta, pp. 125–34.

Rapp, Rayna (1988) 'Is the legacy of second wave feminism postfeminism?' *Socialist Review,* January–March 98: 31–7.

Reebok (1988) *Press Release Package.*

Reebok International Ltd. (1989) *1988 Annual Report.* Canton, MA.

Reebok, *Form 10-K* filed with the Security and Exchange Commission, Washington, DC, for Fiscal Year ending 31 December 1988. Commission file number 1–9340.

Rose, Gillian (1978) *The Melancholy Science: An Introduction to the Thought of Theodor W. Adorno.* New York: Columbia University Press.

Rothenberg, Randall (1989) 'Change in consumer markets hurting advertising industry.' *New York Times,* October 3: A1, D23.

Salomon Brothers (1989) 'Reebok International LTD.—from athletics to fashion and back again' (Stock Research), May 19.

Schudson, Michael (1981) 'Criticizing the critics of advertising: towards a sociological view of marketing.' *Media, Culture and Society*, 3: 3–12.

Schwartz, Tony (1979) 'Hard sell, soft sell, deep sell,' in John W. Wright (ed.) *The Commercial Connection*. New York: Delta, pp. 320–30.

Seeman, Debbie (1981) 'Made-to-odor times are in for changes.' *Advertising Age*, March 2: S-16, 18.

Sennett, Richard (1977) 'Destructive gemeinschaft,' in Norman Birnbaum (ed.) *Beyond the Crisis*. New York: Oxford University Press, pp. 171–97.

—— (1978) *The Fall of Public Man*. New York: Vintage.

Sennett, Richard and Cobb, Jonathon (1972) *The Hidden Injuries of Class*. New York: Vintage.

Sklar, Martin (1969) 'On the proletarian revolution and the end of political-economic society.' *Radical America*, 3: 1–41.

Sloan, Pat (1980) 'Scoundrel is Revlon's latest.' *Advertising Age*, September 1: 1, 59.

Smith, Joan (1981) *Social Issues and the Social Order*. Cambridge: Winthrop.

Smythe, Dallas (1977) 'Communications: blindspot of western Marxism.' *Canadian Journal of Political and Social Theory*, 1, 3: 1–27.

'Spots Put Free Spirits into Reeboks' (1998) *New York Times*, June 17.

Stacey, Judith (1987) 'Sexism by a subtler name?' *Socialist Review*, September–October 96: 7–28.

Tarule, R. (1979) 'The mortise and tenon timber frame: tradition and technology,' in Paul Kebabian and William Lipke (eds) *Tool and Technologies: America's Wooden Age*. Burlington: University of Vermont.

Warner, J. (1988) 'Reebok premieres U.B.U. campaign.' *Adweek*, June 20: 1, 6.

Wernick, Andrew (1984) 'Sign and commodity: aspects of the cultural dynamic of advanced capitalism.' *Canadian Journal of Political & Social Theory*, 8: 17–34.

White, Arthur (1978) 'Business: embattled on two fronts.' *Public Relations Journal*, 34, 1 (January): 16–18.

Williams, Raymond (1977) *Marxism and Literature*. New York: Oxford University Press.

Williams, William A. (1966) *The Contours of American History*. Chicago: Quadrangle.

Williamson, Judith (1978) *Decoding Advertisements: Ideology and Meaning in Advertising*. London: Marion Boyars.

—— (1986) 'Woman is an island: femininity and colonization,' in Tania Modleski (ed.) *Studies in Entertainment*. Bloomington: Indiana University Press, pp. 99–118.

Wilson, John (1988) 'Stages of advertising.' Unpublished paper.

Winship, Janice (1980) 'Sexuality for sale,' in Stuart Hall *et al.* (eds) *Culture, Media and Language*. London: Hutchinson, pp. 217–23.

—— (1987) *Inside Women's Magazines*. New York: Pandora.

'Working Women: Beauty Products Aid Confidence' (1980) *Product Marketing*, Winter: S-56.

Wren-Lewis, Justin (1983) 'The encoding/decoding model: criticisms and redevelopments for research on decoding.' *Media, Culture and Society*, 5: 179–97.

Wuthnow, Robert (1982) 'The moral crisis in American capitalism.' *Harvard Business Review*, March–April: 76–84.

Student Writing

Below you will find the second draft of a student's term paper. Read the draft carefully. Then answer the following questions. Thuy analyzed Levi's jeans as a popular culture statement. She focused on the motivations of those who wear them and on the hidden assumptions that seem to explain these jeans' popularity.

Ly   1

Thuy Ly
Professor Sotiriou
English 103
15 May 1995

The Denim Mythology

1   Talking about popular culture, few can deny the implications of blue jeans introduced by Levi Strauss in 1853. Initially, jeans were noted for their durability and worn exclusively by gold-miners and cowboys. By the turn of the century, they gradually made their way to farmers, manual laborers, and young people. Today, not only have jeans permeated virtually every social category in America, they have actually become a universal fashion statement which is found all over the world and which is embraced by widely diverse cultures. To understand the sprawling popularity of jeans, it makes more effort than an analytical view of their cultural identity. A trace of this origin is equally important. In this regard, I choose to begin my research with a brief "jeaneology," followed by a critical view of the different cultural implications of jeans and the social and psychological effects of different periods that help to propel jeans into a fashion statement. A brief discussion of

Ly   2

jean advertising also is included as a means to further our
understanding of the denim mythology.

2   Unlike other fashion ads which are born out of designers'
artistic whim to meet the psychological need for innovation of
the public, jeans were born to the Wild West to meet the rugged
working conditions in the gold-fields. In 1853, Levi Strauss,
lured by tales of Gold Rush fortunes, traveled from the East
Coast to San Francisco to set up a dry-goods business. As a sort
of sideline, he ran a small shop to make durable trousers from
canvas, which had originally been intended for tents. His pant-
making business became a huge hit because of the great demand
for trousers that could stand the rigors of mining. Back then,
jeans were worn without any special meanings attached to them.
It was functionality and efficiency that warranted their
prolonged popularity among miners and also cowboys, and it was
during this extended period of time that jeans acquired their
ideological baggage necessary to propel them to national fame in
the following century: the rugged, strong, hard-working,
classless identity of gold-miners, and the wild, independent
characteristics of cowboys. This cluster of meanings is deeply
imbued into jeans. Today the gold-rush and the wild prairie have
become parts of the country's legend, yet jeans still retain
their very authentic Western expressions of ruggedness,
naturalness, and freedom. This marks a fundamental difference
between jeans and other fashion items, which obtain their
identities solely through advertising campaigns.

3   The earliest traceable jeans advertisements appeared in the
1930s when Levi Strauss made the first attempt to promote jeans
from an ordinary workwear into the fashion industry. The sales
campaign was initiated by the sudden popularity of Western dude

ranches among Easterners, especially among women who stayed in Nevada for the time it took to get a quick divorce. Levi Stauss's initial ad campaign concentrated on the rugged charm and comfort of jeans and its main target was the female market in the East ("True Blue" 102). In the *Esquire* July 1994 edition, there appears one Levi's ad from the thirties showing a jeans-clad Eastern woman on a ranch vacation. Here jeans adapt perfectly to the shape of her body, expressing individuality and sexuality. Her raised arms give a sense of power and resistance, signifying the durability of jeans under harsh environments. The vast sky and immense pasture behind her stress naturalness and freedom, symbolizing the quality of denim that shrinks to fit the natural shape of the body that stretches easily to allow maximum physical freedom.

4   This is a well organized ad; yet consumer response back then was moderate. The reason for its failure can best be explained by the Fashion Flow Theory proposed by Mary Troxell, Association Professor of Fashion Merchandising at Iowa State University. Troxell suggests that fashions are molded by the force of an era. They mirror the time by reflecting how people think and live. In an upwardly mobile society where the majority seek identification with levels above them, fashion flows downward from upper to lower social classes, and the prevalent apparel is the delicate high fashion of the socially distinguished. Troxell also suggests the fashion has inverted itself since the mid-fifties because of the radical social changes, the increasing fluid and blurred class distinction in American society, and the skeptical view of youths toward upward mobility of earlier generations. New fashion trends usually begin among the young of the lower classes and then move upward, into higher social

Ly 4

levels (Troxell 58). Troxell's theory explains quite
satisfactorily the ineffectiveness of Levi Strauss's advertising
campaign in the socially-upward-mobile thirties when consumer
preference, life style, and dress adoption of the majority were
governed by elitism. Her theory also explains sociologically the
denim craze of the rebellious fifties and sixties when youths
were increasingly cynical about their parent's lifestyle, of
their elitism and conformism. The new generation denied the
importance of hierarchy, status, authority, and position; they
rejected competition. The denim symbolism of ruggedness and
resistance, of informality and nonconformity mirrored exactly
their social dissent. It was the in-tune social and
psychological effects, rather than ad campaigns from Levi
Strauss, that brought about the two-decade long jeans
phenomenon. Troxell maintains:

> *The most common misconception is that fashions are*
> *dictated by designers and retailers who decide what*
> *fashions will be and then force these decisions on*
> *helpless consumers. Instead, consumers themselves dictate*
> *fashion, by their acceptance or rejection of the styles*
> *offered. (3)*

5   In *Understanding Popular Culture*, John Fiske expresses a
similar viewpoint in saying that consumers are not passive and
helpless individuals in a capitalist commodity market. By active
participation in the commodity selection process, they are
actually part of the power structure which shapes our world.
6   Another instance which exemplifies the strength of consumers
in dictating fashion trend appeared in the early eighties when

Ly   5

denim sales dropped drastically. Fiske suggests that the decline
of denim sales reflects the collective resistance of consumers
against the homogenizing force of our mass production society.
He stresses, " . . . the pressures of mass living and the
homogenizing forces that attempt to massify us have produced a
deep need for a sense of individuality and social difference"
(7). Designer jeans merge into the denim market as a response to
consumers' demand for diversity and individuality. Fiske notes
that opposing to the traditional meaning of naturalness and
hard-working generic jeans, designer jeans signify social
sophistication and leisure. The new products stress
individuality by addressing the physicality of the wearer,
especially the rear end. Again it is the in-tune social and
psychological effects that propel the rise of the skin-hugging
jeans.

7   In competition for market share in designer jeans, Levi
Strauss fell behind Jordache, Calvin, and Lee's. According to
Brenda J. Gall of Merrill Lynch, Pierce, Fenner, & Smith, Inc.,
Levi's problems came from "its inability to move beyond the five-
pocket blue jeans" (Calvin 48). In fact, Levi Strauss did invest
in other new jean styles, yet it was not quite successful. In
1984, Levi's decided to retreat from diversifying product lines
to its basic jeanswear 501 and launched an expensive
advertisement nationwide (Calvin 48). The advertisement scored a
huge hit that allowed Levi Strauss to make a U-turn in to the
denim market.

8   At first glance, Levi's advertising success seems to
challenge Troxell's theory stating fashions are molded by the
force of an era, not by sales promotion from the producer (14).
However, close analysis of Levi's advertising campaign reveals
the intricate triangular relationship of the company's ad

Ly 6

strategy, the psychological mode of the era, and the
overwhelming consumer response. In *Reading Ads Socially*,
Robert Goldman, Associate Professor of Sociology at Lewis and
Clark College, provides a careful analysis of Levi's
unconventional ad campaign. Goldman notes that in the mid-
eighties, the American advertising community faced a serious
credibility crisis. Consumers were increasingly skeptical
about the legitimacy of advertising and often expressed
concerns about the manipulation of the advertising industry on
society. They demanded authenticity and unconventionality
(175). By adopting revolutionary techniques such as on-the-
street settings, nonprofessional streetwise characters, open-
ended scripts and grainy photographic style, Levi's ads
addressed directly consumer demand. With streetwise setting
and character, Levi's ads allowed consumers to identify
themselves with characters in the ad. With grainy photographic
style, they invited audience participation in decoding ad
messages. This mental involvement is powerful because most
readers take pleasure in the creative process of supplying
resolution to the contradiction and gap in the text they read.
With anti-hero and self-reflexive individuals, Levi "seemed to
sanction [consumer] resistance to the frame of commodity
hegemony" (173).

9   In this regard, Levi's advertising success comes from its
ability to respond to the psychological tempo of the period
and its ability to articulate consumers' counter-hegemonic
viewpoints and incorporate them into the company commodity
statement. Again, it is the psychological effects that have
reversed denim fashions. It is quite interesting to note that
throughout the entire history of jeans, resistance has been
the major factor that propels them to national fame. In the

Ly 7

fifties, jeans signified resistance to class distinction and
social upward mobility; in the early eighties, resistance to
the mass-production commodity society; in the mid-eighties,
resistance to the pseudo-realism of advertising culture. Fiske
contends that popular culture is the culture of the
subordinated and thus always bears the trace of resistance
within it (4-5). In that sense, jeans are genuine popular
culture because resistance has been their indispensable
symbolism.

Ly 8

Works Cited

Calvin, Peter A. "A Kick in the Pants for Levi's." *Business
      Week* 11 June 1984: 47-48.

Fiske, John. *Understanding Popular Culture.* London: Routledge,
      1994.

Goldman, Robert. *Reading Ads Socially.* London: Routledge,
      1992.

Troxell, Mary D. *Fashion Merchandising.* New York: McGraw-Hill,
      1976.

"True Blue." *Esquire* July 1994: 102-21.

1. Summarize Thuy's argument in paragraph 2. Do you agree with it, or would you want to revise it?

2. Summarize Mary Troxell's theory in paragraph 4. How is Thuy using this theory to develop her argument?

3. Why does Thuy cite John Fiske in paragraph 5? Does the Fiske material further develop Thuy's argument? If so, how?

4. What is the purpose of paragraph 6? Does it logically follow from the previous paragraphs?

5. Reread the concluding paragraph. Does this paragraph tie in with the evidence that Thuy has presented in the previous paragraphs? If so, how?

Peer Responses

Use some or all of these questions to respond to the first draft of your peer's term paper. Comment as specifically as you can so that your peer can use your comments to productively revise her next draft.

There are two sets of questions—one for the first draft and one for the revised draft.

A. Responses to the First Draft

1. Read the beginning of this draft. Locate the argument. Put this argument into your own words. Can you provide any suggestions to improve your peer's argument?

2. Read through the body of the draft. List three sources of evidence that your peer uses to support her argument. Do they effectively sustain her argument, or do they somehow not adequately support it?

3. Locate a particularly well-argued paragraph in the body of the draft. Give your reasons why it is so convincing.

4. Locate a paragraph in the draft's body that needs further development. Provide suggestions for improving this paragraph.

5. Having read the entire draft, now provide three suggestions for improving the next draft.

B. Responses to the Revised Draft

1. Locate the argument of this revised draft. Discuss it with your peer. Are there any aspects of it that can be improved?

2. Reread this draft to see the ways that your peer has supported her argument. Is the evidence representative? Thorough? Accurate? Is there other evidence that you would like your peer to include in the final draft?

3. Locate the section of the body that most strongly speaks to your peer's argument. Why do you believe this evidence to be so convincing?

4. Locate the section of the body that presents the least convincing evidence to support your peer's argument. Why do you believe that this evidence is not convincing?

5. Carefully review this draft to see that the MLA or APA format is being correctly followed. Identify the areas that are not adhering to the proper research format.

Index